gilbert
LAW SUMMARIES

ESTATE & GIFT TAX

Fifteenth Edition

John H. McCord
Professor of Law
University of Illinois

Taxpayer Relief Act Supplement in Back of Book

THE barbri GROUP

HARCOURT BRACE LEGAL AND PROFESSIONAL PUBLICATIONS, INC.
EDITORIAL OFFICES: 176 W. Adams, Suite 2100, Chicago, IL 60603

gilbert LAW SUMMARIES

REGIONAL OFFICES: New York, Chicago, Los Angeles, Washington, D.C.
Distributed by: **Harcourt Brace & Company** 6277 Sea Harbor Drive, Orlando, FL 32887 (800)787-8717

PROJECT EDITOR
Elizabeth L. Snyder, B.A., J.D.
Attorney at Law

QUALITY CONTROL EDITOR
Dawn M. Barker, B.S.

SUMMARY OF CONTENTS

gilbert

capsule summary

estate and gift tax

Text Section

I. INTRODUCTION

A. THE ESTATE TAX

The present estate tax was enacted in 1916 for the purpose of limiting the dynastic accumulation of wealth and is a tax upon the ***transfer*** of property, not upon the property itself . . . . [1]

B. THE GIFT TAX

Enacted in 1932, the present gift tax acts to prevent estate tax avoidance and is also imposed on the transfer of property . . . . [8]

C. COORDINATION OF THE FEDERAL ESTATE AND GIFT TAXES

The Tax Reform Act of 1976 unified the ***computational***, although not the substantive, aspects of the two transfer taxes so that generally the tax will be the same whether property is transferred during life or upon death . . . . [12]

D. THE GENERATION-SKIPPING TRANSFER TAX

First introduced in 1976, this ***separate*** transfer tax was intended to prevent tax avoidance by giving successive life estates. Because of its complexity, application of the tax was continuously deferred and eventually repealed retroactively by provisions of the Tax Reform Act of 1986 which substituted a new generation-skipping tax currently in force . . . . [15]

E. TAXING JURISDICTION

Jurisdictional bases for the taxes are citizenship, residence, and location of the property. As to citizens and residents, taxes reach all property transferred without regard to location. In the case of nonresident aliens, however, tax exposure is dependent upon location of the property within the United States . . . . [22]

II. SUBSTANTIVE ASPECTS OF THE ESTATE TAX

A. GROSS ESTATE

1. **Inclusions in Gross Estate:** I.R.C. sections 2033 through 2046 set forth the types of property and property transfers includible in the gross estate . . . . [26]
2. **Section 2033—Property Owned by Decedent:** All property owned by the decedent at death that is transferred to another on account of his death is included in the decedent's gross estate . . . . [32]
   a. **Transfers taxed:** Taxable transfers include not only transfers by will or intestacy, but also by some other arrangement whereby decedent has effectively directed property that he owns to another as a result of his death [34]
      (1) **Limitations—"ownership" interest "transferred" to another:** Decedent must own property at death and it must be transferred to another. The fact that death is merely the occasion by which a property right arises in another is not enough (*e.g.*, a posthumous, discretionary bonus paid by D's employer to D's family is not taxable in D's estate, because D had no right to the bonus at death) . . . . [35]
   b. **Types of property subject to tax:** All types of property are subject to the tax—real and personal, tangible and intangible, including: . . . . [43]

(1) ***Debts cancelled by will;***
(2) ***Choses in action*** that survive the decedent;
(3) ***Income from income-producing property*** up to the date of decedent's death;
(4) ***Present value of rights to future income;***
(5) ***Post-death payment from decedent's business*** if made in liquidation of his interest in the business (but not post-death profits);
(6) ***Employment benefits payable upon death*** pursuant to a bargained for employment contract;

c. **Types of interests subject to tax:** All types of interests are subject to tax—present, future, vested, and contingent. However, the interest must be ***inheritable*** and it must be ***transferred*** from decedent to another . . . . . . [67]
   (1) **Interests terminating at death:** Interests that terminate on decedent's death, such as a life estate granted to D by another or a remainder contingent upon D's survival, are not "inheritable" and thus ***not taxable.*** [68]

d. **Nature of ownership required for tax:** D must have ***beneficial*** ownership; the estate tax does not reach bare legal title . . . . [74]
   (1) **"Substantial ownership" doctrine:** This doctrine has not been applied to the estate tax. But those situations where it might be used have been accounted for by specific estate tax provisions (discussed *infra*) . . [80]

e. **Relationship between section 2033 and other taxing provisions:** Although not taxable as property owned by the decedent, the gross estate includes certain lifetime transfers by decedent that have a "testamentary" character, and certain types of property interests that "pass" from decedent to a beneficiary at D's death even though there may not be a "transfer" by decedent under technical property law. [I.R.C. §§2035-2042] . . . . [82]
   (1) **Specific statutes take precedence:** As a general rule, the specific taxing provisions take precedence over section 2033 (the general taxing provision). However, specific taxing provisions take precedence only to the extent that the type of transfer or type of property they address is the one intended to be covered by the specific provision . [83]

f. **Impact of state law:** State property law affects the federal estate tax law insofar as it defines the interests and rights a decedent has with respect to property. However, ***federal estate tax law*** determines whether the type of interest or right owned and transferred by decedent is taxable . . . . [85]
   (1) **Determining state law:** In determining the nature of a decedent's interest in property under state property law, federal courts are bound only by state statutes or the decisions of the ***highest court*** of the state. . . . . [86]

3. **Section 2034—Dower or Curtesy Interests:** The interest of a decedent's surviving spouse in the property of a decedent arising from state dower, curtesy, or statutory "forced share" rights is subject to the estate tax . . . . [94]
   a. **No deduction for marital interests:** Property owned at death by D is included at its full value, without a reduction for the surviving spouse's marital interests therein . . . . [95]
   b. **Community property rights:** The vested one-half interest of a surviving spouse in community property is ***not*** included in D's gross estate . . . . [98]
   c. **Effect of marital deduction:** The marital deduction [I.R.C. §2056] operates to remove from the taxable estate most of the property included under section 2034 . . . . [99]

4. **Section 2035—Gifts Made Within Three Years of Death**
   a. **Background**
      (1) **Former tax on transfers in contemplation of death:** Prior to 1977, transfers within three years of death were included in D's estate

only if made "in contemplation of death" (*i.e.*, operative element of the tax was D's subjective intent) . . . . [100]

(2) **1976 Tax Reform Act:** The effect of the 1976 Act was to reduce substantially the need to include deathbed gifts in D's gross estate, since such gifts would be taxed when made and added to the estate tax base to determine the estate tax . . . . [103]

(3) **1981 Tax Act:** The Act eliminates most outright gifts from inclusion in D's gross estate . . . . [106]

(a) **Continued application of section 2035:** Any gift taxes paid or payable with respect to gifts made within three years of decedent's death are included in the gross estate. Also, as noted below, section 2035 interacts with sections 2036, 2037, 2038, 2041, and 2042 so as to include property in D's gross estate . . . . [107]

b. **Relation between section 2035 and other taxing sections:** Section 2035 interacts with other specific taxing sections to produce a tax under those sections if a taxable interest or incident of ownership is transferred, released, or relinquished ***within three years of death.*** In such cases, there is ordinarily included in the gross estate the same amount that would have been included had the transfer or relinquishment not taken place . . . . [114]

(1) **Coextensive interaction:** The substantive provisions of ***both*** section 2035 and the specific taxing section must apply . . . . [118]

(2) **Exception to interaction:** There is no interaction with section 2040. If ***joint tenancy property*** is transferred or severed within three years of death, only the value of any interest retained by the decedent is taxed . . [119]

5. **Section 2036—Transfers with Retained Life Interests:** If decedent makes an inter vivos transfer but retains either a life interest in the property or a power to designate enjoyment of the property during life, the full value of the property transferred is included in the gross estate . . . . [120]

a. **Requirement of a transfer:** Property in which decedent has a life estate or power to affect enjoyment must have been "transferred" by him during his life in order to be taxable under section 2036. "Transfer" includes indirect as well as direct transfers . . . . [130]

(1) **Reciprocal trust doctrine:** If A and B transfer equal amounts on separate irrevocable trusts and A provides that B should enjoy the income for life with remainder to his issue, and B provides for income to A for life, remainder to his issue, A is treated as the actual settlor of the B trust, and B is treated as the actual settlor of the A trust. Consequently, on A's death, the value of the B trust is included in A's gross estate (a transfer with a retained life interest) . . . . [135]

(2) **Time of transfer:** Section 2036 is limited to transfers made on or after March 3, 1931 . . . . [140]

(a) **Outright gifts and gifts on irrevocable trust:** A transfer ordinarily occurs when title passes from the transferor . . . . [141]

(b) **Gifts on revocable trusts:** Courts are split as to the creation of a revocable trust. Some hold the transfer occurs when property is transferred to the trustee; others hold there is no transfer until the power to revoke lapses or is released . . . . [143]

(c) **Additions to trust:** Additions to a trust created prior to March 3, 1931 may result in proportionate taxation . . . . [145]

b. **Requirement that interest or power be retained:** Section 2036 tax attaches only if the transferor retained a requisite interest or power . . . . . . [146]

(1) **Subsequent reconveyance:** Ordinarily, section 2036 does not apply where decedent reacquires an interest after the transfer. However, the interest is treated as having been retained if the donee's subsequent reconveyance was ***prearranged*** . . . . [148]

(2) **Limitation:** A retained interest or power must be in the very property

Text Section

transferred. Thus, tranfers in return for the transferee's promise to pay an annuity to the transferor are treated as the purchase of an annuity (not a reservation of a life estate) .... [150]

c. **Nature of interest retained under section 2036(a)(1):** The requisite interest for taxation is defined as either "***possession or enjoyment*** of the property" or the "***right to income*** from the property" .... [154]

   (1) **Mere fact of possession is insufficient for taxation:** A legally enforceable right to "possession and enjoyment" or "right to income" is not required, but the mere fact of possession is not enough; there must be an understanding or agreement (can be ***inferred*** from possession in certain cases) .... [157]

   (2) **Legally enforceable right to income not required:** Similarly, receipt of income must be pursuant to an "understanding," but such an understanding need not be a legally enforceable obligation as long as it has been performed. And, an understanding can be ***inferred*** from the fact of continued receipt .... [163]

      (a) **Indirect beneficial interests:** "Right to income" may be found whenever income is to be used for the benefit of the transferor during life—*e.g.*, to discharge the transferor's legal obligations .. [165]

      (b) **Discretionary trusts:** The trustee's discretionary power to use trust income for the transferor's benefit will not invoke the tax, as long as the transferor is not a trustee and cannot otherwise compel use of trust property or income for his benefit .... [172]

d. **Nature of the power retained under section 2036(a)(2):** The requisite power is defined as "the right, either alone or in conjunction with any person, to designate the persons who shall possess or enjoy the property or the income therefrom" .... [179]

   (1) **Beneficial power not required:** The power need not be exercisable in the transferor's favor. But nonbeneficial powers must be discretionary; nonbeneficial powers governed by an "ascertainable standard" are mandatory and thus outside the scope of this section .... [183]

   (2) **Form of the power:** Any power that has the effect of designating or shifting enjoyment ***during the transferor's lifetime*** qualifies—*e.g.*, settlor's power to direct accumulation of trust income or to invade corpus for the benefit of the income beneficiary .... [186]

   (3) **Power to affect possession or enjoyment:** Tax also attaches where the decedent retained the power to affect the ***time and manner*** of a beneficiary's possession and enjoyment. But a power to affect only post-death enjoyment (*e.g.*, power is exercisable only by will) is not taxable under section 2036 (but will be taxed under section 2038) ... [190]

   (4) **Administrative powers:** Purely administrative powers are generally not taxable because ***not dispositive or distributive*** .... [197]

      (a) **Retention of voting rights in transferred stock:** Transferred stock is taxable if the decedent retained the right to vote the transferred shares and if at any time within three years of her death, decedent "controlled" the corporation whose shares were given away. "Control" is defined as ownership of twenty percent or more of the voting stock of the issuing corporation. Constructive ownership rules apply .... [199]

   (5) **Decedent reserves access to the power:** D is treated as having retained the power where D reserved indirect access thereto; *e.g.*, trustee's taxable power is attributable to D if D reserved authority to remove the trustee and appoint a successor or veto the trustee's exercise of power .... [205]

   (6) **Contingent powers are taxable** under section 2036 even though

the contingency is without the control of D and has not occurred at D's death .... [207]

e. **Period of retention:** The requisite interest or power must be retained for one of three time periods: (i) for the ***transferor's life***; (ii) for a period ***not ascertainable without reference to the transferor's death***; or (iii) for a period of time that does ***not in fact end with the transferor's death*** .. [208]

f. **Amount includible:** The amount included in the gross estate is the full value of the property subject to the retained interest or power, determined as of the date of decedent's death (or at the alternate valuation date). Where the retained right relates only to a portion of the property, only that portion is taxed .... [216]

 (1) **Intervening estate:** If the retained right is subject to an intervening life estate that cannot be affected by the interest or power, the amount taxable is reduced by the value of the intervening estate .... [218]

 (2) **Power to accumulate income:** If decedent retained the power to direct the accumulation of income, ***both*** the property and the accumulated income it produces are taxed.......................... [219]

g. **Relinquishment or transfer of retained interest or power within three years of death:** Such divestment by decedent causes the entire property to be taxed under section 2036.......................... [220]

6. **Section 2037—Transfers Taking Effect at Death:** A lifetime gift is included in the donor's gross estate if (i) the transferee's possession and enjoyment of the property is contingent upon ***surviving*** the transferor ***and*** (ii) the transferor retained a ***reversionary interest*** in the property ***valued at more than five percent*** of the value of the property (at the time of the transferor's death) ... [222]

a. **Transfer requirement:** Property must be transferred by D during life; and the reversionary interest must be retained by D...................... [236]

b. **Survivorship requirement:** Transferee's ***possession*** and ***enjoyment*** (not "title") must be contingent solely on surviving the transferor .... [239]

 (1) **Effect of alternative event:** Section 2037 is inapplicable if the beneficiary can take upon the happening of some alternative event (unless that event is so extreme as to be "unreal")...................... [242]

c. **Reversionary interest requirement:** The reversionary interest requirement is met where there is any possibility that the property transferred may return to the transferor, or his estate, or be subject to a power of disposition by him .... [245]

 (1) **Exceptions:** A mere expectancy is not a "reversionary interest," nor is a right to receive or dispose of only the income from the transferred property. And a third party's purely discretionary power to distribute all or a part of the property to the transferor will not give rise to the tax. [247]

 (2) **Joint powers:** Such powers are outside the scope of section 2037. [256]

 (3) **Express terms vs. operation of law:** For post-October 7, 1949 transfers, it is sufficient if the reversionary interest arises ***either*** by express terms of the instrument of transfer ***or*** by operation of law, but with respect to pre-October 8, 1949 transfers, the reversionary interest must arise by the express terms of the instrument................ [257]

d. **De minimis rule:** The reversionary interest must ***exceed five percent*** of the value of the property transferred. Value is determined as of the time immediately before the decedent-transferor's death, utilizing standard actuarial and mortality tables .... [261]

e. **The "negative" requirement—power of appointment in another:** Section 2037 will ***not*** apply if, at the time of decedent's death, some other person possesses a taxable power to appoint the property away from decedent to a beneficiary of the present transfer .... [268]

 (1) **Must be a taxable power:** A "taxable power" means one that would result in taxation of the property in the holder's estate under section

Text Section

2041 . . . . [269]

f. **Amount taxable:** Only the value of the interest that is ***dependent on survivorship*** is included in decedent's gross estate . . . . [273]

7. **Section 2038—Revocable Transfers:** Transfers wherein the decedent possesses, at death, a power to alter, amend, revoke, or terminate, either alone or in conjunction with any other person, are includible under section 2038 . . . . [278]

   a. **Transfer requirement:** The property must have been transferred by decedent during her lifetime . . . . [300]

   b. **Power must be exercisable at death:** The requisite power must be exercisable by decedent or by decedent and another at the time of decedent's death . . . . [301]

      (1) **Contingent powers:** A contingent power will not produce a tax under section 2038 where the contingency is outside the transferor's control and has not occurred at the time of the transferor's death. (But such a power may support taxation under section 2036.) . . . . [302]

      (2) **By whom is the power exercisable?** Joint as well as individual powers are taxable, and it is irrelevant that the co-holder of the power is an adverse party. . . . . [306]

      (3) **Indirect access to power sufficient:** Although decedent does not technically possess a power, the tax will attach if the decedent could compel the exercise of a taxable power by another . . . . [309]

      (4) **Source of the power:** As to transfers made after June 22, 1936, it is immaterial whether the transferor retained the power as long as it is exercisable at death. . . . . [312]

   c. **Nature of the taxable power:** Taxable powers under section 2038 include not only powers to revoke a transfer but also powers to alter beneficial enjoyment and to affect the time and manner of a beneficiary's enjoyment; but the power must be ***discretionary.*** Purely administrative powers are not taxable. . . . . [314]

      (1) **"Power to revoke":** This includes any power under which decedent had the right to repossess the property transferred, directly or indirectly (*e.g.*, spouse's right under community property law to set aside improper gift) . . . . [320]

      (2) **"Power to terminate":** This covers any power to end a trust and cause a distribution of trust property before expiration of the specified term. A power to accelerate the time of enjoyment of the trust property is also a taxable power of termination . . . . [324]

      (3) **"Power to alter or amend":** This refers to any discretionary power, the exercise of which will affect beneficial enjoyment of the transferred property (*e.g.*, power to direct accumulation or distribution of income, to substitute or add new beneficiaries) . . . . [329]

   d. **Amount taxable:** Only the value of the interest subject to the taxable power is taxable. . . . . [332]

   e. **Relationship to section 2036(a)(2):** There is considerable overlap in the taxing scope of sections 2036 and 2038; but there are also a number of differences. Principal differences concern the time the transfer is made, the source of the taxable power, powers to control enjoyment of the property after decedent's death, contingent powers, and the amount includible . . . [336]

8. **Section 2039—Annuities:** A surviving beneficiary's interest in an annuity contract or analogous type of arrangement entered into after March 3, 1931 is taxable to the estate of the decedent if (i) the beneficiary's interest is receivable by reason of surviving the decedent and (ii) the decedent was receiving, or had a right to receive, payments under the contract or arrangement . . . . [344]

   a. **Nature of survivor's interest:** A beneficiary's interest is not limited to typical annuity-type payments, but benefits in the nature of life insurance proceeds are ***not*** taxable under section 2039. (However, they may be taxable under section 2042.) Whether a benefit is life insurance turns on whether a "life insurance risk" exists at the date of D's death .... [354]

(1) **Survival of decedent requirement:** Benefits must be payable "by reason of surviving the decedent" but need not be conditioned solely on survivorship .... [359]

(2) **Any form of contract:** The contract or arrangement is not limited to a typical annuity-type contract .... [362]

b. **Nature of decedent's interest:** Decedent must have been receiving, or have had a right to receive, payments under the arrangement, either alone or in conjunction with another, for life or for any period not ascertainable without reference to death or for any period which does not in fact end before death . [367]

(1) **Integrated plan:** Payments under a plan that is technically separate from the survivor's benefits plan will qualify if the separate arrangements form an integrated plan .... [368]

(2) **Annuity or other payment:** Although decedent's interest need not be in the form of an annuity, compensation that the decedent was receiving, or was entitled to receive, at the time of death is excluded—*i.e.*, section 2039 is limited to ***post-employment*** benefits .... [374]

(3) **Right to receive:** If decedent has received ***everything*** she is entitled to receive under the plan, survivor benefits pursuant thereto are not taxed under this section .... [377]

c. **Amount includible:** The amount included in decedent's gross estate is the value of the survivor's benefit that is ***proportionate*** to contributions made by the decedent (or decedent's employer) .... [382]

9. **Section 2040—Joint Interests:** Co-tenancies with ***right of survivorship*** are included in the gross estate of the first joint tenant to die. Tenancies in common and community property are not taxable under section 2040 .... [385]

a. **General rule of inclusion:** The tax reaches the ***full value*** of the property, except that an amount proportionate to the surviving joint tenant's original contribution to the acquisition of the property is ***excluded*** from decedent's gross estate .... [393]

b. **Required nature of survivor's contribution:** Only those amounts that did not originally belong to decedent and that were not transferred from decedent to the survivor for ***less than*** full and adequate consideration in money or money's worth (*e.g.*, gifts) may be attributed to the survivor as an "original contribution" .... [397]

(1) **Income from donated property:** Income derived from donated property is treated as originating with the donee-survivor .... [401]

(2) **Post-gift appreciation:** Profits attributable to ***post-gift appreciation*** in value of the donated property may constitute an original contribution by the donee-survivor .... [402]

(a) **Exceptions:** There is ***no*** exclusion from D's estate where the same property is ***reconveyed*** in joint tenancy or where there is a ***reinvestment*** of joint tenancy property .... [403]

(3) **Assumption of mortgage:** If the survivor jointly assumed a mortgage with decedent in connection with the acquisition of the joint tenancy property, the survivor's proportionate obligation under the mortgage is treated as an original contribution .... [405]

(4) **Burden of proof:** Decedent's estate has the burden of proving what part of the property was contributed by the survivor .... [408]

c. **Relationship to other taxing sections:** Section 2040 generally does not interact with other specific estate tax sections; rather, it ordinarily ***supersedes*** those sections .... [409]

(1) **Severance of joint tenancy:** Section 2040 tax does not attach where the joint tenancy is severed prior to death. However, if D retains an interest as a tenant in common, that interest will be taxed under section

2033 .... [410]

(2) **No interaction with section 2035:** No estate tax will attach if joint tenancy property is transferred within three years of a joint tenant's death .... [411]

d. **Special rule for "qualified joint interests":** As amended by the 1981 Act, section 2040(b) provides that if a qualified joint interest exists (*i.e.*, property held by D and D's spouse as tenants by the entirety or joint tenants with right of survivorship), only one-half of the value of the property is includible in the gross estate of the first to die, without regard as to which co-tenant furnished the consideration at the time of the joint tenancy's creation .... [421]

e. **Compare—community property:** Although community property represents a form of concurrent ownership, the focus for taxation of community property is section 2033. Because each spouse owns a vested interest in one-half of the community property, one-half of the community property is included in the estate of each spouse .... [430]

10. **Section 2041—Powers of Appointment:** Property subject to a ***general*** power of appointment is included in the gross estate of the holder of the power if the power is exercised. And, where the general power was created ***on or after October 21, 1942,*** the property subject to the owner is included in the holder's gross estate whether the power is exercised or not. *Note:* Rules governing the date the power is deemed created are similar to those governing the time property is deemed transferred (*supra*, §§140-145) .... [443]

a. **Nature of the taxable power of appointment:** Section 2041 is limited to ***general*** powers .... [456]

(1) **"General power" defined:** A general power is a power that is exercisable during life or by will in favor of the ***holder, his estate, his creditors,*** or the ***creditors of his estate***. However, an exception is made for powers to invade or appropriate property for the benefit of the holder that are limited by an ascertainable standard relating to health, education, support, or maintenance .... [457]

(2) **Form of the power:** The power need not be in any particular form, and the capacity in which it is exercisable is immaterial. Similarly, the power need not technically lie with D; *e.g.*, D is deemed to possess a general power if he can compel exercise for his benefit .... [460]

(3) **Limited to donated powers:** The tax only applies to donated powers; reserved powers are taxable, if at all, under sections 2036 through 2038 .... [467]

(4) **Direct or indirect benefit:** A general power exists where property may be appointed directly or indirectly for D's benefit. For example, D has a general power where she can appoint property to a trust in which she is beneficiary .... [468]

(5) **Special powers distinguished:** All powers which are not "general" are "special" and are outside the scope of section 2041 .... [471]

b. **Preexisting powers—special rules:** Powers created on or before October 21, 1942 will produce a tax only if exercised. This would include powers exercised by will or powers exercised during life if the property subject to the power would have been included in the holder's gross estate under sections 2035 through 2038 had that property been transferred by decedent .... [474]

(1) **Lapse or release:** Lapse or release of the power is not an exercise and will not support the tax .... [477]

(2) **Joint powers:** A preexisting power granted jointly to D and another is not taxable .... [479]

c. **Post-1942 powers—special rules:** Powers created after October 21, 1942 are taxable ***whether or not exercised.*** However, the power must be exercisable at the date of decedent's death; thus, a power subject to a contingency beyond the holder's control and that has not occurred at date of death is not a taxable power of appointment .... [480]

(1) **Lapse or release:** Lapse or release of a post-1942 power is treated as an exercise. However, the statute makes a special ***exception*** for lapse of ***noncumulative powers to withdraw***: To the extent of the greater of $5,000 or five percent of the value of the property subject to the power, a lapse is not treated as an exercise .... [483]

(2) **Joint powers:** Post-1942 joint powers are taxable unless the coholder is the donor of the power or an adverse party. A permissible appointee is not considered an adverse party. However, if a joint holder is a permissible appointee, only a proportionate amount of the value of the property subject to the power is included in D's gross estate .... [487]

11. **Section 2042—Life Insurance:** Proceeds of life insurance on decedent's life are included in the gross estate if: (i) payable to, or for the benefit of, the estate, or (ii) payable to some other beneficiary and D possessed "incidents of ownership" in the policy at the time of death.. [490]

a. **What constitutes life insurance?** The term "life insurance" is not limited to a commercial life insurance contract. It includes all arrangements that shift or distribute the economic risk of death .... [500]

b. **"Proceeds payable to insured's estate":** This includes all proceeds payable to D's estate or executor and proceeds payable to some other beneficiary if that beneficiary is legally bound to use the proceeds to discharge obligations of the insured's estate .... [507]

c. **Proceeds payable to other beneficiaries:** Proceeds not payable to or for the benefit of the insured's estate are taxable only if decedent-insured possessed ***incidents of ownership*** in the policy at the time of death .. [510]

(1) **"Incidents of ownership":** This includes any right or interest in the policy whereby the insured has the power to control the existence of the policy, to rearrange the economic interests therein, or to affect the benefits payable thereunder.................................. [511]

(a) **Examples:** Incidents of ownership include the right to cancel the policy, to borrow against the policy, to change the beneficiary designations (including contingent beneficiaries), and to affect the time and manner of enjoyment by the selection of settlement options.

(b) **Reversionary interests:** The Code specifically provides that a reversionary interest is an incident of ownership if the value of the interest exceeds five percent of the value of the policy immediately prior to the insured's death .... [517]

(2) **"Possession" of incidents of ownership:** Decedent-insured need ***not*** have retained incidents of ownership; it is sufficient if these incidents are ***possessed*** by and exercisable by D at the time of death (but inability to exercise is immaterial)............................ [518]

(a) **Joint powers taxable:** Taxation is not affected by the fact that concurrence of an adverse party may be required for exercise . [519]

(b) **Examples:** D will be deemed to "possess" incidents of ownership where the incidents are exercisable indirectly as trustee, by virtue of a controlling interest in a closely held corporation, or as a partner.. [524]

d. **Assignment of incidents of ownership:** Proceeds remain taxable to D if the transfer was made under circumstances that would result in inclusion under sections 2035 through 2038 .... [533]

e. **Amount includible:** Ordinarily, the entire value of the proceeds is taxed. But there is some case authority supporting proportionate taxation where the policy is assigned to another within three years of death and the donee thereafter pays all premiums .... [541]

f. **Life insurance and community property states:** An insurance policy is

Text Section

a community asset if purchased with community funds [544]

(1) **Insured dies first:** If the insured dies first, one-half the proceeds is taxable in his or her estate [545]

(2) **Spouse dies first:** If the spouse dies first, his or her one-half interest in the present value of the insurance is taxable under section 2033. Upon the insured's death, all proceeds attributable to premiums paid by him or her are taxable [546]

12. **Section 2043—Consideration:** The estate tax is imposed only upon ***gratuitous*** transfers; transfers for "full and adequate consideration in money or money's worth" are not taxed [551]

    a. **Partial consideration:** Where property is transferred for less than adequate consideration, the amount by which the value of the property exceeds the value of the consideration is deemed a gift [552]

    b. **Measure of consideration:** Consideration that will support a binding contract will not necessarily preclude estate taxation. The consideration must constitute the ***economic equivalent*** of the transferred property [553]

    c. **Consideration moving to decedent:** Additionally, the consideration must move to the decedent; an economic detriment suffered by the transferee in consideration of a transfer will not prevent estate tax exposure [556]

    d. **"Business transaction exception":** Even though consideration received for the transfer is not the economic equivalent of the property, if there is a bona fide business reason for such a transfer and no intent to make a gift, the transfer is not subject to tax. (*Compare:* Ordinarily, donative intent, or lack thereof, is not determinative.) [557]

    e. **Release of marital rights:** The statute specifically provides that the release of dower or curtesy, or of similar marital rights, is not sufficient consideration to preclude estate taxation [562]

13. **Section 2044—Certain Marital Deduction Property:** Property that qualifies for a marital deduction as "qualified terminable interest property" is included in the surviving spouse's estate upon his or her death unless the spouse disposed of the life estate before his or her death under circumstances where a gift tax would attach [567]

14. **Section 2045—Prior Interests:** An interest in property, or powers with respect to property, that will produce estate tax exposure will do so without regard to when the particular transfer, interest, right or power was made, created, exercised, etc., unless otherwise specifically provided [568]

15. **Section 2046—Disclaimers:** Section 2046 incorporates the gift tax rule as to when a disclaimer or renunciation will be effective for federal tax purposes. (*See infra,* §§770 *et seq.*) [571]

B. ESTATE TAX DEDUCTIONS

1. **Introductory Analysis:** Four deductions are allowed under the estate tax: (i) certain expenses of and claims against the estate; (ii) certain losses; (iii) the charitable deduction; and (iv) the marital deduction [573]

2. **Section 2053—Expenses, Indebtedness, and Taxes:** A deduction is allowed for expenses of the estate and for various claims against the estate, including debts and taxes owed by decedent [574]

    a. **Funeral and administrative expenses:** Deductible expenses include funeral expenses and expenses of administration, including executor's commissions, attorneys' fees, and other necessary expenses such as court costs, accountant's fees, etc. [578]

    b. **Claims against the estate:** Debts and other claims assertable against the estate are deductible if they are ***legally enforceable*** obligations of D that existed at the time of death. Thus, income taxes and gift taxes that accrue prior to death are deductible, but death taxes which arise at or after death are not deductible [587]

c. **"Passing" requirement:** This is met where the surviving spouse receives property from decedent or decedent's estate under circumstances where the property transferred is included in decedent's gross estate .... [649]

d. **"Deductible interest":** All interests in property passing to the surviving spouse are deductible interests except: .... [654]
   (1) ***Interests not included in decedent's gross estate;***
   (2) ***Interests that would be deductible under section 2053;***
   (3) ***Interests in property for which a deduction for losses is allowable;*** and
   (4) ***Nondeductible terminable interests.***

e. **The "nondeductible terminable interest" rule:** No deduction is allowed for certain "terminable interests" .... [659]
   (1) **Definition:** A "terminable interest" is an interest in property that will terminate or fail upon lapse of time or the happening of some event. [660]
   (2) **Not all terminable interests are nondeductible:** Terminable interests ***are*** deductible, except in two situations: .... [661]
      (a) **Interests passing to third party:** A terminable interest is not deductible where an interest in the same property has passed from decedent to another person for less than adequate consideration in money or money's worth if, by reason of ownership of that interest, the other person will possess and enjoy the property after the surviving spouse's interest terminates .... [662]
      (b) **Executor required to acquire terminable interest:** A terminable interest is not deductible if decedent's will directs the executor to use estate property to acquire that interest for the surviving spouse .... [663]
   (3) **Interest in unidentified assets:** The "terminable interest" rule also applies where the estate contains a terminable interest that could be used to satisfy the marital bequest. Unless the executor is precluded from funding the bequest with such an interest, the amount of the otherwise allowable marital deduction will be reduced by the value of such interest .... [669]
   (4) **Deductible terminable interests:** Other interests, although technically terminable, are deductible. These include wasting assets, property with limited life, bonds and notes, and estate trusts .... [670]

f. **Five exceptions to "terminable interest" rule**
   (1) **Survivorship exception:** A marital deduction will be allowed even though the interest of the surviving spouse is conditioned upon the spouse surviving the decedent for a period of up to ***six months***, or not dying from a common disaster, as long as the spouse does, in fact, survive the conditional period or does not perish as a result of a common disaster .... [676]
   (2) **Life estate with power of appointment exception:** The marital deduction is allowed if the surviving spouse is entitled to all income from the property (or a specific portion thereof) for life, payable at least annually, ***and*** if the surviving spouse is granted a power to appoint the property (or a specific portion thereof) to himself or his estate, and if this power is exercisable by the surviving spouse alone and in all events.... [679]
   (3) **Insurance settlement exception:** The marital deduction is allowed as to certain interests passing to the surviving spouse in the proceeds of life insurance, endowment, and annuity contracts where conditions similar to the life estate with power of appointment exception are satisfied... [695]
   (4) **Qualified terminable interest property (Q-tip):** This is property that passes from D, in which the surviving spouse has a qualifying income interest for life, and with respect to which D's executor makes

an election to have the property qualify as a Q-tip interest. . . . . [697]

(a) **Qualifying income interest:** The surviving spouse has a qualifying income interest for life if he or she is entitled to all of the income from the property (or a specific portion thereof) payable at least annually; and ***no person*** has a power to appoint any part of the property to anyone other than the surviving spouse (except that the surviving spouse or some other person may be granted a power of appointment if this power is exercisable at or after the surviving spouse's death). . . . . [700]

(b) **Effects of election:** If the Q-tip interest qualifies for the marital deduction in D's estate, the Q-tip property is included in the surviving spouse's gross estate. (Also, the gift tax will apply if the surviving spouse makes a lifetime transfer of his or her income interest in Q-tip property) . . . . [705]

(c) **Partial elections permitted:** The executor may elect to qualify all or any portion of the Q-tip property . . . . [708]

(5) **Charitable remainder trusts:** A marital deduction will be allowed for the value of the income interest passing to a surviving spouse of a decedent if he is the only noncharitable beneficiary of a trust that qualifies as a charitable remainder annuity trust or unitrust . . . . [709]

g. **Disallowance of marital deduction under Rev. Proc. 64-19**

(1) **Requirements:** A marital deduction will not be allowed if: . . . . [710]

(a) The bequest to the spouse is in the form of a ***pecuniary bequest;***

(b) The executor is authorized to ***distribute assets in kind*** to satisfy the bequest;

(c) The executor is authorized to ***select among estate assets*** for the purpose of making the distribution in kind; and

(d) The executor is directed to use ***estate tax values*** in effecting distribution.

(2) **Exceptions**

(a) **Discretion limited:** If applicable state law or the governing instrument requires the executor to distribute assets at least equal in value to the amount of the marital deduction, ***or*** the executor is required to take into account the relative appreciation and depreciation in value of all assets available for distribution, the marital deduction will be allowed . . . . [713]

(b) **Pre-1964 wills:** With respect to wills executed prior to October 1, 1964 (and not republished), the marital deduction will be allowed if the executor and the surviving spouse enter into an agreement requiring the executor to effect distribution in the manner required by the first exception. . . . . [714]

h. **Disallowance of marital deduction where surviving spouse is not a United States citizen:** No marital deduction is allowed if the surviving spouse is not a United States citizen, even though the decedent ***is*** a citizen. [718]

(1) **Exception:** A marital deduction ***will*** be allowed to the estate of the citizen-spouse if the otherwise qualifying interest passes to a "qualified domestic trust" . . . . [719]

III. SUBSTANTIVE ASPECTS OF THE GIFT TAX

A. TAXABLE GIFTS

1. **Four Basic Elements of a Taxable Gift** . . . . [727]

a. ***The identity and capacity*** of donor and donee;

b. ***Subject matter*** of the gift;

c. ***Sufficiency of the transfer*** that will attract the tax; and

Text Section

d. ***Lack of adequate consideration.***

2. **Donor and Donee**

 a. **Donor**

  (1) **Beneficial owner:** The transfer is taxable to the person or persons who owned a ***beneficial interest*** in the property transferred .... [730]

  (2) **Nonresident aliens:** Nonresident aliens are only taxed on gifts of property located in the United States, and transfers of intangible property by nonresident aliens are generally not subject to gift tax at all ... [731]

  (3) **Void gifts:** Void gifts are not taxable .... [733]

  (4) **Identity of donor:** The tax is imposed on the ***actual*** owner and transferor (not simply the nominal transferor). (*Cf.* "reciprocal trust" doctrine, *supra,* §§135-139) .... [734]

  (5) **Agent of donor:** A gratuitous transfer made by an agent or legal representative of the owner of property is a taxable gift by the owner if the agent or representative has authority to make such transfer .... [735]

 b. **Donee:** The donee need not be identified or ascertained. A gift to an entity is treated as a gift to persons who own beneficial interests in the entity .... [736]

3. **Subject Matter of the Gift:** The gift tax is imposed upon transfers of property .. [740]

 a. **Definition of property:** The term "property," for gift tax purposes, generally includes ***any type*** of interest in property, real or personal, tangible or intangible, and encompasses equitable, future, and contingent interests .. [741]

 b. **Types of property subject to tax**

  (1) **Debts:** Forgiveness of a debt and payment of the debts of another are taxable as gifts. A gratuitous transfer of the donor's own note or check is not taxable until the donee cashes the check or collects the note ... [751]

  (2) **Promise to transfer property in the future:** Assumption of a legal obligation to transfer property in the future is a taxable gift .... [754]

  (3) **Gifts of income:** A gratuitous transfer of a right to receive income from property is a taxable gift .... [755]

  (4) **Annuities:** In general, the transfer of an annuity or the irrevocable designation of the beneficiary of an annuity is a taxable gift of the value of the contract or benefits .... [757]

  (5) **Disposition of life estate in Q-tip property:** If the spouse disposes of the life interest during his or her lifetime, the spouse will be treated as having made a gift of the ***full value*** of the property to which the interest relates, not just the life interest itself .... [758]

 c. **Performance of personal services:** The gratuitous performance of services for another is not subject to the gift tax .... [759]

 d. **Right to use property:** Most authorities had held that allowing another to use money or property without paying interest or rent does not result in a taxable gift. However, the Supreme Court has held that an ***interest free loan*** can be a taxable gift of the reasonable value of the use of the money lent .... [761]

 e. **Lapsing rights:** Where someone transfers an interest in property by gift but retains valuable rights with respect to the property and then permits or causes such rights to lapse, the lapsing rights are considered gifts under the 1990 Act .... [763]

4. **Sufficiency of Transfer:** While no specific form of transfer is required, property owned by the donor must be irrevocably transferred to the donee for the gift tax to attach .... [764]

 a. **Form of transfer**

  (1) **Direct and indirect gifts:** Taxable gifts may be made directly or indirectly. Thus, if A transfers property worth $20,000 to B on condition

that B transfer property worth $5,000 to C, A has made two taxable gifts: a gift of $15,000 to B and a gift of $5,000 to C. . . . . [766]

(2) **Powers of appointment:** Section 2514 specifically provides that the exercise of a ***general*** power of appointment or, in the case of post-1942 powers, the exercise or ***release*** of a general power of appointment, is treated as a transfer of the property subject to the power and is taxable as a gift. . . . . [768]

(3) **Disclaimers:** An effective disclaimer (unqualified refusal to accept property) is ***not*** a transfer . . . . [770]

(a) **Requirements:** Under section 2518 (introduced by 1976 Tax Reform Act), a disclaimer is effective for federal gift and estate tax purposes if: . . . . [772]

1) The disclaimer is in ***writing;***

2) The disclaimer is ***received by donor*** (or the estate) ***within nine months*** of the date of transfer (or within nine months of the day donee reaches age twenty-one);

3) The donee has ***not accepted*** the interest or any of its benefits; and

4) As a result, the interest ***passes to someone other than the disclaimant without any direction on the disclaimant's part.***

(b) **1981 amendment:** A disclaimer will be effective for federal tax purposes even though technically invalid under state law if requirements 2) and 3) above are satisfied, and if a written transfer of the property is made to those persons who would have received the property had the disclaimer in fact been valid. . . . . [778]

b. **Complete vs. incomplete transfers:** Only ***complete*** transfers are subject to the gift tax. . . . . [779]

(1) **Categories of incomplete transfers**

(a) **Retained interests:** To the extent that the donor retains an interest in the property, the transfer is incomplete . . . . [781]

(b) **Revocable transfers:** If the donor can revoke the transfer without the consent of an adverse party, the gift is incomplete . . . . . [782]

(c) **Power to alter:** Even though the donor retains no interest or power to revoke, a retained power to change beneficiaries (alter or amend the transfer) renders the gift incomplete . . . . [783]

(2) **Payments made under an incomplete trust:** Even though a gift is incomplete, if the income is paid over to a beneficiary there is a completed gift of that income . . . . [796]

(3) **Incomplete transfer made complete:** An incomplete transfer is completed and a taxable gift is made when and if the donor relinquishes the interest or power that rendered the gift incomplete in the first instance. [797]

c. **Correlation with estate tax:** The principal purpose of the gift tax is to prevent estate tax avoidance. Thus, transfers for less than full consideration not subject to estate tax will be taxed under the gift tax. (However, many transfers are subject to both taxes.) . . . . [798]

5. **Consideration:** For purposes of the gift tax, a gift is a transfer for ***less than adequate and full consideration in money or money's worth***. . . . . [801]

a. **Measure of consideration:** As with estate tax provisions, consideration must be measurable in ***monetary terms*** and must ***move to the transferor***; and release of dower, curtesy, or similar marital rights is not sufficient consideration to prevent gift tax exposure. . . . . [802]

b. **Business transaction exception:** Business motivated transfers that proceed from arm's length negotiation and are free from donative intent are not taxed as gifts even though not supported by sufficient consideration . . . . . [807]

c. **Involuntary transfers:** Generally, the gift tax reaches only ***voluntary*** transfers . . . . [811]

(1) **Divorce settlements:** It has been held that where the parties' agreement settling property and marital rights is incorporated in the decree, and where the court has power to modify the terms of the agreement, transfers pursuant to the agreement are ***not*** taxable gifts; they are made by force of the decree and not the voluntary agreement . . . . . . [812]

(2) **Statutory relief:** Section 2516 specifically provides that transfers pursuant to a written agreement between spouses in settlement of marital property rights or to provide a reasonable allowance for support of minor children are not taxable gifts, provided a divorce actually occurs within a three-year period beginning one year prior to the execution of the agreement . . . . [813]

d. **Widow's election in community property states:** Decedent-spouse's disposal of the entire community property by will may result in a taxable gift by the surviving spouse if he or she consents to the testamentary scheme. There are no gift tax consequences where the widow elects to take against the will . . . . [818]

6. **Treatment of Concurrent Interests in Property**

a. **Creation of concurrent interests:** In general, the basic rules of the gift tax govern in determining whether there has been a taxable gift. If property is acquired in co-tenancy, there is a taxable gift to the extent that the value of the undivided interest acquired by one co-tenant exceeds what he or she contributed to the purchase price . . . . [821]

(1) **Exception for certain revocable joint interests:** However, if the concurrent interest is "revocable" by the donor, there is not a complete gift, and thus, no gift tax exposure. Examples of "revocable" concurrent interests include joint bank accounts, joint brokerage accounts, and United States Savings Bonds registered in a form of joint ownership. [824]

(2) **Real property acquired by spouses:** Prior to 1982 (and after 1954), the creation of a tenancy by the entirety or a joint tenancy between spouses in real property was not treated as a taxable gift to any extent unless the donor-spouse elected to treat it as such at the time the joint tenancy was created. The creation of such joint tenancies after 1981 may constitute taxable gifts, but any gift is completely offset by the marital deduction . . . . [825]

b. **Termination of concurrent interests:** If the creation of a concurrent interest was a taxable gift, a later severance will not produce a second taxable gift, provided each co-tenant receives his or her share of the property. But a transfer of a concurrent interest by the co-tenants to a third party is treated as a gift by each co-tenant of his or her undivided interest . . . . [828]

(1) **Special rule where creation of a joint tenancy was not a taxable gift:** Where creation of the concurrent interest was not a taxable gift, a severance ***will*** be a taxable gift unless the donor receives the entire property or proceeds of its sale . . . . [833]

(2) **Application of special rule:** Where co-tenants are husband and wife, the taxable gift that may result from the severance will be fully deductible under the gift tax marital deduction to the extent that there is a technical transfer from one spouse to the other. . . . . [835]

7. **The Annual Exclusion:** The first $10,000 of gifts (other than gifts of "future interests") given by a donor to any single donee in any calendar year is excluded in computing the donor's taxable gifts . . . . [841]

a. **Exclusion not allowed for gifts of "future interest":** For this purpose, a future interest is any interest, whether vested or contingent, that is limited to commence in use, possession, or enjoyment at a future date, or is subject to the will of some other person (*e.g.*, the interest of a discretionary distributee) . . . . [847]

(1) **Exception for minor's trusts:** Even though technically a "future interest," the annual exclusion is allowed for gifts on trust for the benefit of a minor if the property and the income must be used for the minor's benefit until age twenty-one (the excess may be accumulated) and the property and any accumulated income must be distributed to the minor upon the minor's attaining age twenty-one . . . . [857]

(2) **Income interest may qualify separately:** In the case of a qualified minor's trust, the income interest may separately qualify for the annual exclusion where income must be used for the benefit of the minor during minority and the accumulated income distributed at age twenty-one, even though the property itself will not qualify for the annual exclusion under this exception because it is to be distributed to the minor at some later date . . . . [859]

b. **Exclusion not allowed if the value of present interest is not ascertainable:** The identity and number of the donees must be ascertainable. Moreover, there must be ***no condition or power*** that could operate to impair or destroy the gift . . . . [861]

8. **Exclusion for Certain Transfers for Educational or Medical Expenses:** The 1981 Act allows an ***unlimited*** exclusion for payments made to an institution or person furnishing education or medical services to another person . . . . [865]

9. **Gift Splitting Between Spouses:** Section 2513 provides that a gift made by one spouse to a third party may be treated as being made one-half by each spouse if the nondonor spouse consents to "split" the gift . . . . [869]

a. **Limitation:** Consent must extend to ***all*** gifts made by spouses during that calendar year . . . . [872]

b. **Exception for gifts to spouse:** Gift-splitting is not allowed where the donor grants the spouse a general power of appointment with respect to the property transferred . . . . [873]

B. GIFT TAX DEDUCTIONS

1. **Introduction:** Two deductions are allowed under the gift tax: (i) the charitable deduction; and (ii) the marital deduction. The former lifetime exemption of $30,000 was abolished by the 1976 Reform Act for all transfers made after December 31, 1976. . . . . [875]

2. **The Charitable Deduction (Section 2522):** The gift tax charitable deduction is virtually identical to the estate tax charitable deduction . . . . [879]

a. **Requirements:** It is allowed for the net value of property transferred to a ***qualified*** charitable object. However, the deduction is limited to the amount of the "taxable gift" (*i.e.*, the gross amount of the gift less the annual exclusion) . . . . [881]

b. **Split interest gifts:** As with the estate tax, charitable remainder gifts or charitable lead gifts must be made in the form of qualified "annuity trusts," "unitrusts," or "pooled income funds" . . . . [884]

3. **The Marital Deduction (Section 2523):** In computing "net gifts," a deduction is allowed for the value of any property transferred by the donor to the spouse. . [887]

a. **Requirements:** The basic rules are virtually identical to those governing estate tax marital deduction. It is allowed only in the case of United States citizens or resident donors; only for gifts to the donor's spouse; and only if the interest given to the spouse is a deductible interest . . . . [889]

(1) **Community property:** Community property qualifies as a "deductible interest" to the same extent as separate property. . . . . [893]

(2) **Nondeductible terminable interest rule:** A terminable interest (defined the same as under the estate tax, *supra*, §§659 *et seq.*) is nondeductible where the interest in the same property is given to a third party and, as a result of ownership of this interest, the third party may possess and enjoy the property after the interest of the spouse terminates . [895]

(a) **Donor retains an interest or has power to appoint an interest:** A terminable interest is also nondeductible under the gift tax if the donor retains an interest in the property that would allow the donor to possess or enjoy the property after the donee spouse's interest terminates or the donor has the power to appoint an interest in the property that he can exercise in such a manner that the appointee may possess or enjoy the property after the termination of the spouse's interest .... [896]

(b) **Joint interests:** The fact that the donor spouse has an interest in the property as a co-tenant with right of survivorship will not prevent allowance of the deduction for the undivided interest transferred to the spouse .... [897]

(c) **Interest in unidentified assets:** Like the estate tax, the nondeductible terminable interest rule under the gift tax is extended to situations where a nondeductible interest in an unidentified group of assets could be distributed to the spouse .... [898]

(3) **Exceptions:** Unlike the estate tax, the gift tax does not contain an exception for survivorship nor for insurance proceeds .... [899]

(a) **Life estate with power of appointment:** The life estate with power of appointment exception also applies to the gift tax marital deduction; the requirements are identical to those under the estate tax .... [900]

(b) **"Q-tip" interests:** The gift tax allows a deduction for "qualified terminable interest property" given to one's spouse. This exception tracks the Q-tip exception under the estate tax .... [901]

(c) **Charitable remainder trusts:** The gift tax allows a deduction, like that allowed under the estate tax, for the value of the income interest given to one's spouse in a qualified charitable remainder annuity trust or unitrust.................................... [905]

b. **Maximum allowed:** The gift tax marital deduction is allowed for the full value (100 percent) of the property transferred to the donee-spouse, subject to two limitations .... [906]

(1) **Net value:** If the property is subject to an encumbrance, or if the donee incurs some obligation as a condition of receiving the gift, the deduction is limited to the net value of the property .... [907]

(2) **Annual exclusion:** The allowable marital deduction must be reduced by the amount of any allowable annual exclusion.................. [908]

(3) **Note—prior law:** Prior law will govern gifts made before 1982 .... [909]

IV. VALUATION

A. INTRODUCTION

Estate and gift taxes are both measured by the ***"fair market value"*** of property transferred. However, different rules concerning valuation date and property subject to tax may apply for estate and gift tax purposes .... [913]

B. RULES OF LAW RELATING TO VALUATION

1. **Valuation Date**

a. **Gift tax:** Taxable gifts are valued as of the ***date the gift is made*** ..... [917]

b. **Estate tax:** Property included in the gross estate, for estate tax purposes, is valued as of the date of the decedent's death ***or*** the executor may elect, under section 2032, to value estate assets at the "alternate valuation date" (six months after the date of the decedent's death). However, valuation changed solely by lapse of time is disregarded if the alternate valuation date is elected.. [918]

(1) **Application of sections 2035-2038:** Assets included in D's estate under sections 2035 through 2038 are valued on the basis of their value at the date of D's death (or alternate valuation date), not their value at the time of transfer . . . . [923]

2. **Fair Market Value:** The standard for valuation is "fair market value," generally defined as the price that a willing buyer would pay a willing seller after arm's length bargaining where there is no compulsion to buy or sell and where both parties are aware of all relevant facts. The burden of proof as to valuation is upon the taxpayer . . . . [928]

a. **Special use valuation for estate tax purposes:** In certain circumstances, farmland or real property used in a closely held trade or business may be valued for estate tax purposes at less than "fair market value" [I.R.C. §2032A] . . . . [931]

b. **Special valuation rules designed to limit "estate tax freezes":** New Chapter 14 represents a legislative attempt to address the problem of "freezing" the value of property that is expected to appreciate and giving away the anticipated appreciation free of gift or estate tax liability. The problem is treated essentially as a gift tax valuation issue . . . . [937]

(1) **Transactions affected:** Chapter 14 affects four types of situations: . . [940]

(a) **Transfer of interests in corporations or partnerships:** Section 2701 generally applies where a person transfers an interest in a corporation or partnership to or for the benefit of a family member, and the transferor or an "applicable family member" retains an interest in the same corporation or partnership. Exceptions include situations in which: (i) market quotations are readily available for the transferred stock or retained interest; (ii) there is only one class of interest (or if two classes, they differ only as to voting rights); or (iii) there is a proportionate transfer of all classes of interest . . . . [941]

1) **Valuation rules:** The transferred interest is valued by subtracting the value of the retained interest from the proportionate fair market value of the entire enterprise. If the retained interest is an "applicable retained interest" (*i.e.*, a distribution right, or a liquidation, put, call, or conversion right), it is assigned a value of zero . . . . [943]

a) **Exceptions to zero value rule:** The zero value rule does not apply to the following: . . . . [945]

1/ Where the transferor (or applicable family member) does not hold at least ***50%*** of the value or voting power of the entity immediately before the transfer;

2/ Distribution rights in the form of ***qualified payments***;

3/ Distribution rights with respect to a ***retained junior equity interest***; and

4/ A right that must be exercised at a ***specific time and in a specific manner***.

b) **Minimum value rule:** If there is a transfer of a junior equity interest, the proportionate value of such interest is determined by valuing all junior equity interests at not less than 10% of the total value of all equity interests in the entity, ***plus*** the total amount of any indebtedness of the entity to the transferor (or to an applicable family member) . . . . [946]

(b) **Transfers of interests in trusts:** A "grantor retained income trust" (GRIT) is valued at zero for purposes of determining the value of the taxable gift of the remainder. However, a value ***is*** assigned if the retained interest is a qualified interest (*i.e.*, a grantor retained annuity trust (GRAT) or a grantor retained unitrust (GRUT)) [951]

1) **Applies to term interests also:** If a transferor gives a term interest but retains a remainder, the remainder is valued at zero unless the remainder is noncontingent, and the term interests are either GRATs or GRUTs . . . . [952]

2) **Exceptions:** The zero value rule of this section does not apply to: . . . . [953]

a) Transfers to ***nonfamily members***;

b) ***Incomplete gifts***; and

c) Transfer of an interest in property that is to be used as a ***personal residence*** by the persons holding the term interests.

(c) **Property subject to restrictions:** Various burdens on property (*e.g.*, restrictions on its transfer) might be used to reduce its fair market value. To remedy this, section 2703 mandates that such restrictions be disregarded for purposes of estate, gift, and generation-skipping taxes . . . . [955]

1) **Exception—bona fide business agreements:** The rule of section 2703 does not apply to an option, agreement, right, or restriction that meets the following requirements: . . . . [957]

a) There is a ***bona fide business arrangement***;

b) The agreement is not a device to transfer property to members of the decedent's family for ***less than full and adequate consideration*** in money or money's worth; and

c) The terms are comparable to similar arrangements entered into by persons in an ***arm's length transaction***.

(d) **Lapsing rights and restrictions:** Prior to 1990, the gift and estate tax was unable to cover situations in which someone transferred an interest in property by gift, while retaining valuable rights with respect to the property, and then permitted or caused these rights to lapse . . . . [959]

1) **Taxable transfer:** The lapse of a voting or liquidation right in a corporation or partnership is treated as a transfer by gift or as a transfer includible in the decedent's gross estate. [961]

a) **Limitation—control:** The lapse is treated as a transfer only if the person holding the right immediately before the lapse and members of that person's family (both before and after the lapse) control the corporation or partnership . . . . [962]

b) **Amount of transfer:** The taxable amount is the difference between the value of the interest retained immediately prior to the lapse and its value immediately after the lapse . . . . [963]

C. VALUATION METHODS

There are, essentially, three general methods of valuation commonly used . . . . [966]

1. **Market Price Method:** Where market prices for identical property are known. *e.g.,* in the case of listed securities, these prices may be used to value the same property included in the gross estate. Similarly, appraisal may be based on "comparable sales" . . . . [967]
2. **Actuarial Valuation:** The value of life estates, remainders, terms for years, annuities, etc., is based upon actuarial tables prescribed by the Regulations . . [969]
3. **Capitalization of Earnings Method:** Market value may be estimated by capitalizing the known earnings derived from the property . . . . [970]

D. VALUATION OF SOME SPECIFIC ITEMS

1. **Real Property:** This is usually valued on the basis of comparable sales. Generally, an appraisal must take into account the property's ***"highest and best use"***. [971]
2. **Stocks and Bonds**
   a. **Listed securities:** Fair market value is the mean between the highest and lowest selling price on the valuation date or nearest trading date .... [973]
   b. **Unlisted securities:** Valuation must take into account all recent sales, corporate net worth, earning capacity, etc. .... [976]
   c. **Mutual fund shares:** This is valued at "net asset value" (*i.e.*, asking price less any sales commission or "load") .... [978]
   d. **Bonds, notes, evidences of indebtedness:** These are valued at face value plus accrued interest, unless evidence is introduced justifying a discount .... [979]
3. **Life Estates, Annuities, Remainders, Reversionary Interests, etc.:** Annuities issued by a company regularly selling annuity contracts are valued by reference to the present cost of purchasing a similar contract. All other annuities, life estates, etc., are valued under the Regulations' "present worth tables" .... [980]

V. COMPUTATION OF TAX

A. GIFT TAX COMPUTATIONS

1. **Computational Procedure:** The gift tax is computed by applying the unified tax rates to the total of current and prior taxable gifts made by a donor, and then subtracting a figure obtained by applying the same rates of tax to the sum of all prior taxable gifts. Effective for transfers made after December 31, 1976, the same tax rate schedule is applied to both lifetime and testamentary transfers . [982]
2. **Cumulative Nature of Tax:** The gift tax is imposed on a cumulative basis to all gratuitous transfers made by an individual during life. The effect is to expose current taxable gifts to higher marginal rates. .... [991]
3. **Unified Gift Tax Credit:** From the tax determined by the cumulative computation, the "unified credit" may be subtracted—to the extent that the unified credit was not previously allowable to the taxpayer. .... [994]
   a. **Amount of credit:** By 1987, a credit in the amount of $192,800 may be claimed. Between 1982 and 1987, there is a six-year phase-in of the augmented unified credit .... [995]
   b. **Limitation:** The credit must be claimed against gifts in the order of time they are made or it is forfeited .... [1000]

B. ESTATE TAX COMPUTATIONS

1. **Computational Procedure:** Under present law, the estate tax is computed by applying the unified rates of tax to the total of taxable estate and all "adjusted taxable gifts," and then subtracting "taxes payable," an amount obtained by applying the same rates of tax to the total of the taxable gifts that were included in the first computation .... [1008]
   a. ***"Adjusted taxable gifts"*** means all taxable gifts made ***after*** December 31, 1976, that are not included in the taxable estate .... [1010]
   b. ***"Taxes payable"*** includes gift taxes with respect to "adjusted taxable gifts" ***and*** any taxable gifts that were included in the gross estate .... [1011]
2. **Unified Estate Tax Credit:** From the tax thus determined, the "unified credit" may be subtracted. The result is the tax liability. The credit is identical in amount and phase-in to the unified gift tax credit .... [1014]
3. **Other Credits Allowed Against Estate Tax:** In addition to the unified estate tax credit, four other credits are allowed: .... [1017]
   a. ***Credit for state death taxes paid***;
   b. ***Credit for certain pre-1977 gift taxes paid***;

c. ***Credit for taxes paid on a prior estate*** (property previously taxed to another); and
d. ***Credit for certain foreign death taxes paid*** to another country that relate to property also included in the gross estate of a citizen-decedent.

VI. RETURNS AND PAYMENT OF TAX

A. GIFT TAX

1. **Returns:** A gift tax return must be filed for any calendar year in which a gift is made. . . . . [1028]
   a. **Exceptions:** A gift tax return need not be filed if the only transfers made during the year are fully exempt from the tax or are nontaxable because of the 100 percent marital deduction . . . . . [1029]
2. **Payment of Tax:** The donor is primarily liable for payment of the tax. It is due at the same time the return must be filed . . . . . [1034]
   a. **Transferee liability:** If the donor does not pay the tax, the government has a ***lien*** on the property to the extent of the tax due and also a right to hold the ***donee*** liable for the unpaid gift tax to the extent of the value of the property received. . . . . [1035]
3. **Special Rules for Split Gifts:** If a gift of future interest is split, both spouses must file a return, reporting one-half the property's value. If a present interest gift is split, the actual donor must file if the gift exceeds $10,000; the other spouse need not file unless the one-half value attributed to that spouse exceeds $10,000. Both spouses are jointly and severally liable for payment of the tax . . . . . [1039]

B. ESTATE TAX

1. **Returns:** The estate tax return must be filed by the decedent's executor within nine months of the date of the decedent's death . . . . . [1042]
   a. **Limitation—filing amount:** No return need be filed if the gross estate does not exceed certain specified amounts. Since 1987, the specified amount has been $600,000 . . . . . [1045]
2. **Payment of Tax:** The executor is primarily responsible for payment of tax. It is due at the same time the return must be filed . . . . . [1049]
   a. **Transferee liability:** If the executor fails to pay, persons holding legal or beneficial interests in the property included in the gross estate are liable for the payment of the tax to the extent of the value of their interest . . . . . [1053]
   b. **Extensions of time for payment:** Such extensions are available at the executor's election for certain reversionary or remainder interests that are included in the decedent's gross estate. They may also be granted upon showing of cause. . . . . [1055]
      (1) **Installment payments:** In certain circumstances where an estate is substantially comprised of an interest in a "closely held business," the executor may elect to pay the estate tax related to the business interest in installments . . . . . [1057]
   c. **Apportionment:** The burden of estate taxation generally follows the order of abatement prescribed by state law. . . . . [1061]

VII. TAX ON GENERATION-SKIPPING TRANSFERS

A. INTRODUCTION

1. **Definition:** A generation-skipping transfer is, generally, a gift or bequest of an interest in property (on trust or otherwise) to persons who are assigned to a generation more than one generation younger than that of the donor or decedent ("skip person") . . . . . [1062]

2. **When Imposed:** A generation-skipping transfer tax was not imposed at the time the generation-skipping transfer was created. Rather, it was imposed at the time present enjoyment of the property shifted to a younger generation either because of the termination of an older generation beneficiary's interest or because there was a distribution made to younger generation beneficiaries. It was designed to produce essentially the same transfer tax result as would obtain if the transferred property had been given or bequeathed outright through succeeding generations. [1064]
3. **Repeal and Replacement in 1986:** Originally enacted in 1976, this tax was never applied because of its complexity. Congress retroactively repealed the 1976 provision and, in 1986, replaced it with a new generation-skipping transfer tax. The new tax is substantively the same tax with simplified computations except that it also applies to "direct skips" . . . . [1069]

B. TRANSFERS TO WHICH THE TAX APPLIES

The tax applies to "every generation-skipping transfer," including taxable distributions, taxable terminations, and direct skips . . . . [1075]

1. **Definitions**
   a. **Taxable distribution:** This is any distribution from a trust (or any arrangement having a trust effect) to a "skip person," except for distributions considered taxable terminations or a direct skip . . . . [1077]
   b. **Taxable termination:** This involves any termination (*e.g.,* by death) of an interest in trust property except where a non-skip person has an interest in the property immediately following termination ***or*** if no distribution may afterwards be made to a skip person . . . . [1078]
   c. **Direct skip:** This involves a transfer that is subject to gift or estate taxes but is made to a skip person . . . . [1079]
   d. **Interest:** A person has an interest if she either (i) has a right to receive income or corpus from the trust or (ii) is a permissible recipient of income or corpus. A trust is treated as a skip person if all trust interests are held by skip persons or if no person holds a present interest but all future distributions must be made to skip persons . . . . [1082]
   e. **Ascertaining generations:** Generations are generally determined along family lines—*i.e.,* grantor, grantor's spouse and grantor's siblings would be one generation; their children (including adopted children) would be assigned to the first younger generation; and grandchildren would be assigned to the next younger generation, etc. Nonfamily generations are assigned on the basis of the difference in age between the beneficiaries and the grantor: a person born more than 12½ years after the grantor would be in the first younger generation, and thereafter generations are determined on the basis of twenty-five years . . . . [1085]
2. **General Exceptions:** The generation-skipping tax does not apply to a transfer to the extent that: (i) the property was subject to a prior generation-skipping tax; (ii) the prior taxable transfer was to a transferee assigned to a generation the same as or lower than that of the present transferee; and (iii) the transfer does not have the effect of avoiding the generation-skipping tax. Transfers for ***educational or medical expenses*** are also not taxable . . . . [1090]
3. **Special Exception for Direct Skips:** A transfer to a grandchild of the transferor (direct skip) is not taxable if the granchild's parent (i.e., transferor's child) is dead . . . . [1093]

C. AMOUNT TAXABLE

1. **Taxable Distributions:** The taxable base is the value of the property ***received*** by the transferee minus any related expenses incurred by the transferee. If the tax is paid by a trust for the recipient of a taxable distribution, that tax is considered a taxable distribution . . . . [1098]

2. **Taxable Terminations:** The taxable amount is the value of all property subject to the taxable termination minus certain expenses allowable as estate tax deductions .... [1100]
3. **Direct Skips:** Tax is imposed on the value of the property received by the transferee........ [1101]
4. **Valuation Rules:** The property is valued at its fair market value at the time of the transfer minus any consideration furnished by the transferee .... [1102]
   a. **Time of transfer:** Taxable distributions or a lifetime direct skip occurs on the date of the distribution or gift. The transfer date of a direct skip by bequest is the date of decedent's death. A taxable termination occurs on the date of termination .... [1103]
5. **GST Exemption:** There is an exemption of $1 million that may be allocated by the transferor among her transferred property. This is ***not*** an exclusion ...... [1105]

D. COMPUTATION OF TAX

The taxable amount of the generation-skipping transfer is multiplied by the applicable rate—*i.e.,* the ***maximum federal estate tax rate*** in effect on the transfer date, multiplied by the inclusion ratio .... [1107]

E. PAYMENT OF TAX

For taxable distributions, the transferee pays the tax. For taxable terminations, the trustee is liable for the tax; if there is no formal trust, "trustee" is the person in actual or constructive possession of the property. The transferor pays the tax in cases of direct skips .... [1111]

TEXT CORRELATION CHART

Gilbert Law Summary **Estate and Gift Tax**	Bittker, Clark **Federal Estate and Gift Taxation** 1990 (6th ed.)	Campfield, Dickinson, Turnier **Taxation of Estates, Gifts and Trusts** 1991-1993	Stephens, Maxfield, Lind, Calfee **Federal Estate and Gift Taxation** (Student Edition) 1991 (6th ed.), 1992 Supp.	Surrey, McDaniel, Gutman **Federal Wealth Transfer Taxation** 1987 (Successor Edition)
I. INTRODUCTION				
A. The Estate Tax	1-38	3-28	(1) 2-17; Supp. (S1) 1-2	35-36
B. The Gift Tax	1-38	3-28, 31-34	(1) 17-26; Supp. (S1) 2	37-38
C. Coordination of the Federal Estate and Gift Taxes	22-27	6-8, 11	(1) 25-26	8-14
D. The Generation-Skipping Transfer Tax	30-31	12-13	(1) 26-34	38-41
E. Taxing Jurisdiction				15-22
II. SUBSTANTIVE ASPECTS OF THE ESTATE TAX				
A. Gross Estate				
1. Inclusions in Gross Estate—General Overview	20-22	279-280	(4) 6-8; Supp. (S4) 3	71-73
2. Section 2033—Property Owned by Decedent	145-179	280-313	(4) 96-118; Supp. (S4) 14-17	71-128
3. Section 2034—Dower or Curtesy Interests	179-183		(4) 118-120	218-228, 230, 233
4. Section 2035—Gifts Made Within Three Years of Death	195-204	573-597	(4) 121-136; Supp. (S4) 17-19	260-275
5. Section 2036—Transfers With Retained Life Interests	247-269	387-448	(4) 136-238; Supp. (S4) 19-24	302-367
6. Section 2037—Transfers Taking Effect at Death	299-323	483-509	(4) 238-253	286-302
7. Section 2038—Revocable Transfers	204-247	449-482	(4) 254-277; Supp. (S4) 24-26	282-284
8. Section 2039—Annuities	324-340	511-541	(4) 277-291; Supp. (S4) 27	431-457
9. Section 2040—Joint Interests	183-193	315-335	(4) 291-309; Supp. (S4) 27-28	457-489
10. Section 2041—Powers of Appointment	382-410	543-572	(4) 309-336; Supp. (S4) 28	489-520
11. Section 2042—Life Insurance	341-382	337-386	(4) 336-362; Supp. (S4) 29-30	524-606
12. Section 2043—Consideration	63-71	599-614	(4) 362-375	381-395
13. Section 2044—Certain Marital Deduction Property		173-175	(4) 376-377; Supp. (S4) 31	840-844
14. Section 2045—Prior Interests			(4) 377-378	96-107, 914-923 151-158, 501, 516, 524, 705, 776
15. Section 2046—Disclaimers		758-759	(4) 378	
B. Deductions				
1. Introductory Analysis	423		(5) 3-4	607-610
2. Section 2053—Expenses, Indebtedness and Taxes	423-443	615-639	(5) 4-32; Supp. (S5) 2-4	611-631

TEXT CORRELATION CHART—continued

Gilbert Law Summary Estate and Gift Tax	Bittker, Clark **Federal Estate and Gift Taxation** 1990 (6th ed.)	Campfield, Dickinson, Turnier **Taxation of Estates, Gifts and Trusts** 1991-1993	Stephens, Maxfield, Lind, Calfee **Federal Estate and Gift Taxation** (Student Edition) 1991 (6th ed.), 1992 Supp.	Surrey, McDaniel, Gutman **Federal Wealth Transfer Taxation** 1987 (Successor Edition)
3. Section 2054—Deductions for Losses	444-445		(5) 32-36	696-733
4. Section 2055—The Charitable Deduction	445-469	641-672	(5) 36-66; Supp. (S5) 4-9	754-867
5. Section 2056—The Marital Deduction	469-522	673-761	(5) 67-131; Supp. (S5) 9-22	
III. SUBSTANTIVE ASPECTS OF THE GIFT TAX				
A. Taxable Gifts	39-144	31-134	(9) 11-46, (S10) 3-98 Supp. (S9) 2-6, (S10) 2-13	129-218, 301, 396-423, 457, 479-486, 520-524, 575-583, 868-871
B. Deductions	469-523	135-175	(11) 1-25; Supp. (S11) 1-4	217-218, 631-683, 709-714, 867-868
IV. VALUATION				
A. Introductory Comments	531-533	183-184		930
B. Rules of Law Relating to Valuation	533-540, 570-571	184-189, 199-269	(4) 8-96, (10) 37-59; Supp. (S4) 3-14, (S4A) 2-24, (S10) 7-9	930-940
C. Valuation Methods		191-197	(10) 41-49; Supp. (S10) 7-8	940-1040
D. Valuation of Some Specific Items	560-569	271-275	(4) 10-34; Supp. (S4) 4-8	168-182, 301, 400-401, 583-592, 931-934, 940-1038
V. COMPUTATION OF TAX				
A. Gift Tax Computations	22-27	9-16	(1) 24-25, (9) 8-10	37-38
B. Estate Tax Computations	22-27	9-16	(1) 14, (2) 3-4; Supp. (S2) 1-2	35-37
VI. RETURNS AND PAYMENT OF TAX				
A. Gift Tax	590-591	177-180	(1) 26, (9) 34-36; Supp. (S9) 4-5	23-24
B. Estate Tax	573-590	763-779	(1) 16-17, (2) 10-22; Supp. (S2) 2-8	22-23
VII. TAX ON GENERATION-SKIPPING TRANSFERS				
A. Background and Introduction	30-31, 411-412	783-789	(1) 26-34, (12) 1-5, (13) 2-9	880-884
B. Transfers to Which the Tax Applies	412-417	789-791	(13) 9-65, (15) 1-21; Supp. (S15) 1-2	887-901
C. Amount Taxable	417-419	790-792	(12) 5-8, (14) 1-16, (15) 1-21; Supp. (S14) 1, (S15) 1-2	892-894
D. Computation of Tax	419-420	792-793	(1) 31-34, (16) 2-51; Supp. (S16) 1-2	38-41, 889-891
E. Payment of Tax	591		(1) 34, (12) 8-13	24, 896-897

approach to exams

In dealing with exam questions concerning federal estate, gift, or generation-skipping transfer tax issues, you must first recognize that a problem in the area exists, then focus on and analyze the specific tax issues presented and, finally, apply the relevant rules of law to resolve the issues in the specific context in which they are presented.

A. RECOGNIZING A PROBLEM

In every area of law, there are certain types of events, transactions, etc., that "flag" the existence of a relevant legal issue. For example, in torts, someone is ***injured***; in contracts, someone has ***agreed*** to do something.

1. **Transfer Taxes:** The three taxes that are the subject of this Summary are all transfer taxes: They are imposed upon the transfer of property. The "flag" for you to watch for is a ***transfer.***

2. **What Kind of Transfer?** Only ***gratuitous transfers*** are taxed. Thus, when money, property, or services of equivalent value are received by the transferor in exchange for the property transferred, an income tax issue may arise but a transfer tax issue is ordinarily ***not*** present.

3. **Scope of the Transfer Concept:** Taxable transfers can be quite subtle. Be alert for a transfer tax issue whenever ***beneficial enjoyment of property,*** or some ***power to control beneficial enjoyment, shifts*** from one person to another.

4. **Lifetime vs. Testamentary Gifts:** Generally, the subject of the gift tax is lifetime transfers, while the subject of the estate tax is transfers that occur as a result of a person's death. However, some lifetime gifts are exposed to the estate tax, either because the transfer is effectively completed by the transferor's death (*e.g.*, a lifetime gift of a remainder following a reserved life estate), or because estate tax exposure is necessary to prevent tax avoidance (*e.g.*, "deathbed gifts").

5. **Correlation of the Transfer Taxes:** The three taxes are designed to assure that gratuitous transfers, whenever or however made, will be subject to tax and, with the introduction of the unified tax scheme in 1976, that they will be exposed to the same graduated rates of tax—whenever or however made. For the most part, the taxes are ***mutually inclusive***; *i.e.*, a transfer that is not exposed to the estate tax will be exposed to the gift tax. But, as will be seen, the taxes are ***not mutually exclusive***; *i.e.*, some taxable gifts may also be exposed to the estate tax, necessitating adjustments in the form of tax credits to relieve double taxation.

B. ANALYZING THE TRANSFER TAX ISSUE

A detailed understanding of the pertinent provisions of the Internal Revenue Code is, of course, essential for identification and analysis of the particular issue or issues. Sometimes, the issues may be highlighted for you: *e.g.*, "Did A make a taxable gift?" or "Is A entitled to any deduction in connection with the bequest to the surviving spouse?" Frequently, however, you will be required to identify issues in addition to presenting reasoned conclusions: *e.g.*, "Discuss the estate and gift tax consequences, if any."

In general, transfer tax issues fall into the following six general categories (the first four of which are the most common). Ask yourself:

1. **Is the Transfer Taxable at All?**

   a. Is the apparent shifting of beneficial ownership or enjoyment of a type that is subject to one or more of the general or specific provisions of the transfer taxes?

   b. Is the transfer gratuitous, in whole or in part, or is it for a full consideration that is recognized as "adequate" for transfer tax purposes?

2. **Under Which Tax Does the Transfer Fall?**

   a. If made during the donor's lifetime, does it fall within the definition of a "taxable gift" for gift tax purposes?

   b. Even though made during the donor's lifetime, is it the kind of lifetime gift that is deemed "testamentary" in nature so that it may also be taxable for estate tax purposes?

   c. If the transfer occurs at the time of death, did the decedent have a sufficient "interest" in the property so that it should be taxed in the estate for estate tax purposes?

   d. If the decedent held only a lifetime interest, is there "generation skipping" involved so as to subject the property to the generation-skipping transfer tax?

3. **What Is the Value of the Property Transferred?**

4. **Are Any Exemptions or Deductions Allowable With Respect to the Transfer?**

5. **How Is the Tax to Be Computed?**

   a. Should any prior transfers be taken into account in applying the graduated rates of tax?

   b. Are any credits against tax allowable in computing the ultimate tax liability?

6. **Who Is Liable for Payment of the Transfer Taxes?**

C. APPLY RELEVANT RULES TO SPECIFIC SITUATIONS

Ordinarily, it is not enough that you simply identify the issues and state the rules of law; rather, you must ***apply*** the issues and rules in the context of the specific factual situations presented by the problem. Keep in mind the following:

1. **Do Not Fight the Facts:** Accept the facts as given. For example, if you are told that "A gave property to B," do not dwell on the adequacy of consideration for the transfer—unless other facts raise the issue of consideration.

2. **Multiple Theories:** Sometimes (particularly under the estate tax) a tax might attach under more than one section of the Code. Be alert to this and discuss all relevant theories under which the transfer might be taxed. At the same time, do ***not*** discuss theories of taxation that are not raised by the problem; a proper answer should not be a summary of the course.

3. **Alternative Positions:** Sometimes there is no clear-cut "answer" to a particular issue raised; *i.e.*, an argument can be made either for or against imposition of the tax. If so, discuss both positions fully. At the same time, do not manufacture alternative positions.

I. INTRODUCTION

chapter approach

Questions involving the history, nature, and constitutionality of the federal transfer taxes (the estate tax, gift tax, and generation-skipping transfer tax) rarely appear on examinations. However, the ***purpose*** and ***interrelationship*** of the three transfer taxes are important to know as they are frequently relevant to questions relating to whether one or more of the taxes may be applicable to a particular transfer.

A. THE ESTATE TAX

1. **Brief History:** [§1] The federal government imposed death taxes of various sorts prior to the beginning of the twentieth century. However, these early federal death taxes were only temporary expedients designed to meet some emergency need for federal revenue (*e.g.*, prosecution of the Civil War) and were repealed when the emergency need ceased.

   a. **Origin of present estate tax—Revenue Act of 1916:** Similarly, the need for revenues to wage World War I prompted a federal estate tax imposed by the Revenue Act of 1916. But here, the termination of hostilities did not produce a termination of the tax. Although its provisions have been refined by amendment over the years, the essential scope and thrust of that estate taxing scheme persist today in sections 2001 through 2209 of the 1954 Code.

2. **Purpose:** [§2] While the federal estate tax raises a substantial amount in terms of absolute dollars, the percentage of federal revenues it produces is relatively insignificant. Proponents of the first federal estate tax were more concerned with socio-economic matters than fiscal effects; they saw the federal estate tax as a means of limiting and reducing the accumulation of wealth by American family "dynasties." Interestingly enough, this result has been achieved more through the income tax than the estate tax. However, the estate tax remains as an "ultimate" tax which adds the final element of progressivity to the federal revenue system—*i.e.,* where a taxpayer has been able to accumulate substantial wealth in spite of the income taxes, the estate tax (applied at progressively graduated rates) exacts a final levy.

3. **Types of Death Taxes:** [§3] State and federal death taxes are of two types: estate taxes and inheritance taxes. Simply stated, an estate tax is a tax upon the value of all property owned by a decedent that is ***transferred*** or transmitted to the decedent's heirs or beneficiaries upon the decedent's death. On the other hand, an inheritance tax is a tax upon the value of property ***received*** by an heir or beneficiary on account of a decedent's death.

   a. **Estate tax computation:** In the case of an estate tax, a ***single set*** of deductions, exemptions, and graduated rates are applied to the decedent's estate; with few exceptions, it does not matter how many heirs or beneficiaries share in the estate, or who they are.

b. **Inheritance tax computation:** In the case of an inheritance tax, however, ***separate*** exemptions and rates are applied to the share received by each beneficiary and, typically, the rates of tax and allowable exemptions vary according to the relationship of the beneficiaries to the decedent.

4. **Overview of State Death Taxes:** [§4] All states except Nevada impose death taxes, some under an estate tax system, others under an inheritance tax system or a combined inheritance-estate tax system. Some state death tax schemes are tied directly to the federal estate tax (*i.e.,* the state tax is effectively based upon the taxable estate as defined by federal tax law). But even where there is not a direct tie-in, the scope of state death taxes is generally very similar to that of the federal estate tax in terms of what types of property and what types of transfers are subject to the tax. Thus, a thorough understanding of the federal estate tax will facilitate an understanding of the relevant state death tax. Moreover, tax planning with a view to the federal estate tax will, in general, achieve satisfactory tax results under the state death tax as well.

5. **Nature of the Federal Estate Tax:** [§5] Although the federal estate tax is measured by the value of the property transferred, it is not deemed to be a property tax, but rather an excise or privilege tax. That is, the tax is imposed upon the transfer of the property, not on the property itself; or, stated another way, the tax is not upon the ownership of property but upon the ***privilege of transferring property*** by devise, bequest, or inheritance.

   a. **Constitutionality:** [§6] This distinction—between a tax on property and on a transfer of property—has important legal significance. Under Article I, Section 9, Clause 4 of the United States Constitution, direct (property) taxes must be apportioned among the several states according to population, whereas indirect (transfer) taxes are subject only to the constitutional requirement of uniformity. Thus, by finding that the federal estate tax was imposed upon the ***transfer*** of property at death, not on the property itself, the United States Supreme Court was able to uphold the validity of the tax against the assertion that it was unconstitutional because not apportioned. [New York Trust Co. v. Eisner, 256 U.S. 345 (1921)]

6. **Nonretroactive Application of Federal Estate Tax:** [§7] It is well settled that the federal estate tax "should not be construed to apply to transactions already completed." [Nichols v. Coolidge, 274 U.S. 531 (1926)] Hence, even where it might be constitutionally permissible to apply estate tax amendments retroactively, Congress has, as a matter of ***policy***, limited amendments to prospective application only. As a consequence, the estate tax law in effect at the date of the transaction in question governs—even though the law may subsequently have changed. (Accordingly, throughout this summary, references are made to prior law wherever significant distinctions exist in the present law.)

B. THE GIFT TAX

1. **Brief History:** [§8] The first federal gift tax was enacted in 1924. [Revenue Act of 1924, §§288-293] However, this tax was generally ineffective and was repealed in 1926. The flaw in the 1924 tax was traceable not only to the substantial exemptions it allowed,

but also to the fact that it operated annually (like the income tax) rather than cumulatively, thereby failing to take the donor's previous gifts into account.

a. **Origin of present gift tax—Revenue Act of 1932:** The present gift tax has its origins in the Revenue Act of 1932. Its provisions have been refined by amendment over the years, but its essential thrust and scope persist today in sections 2501 through 2524 of the 1954 Code.

2. **Purpose:** [§9] The federal gift tax serves several purposes, one of which is to discourage avoidance of the federal income tax by the device of giving away income-producing property to those in lower income tax brackets. The gift tax exacts a "price" for this opportunity at the time the transfer is made.

a. **Curtailing estate tax avoidance:** However, the principal purpose of the gift tax is to limit avoidance of the ***estate tax*** by the device of lifetime gifts which would remove the transferred property from estate tax exposure on the donor's death. This is important to bear in mind since the scope of the gift tax and the interpretation of what transfers constitute taxable gifts are frequently based on consideration of the essential purpose of the tax.

3. **State Gift Taxes:** [§10] While a number of states impose taxes upon lifetime gifts in addition to estate or inheritance taxes, many do not. However, in those states that have adopted a gift tax, the scope is generally similar to that of the federal gift tax.

4. **Nature and Constitutionality of Federal Gift Tax:** [§11] The federal gift tax, like the federal estate tax, has been interpreted to be a type of excise tax—*i.e.*, a tax upon the ***transfer*** of property rather than upon the property itself. Thus, just as in the case of the estate tax, the gift tax has been held to be an indirect tax and hence not subject to the constitutional provision requiring apportionment of direct taxes. [Bromley v. McCaughn, 280 U.S. 124 (1929)]

C. COORDINATION OF THE FEDERAL ESTATE AND GIFT TAXES

1. **Background:** [§12] Although the federal estate and gift taxes are related in purpose (above) and the separate provisions are frequently read "in pari materia" (*i.e.,* construed together), differences do exist in the substantive scope of the taxes. Generally, the estate and gift taxes are ***mutually inclusive***—so that a transfer not taxed under one of the tax schemes will be taxed under the other. On the other hand, the two taxes are ***not mutually exclusive***; *i.e.,* some transfers may be taxed under ***both*** taxing schemes (although adjustments in the form of credits serve to eliminate double taxation).

a. **Former dual tax schemes:** [§13] Prior to 1977, a true dual system of estate and gift taxation existed:

(1) ***Separate graduated rates*** were applied under the estate and gift taxes, the gift tax rates being fixed at three-fourths of those of the estate tax within the same tax bracket.

(2) ***Separate exemptions*** applied to the two taxing schemes. This allowed for an optimum level of tax-free transfers—*i.e.*, a person could make lifetime gifts which would utilize the gift tax specific exemption ($30,000) without any reduction in the estate tax exemption ($60,000).

(3) ***Most importantly, the estate taxes were applied only to property taxable under the estate tax***—not cumulatively to all gratuitous transfers. Thus, even though a person may have made substantial lifetime gifts, upon death his estate got a "new start" through the graduated estate tax rates.

2. **The "Unified Tax" of the 1976 Tax Reform Act:** [§14] The Tax Reform Act of 1976 did ***not*** unify the substantive aspects of the federal estate and gift taxes—numerous substantive differences in thrust and scope still remain. However, it ***did*** unify the ***computational*** aspects of the two transfer taxes and eliminated the dual system of rates and exemptions described above.

   a. **General operation:** Under the Tax Reform Act, ***a single set of graduated rates*** is applied to both lifetime and deathtime transfers. Further, the separate gift and estate tax exemptions (above) were repealed and a ***single "unified credit"*** was enacted which, in effect, operates cumulatively to both lifetime and deathtime transfers. Moreover, the new unified tax computation requires the estate tax to take into account lifetime gratuitous transfers, so that ***all*** gratuitous transfers are now taxed ***cumulatively***. (*See infra*, §§1003 *et seq.*, for detailed discussion and illustrative computations.)

D. THE GENERATION-SKIPPING TRANSFER TAX

1. **Background:** [§15] Prior to 1976, there was opportunity for considerable estate tax avoidance through the use of so-called generation-skipping transfers. This was made possible by the fact that the estate tax does not apply to property in which the decedent possessed only a life interest or special power of appointment (*see infra*, §§36, 471-472). Therefore, by granting successive life estates and special powers of appointment, estate tax exposure could be avoided through succeeding generations (limited only by the Rule Against Perpetuities), even though each succeeding generation enjoyed the use of the property and considerable power with respect to its disposition. This potential for tax avoidance was long recognized as a significant flaw in the scheme of estate and gift taxation.

2. **The Tax Reform Act of 1976:** [§16] The 1976 Tax Reform Act introduced a completely new transfer tax—the "Generation-Skipping Transfer Tax." This tax was intended to eliminate the above mentioned opportunity for tax avoidance.

   a. **Separate tax:** [§17] The generation-skipping transfer tax was not an amendment to, or modification of, the estate or gift tax. Rather, it was an entirely ***separate system*** of transfer taxation; *i.e.*, a tax is imposed upon the value of property at the time an interest therein shifts from one generation to a succeeding generation.

b. **Correlation with estate and gift taxes:** [§18] Nonetheless, the generation-skipping transfer tax was directly related to the estate and gift taxes insofar as it was designed to produce essentially the same tax result in the case of generation-skipping transfers as would have occurred had the property passed through successive generations by way of straightforward gifts or bequests. And, the tax was computed with reference to related estate or gift tax exposure.

3. **The Tax Reform Act of 1986:** [§19] The generation-skipping transfer tax provisions of the 1976 Act were perceived as "unduly complicated." As a result, Congress continually deferred the effective date for application. In 1986, Congress repealed the 1976 tax, but replaced it with a new generation-skipping tax.

a. **Essential difference:** [§20] The substantive provisions of the generation-skipping tax, as originally enacted in 1976, remain intact in the 1986 Code. The essential differences are:

(1) ***The new tax is computed by applying a flat rate*** of tax to the actual amount of the generation-skipping transfer. (Under the 1976 Act, the estate and gift tax ***graduated*** rates were applied to the amount of the generation-skipping transfer ***as cumulated with*** the transferor's taxable gifts and taxable estate.)

(2) ***The circumstances in which the tax will apply have been expanded.***

b. **Pre-1986 generation-skipping transfers:** [§21] Recognizing the confusion that was caused by the continued deferral of the 1976 tax, this tax was repealed retroactively. Thus, generation-skipping transfers occurring after the 1976 Act but before the 1986 Act are ***exempt*** from generation-skipping taxes.

E. TAXING JURISDICTION

1. **Jurisdictional Bases for Estate and Gift Taxation:** [§22] A number of bases for taxing jurisdiction are accepted under the Constitution as well as under conventional international law. But for estate and gift tax purposes, the jurisdictional bases are citizenship or residence, and the location of property.

a. **Citizens and residents:** [§23] The estate tax reaches all property owned by a citizen or resident of the United States ***without regard to its location***. [I.R.C. §2031] (Prior to 1962, the statute excepted real property located outside the United States, but this exception was repealed.) Similarly, the gift tax reaches all property transferred by a citizen or resident. [I.R.C. §2501]

b. **Nonresident aliens:** [§24] However, in the case of nonresident aliens, only property ***located in the United States*** is subject to the federal estate tax. *Rationale:* Since no "personal" relationship exists between the decedent and the United States, taxing jurisdiction must be based upon the property's presence within the United States. [I.R.C. §2103]

(1) **Compare:** Gift tax exposure likewise depends upon location of the property within the United States. In addition, section 2501 generally exempts from the gift tax transfers of ***intangible*** property by nonresident aliens.

2. **The Generation-Skipping Transfer Tax:** [§25] The same rules apply to citizens and residents under the 1986 Act (*see supra*, §23). This Act requires the Treasury to issue regulations providing for the application of the generation-skipping tax to nonresident aliens. Such regulations are to be "consistent with the principles of chapters 11 and 12." [I.R.C. §2663(2)] The rule then for nonresident aliens would be as outlined in §24, above.

II. SUBSTANTIVE ASPECTS OF THE ESTATE TAX

chapter approach

The estate tax is imposed upon the "taxable estate." [I.R.C. §2001] This is defined as the "gross estate" less any allowable deductions. [I.R.C. §2051] To determine estate tax liability, you need to determine:

1. **The gross estate:** What transfers or property are subject to the estate tax, or as it is usually expressed, what transfers are "included in the gross estate"?

2. **Any allowable deductions:** After you have determined the total value of the gross estate, you need to identify any and all allowable deductions.

These functional aspects of computing estate tax liability also define the two basic substantive areas of the estate tax law: the gross estate and allowable deductions.

A. GROSS ESTATE

1. **Inclusions in Gross Estate—General Overview:** [§26] Sections 2033 through 2046 of the Internal Revenue Code set forth the types of property and property transfers that are included in the gross estate. These provisions may be divided into five categories:

   a. **Property owned by decedent:** [§27] By virtue of sections 2033 and 2034, the value of all property owned by the decedent at death is included in the gross estate.

   b. **Property not owned by decedent:** [§28] Moreover, property given away during life by the decedent and thus not "owned" at death, may, under certain circumstances, be included in the gross estate. Sections 2035 through 2038 detail the situations in which the estate tax reaches inter vivos transfers.

   c. **Special types of property and transfers:** [§29] Certain property interests, rights, or powers give rise to a type of transfer upon the death of the decedent and have a "testamentary" flavor, and yet might fall outside the scope of the above taxing sections because of technical, property law notions of "ownership" or "transfer." Sections 2039 through 2042 address the possible estate tax exposure of four such special types of property: annuities [I.R.C. §2039]; joint tenancies [I.R.C. §2040]; powers of appointment [I.R.C. §2041]; and life insurance [I.R.C. §2042].

   d. **Transfers for consideration:** [§30] Only ***gratuitous*** transfers are subject to the estate tax, not bargained-for sales or exchanges for consideration. Section 2043 outlines the nature and adequacy of consideration that will, for federal estate tax purposes, prevent a transfer (in whole or in part) from being considered gratuitous and thus insulate the transfer from the estate tax.

e. **Miscellaneous provisions related to the gross estate:** [§31] These include the following:

(1) **Certain marital deduction property:** Under the Revenue Act of 1981, certain property may qualify for the marital deduction even though the surviving (or donee) spouse is granted a limited interest which would not be taxable to the spouse under general rules of the estate tax. Section 2044 requires that this property be included in the spouse's gross estate.

(2) **General rule of inclusion:** Section 2045 sets forth a general rule of comprehensive inclusion. The substantive inclusion provisions of sections 2034 through 2042 (above) operate without regard to when a transfer was made or when a property interest arose, except as otherwise specifically provided by law.

(3) **Disclaimer or renunciation:** As will be seen, a valid disclaimer or renunciation of property is not a "transfer" for estate tax purposes (*infra*, §571). Section 2046 incorporates the gift tax rules of section 2518 relating to the circumstances in which disclaimers or renunciations will be effective and thus outside the purview of the estate tax.

2. **Section 2033—Property Owned by Decedent:** [§32] Section 2033 is the basic provision of the Code dealing with the gross estate. It is deceptively simple: "The value of the gross estate shall include the value of all property to the extent of the interest therein of the decedent at the time of his death."

a. **Introductory analysis:** [§33] For purposes of analysis, issues raised by section 2033 are typically divided into the following three categories and will be treated accordingly herein:

(1) ***The fundamental issues***—*i.e.*, the types of ***transfers, property,*** and ***interests*** subject to section 2033, as well as the nature of ownership within its scope;

(2) ***The relationship of section 2033*** (the general taxing provision) ***to the more specific taxing sections*** which follow; and

(3) ***The impact of state law*** upon the federal taxing scheme.

b. **Transfers taxed:** [§34] Clearly, section 2033 reaches property transferred by will or intestacy. However, it is not limited to such transfers. As long as the decedent ***owns*** an interest in property ***at death,*** which is ***transmitted*** to another on account of the decedent's death, the property is included in the decedent's gross estate.

(1) **Example—employee death benefits:** Under D's contract of employment, D's employer agreed that if D should die while in its employ it would pay to a person designated by D the sum of $5,000. D died while employed and her employer paid $5,000 to D's designee, A. Although the amount transmitted to

A "passed" by contract, rather than by will or intestate succession, it is includible in D's gross estate under section 2033. *Rationale:* D's unqualified contract right to designate the recipient of the payment gave her an "interest in property" which passed to another by reason of her death. (*See* further discussion *infra*, §61.)

(2) **Limitations—"ownership" interest "transferred" to another:** [§35] For a tax to attach under section 2033, the property must be ***"owned" by the decedent at death*** and it must be ***"transferred" from the decedent to another.***

(a) **Property "owned":** [§36] The mere fact that a decedent's death is instrumental in someone acquiring an interest in property is not enough to support imposition of the tax. The decedent must have had an ***interest*** in the property at death.

1) **Example:** A ***discretionary*** bonus awarded an employee ***after*** his death and paid over to the employee's executor is not taxable in the employee's gross estate. Since the payment was a matter of discretion only, the decedent neither had a right to, nor interest in, the bonus; it is therefore immaterial that his death may have occasioned the transfer. [Rev. Rul. 65-217, 1965-2 C.B. 214]

(b) **"Transfer by decedent"—interests terminating at death:** [§37] Although a literal reading of section 2033 might suggest that an interest owned at death is included in the gross estate even though that interest does not pass from the decedent to another, the proper and accepted interpretation of the statute is that it applies only to ***inheritable interests*** which are transferred at death. Hence, interests that terminate upon death (*e.g.,* a life estate) are ***not taxable*** under section 2033.

1) **Example:** A transferred Blackacre to D for life, remainder to X and his heirs. D died. Although D "owned" a life estate in Blackacre at death, his death extinguished this interest and X's remainder passed not from D but from A. Thus, there is no tax exposure to D's estate under section 2033. [Williams v. United States, 41 F.2d 895 (Ct. Cl. 1930); *see also* Helvering v. Rhodes' Estate, 117 F.2d 509 (8th Cir. 1941)—life income interest in trust; Commissioner v. Rosser, 64 F.2d 631 (3d Cir. 1933)—contingent remainder conditioned upon survival]

2) **Distinguish—life estate for life of another:** [§38] If decedent enjoys a life estate measured by the life of some other person and dies before the termination of the measuring life, the remaining term of that life estate ***is*** an inheritable interest includible under section 2033.

a) **Note:** The remaining portion of a term of years is likewise inheritable and thus included in the tenant's gross estate under this section. [Millard v. Malony, 121 F.2d 257 (3d Cir. 1941), *cert. denied,* 314 U.S. 636 (1941)]

b) **And note:** A similar result is reached with future interests not contingent upon survival; the contingency goes to the question of valuation rather than inclusion. [Rev. Rul. 67-370, 1967-2 C.B. 325]

3) **Compare—transfer by decedent subject to retained life estate:** [§39] The rule that interests terminating on death are not taxable applies only to interests conveyed to the decedent by another. Transfers ***by*** the decedent with a ***retained*** life estate are taxable in the decedent's estate under section 2036, discussed *infra,* §§120 *et seq.*

4) **Joint tenancies:** [§40] Although joint tenants have ownership interests in property and the death of one is instrumental in the transmission of the decedent's interest to the survivor(s), there is ***no "transfer"*** from a deceased joint tenant to the survivor(s). Rather, upon the decedent's death her interest is extinguished, and it passes to the surviving joint tenant(s) by "right of survivorship." (*See* Property Summary.) Thus, there is no tax exposure under section 2033.

a) **Cross-refer—section 2040:** Note, however, that section 2040 specifically addresses the taxation of these forms of concurrent ownership. (*See infra,* §§385 *et seq.*)

b) **Distinguish—tenancies in common:** [§41] Those forms of concurrent ownership that do not carry survivorship rights (*e.g.,* tenancy in common) are taxable under section 2033 since the undivided interest of a deceased co-tenant is inheritable. [Harvey v. United States, 185 F.2d 463 (7th Cir. 1950)]

5) **Compare—generation-skipping transfers:** [§42] As indicated earlier (*supra,* §15), prior to 1976, estate taxes could be avoided for an extended period of time through the use of a long-term trust or similar device in which several successive generations of beneficiaries were given life interests, with remainders in fee reserved for subsequent generations. Since each generation of beneficiaries held only life estates, nothing was taxable on their deaths; the income and enjoyment of the property effectively shifted to the next generation free of any estate tax. To eliminate this opportunity for tax avoidance, the generation-skipping transfer tax imposes a tax each time the interest or powers of the successive generation of trust beneficiaries terminate. (*See* detailed discussion *infra,* §§1062 *et seq.*)

a) **But note:** Recall that this "generation-skipping transfer tax" is a separate system of transfer taxation and does not affect the estate tax rules.

c. **Types of property subject to tax:** [§43] All types of property—real or personal, tangible or intangible—are subject to the estate tax, including notes or other claims owned by the decedent, choses in action that survived the decedent's death, and accrued salary, rent, interest, dividends, or other accrued rights to income owned by the decedent. [Treas. Reg. §20.2033-1]

(1) **Debts cancelled by will:** [§44] If a decedent holds a note or otherwise has a claim against another, the amount thereof is taxable under section 2033 even though the obligation is cancelled by decedent in the will. In other words,the cancellation is treated as if decedent had bequeathed the amount of the debt to the debtor. [Treas. Reg. §20.2033-1(b)]

(a) **Compare—self-cancelling installment notes:** With self-cancelling installment notes ("SCIN's"), the result is different. For example, in *Moss v. Commissioner*, the decedent sold stock during his life, taking back an installment note that recited that: "Unless sooner paid, all sums, whether principal or interest, shall be deemed cancelled and extinguished as though paid as of the death of [the seller-decedent]." The Tax Court held that the installment buyer's obligation and hence any right to payments on the part of the decedent or his estate was thus extinguished by the decedent's death. (*See supra*, §32.) Therefore, the unpaid balance on the note was ***not includible*** in the decedent's estate. [Moss v. Commissioner, 74 T.C. 1239 (1980)]

(2) **"Tax exempt" bonds, etc.:** [§45] According to the Regulations, statutory provisions exempting bonds, notes, bills, and certificates of indebtedness, as well as the interest thereon, from taxation are generally ***not applicable*** to the estate tax. *Rationale:* Such tax is an excise tax on the transfer of property at death, not a tax on the property transferred. [Treas. Reg. §20.2033-1(a)]

(3) **Injury and death claims**

(a) **Causes of action for wrongful death:** [§46] Although the Service has long agreed that wrongful death actions vested in a decedent's heirs are not property "owned" by the decedent and thus not taxable, for many years it insisted such claims were taxable under section 2033 if they accrued to the decedent's estate. However, the Service has reversed itself on the latter point, conceding that in ***no*** event is the value of wrongful death claims (or the proceeds) taxable. [Rev. Rul. 75-127, 1975-1 C.B. 297]

1) **Rationale:** "Simple logic mandates the conclusion that an action for wrongful death cannot exist until the decedent has died, at which point he is no longer a person capable of owning any property

interests." [Connecticut Bank & Trust Co. v. United States, 465 F.2d 760 (2d Cir. 1972)]

(b) **Compare—actions that survive plaintiff's death:** [§47] On the other hand, any claims or causes of action owned by the decedent at the time of death and which survive his death are includible in the gross estate under section 2033. [Maxwell Trust v. Commissioner, 58 T.C. 444 (1972)]

(4) **Life insurance:** [§48] The includibility of the ***proceeds*** of life insurance in the estate of the insured is subject to special rules under section 2042 of the Code. (*See infra,* §§490 *et seq.*) However, section 2033 does bring the ***contract*** of insurance into the policy owner's gross estate if the owner is a person other than the insured—*e.g.*, where one spouse owns a contract of insurance on the life of the other spouse.

(a) **Amount taxable:** [§49] If the insured is dead at the time the policy owner dies, the entire proceeds are taxable in the decedent's gross estate since the policy has matured. However, if the insured is still alive, only the value of the policy—measured by its replacement cost—is includible. [DuPont's Estate v. Commissioner, 233 F.2d 210 (3d Cir. 1956)]

(b) **Simultaneous death:** [§50] What happens if the insured and beneficiary (owner) die in a common disaster, and it is impossible to determine who died first? State law generally provides a presumption that the insured survived the beneficiary, so that the insurance proceeds can be paid to the alternate or secondary beneficiary. Even so, the original beneficiary ***was*** the owner of the policy at the time of death. Hence, although the chances of ever collecting anything were zero, the policy is taxable in the owner's estate on the basis of its replacement value. [Chown v. Commissioner, 428 F.2d 1395 (9th Cir. 1970)]

(5) **Income-producing property:** [§51] Where decedent owned income-producing property at death—*e.g.*, rental real estate, stocks, or bonds that pay interest—there is included under section 2033 not only the value of that property, but also the income therefrom that has accrued at the date of decedent's death. [Treas. Reg. §20.2033-1(b)] On the other hand, income accruing ***after*** death is ***not*** included in the gross estate (although it is taxable to the recipient estate or beneficiary under the income tax).

(6) **Rights to future income:** [§52] If the decedent owned at death a right to receive income in the future, the ***present value*** of that right is included in the gross estate. The present value is computed by reducing the amount of the expected payments to reflect the fact that money that will not be received until some future date is "worth" less than money presently in hand (since one will not enjoy the earning power of the future payments until they are received). This process, called "discounting," is accomplished by using discount tables specified by the Regulations. [Treas. Reg. §20.2031-7]

(a) **Example:** D agreed to play ball for a professional football club. His contract obligated the club to pay him, in addition to an annually negotiated salary, $50,000 per year for ten years irrespective of whether D was able to play; and if D died during the ten-year period, payments would continue to be made to his estate. D was killed in the first year's spring training, before collecting any of the deferred "bonus" payments. The present (discounted) value of the payments is taxable to his estate under section 2033.

(b) **Income derived from property vs. rights to future income:** [§53] It is important to distinguish "rights" to future income that derive from the ownership of income-producing property (*supra*, §51) from rights to future income where the right itself is the property "owned" (*supra*, §52). In the former case, unearned income is not taxed under section 2033; however, this anticipated income does affect the valuation of the underlying property, which ***is*** taxed. In the latter case, the right to income has been "earned" and the right itself is the property taxed.

(7) **Post-death payments from decedent's business:** [§54] Whether payments made from decedent's business subsequent to death are includible in the gross estate depends upon the nature of those payments.

(a) **Liquidation payments:** [§55] Payments made in liquidation of decedent's interest in the business are a "substitute" for that interest—*i.e.*, property owned by the decedent at death—and are taxable under section 2033.

(b) **Post-death profits:** [§56] However, where payments represent business profits accruing after decedent's death and are paid to the estate or beneficiary because the decedent's successor continues to own the business interest, only the ***business interest*** is included in the decedent's gross estate, ***not the future profits***.

(c) **Application:** [§57] The above rules are merely specialized demonstrations of the general rules relating to income-producing property (*supra*). However, there may be some confusion in their application:

1) **Survivor's benefits:** [§58] Where business profits are paid to the decedent's beneficiary pursuant to a contract entered into by decedent and the business entity prior to the decedent's death, under the better view the value of these survivor's benefits is included in the decedent's gross estate. *Rationale:* The decedent owned a ***contractual right*** at death; *i.e.*, the amounts to be paid to the beneficiary are pursuant to a contract which is distinct from the ownership of the business interest itself. [McClennen v. Commissioner, 131 F.2d 165 (1st Cir. 1942); Rev. Rul. 66-20, 1966-1 C.B. 214; *but cf.* Bull v. United States, 295 U.S. 247 (1935)—benefits belong to survivor, hence not taxable in decedent's estate]

2) **Partnership liquidation agreements:** [§59] Many partnership agreements provide that, upon the death of a partner, the partnership will not be dissolved and its assets distributed to the partners. Rather, in lieu of any distribution of a deceased partner's interest in specific partnership property, the partnership agrees to pay that partner's estate or designated beneficiary a percentage of partnership earnings for a specified period of time. The better view is that such rights to future payments are taxable under section 2033 where the substance of the arrangement is that the partner's death extinguishes his partnership interest and his estate is left with the contractual right to future payments in lieu of any claim against the partnership for a distribution of the deceased partner's capital; it is only this contract right that the decedent owns at death. [Estate of Riegelman v. Commissioner, 253 F.2d 315 (2d Cir. 1958); *but cf.* Bull v. United States, *supra*]

(8) **Employment benefits**

(a) **Voluntary payments:** [§60] It is clear enough that voluntary payments made by an employer to a deceased employee's surviving spouse or family are not taxed under section 2033: even though the death may have prompted the payments, the employee had no right to or interest in such payments before or at death.

(b) **Benefits pursuant to contract:** [§61] On the other hand, if death benefits are paid to specified beneficiaries as part of the bargained-for employment contract, they are included in the deceased employee's gross estate; even though the employee did not receive the payment, she possessed at death a contractual right that such payments would be made to her designated beneficiaries.

(c) **Other arrangements:** [§62] Between the above two situations, a number of other employment-benefit possibilities exist—*e.g.*, contractual arrangements under which the employee has no choice in the designation of beneficiaries; survivor benefit plans that are forfeitable; benefit plans that are terminable at the will of the employer; etc. However, these other arrangements have been most troublesome from the viewpoint of the estate tax and section 2033, producing a split of authority between the courts and the Service.

1) **Case law:** [§63] Although, as a practical matter, such survivor benefit plans were found to represent a valuable "expectancy" during the life of the employee and in fact were paid to the surviving spouse or family after death, some courts were unable to find a sufficient property interest in such "expectation" for section 2033 purposes. Absent a finding that the deceased employee had a right to or interest in the payments there could be no tax (it being irrelevant

that the employee's death was instrumental in vesting the benefit in the survivors; *see supra*, §36). [*Compare* Goodman v. Granger, 243 F.2d 264 (3d Cir. 1957) *with* Wadewitz v. Commissioner, 39 T.C. 925 (1963); *and see* Tully v. United States, 528 F.2d 1401 (Ct. Cl. 1976)]

2) **Service position:** [§64] On the other hand, the Service asserted that it would undertake to tax such survivor benefits if the plan was not in fact terminated or forfeited before death and if the benefits were actually paid to the survivors. [GCM 27242, 1952-1 C.B. 160] This administrative ruling, in effect, adopted a practical view—since such plans constitute bargained-for employee fringe benefits, and since it is unlikely that the plans would be arbitrarily terminated (given the negative effect this would have on employee morale), the employee's interest in the plan benefits is not so tenuous as to be a mere "expectancy."

3) **Effect of section 2039:** [§65] Section 2039 (entitled "Annuities") was added to the Code in 1954 primarily to clarify the estate tax exposure of survivor's benefits under employment related plans and, since its enactment, has been the principal focus for the taxation of such plans. Consequently, the development of this area of the law under section 2033 has been limited; most typical employee-survivor benefit plans are taxed under section 2039 so that the government need not resort to section 2033. (*See* detailed discussion *infra*, §§344 *et seq.*)

(9) **Statutory benefits:** [§66] As distinguished from private, contractual benefit plans (above), survivor benefits under various types of social welfare legislation are ***not taxable*** under section 2033. Examples include Social Security payments, benefits under the Railroad Retirement Act of 1937, and Workers' Compensation awards. [Rev. Rul. 67-277, 1967-2 C.B. 322]

(a) **Rationale—not "owned at death":** Decedent owns no interest in statutory benefits payable to certain survivors from funds produced by taxes.

d. **Types of interests subject to tax:** [§67] All types of interests in property, in the general property law sense, are subject to section 2033. It does not matter what the interest is called as long as it is an inheritable interest that was owned by the decedent at death and is transmitted by the decedent to another (*supra*, §37).

(1) **Life estates and analogous interests:** [§68] As noted earlier, a life estate (in trust or otherwise) measured by decedent's own life is ***not taxed*** under section 2033 since the decedent's death extinguishes her interest. (*See supra*, §37.) Similarly, life interests under an annuity contract (purchased by the decedent or another) that has no refund or survivor feature are not included in the gross estate since all interests and rights in the contract terminate upon the life annuitant's death. (Distinguish, however, life estates

for the life of another and terms for years, which are subject to section 2033; *see supra*, §38.)

(2) **Refund annuities:** [§69] A "refund annuity" is an annuity for life that provides that a certain number of payments are "guaranteed." If the annuitant does not live long enough to collect the full guaranteed amount, the remaining, unpaid guaranteed payments are refunded to the annuitant's estate. This right to a refund is "property owned" by decedent and ***is taxable*** under section 2033.

(a) **Survivor annuities:** [§70] Under survivor annuities, benefits are typically payable to the annuitant (or joint annuitants) for life, and then to another (or the other joint annuitant) upon the death of the primary annuitant. Historically, much difficulty was encountered in taxing survivor annuitant's benefits under section 2033; unlike refund annuities, above, it is difficult to find that the decedent has any "interest" in the contract that survived her death, or that she "transferred" the benefits to the survivor since, in legal contemplation, the survivor's benefits were established (and thus "transferred") at the time the contract was purchased. Today, however, such annuities are clearly taxed under section 2039 (*infra*, §§344 *et seq.*).

(3) **Future interests:** [§71] Interests in property that have not yet vested in possession (*i.e.*, future interests, such as reversions and vested remainders) generally ***are taxed*** under section 2033 just like possessory interests. Thus, the present value of such interests is included in the gross estate. [Frazier v. United States, 322 F.2d 221 (5th Cir. 1963)—valuation being made by use of actuarial tables prescribed by the Regulations; Treas. Reg. §20.2031-7]

(a) **Contingent interests:** [§72] The fact that a future interest is contingent (either subject to a condition precedent or vested subject to divestment upon the happening of a condition subsequent) does not prevent its inclusion in the gross estate. The contingency, however, will affect the ***value*** of the interest. [Rev. Rul. 67-370, 1967-2 C.B. 325]

1) **Computing value:** Some contingent interests can be valued by use of standard actuarial tables, while others are not susceptible of valuation by standard methods. If the value of an interest is not ascertainable—*e.g.*, because highly speculative—although it is includible in the gross estate and should be scheduled on the estate tax return (since it ***is*** an interest in property owned at death), the value assigned will be zero. [Smith v. Shaughnessy, 318 U.S. 176 (1943)]

(b) **Limitation—future interests contingent on survival:** [§73] Distinguish, however, future interests that are contingent upon decedent's survival. If the decedent fails to survive, the interest is extinguished and thus not taxed under section 2033 (*supra*, §37).

1) **Example:** A conveys Whiteacre to B for life, remainder to D if D survives B, and remainder to C if D does not survive B. If D predeceases B, she has no interest in Whiteacre that can be taxed to her estate.

e. **Nature of ownership required for tax:** [§74] The "ownership" required by the statute is ***beneficial ownership***; technical legal title is not subject to the estate tax. [Treas. Reg. §20.2033-1] Thus, for example, if D holds legal title to property as trustee for another but has no beneficial interest herself, the property is not taxed in D's estate.

(1) **Transfers void under local law:** [§75] One who makes a transfer of property that is absolutely void under local law has not parted with beneficial ownership; hence, the property remains taxable in the transferor's estate under section 2033. [City National Bank v. United States, 383 F.2d 341 (5th Cir. 1967)] On the other hand, property ***received*** in a transfer that is void under local law is ***not taxed*** in the transferee's estate (because the transferee has never acquired beneficial ownership).

(2) **Voidable transfers:** [§76] If a transfer is voidable by the decedent-transferor, the property is taxable under section 2038 as a revocable transfer (*infra*, §§278 *et seq.*); hence, the issue of taxation under section 2033 is not likely to arise. [*See* Commissioner v. Allen, 108 F.2d 961 (3d Cir. 1939), *cert. denied*, 309 U.S. 680 (1940)]

(a) **Compare—transfer voidable by third person:** [§77] On the other hand, if a transfer is voidable by persons other than the decedent (*e.g.*, transfer in fraud of creditors), the property is neither taxed under section 2033 (since the decedent has no interest in or claim to the property) ***nor*** under section 2038 (since the "power to revoke" resides in a third party). [*Cf.* McCann v. Commissioner, 87 F.2d 275 (6th Cir. 1937)]

(b) **Decedent as recipient of voidable transfer:** [§78] A voidable transfer made ***to*** decedent that is rescinded on or before the decedent's death clearly should ***not*** be included in decedent's gross estate. But the result is not so clear where the power to avoid the transfer remains ***unexercised*** at decedent's death so that decedent holds the title subject to the possibility of divestment. It might be argued that since the decedent owned a transferable interest at death, and since the power to rescind might never be exercised or may lapse, the property should be included in the gross estate with the power to avoid the transfer taken into account only in valuing the property. However, it is also arguable that the outstanding power to rescind reduces the decedent's interest to bare legal title not subject to tax—in effect, the decedent is no more than a constructive trustee for the power holder, with only a nontaxable "expectancy" that the legal title may ripen into beneficial ownership upon waiver or lapse of the right to rescind. [*Cf.* McCann v. Commissioner, *supra*] Either position is reasonable, but there is no definitive authority on point.

(3) **Expectancies:** [§79] An "expectancy" is not an interest in property. Consequently, the possibility, or even the likelihood, that a decedent or her estate may receive property under a will, under the laws of intestate succession, or as a (revocable) beneficiary under a life insurance policy on the life of another is ***not*** taxable.

(4) **The "doctrine" of substantial ownership:** [§80] In *Helvering v. Clifford,* 309 U.S. 331 (1940), the Supreme Court held that for ***income*** tax purposes, the income from transferred property remains taxable to the transferor where the transfer was for a short term with the property to revert to the transferor, and the transferor retained extensive powers to affect beneficial enjoyment of the property and its management. In other words, even though a technical transfer has been made, a person may be treated as the "***substantial owner***" of property and taxed accordingly.

(a) **Application to estate tax:** [§81] Subsequent to the *Cifford* holding, the Service sought to apply the substantial ownership doctrine to the estate tax. In *Helvering v. Safe Deposit & Trust Co.*, 316 U.S. 56 (1942), the decedent had been granted a life estate in property with the power to appoint the remainder to whomever he wished, including himself (*i.e.*, a general power of appointment). The Service argued that decedent's lifetime enjoyment and free power of disposition were the equivalent of "substantial ownership," thereby exposing the property to tax under the predecessor of section 2033. But the Supreme Court disagreed, refusing to sustain the tax on this theory.

1) **Rationale—intent not to tax implied:** The Court reasoned that since Congress had enacted an estate tax provision specifically taxing general powers of appointment that were ***exercised*** by a decedent, this indicated an intention not to tax powers, such as the one in the instant case, that were ***unexercised.*** The specific taxing provision and the congressional intent inferred therefrom were held to supersede the general taxing provision of section 2033. (*See infra,* §§82 *et seq.*)

2) **Effect—doctrine still viable for estate tax purposes?** Note that the Court did not reject the proposition that the doctrine of substantial ownership may be applicable to the estate tax. However, since most situations that might support use of the doctrine have been taken into account by specific provisions of the estate tax, there is seemingly little room left for its application under the general provision of section 2033. [*See* I.R.C. §§2036-2038]

f. **Relation between section 2033 and other taxing provisions—canon of construction:** [§82] It is generally accepted that where a specific statutory provision states the legislature's announced rule of law with respect to a specific situation or transaction, the ***specific provision takes precedence*** over a more general statutory provision. This is well demonstrated by the Supreme Court's holding in *Helvering v. Safe Deposit & Trust Co., supra; i.e.,* since Congress had specifically enacted a section taxing the testamentary ***exercise*** of a power of appointment, thereby evidencing an intention not to tax unexercised powers, an unexercised general power could not be taxed under the more specific section or the general taxing provision of section 2033. (*But note:* Unexercised general powers of appointment are taxed today under section 2041; *see infra*, §§451 *et seq.*)

(1) **Background:** *Helvering v. Safe Deposit & Trust Co.* should be read in light of *United States v. Field,* 255 U.S. 257 (1921), where the Supreme Court had held that property subject to a power of appointment (whether or not exercised) could not be taxed under the predecessor of section 2033 since, under technical property law, property subject to a power does not "pass" from the donee of the power (decedent) to his appointee or to a taker in default but rather is deemed to pass from the original grantor to the ultimate taker. When Congress subsequently imposed a tax on ***exercised*** powers of appointment, this did not affect the rule and rationale of *Field* as to unexercised powers. Moreover, while the *Clifford* case and the development of the doctrine of substantial ownership occurred later, by the time the issue was presented in *Helvering v. Safe Deposit & Trust Co.*, the Court was apparently unwilling to interfere with the long history of limited taxation of powers of appointment by extending application of the substantial ownership doctrine to section 2033.

(2) **Application—canon of construction not rigidly applied:** [§83] The principle that specific statutes take precedence over general statutes is not an inflexible rule of law but rather a rule for ascertaining legislative intent and, as such, should not be read too broadly. The fact that a specific statute addresses certain interests in property does not necessarily mean that other interests are beyond the reach of another taxing provision. For example, under certain circumstances, section 2042 taxes the ***proceeds*** of life insurance in the estate of the insured (*infra*, §§490 *et seq.*). Although more "specific" than section 2033, it does not preclude inclusion of the insurance ***contract*** in the gross estate of the owner who is one other than the insured (*supra*, §48).

(a) **Section 2033 not a "fallback":** [§84] At the same time, courts continue to be reluctant to apply section 2033 as a "fallback" where the government is unable to apply a more specific section. [*See* Estate of Tully v. Commissioner, 528 F.2d 1401 (Ct. Cl. 1976)]

g. **Impact of state law:** [§85] The nature of an individual's interest in property is defined by the law of the state in which the property is located, and since imposition of the estate tax depends upon the nature of decedent's interest, the resolution of federal estate tax issues often calls for reference to local law. At the same time, however, local law does not define the ***scope*** of federal tax law—whether an interest in property or a transfer is taxable (or a claim is deductible) is a matter of federal tax law, to be resolved by a federal administrative agency or the federal courts. Stated more simply, ***local law*** defines a person's rights, obligations, privileges, and powers with respect to property; whereas ***federal tax law*** defines whether those rights, etc., give rise to imposition of the estate tax (or allowance of an estate tax deduction).

(1) **Determination of state law:** [§86] Given the relation between local law and the federal tax law, the issue arises as to how the federal institutions determine the relevant local law question.

(a) **Where general rule of law applies:** [§87] The resolution of this issue is relatively simple where a general rule of local property law, promulgated by a state statute or by the state's highest court as a matter of common law, is clearly applicable. Absent conflicting federal law (*e.g.*, Treasury Regulations governing U.S. Savings Bonds; below), the federal authority will follow the state law.

1) **Example:** A granted property "to D for life, remainder to D's heirs." If the Rule in Shelley's Case is followed in the state in which the property is located, D has a fee simple interest and the property will be included in his gross estate. (*See* Property Summary.) But, if the state has repudiated the Rule, no tax will attach since D's interest is a life estate which was extinguished at death.

(b) **Where interpretation of state law required:** [§88] Where the question involves the interpretation of state law and its application to a specific situation, and where the specific issue has ***not*** been adjudicated by a state court, the federal institution (the I.R.S. or a federal court) must undertake to interpret and apply the local law itself.

1) **Example:** Under local law, "delivery" of property to the donee is required for a completed lifetime gift. Prior to death, D endorsed certain securities to A and placed them in D's safe deposit box. At the same time, D wrote to A advising her that, "I have endorsed certain securities over to you this day as a gift and have placed them in my safe deposit box for safekeeping. Stop by at your convenience, and we will go to the bank to get them." D died before A came for the securities. Assuming that no local authority addresses the issue of whether endorsement of securities and notification to the donee of the purported gift, under the circumstances recited, satisfies the delivery requirement, the federal institution must make its own determination in order to ascertain whether D owned the securities at death or had made a completed gift, thereby divesting himself of all interest in the securities prior to death.

(2) **Effect of prior state court determination:** [§89] A difficult question arises where a lower state court has adjudicated the specific property rights: To what extent is the federal institution ***bound*** by that determination? For example, suppose in the above example that the probate court had determined, upon petitions of A and D's executor, that delivery to A had been completed, so that A was the owner of the securities at D's death and they were not part of D's

probate estate. Neither party appeals and the decision becomes final. Does this final determination of the probate court conclusively settle the question of whether the securities are subject to tax under section 2033?

(a) **Former conflicting views:** [§90] Prior to 1967, there were at least three differing views on this issue: (i) The state court's determination, which bound the parties in interest, ***also bound the federal court*** addressing the federal tax issue. (ii) The state court's determination was binding ***unless procured by fraud or collusion.*** (iii) The state court's determination was binding only if the federal court found that the issue was ***fairly presented*** by opposing parties and ***fairly litigated*** in the state court proceedings.

(b) **The *Bosch* case—lower court decisions not binding:** [§91] The Supreme Court finally resolved the conflict in 1967, adopting a rule reminiscent of that applied in diversity litigation under *Erie Railroad v. Tompkins,* 304 U.S. 64 (1938) (*see* Civil Procedure Summary). It held that, in addressing a federal tax question turning upon a question of local property law, federal courts are only bound by the decisions of the ***highest court of the state*** (because "the state's highest court is the best authority on its own law"). State lower court decisions, on the other hand, need only be given "proper regard": *i.e.*, the federal authority is in effect "sitting as a state court"; it is not bound by the lower court decision but rather can decide the matter as it believes the state's highest court would decide it. [Commissioner v. Estate of Bosch, 387 U.S. 456 (1967)]

1) **Criticism—potential for unjust results?** [§92] Where a federal court "sits as a state court" in a diversity case, its decision is final as to all matters in controversy. However, in federal tax cases, the federal court decision is only final as to the tax issue; it does not determine property rights of the parties under the state law. Thus, under the *Bosch* decision, one party (A in the example above) may be finally determined to be the legal owner of property by a state court, while another party (D in the example above) may be treated as the owner for estate tax purposes!

(3) **Limitation—regulations superseding general property law:** [§93] There are numerous situations where special regulations relating to registration of title govern the legal effect of an attempted transfer of property. If state law is found to be superseded by such regulations, the federal authority is not bound by state court determinations on the matter.

(a) **Application—transfers of U.S. Savings Bonds:** The question of whether these regulations override general property law has been litigated extensively in connection with United States Savings Bonds (Treasury Regulations requiring reregistration in order to transfer the bonds). Lower courts formerly split on the issue. [Silverman v. McGinnes, 259 F.2d 731 (3d Cir. 1958)—state law controls; *but see* Curry v. United States, 409 F.2d 671 (6th Cir. 1969)—contra] However, in 1973, the Supreme Court held that the Treasury Regulations do supersede all contrary state law so that a transfer of U.S. bonds pursuant to state law may nevertheless be taxed in the donor's estate should it fail to satisfy Treasury Regulation requirements. [United States v. Chandler, 410 U.S. 257 (1973)]

3. **Section 2034—Dower or Curtesy Interests:** [§94] Section 2034 of the Code includes in the decedent's gross estate "the value of all property to the extent of any interest therein of the surviving spouse, existing at the time of the decedent's death as dower or curtesy, or by virtue of the statute creating an estate in lieu of dower or curtesy."

   a. **Effect—no deduction for marital interests:** [§95] Property owned by the decedent at death is included at its ***full value*** without any reduction for the surviving spouse's marital interests therein. [Treas. Reg. §20.2034-1]

   b. **Background and analysis:** [§96] This section is more a clarification of legislative intent than a substantive taxing provision. It was enacted in 1918 (two years after the predecessor of section 2033) simply to make clear that if property is subject to tax under section 2033, its full value is to be included in the gross estate; this is so even though an argument might be made that the property is not freely transferable by the decedent to the extent that it is subject to the surviving spouse's dower, curtesy, or statutory "forced share" rights.

      (1) **Note:** The above principle (precluding reduction of the gross estate to the extent of such marital "claims" against the estate) is consistent with other provisions of the statute that deny that marital rights constitute adequate consideration either to prevent classification of a transfer as "gratuitous" [I.R.C. §2043(b)], or to support a deductible claim against the estate [I.R.C. §2053(e)]. *(See infra*, §§562, 595.)

   c. **Release of interest:** [§97] Moreover, section 2034 cannot be avoided by substitution of a contractual obligation to pay an amount in lieu of dower or curtesy [Empire Trust Co. v. Commissioner, 94 F.2d 307 (4th Cir. 1938)]; or by the surviving spouse's release of dower or curtesy rights in lieu of a legacy in the decedent's will [Mayer v. Reinecke, 130 F.2d 350 (7th Cir. 1942)].

   d. **Compare—community property rights:** [§98] Dower and curtesy are not vested interests, but mere expectancies in the property of the other spouse. On the other hand, in community property states each spouse is treated as owning a present, undivided one-half interest in the community assets. The result is that on the death of either spouse, ***only his or her one-half is includible*** in the gross estate; the other half belongs to the surviving spouse and is not includible (*infra*, §431).

e. **Effect of marital deduction:** [§99] The importance of section 2034, requiring the inclusion of dower and curtesy interests, is greatly offset by the marital deduction. [I.R.C. §2056] As will be seen (*infra*, §§628 *et seq.*), the marital deduction operates to take out of the taxable estate most of the property included therein under section 2034.

4. **Section 2035—Gifts Made Within Three Years of Death:** [§100] The estate tax cannot reach property that was the subject of a completed gift during the decedent's life. Thus, to prevent easy avoidance of the estate tax by "deathbed transfers," the estate tax has always provided for the taxation of gifts made shortly before death.

a. **Background**

(1) **Former tax on transfers "in contemplation of death":** [§101] Prior to 1977, a completed gift made by the decedent during life was exposed to the estate tax if made ***"in contemplation of death."*** The operative element for taxation was the ***subjective intent*** or motive of the decedent at the time of the transfer.

(a) **Proof of transferor's intent—presumptions:** [§102] Intent or motive is essentially a factual question, always difficult to resolve. And, it is made even more difficult when one is called upon to ascertain the subjective intent of a person who is now dead. In order to reduce these administrative problems, the statute has always included a presumption that transfers within a certain period prior to death would be deemed to have been made in contemplation of death.

1) **Conclusive presumptions and *Heiner v. Donnan*:** From 1916 until 1926, the statutory presumptions could be rebutted upon showing absence of the requisite motive. The conflicts and controversies this produced prompted Congress, in 1926, to enact a ***conclusive*** presumption that transfers in excess of $5,000 made within two years of the decedent's death were made in contemplation of death. However, in *Heiner v. Donnan*, 285 U.S. 312 (1932), the Supreme Court held this presumption constitutionally invalid as a violation of the Due Process Clause of the Fifth Amendment insofar as it established an arbitrary classification for taxation of certain transfers (within two years of death) while others (made before that time) escaped tax.

2) **Viability of a conclusive presumption today:** Although *Heiner v. Donnan* has never been overruled, it is felt that a conclusive presumption could survive constitutional attack today. Over the years, the Supreme Court has been more willing to uphold objective guidelines for imposition of the tax, on the theory that they are reasonable

and necessary for the effective administration of the tax and thus not arbitrary classifications. (This was the theory urged, unsuccessfully, by the dissent in *Heiner v. Donnan.*)

3) **Presumptions under the 1954 Code:** Prior to its amendment in 1976, the 1954 Code contained two presumptions:

a) A ***rebuttable*** presumption that transfers made within three years of death were made in contemplation of death; and

b) A ***conclusive*** presumption that transfers made more than three years before death were ***not*** in contemplation of death.

(2) **1976 Tax Reform Act amendment:** [§103] Under the Tax Reform Act of 1976, any inter vivos transfer, in trust or otherwise, made by the decedent after December 31, 1976, was included in his gross estate if the decedent died within three years of the transfer; *i.e.,* the amendment dictated ***automatic*** inclusion in the donor's gross estate of gifts made ***within three years of death***.

(a) **Constitutionality:** [§104] Despite any lingering vitality of *Heiner v. Donnan,* the Committee Reports support the constitutionality of this approach. The amendment did not establish a conclusive presumption of subjective intent but, rather, provided a rule of law as to the scope of the estate tax which would be applied uniformly to all taxpayers without regard to intent. (*See also supra,* §102.)

(3) **Limited taxation of "deathbed gifts" under the 1981 Act:** [§105] As previously noted, the 1976 Act "unified" the gift and estate tax rates and credits, and provided that all lifetime transfers be taken into account in determining the marginal rates of tax that would be applied to the decedent's estate. (*See supra,* §14.) The effect of these provisions was substantially to reduce the need to ***include*** deathbed gifts in the gross estate of a decedent, since such gifts would be taxed under the gift tax when made (using the same rate schedule as the estate tax) and would be added to the estate tax base for the purpose of determining the estate tax. (*See infra,* §§1008, 1010.) In effect there would be no difference in the total taxes paid, whether or not such gifts were included in the decedent's gross estate, except: (i) if the property appreciated substantially between the date of the gift and the donor's death (within three years), and (ii) to the extent that any gift tax annual exclusion was applicable to the gift. (*See infra,* §§841 *et seq.*)

(a) **Outright gifts excluded:** [§106] Congress was persuaded that the unification of the transfer taxes thus made the tax avoidance potential of most deathbed gifts quite negligible, and this negligible fiscal effect did not justify the time and cost required to assure that all of such gifts were reported and to undertake a second appraisal and valuation of the property transferred. Consequently, the 1981

Act amended section 2035 so as to eliminate most outright gifts from inclusion in the donor's gross estate. [I.R.C. §2035(d)(1)]

(b) **Continuing major impact of section 2035:** [§107] However, section 2035 was ***not*** repealed. It continues to operate and have a major impact in two very important areas:

1) **"Gross-up rule":** [§108] Although a gift made within three years of death is not included in the donor's estate, any gift taxes paid or payable with respect to such gifts ***are*** included. [I.R.C. §2035(c)] (*See infra*, §§110 *et seq.*)

2) **Transfer or release of taxable "strings":** [§109] If the decedent possessed or retained a taxable interest or power with respect to certain property which would result in the inclusion of the subject property in the decedent's estate under section 2036, 2037, 2038, or 2042, the transfer or release of the taxable power or interest within three years of death will be ineffective to preclude estate taxation of the property; *i.e.*, section 2035 continues to interact with these other sections so as to include in the gross estate property that would have been included if the transfer or release had not occurred within the three-year period. [I.R.C. §2035(d)(2)] (*See infra*, §§114 *et seq.*)

b. **Gift taxes paid by decedent on inter vivos gifts also included ("gross-up" rule):** [§110] There is also included in decedent's gross estate the amount of any gift tax paid by the decedent or his estate with respect to any gifts made within three years of death. [I.R.C. §2035(c)]

(1) **Purpose:** [§111] Without this rule, it would be advantageous for a donor to make deathbed gifts: the payment of related gift taxes would reduce his gross estate since, if the decedent paid the taxes, the amount would not be in his estate, and if the executor paid the taxes, the estate would be entitled to a deduction therefor. [*See* I.R.C. §2053; *infra*, §591] The "gross-up" rule eliminates this opportunity for tax avoidance.

(2) **Applies to spouse's gifts too:** [§112] Moreover, the "gross-up" rule also applies to gift taxes paid by the decedent (or decedent's executor) with respect to gifts made by decedent's spouse within three years of the decedent's death; *i.e.*, gifts of the spouse's separate property that are "split" with the decedent under section 2513. ("Gift splitting" is discussed *infra*, §§869-874.)

(3) **Also applies where donee pays gift tax:** [§113] In *Estate of Sachs v. Commissioner*, 88 T.C. 769 (1987), a gift made within three years of the donor's death was conditioned on the donee paying the donor's gift tax liability—a "net gift" situation. The Tax Court held that the gift tax, even though paid by the donee, was includible in the donor's estate under section 2035(c).

c. **Relation of section 2035 to other taxing sections—release of taxable interests within three years of death:** [§114] With the exception of section 2040, which taxes joint tenancy property, section 2035 interacts with the other specific taxing sections of the Code to produce a tax under those sections if a taxable interest or incident of ownership is ***transferred, released, or relinquished within three years of death.*** [I.R.C. §2035(d)(2)]

(1) **Basis for interaction:** [§115] Prior to 1981, this interaction was specifically provided for in certain of the other taxing provisions [*e.g.*, I.R.C. §§2038, 2041], or was developed by judicial authorities as a matter of statutory interpretation based upon principle and apparent congressional intent [*see, e.g.*, Allen v. United States, 293 F.2d 916 (10th Cir. 1961), *cert. denied*, 368 U.S. 944 (1961)]. The 1981 amendment of section 2035 specifically provides that this section will continue to interact with sections 2036, 2037, 2038, and 2042. Also, section 2041 continues to interact with section 2035 by virtue of section 2041(a)(1)(B) and (a)(2). (*See infra*, §476.)

(2) **Example—gift of retained life estate within three years of death:** [§116] Ten years ago, D transferred property to X but reserved a life estate. Two years before death, D transferred his life estate to X. Section 2036(a)(1) taxes transfers during life where the transferor retained a life interest in the property; and section 2035, as amended, continues to operate where a retained life estate is transferred within three years of death. Thus, it is not the life interest alone which will be taxed (under section 2035) but, by the interaction of sections 2035 and 2036(a)(1), the ***full value*** of the property. In effect, section 2035 operates to permit a tax under section 2036(a)(1) just as if D's life interest persisted until his death.

(3) **Example—sale of interest within three years of death:** [§117] Moreover, where decedent ***sells*** his retained life estate to the holder of the remainder within three years of death, at least one court has held that the full value of the property (less the consideration received for the transfer) is taxable in decedent's estate by virtue of sections 2035 and 2036(a)(1). [Allen v. United States, *supra*]

(a) **Rationale:** Even though there was "full and adequate consideration" for the transfer of the life estate (note that the estate tax only applies to "gratuitous" transfers, *infra*, §551), the consideration paid was negligible when compared to the value of the property which taxpayer, by this device, hoped to remove from taxation under section 2036(a)(1). Congress clearly intended to tax the full value of property transferred subject to a retained interest that persists until death or that is relinquished within three years of death, and the court refused to allow this intent to be frustrated by a transfer within three years of death for a consideration inadequate when compared to the value of the property potentially subject to tax.

(4) **Limitation—coextensive interaction:** [§118] Where section 2035 interacts with another specific taxing section, the substantive provisions of ***both*** sec-

tions must apply for a tax to result; the interaction neither adds to nor reduces the scope of the substantive provisions.

(a) **Example:** If, in the above example, D transferred his retained life interest to X ***four years*** before death, no estate tax would result since, under section 2035, transfers more than three years prior to death are not taxed and, under section 2036(a)(1), a retained life interest will not produce a tax if the life estate is transferred or relinquished before death (*see infra,* §220). Likewise, if the life estate had not been retained by D but rather, had been ***granted to him*** by another, a transfer within three years of death would not produce a tax, since a life estate granted to the decedent by a third party is not taxable under section 2036(a)(1); ***section 2035 does not add to the scope of other taxing sections.***

(5) **Exception—joint tenancy property:** [§119] Section 2035 does not interact with section 2040. Section 2040 taxes the full value of property held in joint tenancy with right of survivorship to the estate of the first to die, unless it is proven that the survivor made an original contribution to the acquisition of the property (*see infra,* §§385 *et seq.*). Where, within three years of death, the joint tenancy was severed by transfer of the property to another or by conversion into a tenancy in common, the courts held that only the value of the decedent's interest was subject to the estate tax on the theory that section 2040 only operates where the property is in fact held in joint tenancy at death; and section 2035 only reached the value of the interest transferred by the decedent, *i.e.,* the undivided interest that decedent transferred. [Sullivan's Estate v. Commissioner, 175 F.2d 657 (9th Cir. 1949)] Although this result (under prior law) was much criticized, the 1981 amendment to section 2035 fails to specify any interaction between this section and section 2040 and thus preserves the exception. (*See infra,* §411 for further discussion.)

5. **Section 2036—Transfers With Retained Life Interests:** [§120] Under section 2036 of the Code, a tax is imposed upon any inter vivos transfer made by a decedent "under which he has retained for his life or any period not ascertainable without reference to his death or for any period which does not in fact end before his death—(1) the possession or enjoyment of, or the right to income from, the property, or (2) the right either alone or in conjunction with any person, to designate the persons who shall possess or enjoy the property or the income therefrom."

a. **Historical background:** [§121] This section (as well as sections 2037 and 2038, discussed *infra*), derives from the Revenue Act of 1916 which imposed an estate tax upon lifetime transfers "intended to take effect in possession or enjoyment at or after" the transferor's death. Sections 2036 through 2038 codified the intended scope and thrust of this rather obscure phrase and, for the most part, addressed what were at first very restrictive and later quite expansive interpretations of that phrase by the Supreme Court.

(1) **Transfers with retained life estates held not taxable:** [§122] It had always been assumed that a transfer with a reserved life estate was clearly within the

intendment of the statutory language taxing transfers "intended to take effect in possession and enjoyment at or after" the transferor's death. State courts, interpreting identical language in state inheritance tax laws, had consistently so held, and the Supreme Court, in *Reinecke v. Northern Trust Co.*, 278 U.S. 339 (1929), had so implied (*see infra*, §§281-287). It therefore came as quite a surprise when the Supreme Court held, in *May v. Heiner*, 281 U.S. 238 (1930), that such transfers were ***not*** subject to the estate tax. The Court's theory was that the transfer to the owner of the remainder occurred at the time of the original grant, not upon the transferor's death; the remainder was already vested and death merely extinguished the intervening interest. Thus, the words "intended" and "possession and enjoyment" were effectively read out of the statute, the Court insisting that a transfer from the decedent at death was required.

(2) **Congressional reaction—the 1931 Joint Resolution and the 1932 Act:** [§123] On March 2, 1931, the Supreme Court reaffirmed its position in *May v. Heiner*. However, Congress responded the next day with a Joint Resolution specifically taxing transfers with a reserved life estate. This provision was subsequently clarified and refined in the Revenue Act of 1932.

(a) **Limitation—prospective operation only:** [§124] It is important to note that Congress limited the provisions of both the Joint Resolution and the 1932 Act to prospective application only. Thus, transfers prior to the effective date of the Joint Resolution (March 4, 1931) are not taxed; and transfers between that date and the effective date of the 1932 Act (June 7, 1932) are taxed under the more limited provisions of the Joint Resolution.

(b) **Substantive changes:** [§125] The 1932 Act contained four modifications, two of which were considered substantive ***without retroactive effect***: (i) the addition of "for any period not ascertainable without reference to [the tranferor's] death" to the time periods for which an interest must be retained in order to incur the tax; and (ii) the imposition of the tax when the decedent retained the power to designate income "either alone or in conjunction with any person."

(c) **Clarifying changes:** [§126] On the other hand, two changes were deemed to be merely clarifying and declaratory of prior law: (i) the substitution of the phrase "for any period which does not in fact end before his death" for the language of the Joint Resolution "for any period not ending before his death"; and (ii) substituting "the right to income" for "the income."

(3) **Later developments—*May v. Heiner* overruled:** [§127] In *Commissioner v. Church's Estate*, 335 U.S. 632 (1949), the Supreme Court overruled *May v. Heiner*. And, while the decision had little impact on transfers with reserved life estates after 1931, it did expose pre-1931 transfers to tax under the "intended to take effect" language which was still part of the Code in 1949.

(a) **Effect of section 2036(c) of the 1954 Code—1931 cut-off date:** [§128] However, the tax on the pre-1931 transfers was not long lived. With the passage of the 1954 Code, Congress provided (under section 2036(c)) that the tax will ***not*** reach transfers made prior to the effective date of the Joint Resolution, and transfers between that date and the effective date of the 1932 Act will be taxed only if they would have been taxed under the Joint Resolution.

b. **Introductory analysis:** [§129] On its face, section 2036(a) specifies four requirements for taxation:

(1) **Transfer:** Decedent must have made an inter vivos transfer of property or an interest in property (on trust or otherwise).

(2) **Retained interest:** At the time of the transfer, decedent must have retained certain interests in or powers over the property.

(3) **Taxable interests or powers:** The interests or powers retained must be either:

(i) ***The possession or enjoyment*** of, or a right to income from, the property; or

(ii) ***The right to designate who shall possess or enjoy*** the property or its income.

(4) **Time periods:** The taxable interests or powers must be retained for one of three time periods:

(i) For ***life;*** or

(ii) For a period other than life if the period ***cannot be determined without reference to the transferor's death;*** or

(iii) For a period of time other than life if ***in fact the decedent dies before the end of that period.***

(5) **Comment:** For purposes of this Summary, analysis of the scope and thrust of section 2036 follows the above four taxation requirements. It should be noted, however, that the interpretative authorities frequently cross categories. For example, the issue of whether a taxable interest or power has been ***retained*** may merge with the issues of whether it is the decedent who made the ***transfer*** of property and whether the decedent has a "right" to possession or to income.

c. **Requirement of a transfer:** [§130] For purposes of taxation under section 2036, it is insufficient that the decedent possess a life estate in property or a special power with respect to property. Rather, the property to which the life estate or power relates must have been "transferred" by the decedent during life.

(1) **Transfers—in general:** [§131] The term "transfer" applies, of course, to the conveyance of any property, on trust or otherwise. It also applies to any expenditure made by a decedent during life for the purpose of having a third person convey property to a donee (*see* below). And, it includes the relinquishment of an interest or incident of ownership (*see supra,* §114) or the exercise or release of a taxable power of appointment (*see infra,* §§442 *et seq.*). These notions of "transfer" are applicable, directly or by analogy, to the transfer requirement under section 2036. Additionally, some other transfer issues have been addressed by the courts with specific reference to section 2036.

(2) **Life insurance settlement options:** [§132] If a beneficiary under a life insurance policy on the life of another is entitled to receive the proceeds upon the death of the insured but elects a settlement option under which the company retains the proceeds, paying the electing beneficiary interest on the fund for life and distributing the retained proceeds to the beneficiary's designee upon the beneficiary's death, it has been held that the beneficiary has made a ***transfer of the proceeds*** reserving a right to income, which is taxable under section 2036. It is immaterial that the settlement option was elected prior to or upon the death of the insured. [Pyle v. Commissioner, 313 F.2d 328 (3d Cir. 1963)]

(a) **Compare—insured's election:** [§133] But where the ***insured*** elects this type of settlement option for the beneficiary, and the beneficiary has no right or power to modify the same, the result is contra. Here, the beneficiary has not made a "transfer," and hence the proceeds are not taxable to her estate. [Minotto v. Commissioner, 9 T.C.M. 556 (1950)]

(3) **Community property election:** [§134] In community property states, a surviving spouse may elect, pursuant to a provision in the deceased spouse's will, to take a life estate in all the community property in lieu of the survivor's own vested fee interest in one-half the community property. If such an election is made, the survivor is treated as having transferred her vested one-half interest while reserving a life estate therein. [Gregory v. Commissioner, 39 T.C. 1012 (1963)]

(a) **Compare:** The survivor is not deemed to have made a transfer of the ***deceased*** spouse's interest, and since the survivor possessed only a life estate therein, at death it is not taxed in her estate (*supra,* §37).

(b) **And note:** The "widow's election" cases under section 2036 are complicated by the issue of consideration. Since the "transfer" by the survivor is in consideration of the life estate in the property of the deceased spouse, the value of the property transferred for purposes of tax under section 2036 must be reduced by the value of the life interest. (*See* detailed discussion of "widow's election," *infra,* §§434-442.)

(4) **Who is the transferor:** [§135] Ordinarily, in assessing tax consequences, the ***substance*** of transactions, rather than mere form, controls. For example, suppose D were to purchase property from A and direct A to transfer a life estate in the property to D with a remainder to X; or suppose D were to transfer property to A with the understanding that A would immediately thereafter transfer that same property on trust naming D the life income beneficiary with remainder to A (or another). In both cases, A is the formal or nominal transferor of the property in which D enjoys a life estate but, clearly, D is the actual transferor. And in both cases, the tax law would treat D as the transferor of the property in which the life estate was reserved.

(a) **Application—reciprocal trusts:** [§136] The above principle (*i.e.*, that substance rather than form determines who is the transferor) is well illustrated by the "reciprocal trust doctrine."

1) **Example:** Two brothers (A and B) transferred equal amounts of property on separate irrevocable trusts. The trust established by A provided that B should enjoy the income for his life with remainder to his issue. The trust established by B was identical, but reciprocal, in its terms, providing for income to A for life, remainder to his issue. The court found that the trusts were in consideration of each other so that A was to be treated as the actual settlor of the trust nominally established by B, and conversely. Thus upon A's death, the value of the B trust—which A was deemed to have established—was included in A's gross estate because of the "retained" life estate which A had in that trust. [Lehman v. Commissioner, 109 F.2d 99 (2d Cir. 1940), *cert. denied*, 310 U.S. 637 (1940)]

2) **When are trusts deemed "reciprocal"?**

a) **Background—husband and wife reciprocal trusts:** [§137] At one time, problems were experienced in taxing reciprocal trusts between husband and wife. Outside of interspousal arrangements, the authorities had emphasized consideration as the touchstone for determining the actual, substantial transferor; but where the reciprocal settlors were husband and wife, it was difficult to find a technical, common law consideration. Thus, prior to 1969, many courts refused to apply the reciprocal trust doctrine between spouses, reasoning that the trusts were merely a mutual division of family property and were not created in consideration of each other. [Newberry's Estate v. Commissioner, 201 F.2d 874 (3d Cir. 1953)]

b) **Consideration not required:** [§138] However, the Supreme Court has since eliminated the notion of consideration as a critical element on the theory that "'consideration,' in the traditional legal sense, simply does not normally enter into such intrafamily transfers." Rather, "application of the reciprocal trust doctrine requires only that the trusts be ***interrelated*** and that to the extent of mutual value, leave the settlors in approximately the ***same economic position*** as they would have been in had they created the trusts naming themselves as life beneficiaries." [United States v. Grace, 395 U.S. 316 (1969)]

c) **Comment:** [§139] Presumably, *Grace* does not stand for the proposition that consideration is irrelevant, but rather that the reciprocal trust doctrine may be applied even though technical legal consideration is absent. However, in resolving one issue, *Grace* opens up others. For example, is the Court's rule subjective insofar as it speaks of the "interrelationship" of the trusts (which suggests an intent to interrelate), or is it objective insofar as it speaks of no effective change in the parties' economic position (which can be detected by objective observation of the result)? [*See* Bischoff v. Commissioner, 69 T.C. 32 (1977)—concurring opinion suggests that the *Grace* case requires an ***intended*** interrelationship]

(5) **Time of the transfer:** [§140] Since section 2036 does not reach transfers prior to the effective date of the 1931 Joint Resolution, it may be important to determine precisely when a transfer is deemed made. The general rules may be summarized as follows:

(a) **Outright gifts:** [§141] Where a gift is made outright, the transfer occurs when title passes from the transferor.

(b) **Gifts on irrevocable trust:** [§142] Similarly, the passing of title is the critical time as to gifts on trust. The fact that signatures are later added to the trust agreement does not alter the effective transfer date, but merely signifies the signer's acquiescence to a transfer previously made. [Commissioner v. Henry, 161 F.2d 574 (3d Cir. 1947)]

1) **And note:** It has also been held that a transfer is complete upon delivery of the deed of trust, even though the trust property was not given to the trustee until a later date. [Farnum v. Commissioner, 14 T.C. 884 (1950)]

(c) **Gifts on revocable trusts:** [§143] On the other hand, where the trust is ***revocable*** the authorities are in conflict. The Tax Court adopts the position that the transfer is made at the time the property is transferred to the trustee [Canfield v. Commissioner, 34 T.C. 978 (1960), *aff'd*, 306 F.2d 1 (2d Cir. 1962)], while the Court of Claims and the Fourth Circuit have held that the transfer does not occur until the power to revoke lapses or is released [Smith v. United States, 139 F.2d 305 (Ct. Cl. 1956); Commissioner v. Talbott, 403 F.2d 851 (4th Cir. 1968), *rev'g* 48 T.C. 271 (1967), *cert. denied*, 393 U.S. 1022 (1969)].

1) **Comment:** [§144] The better position seems to be that of the Tax Court, since it is in accord with the generally accepted rule of when a power of appointment is created and, thus, provides consistent, albeit not conceptually necessary, treatment. (*See infra,* §454.)

(d) **Additions to trust:** [§145] Even though a trust was created prior to March 3, 1931, ***additions*** to the trust made after that date may result in proportionate taxation of the trust corpus under section 2036. For example, if D transferred $80,000 on trust in 1930, reserving a right to trust income for life, and then transferred $100,000 to the trustee of this trust in 1940 (at which time the previously transferred corpus had appreciated in value to $100,000), one-half of the trust corpus would be exposed to the estate tax under section 2036 on the theory that the added property was "transferred" after the cut-off date.

d. **Requirement that the interest or power be retained:** [§146] For the tax to attach under section 2036, it is ***not*** sufficient that the taxable interest or power be possessed by the decedent at death. Rather, the decedent must have ***retained*** the interest or power in connection with the inter vivos transfer. (Note that this issue can merge with that of identifying the transferor, discussed above. Thus, *e.g.*, where a person provides the consideration for a transfer by another, the courts not only find that the transfer was, in substance, that of the decedent, but also that, in substance, the decedent retained the taxable interest in the property.)

(1) **Use of collateral documents:** [§147] Apparently, the taxable interest or power need not be expressly retained in the specific instrument of transfer. It is sufficient that the "retention" appear in some other document, as long as that collateral document is directly related to the transfer and may be read as part thereof. [*See* McNichol v. Commissioner, *infra,* §149]

(2) **Subsequent reconveyance of interest:** [§148] However, section 2036 will ***not*** apply where the decedent ***reacquires*** an interest in the property subsequent to the transfer. For example, if D made an outright gift of property during his lifetime and the donee later—without prearrangement—reconveyed to him a life estate therein, D does not have a "retained" life estate, and the transfer would not be taxable. [*See* Estate of Uhl v. Commissioner, 241 F.2d 867 (7th Cir. 1957)]

(3) **Compare—prearranged reconveyance:** [§149] To be distinguished from the above situation are cases where the donee's subsequent reconveyance was prearranged. The Regulations maintain that "an interest or right is treated as having been retained or reserved if at the time of the transfer there was an understanding, express or implied, that the interest or right would later be conferred." [Treas. Reg. §20.2036-1(a)]

(a) **Significance—tax avoidance forestalled:** This position is clearly reasonable and necessary to prevent the tax avoidance that would otherwise result through transfers with no apparent retained interest but which are made with the clear understanding that such an interest will be conferred upon the transferor. Indeed, the same rule obtains where the understanding was not legally enforceable but was, in fact, carried out.

(b) **Example:** D transferred income-producing property to his children upon an oral understanding that he would continue to receive all the rents until he died. Pointing out that the "retention" need not be expressed in the instrument of transfer, the court found that even though the oral understanding was unenforceable under local law, it was sufficient for taxation purposes when coupled with the fact that D did collect the income for life. [McNichol v. Commissioner, 265 F.2d 667 (3d Cir. 1959), *cert. denied*, 361 U.S. 829 (1959)]

(4) **Limitation—interest must be retained in property transferred; annuities:** [§150] The retained interest or power must be in the ***very property*** transferred; hence, transfers solely in return for the transferee's promise to pay an ***annuity*** to the transferor are usually treated as the purchase of an annuity, not the reservation of a life estate in the conveyed property.

(a) **Example—transfer for annuity:** [§151] D, along with her husband and son, had transferred property to a trustee, directing the trustee to liquidate the trust property and purchase annuities for the beneficiaries. (Specifically, D was to receive an annuity paying her $10,000 per year for life.) Until the property could be liquidated in an orderly manner and the annuities purchased, the trustee was authorized to hold the property and pay D up to $10,000 per year. D died before any annuities were purchased but for over ten years received approximately $10,000 per year from the trust. The Tax Court held that D's portion of the trust property (to the extent necessary to produce $10,000 of income per year) was taxable under section 2036(a)(1). However, the Seventh Circuit reversed, finding that the transfer was in consideration of an agreement to pay an annuity of $10,000 per year and there was no retained interest in the property transferred. [Becklenberg v. Commissioner, 273 F.2d 297 (7th Cir. 1959)]

(b) **Example—transfer held reserved life estate:** [§152] Taxpayers transferred closely held stock to trust for an "annuity" calling for payment of $75,000 annually for their lives. The trustee then sold the stock for $1,000,000 (payable in ten years) with annual interest of $75,000. The court held that in substance the taxpayers had reserved a life estate in the property transferred on trust. [Lazarus v. Commissioner, 513 F.2d 824 (9th Cir. 1975); ***and see*** Ray v. Commissioner, 762 F.2d 1361 (9th Cir. 1985)—transfer on trust was held ***not*** to be a transfer for an annuity because, on the facts, no exhaustion of the principal would ever be required to pay the fixed monthly amount reserved by the transferor]

(c) **Annuity-life insurance package:** [§153] Decedent, who was uninsurable, purchased an "annuity-life insurance package" for a single premium of $350,000 and then assigned the insurance policies to a trust for her children. For all practical purposes, the face amount of the life insurance was approximately equal to the single premium paid, and the annuity payments were approximately equal to the income that that premium could be expected to earn, less an amount that the insurance company would take as its profit. The government asserted that this agreement was really a transfer with the reservation of a life interest, but the Supreme Court disagreed, holding that the annuity and life insurance contracts were technically two separate contracts and thus two separate properties. The straight life annuity which ended at Decedent's death was not taxable under section 2033 (*see supra*, §68); the life insurance was not taxable under section 2042 since Decedent retained no incidents of ownership in the policy (*infra*, §§511 *et seq.*); and there could be no tax under section 2036 since Decedent's annuity contract (which was retained) represented an interest neither in the property transferred (the premium paid) nor in the separate life insurance contract. [Fidelity-Philadelphia Trust Co. v. Smith, 356 U.S. 274 (1958)]

1) **Note:** This rather transparent tax avoidance scheme is now forestalled by section 2039 ("Annuities") as applied in *Montgomery v. Commissioner, infra*, §372.

e. **Nature of interest retained under section 2036(a)(1):** [§154] Section 2036(a)(1) requires retention of a beneficial interest in the property: Decedent must retain ***"possession or enjoyment"*** of, or ***"the right to income"*** from, the property. Apparently the retention of both possession or enjoyment and the right to income is not required, although from an economic perspective these elements frequently merge (*i.e.*, a right to income from the property connotes enjoyment of it, and possession or enjoyment implies a lifetime access to its economic potential). [*Cf.* McNichol v. Commissioner, *supra*, §149—where the court identified a decedent's collection of rents under the informal understanding with his children as "possession or enjoyment" of the property]

(1) **Non-income producing property:** [§155] Since the retention of possession or enjoyment is sufficient to attract the tax, it is not necessary that the property be income producing. Thus, if D gives certain works of art to A, but retains possession for life, the value of the works of art is taxable to D under section 2036(a)(1) simply because of retained possession; one need not resort to economic niceties to find some "right to income" from this non-income producing property.

(2) **Contingent interests—secondary life estates:** [§156] As a general proposition, actual possession or enjoyment during life is required; a retained reversionary interest would be taxed under section 2033 but probably not under section 2036. However, a retained right to income will produce a tax under section 2036 even though the decedent was not receiving income at the time of death. According to the Committee

Reports that accompanied the 1932 Act, this was the thrust of the clarifying amendment inserting "right to income" for "the income." Moreover, the retention of a secondary life estate after the death of a primary life tenant will produce a tax even though the decedent dies before the primary life tenant. [Treas. Reg. §20.2036-1(b)(ii); *and see* Arents v. Commissioner, 297 F.2d 894 (2d Cir. 1962), *cert. denied*, 369 U.S. 848 (1962)]

(3) **Possession or enjoyment:** [§157] As previously noted, section 2036 will apply even though the decedent retained no legal ***right*** to lifetime possession and enjoyment. However, the mere fact of possession is apparently ***not*** sufficient to attract the tax; there must also exist some ***understanding*** or agreement between the decedent and the transferee that the decedent should be entitled to enjoy possession for one of the requisite time periods. [Treas. Reg. §20.2036-1(a); *and see supra,* §149]

(a) **Inferring an understanding from possession:** [§158] In a number of cases where the decedent transferred a personal residence to a spouse or children but continued to live in the residence until death, the Service contended that an understanding or agreement should be inferred from the fact of continued possession.

1) **Intra-spousal transfers:** [§159] However, in cases involving transfers between spouses, this position did not meet with success [*see, e.g.*, Gutchess v. Commissioner, 46 T.C. 554 (1966), *acq.* 1967-1 C.B. 2], and in 1970, the Service announced that "continued occupancy by the donor spouse along with the donee spouse will not normally give rise to an inference that an understanding or agreement exists." [Rev. Rul. 70-155, 1970-1 C.B. 189]

2) **Other transfers—exclusive possession test?** [§160] On the other hand, continued occupancy of a residence given to other persons (usually children) frequently has been held to create an inference that an "understanding" existed, thus supporting a tax on the value of the residence under section 2036. A comparison of two cases suggests that a critical factor giving rise to this inference is the exclusive occupancy of the donor. [*See* Linderme, Sr. v. Commissioner, 52 T.C. 305 (1969)—property taxed; donor's exclusive occupancy emphasized; Diehl v. United States, 21 A.F.T.R.2d 1607 (1967)—jury verdict for taxpayer; decedent continued to reside in residence with donees, his children]

(b) **Inferring an understanding from transfer to passive trustee:** [§161] Similarly, the requisite "understanding" has been inferred where decedent makes a transfer on trust and, regardless of the trust terms, continues to beneficially enjoy the transferred property.

1) **Example:** D transferred property on trust, the income to be paid to his wife for life with remainder to his children. The trust was ostensibly irrevocable and, for purposes of this issue, no interest or power was retained. However, the evidence indicated that D's wife never directly received any income from the trust, that the beneficiaries were only vaguely aware of the existence of the trust but not of its terms or the identity of the trustee, and that the trustee, in fact, distributed income and corpus at D's direction and request and principally to D for his benefit. Finding that the dealings raised an inference of a prearrangement that D should retain control for his benefit until death, the court held that D had retained possession and enjoyment during his life and imposed a tax on the property under section 2036(a)(1). [McCabe v. United States, 475 F.2d 1142 (Ct. Cl. 1973)]

(c) **Gift and leaseback:** [§162] A gift of property followed by a "lease" back to the donor, allowing him to use the property for the balance of his lifetime by paying a nominal "rent," is nothing more than a disguised life estate and is fully taxed in the "tenant's" estate. [Estate of DuPont, 63 T.C. 746 (1975)]

(4) **Right to income:** [§163] Just as "possession and enjoyment" does not require a legally enforceable right, neither does the "right to income." The term "right" was added by the Revenue Act of 1932, not to limit the scope of this taxing provision but to clarify that property can be taxed even though the decedent is not receiving the income if he has a right to the income. As discussed above, the Regulations suggest that "right" is to be interpreted as including an "understanding, express or implied"; and judicial authorities have held that the tax attaches under section 2036(a)(1) if the decedent is in fact receiving the income pursuant to some understanding with the donee even though the understanding is not legally enforceable. [*See* McNichol v. Commissioner, *supra,* §149]

(a) **Inference of retained right from fact of continued receipt:** [§164] Apparently, there is a greater willingness to infer an understanding from the fact of continued receipt of income than from the fact of continued possession of non-income producing property. The authority of, *inter alia, Gutchess, supra*—involving continued occupancy of the family residence by donor and donee spouses—caused no problem to the court in *McCabe, supra,* which involved continued enjoyment by the donor spouse of the income from property seemingly transferred to the donee-spouse.

(b) **Indirect beneficial interests:** [§165] The "right to income" is not limited to situations where the decedent personally collects or receives the income. So long as the income is to be used for the ***benefit of the transferor*** during life, a retained right to income may be found.

1) **Discharge of legal obligations:** [§166] Thus, if income from property transferred on trust is to be used, or may be used, to discharge the transferor's legal obligations, this retained beneficial interest is clearly treated as a "right to income." [Treas. Reg. §20.236-1(b)(2)]

   a) **Contingent obligations:** [§167] However, it is not entirely clear whether payments made on an obligation for which the settlor was only ***contingently*** liable will support taxation of the trust property in the settlor's estate.

      1/ At least one case suggests that the income must be used to discharge a primary liability of the transferor. Thus, where decedent transferred mortgaged property on trust with directions that the income from the property be used to pay off the mortgage, even though the decedent was personally liable to pay the mortgage note the court held that there was no "right to income" retained. *Rationale:* There had been a complete and irrevocable transfer of the property for the benefit of others, and the primary obligation for the discharge of the mortgage was that of the donee, not the donor who was only secondarily liable; therefore, application of the income to this purpose was for the benefit of the trust and beneficiaries, not the decedent. [Hays v. Commissioner, 181 F.2d 169 (5th Cir. 1950)]

2) **Support trusts:** [§168] Where decedent creates a trust, the income from which is to be used during his life to fulfill his legal obligation of support, he has retained a "right to income." For example, a trust is taxable under section 2036(a)(1) where the income is payable to the decedent's wife for family and joint living expenses and for her support. [Helvering v. Mercantile-Commerce Bank & Trust Co., 111 F.2d 224 (8th Cir. 1940), *cert. denied*, 310 U.S. 654 (1940); *and see* Commissioner v. Dwight's Estate, 205 F.2d 298 (2d Cir. 1953), *cert. denied*, 346 U.S. 871 (1953); Estate of Gorkey v. Commissioner, 72 T.C. 721 (1979), *aff'd as to this issue*, 735 F.2d 1367 (7th Cir. 1984)]

3) **Transfers under Uniform Transfers to Minors Act:** [§169] Similarly, a transfer to children under the Uniform Gifts to Minors Act (the donor-parent acting as custodian) was included in the transferor's estate, since the Act authorized application of the income for the support of the minor. [Prudowsky v. Commissioner, 55 T.C. 890 (1971), *aff'd*, 465 F.2d 62 (7th Cir. 1972)] The same result will obtain under the newer Uniform Transfers to Minors Act.

4) **Compare—transfers extinguishing support obligation:** [§170] However, where property is transferred to ***extinguish*** any further support obligation (*e.g.*, alimony trust created by D to discharge alimony owing to ex-wife), the payments are no longer deemed attributable to D's continuing legal obligation and hence the transfer is not includible in his estate. [National Bank of Commerce v. Henslee, 179 F. Supp. 346 (M.D. Tenn. 1959)] Rather, it is treated as a transfer for consideration and is excluded from tax.

5) **Cross-refer—period of retention:** [§171] In addition to the "right to income" issue, support trusts or custodial gifts for minors also present issues of whether the interest or right of the decedent has been retained for one of the requisite time periods; *see infra,* §215.

(c) **Discretionary trusts:** [§172] As long as the transferor is not a trustee and cannot otherwise compel the use of the trust property or income for his benefit, the fact that the trustee has discretionary power to so use the income will not, apparently, cause the trust property to be taxed under section 2036(a)(1). [*See* Chrysler v. Commissioner, 44 T.C. 55 (1965), *rev'd on another issue*, 361 F.2d 508 (2d Cir. 1966); *and see* Mitchell v. Commissioner, 55 T.C. 576 (1970), *acq.*, 1971-2 C.B. 3] And this is true even if the trustee is given discretion to make payments directly to the settlor. [*See* Commissioner v. Irving Trust Co., 147 F.2d 946 (2d Cir. 1945)]

1) **Caution—prearrangement?** [§173] However, the courts may imply a retention of a right to income from continued discretionary distribution to the settlor. For example, where the property transferred was D's sole source of income, and after the transfer the trustee paid all of the income to D, a prearrangement may be inferred even though the instrument recited that the trustee had "absolute discretion" regarding payments. [Skinner v. United States, 316 F.2d 517 (3d Cir. 1963)]

2) **Compare—where settlor can compel exercise of discretion:** [§174] And, even though a trustee is given discretion to make payments to the settlor, if the settlor can compel exercise of this discretion in his favor, a "right to income" will be deemed to exist. For instance, where the standards governing the exercise of discretion are vague (*e.g.*, a direction to distribute "such income as may be necessary for the comfort and happiness" of the settlor) the settlor could presumably enlist the aid of a court to compel the trustee to make distribution to him. Moreover, even where the standards governing the exercise of discretion are definite and ascertainable (*e.g.*, to distribute "such income as may be necessary for the support, maintenance and welfare" of the settlor), the settlor could compel the exercise of the trustee's discretion in his own favor and, hence, has retained a "right to income."

(d) **Family annuity agreements:** [§175] A "sale" of property in which the "buyer" contracts to make payments on the purchase price out of the income to be derived from the property during the balance of the transferor's life is not likely to be treated as a sale for estate tax purposes.

1) **Example:** Suppose that D sells Blackacre to his son for $50,000, the property's fair market value, but it is provided that the purchase price shall be payable "in annual amounts equal to the net income derived from the property; any unpaid balance on the purchase price owing at my death shall be forgiven." This is nothing more than a gift of the property with D retaining the right to income for life, and the transfer is therefore includible in D's estate. [Schwartz v. Commissioner, 9 T.C. 229 (1947); Lazarus v. Commissioner, *supra*, §152]

2) **Compare—qualified "private annuities":** [§176] If, however, the payments were based upon D's ***life expectancy***—as opposed to income to be derived from the property—the transaction might be treated as a transfer of property for a "private annuity." The transferee's potential obligation to pay in excess of any income derived from the property may constitute sufficient consideration to take the property out of D's estate; *see supra,* §150.

(e) **Transfer of stock coupled with employment contract:** [§177] Where stock is transferred by gift and, in connection therewith, the transferor enters into an "employment contract" with the corporation which provides for a "salary" in an amount likely to and which does absorb all the corporate profits, and which is to be paid to the transferor for the transferor's life without regard to services rendered, the transaction may be treated as a transfer of stock reserving a right to income. [Holland v. Commissioner, 47 B.T.A. 807 (1942)]

1) **Compare—bona fide employment contract:** [§178] But, where the employment contract represents reasonable compensation for services actually rendered by the transferor, it has been held that the tax will not attach under section 2036(a)(1). [Hofford v. Commissioner, 4 T.C. 542 (1945)]

f. **Nature of power retained under section 2036(a)(2):** [§179] Section 2036(a)(2) exposes to the estate tax any property transferred by the decedent wherein there was retained "the right, either alone or in conjunction with any person, to designate the persons who shall possess or enjoy the property or the income therefrom."

(1) **In general—power vs. interest:** [§180] This provision pertains to retention of a ***power*** with respect to the property rather than an interest in the property or its income. However, most of the substantive rules applicable to retained interests are applicable, by analogy, to retained powers.

(a) **Transfer and retention:** [§181] Thus, the issues and principles considered in connection with the requirements that there be a "transfer" and that the interest or power be "retained" apply equally to retained interests under section 2036(a)(1) and retained powers under section 2036(a)(2). (*See* discussion *supra*, §§130 *et seq.*)

(b) **Contingent powers included:** [§182] Even though the exercise of the power is contingent upon the happening of an event beyond the control of the transferor and which has not occurred at the time of her death, the property is subject to tax. [Treas. Reg. §20.2036-1(b)(3)(iii)]

1) **Compare:** An analogy may be made here to retained secondary life estates. Recall that such retained interests will expose the transferred property to taxation even where the decedent dies before the primary life tenant—*i.e.*, before the retained interest is enjoyed by the decedent (*supra*, §156). A retained power is similarly taxable under section 2036(a)(2) even though the power was not exercisable by the decedent at her death because a stated contingency had not occurred.

(c) **Beneficial power not required:** [§183] It is not necessary that the power be exercisable in favor of the transferor. If the transferor has power to designate the possession or enjoyment by others, the tax will attach despite the fact that she could not have exercised the power so as to secure a personal economic benefit. [*See, e.g.*, Yawkey v. Commissioner, 12 T.C. 1164 (1949)]

(d) **Joint powers included:** [§184] Nor does it matter that a power is exercisable by the decedent only jointly or with the consent of another. Moreover, the fact that the co-holder of the power (or person whose consent may be required) enjoys a beneficial interest in the property that would be adversely affected by its exercise does not prevent taxation. The phrase "any person" in the statute means ***any*** person, even an adverse party. [Helvering v. City Bank Farmers Trust Co., 296 U.S. 85 (1935)]

(e) **Capacity in which power exercisable:** [§185] If the requisite power is retained, the capacity in which it is exercisable is immaterial. For instance, the fact that the power is exercisable by the decedent in a fiduciary capacity as trustee will not prevent taxation.

(f) **Form of the power:** [§186] The retained power need not specifically authorize a designation or shifting of enjoyment; any power having this effect is within the scope of the statute.

1) **Power to accumulate:** [§187] Accordingly, section 2036(a) applies to any transfer on trust in which the settlor has retained the power to direct the accumulation of trust income during her lifetime

because such accumulation would ***divert the income*** from the income beneficiary to the owner of the remainder. In other words, the accumulation of income operates as a "silent" transfer to corpus, thus enlarging the remainder interest. [United States v. O'Malley, 383 U.S. 627 (1966)]

a) **Nonexercise of right immaterial:** Note that the mere ***retention*** of such a power makes the transfer taxable, regardless of whether any accumulation was ever directed by the settlor.

2) **Power to encroach:** [§188] A similar result follows where the settlor retains the power to invade or encroach upon the corpus for the benefit of the income beneficiary (at the expense of the owner of the remainder). The retention of such power to shift beneficial enjoyment makes the trust corpus taxable in the settlor's estate, whether or not the power was ever exercised. [Commissioner v. McDermott's Estate, 222 F.2d 665 (7th Cir. 1955)]

3) **Power to allocate ("sprinkle"):** [§189] Likewise, if the settlor retained the power to direct the allocation of trust income among various beneficiaries, the property transferred remains taxable to her estate. [Industrial Trust Co. v. Commissioner, 165 F.2d 142 (1st Cir. 1947)]

(2) **Power to affect possession or enjoyment**

(a) **Shifting of economic enjoyment not required:** [§190] Clearly, the power to shift possession or enjoyment of the property or its income from one party to another is taxable (above); however, this is not essential. Section 2036(a)(2) will also apply where decedent has retained the power to affect the ***time and manner*** of a single beneficiary's possession and enjoyment.

1) **Example:** D created certain inter vivos trusts for her children. As co-trustee she had the power, in conjunction with the other trustees, to accumulate the income or distribute it currently to the designated income beneficiary. Upon her death, the trusts would terminate and the corpus and any accumulated income was to be distributed to the beneficiary or to his or her estate. Each trust had a single income beneficiary who also owned the remainder so that, in any event, the beneficiary of each trust was assured of receipt of all the income and the property. Although D had no power to shift economic enjoyment, the trusts were held taxable under section 2036(a)(2). *Rationale:* D was able to affect the time and manner of beneficial enjoyment by exercising her power (retained as co-trustee) to accumulate income during her life rather than distributing it currently. [Struthers v. Kelm, 218 F.2d 810 (8th Cir. 1955); *see also* Lober v. United States, 346 U.S. 335 (1953)—dealt with a similar question under

the predecessor of section 2038 ("Revocable Transfers"), discussed *infra*, §328]

(b) **Limitation—power must be exercisable during transferor's life:** [§191] However, the power must be one that will affect possession or enjoyment of the income or property ***during the transferor's lifetime***. Thus, for example, if the power to designate is exercisable only by will, it will not be taxed under this section. [Treas. Reg. §20.2036-1(b)(3)]

1) **But note:** A power to affect post-death enjoyment ***is taxable*** under section 2038. (*See infra*, §339.)

(c) **Limitation—nonbeneficial power must be discretionary:** [§192] Where the power in question is to designate possession or enjoyment ***of another***, it must be a ***discretionary*** power. Consequently, if the transferor is the trustee of a trust that ***requires*** the distribution of income to A for life with remainder to B, the transferor has no "power" to designate income or possession.

1) **Power limited by ascertainable standard:** [§193] Similarly, if the exercise of a power to accumulate or distribute income or to invade corpus is governed by an ***ascertainable standard,*** the power is not discretionary but, rather, is in substance a mandatory direction. [*See* Jennings v. Smith, 161 F.2d 74 (2d Cir. 1947)]

a) ***"Ascertainable standards"*** are those that identify a reasonably objective circumstance that will govern the exercise of the power. Typically accepted as ascertainable standards are: support, education, health or medical needs, maintenance according to one's accustomed standard of living, etc.

2) **Discretionary standards:** [§194] In contrast, where an apparent standard governing exercise of the power cannot be reasonably related to some objective circumstance, it does not effectively limit or mandate exercise of the power and thus leaves the power discretionary. For example, a power remains fully discretionary even though its exercise is subject to such vague guidelines as "happiness," or "comfort and happiness."

3) **Mixed standards:** [§195] And, if a "discretionary" standard is included among "ascertainable" standards, the power remains discretionary; *e.g.*, a power governed by "support, maintenance, welfare ***and happiness***" is discretionary. On the other hand, a "discretionary" standard may be so limited as to become an ascertainable standard—*e.g.*, "reasonable comfort according to one's accustomed manner of living."

4) **Compare—beneficial power:** [§196] Note that an ascertainable standard (nondiscretionary power) will prevent taxation only where the power is ***nonbeneficial,*** *i.e.*, where decedent could not personally benefit by its exercise. If the power is a beneficial one, the fact that it is enforceable by the decedent—either because it is mandatory or subject to ascertainable standards—clearly makes it a right to income, taxable under section 2036(a)(1) (*see supra*, §174).

(d) **Administrative powers:** [§197] The statute, in designating for taxation those retained powers that would affect possession and enjoyment, is qualitatively limited to ***dispositive or distributive powers,*** not those relating solely to the management and administration of the property or investment of trust funds. However, it is arguable that administrative powers can affect possession or enjoyment. For example, broad powers of investment conceivably might permit the trustee (decedent) to invest entirely in unproductive property, thereby shifting enjoyment from the current income beneficiary to the remainderman.

1) **The "*State Street Trust* doctrine":** [§198] Thus, in *State Street Trust Co. v. United States,* 263 F.2d 635 (1st Cir. 1959), the court held that the broad investment powers retained by the decedent as trustee of the trust he created were the equivalent of the power to designate possession or enjoyment of income insofar as the decedent might, through selection of investments, benefit one beneficiary to the detriment of others. It rejected the taxpayer's argument that fiduciary restraints imposed by state law would prevent such shifting of economic benefits under the guise of exercising administrative powers as to trust investments.

a) ***State Street Trust*** **overruled:** But the "*State Street Trust* doctrine" was, in fact, never followed; subsequent cases were always distinguished on the facts. And, in 1970, the First Circuit overruled its eleven-year-old opinion. [*See* Old Colony Trust Co. v. United States, 438 F.2d 684 (1st Cir. 1970)] *Rationale:* The principle that the fiduciary must be impartial and serve all beneficiaries, coupled with the power of all beneficiaries to enlist the aid of the courts to enforce compliance with this principle, gainsays any discretionary "power" in a trustee to improperly use administrative powers to affect beneficial enjoyment.

2) **Retention of voting rights in transferred stock**

a) **Former rule—section 2036 inapplicable:** [§199] Prior to the 1976 Tax Reform Act, mere retention of voting control over shares of a closely held corporation transferred on trust was not considered a "power to designate," and hence did not result in taxation of the shares in the transferor's estate. [United States v. Byrum, 408 U.S. 125 (1972)]

1/ ***Byrum* case:** D owned 71 percent of the stock of three corporations. He transferred a portion of this stock on trust for his children, retaining the power to vote the stock, to veto its sale or exchange, and to replace the trustee. The government argued that D's power to vote the transferred stock, when viewed in light of the voting power of the retained stock, amounted to a retention of enjoyment of the property transferred (control of the corporation) which was taxable under section 2036(a)(1), and also effectively gave the decedent power to control the dividend policy and income flow, thus amounting to a power to designate who shall possess or enjoy the income from the property which was taxable under section 2036(a)(2).

2/ **Holding:** Over the dissent of Justice White, the Supreme Court held that administrative powers, however broad, were not taxable under section 2036. Citing *Reinecke v. Northern Trust Co.* (*infra*, §281), it reasoned that fiduciary restraints (here imposed upon corporate directors) prevented the administrative powers from being viewed as discretionary distributive or dispositive powers.

b) **The "anti-*Byrum*" amendment:** [§200] An amendment intended legislatively to overrule the *Byrum* decision was passed as part of the Tax Reform Act of 1976, but it was so flawed in purpose and effect that within two years a completely new "anti-*Byrum*" amendment was substituted by the Revenue Act of 1978. Under section 2036(b), a person will be considered to have retained the "enjoyment" of stock transferred during life (*i.e.*, it will be included in her estate under section 2036(a)(1)) if the donor ***retains the right to vote the transferred shares and*** if at any time within three years of her death, the donor ***"controls" the corporation*** whose shares were given away.

1/ **Retention of voting rights:** Although the statutory language is somewhat obscure, the Committee Reports make it clear that inclusion in the gross estate will occur only if the right to vote the stock transferred is retained. Thus, a 100 percent shareholder could give away 49 percent of the corporate stock, retain control through ownership of the retained 51 percent, but avoid estate tax upon the stock transferred if the power to vote that stock was not retained. Or, a controlling shareholder may retain control but avoid any estate tax upon nonvoting shares that are transferred.

2/ **Control requirement:** Under subsection (b)(1), "control" is defined as ownership of 20 percent or more of the voting stock of the issuing corporation.

a/ Note that the decedent-transferor need not ***retain*** control; it is sufficient if the decedent possesses the requisite control at any time within three years of death.

b/ And, for purposes of the control requirement, the "constructive ownership rules" of section 318 are applicable—*i.e.*, any stock owned directly or indirectly by the decedent's parents, spouse, children, or grandchildren, and any stock owned by certain entities, *e.g.*, trusts, estates, partnerships, or controlled corporations, is attributed to the decedent. (*See* further discussion of "attribution" in Income Tax II Summary.)

3/ **Comment:** [§201] As noted above, the government's theory in *Byrum* (and in Revenue Ruling 67-54, 1967-1 C.B. 269 which involved a gift of ***nonvoting*** stock by a controlling shareholder) rested upon the element of substantial retained control whereby the donor could personally enjoy the perquisites of corporate proprietorship during life and affect (through this control) the beneficial enjoyment by donees of the proprietary and financial perquisites of stock ownership.

a/ Under the government's theory, retention of voting power in the transferred stock was not critical as long as the decedent otherwise retained ***control*** through, *e.g.*, continued ownership of a controlling block of stock. And, the government urged in *Byrum* that it was concerned with ***control***, not an "insignificant minority interest."

b/ By requiring retained voting rights in the stock transferred, the amendment permits the retention of control by a major shareholder as long as the subject of the gift is of a minority interest (in which voting rights are not retained) or is of nonvoting stock. On the other hand, by defining "control" at such a low level as 20 percent of voting power, the statute embraces minority interests with which the government may not have been concerned.

3) **Lapse of right to vote stock:** [§202] Suppose that the decedent did not ***retain*** the right to vote any of the stock given away during life, but continued to control the corporation through the power to vote, *e.g.*, 60 percent of the common stock, which was not transferred. Suppose further that the corporation's Articles of Incorporation provided that the right to vote stock would cease upon the death of the shareholder.

a) **Prior law:** [§203] The stock transferred would not be included in the decedent's gross estate under section 2036(c) because the right to vote that stock was ***not retained***. (*See supra*, §200.) And prior to 1990, a tax-free transfer could be effected to the extent that the lapse of the voting rights upon death enhances the value of the original donee's stock and decreases the value of the retained stock which is included in the dededent's estate under section 2033.

b) **Compare—under 1990 Act lapsing rights treated as transfers for estate tax purposes:** [§204] Section 2704 of new Chapter 14 now treats such a lapse of voting rights as a transfer at death, includible in the gross estate of the decedent-donor. (*See infra*, §§959 *et seq.*, for discussion of this and related provisions of new Chapter 14.)

(3) **In whom power vested?** [§205] If the power is a beneficial one, it will usually result in taxation whether possessed by the decedent or by another. However, if the power is (i) ***purely discretionary***, (ii) ***exercisable solely by another person***, and (iii) the ***decedent had no right or power to compel its exercise in his favor***, there will be no tax under section 2036. [Commissioner v. Irving Trust Co., 147 F.2d 946 (2d Cir. 1945)]

(a) **Taxation of nonbeneficial power:** [§206] But a nonbeneficial power will be taxable under section 2036(a)(2) if it is exercisable by the decedent or the decedent is otherwise in a position to compel its exercise.

(b) **Effect of access to the power:** [§207] Even though the decedent does not technically possess the power, she will be deemed to have retained the power (where this is necessary for taxation) where she has reserved indirect access thereto.

1) **Example—power to remove trustee:** Accordingly, a power vested in a trustee which, if retained by the decedent, would be a taxable power, will be deemed possessed by the decedent (and the property will be taxed) if she has reserved authority to remove the trustee and appoint a successor, since, by so doing the decedent is able to "shop around" for a trustee amenable to her wishes. [Treas. Reg. §20.2036-1(b)(3); *see also* Rev. Rul. 79-353, 1979-2 C.B. 325]

2) **Example—right to veto exercise of power:** Likewise, if the decedent retains a right to consent to the trustee's proposed exercise of a (taxable) power, she will be treated as having retained the power purportedly granted to the trustee. The law refuses to give any effect to the technical distinction that the trustee must initiate action, while the decedent is limited to exercising a veto. [*Cf.* Thorp v. Commissioner, 164 F.2d 966 (3d Cir. 1947), *cert. denied*, 333 U.S. 843 (1948)]

g. **Period of retention:** [§208] The interest or power must be retained for one of three time periods: (i) for the ***transferor's life;*** (ii) for a period ***not ascertainable without reference to transferor's death;*** or (iii) for a period of time that does ***not in fact end with death.***

(1) **For life:** [§209] The first period, "for life," is self-explanatory and usually quite obvious. Recall that the decedent need not be actually enjoying the property during life or in fact be able to exercise a power to designate during life. A retained secondary life estate or retained contingent power to designate possession or enjoyment will result in taxation even though the decedent dies before the primary life tenant or before the occurrence of a contingency governing exercise of the power. (*See supra,* §§156, 182.)

(2) **Period not ascertainable without reference to death:** [§210] This time period is apparently designed to assure that a tax will be imposed under section 2036 even though a person does not technically reserve an interest or power "for life"—as long as the life or death of the transferor is the critical limitation upon the continuation of the retained interest or power.

(a) **Example:** D transfers property to A, reserving the right to receive the income therefrom in quarterly payments, with the proviso that no part of the income between the last quarterly payment and the date of D's death is to be received by D or D's estate. Since the period for which the income was retained is "not ascertainable without reference to his death," the transfer is taxable in D's estate. [*See* Treas. Reg. §20.2036-1(b)(1)(i)]

(b) **Example:** Similarly, it is this time period that provides the basis for taxing property wherein the decedent retained a secondary life estate but dies before the primary life tenant. [*See* Treas. Reg. §20.2036-1(b)(1)(ii)]

(3) **Period that does not in fact end before death:** [§211] The Committee Report accompanying the 1932 Act illustrated this time period with an example of a very elderly person who reserved a long term of years in the transferred property. Based upon this illustration, the Regulations under the 1939 Code interpreted this phrase as comprehending a transfer where an interest or power is retained "for such period as to evidence his intention that it should extend for at least the duration of his life, and his death occurred before the expiration of such period." [Treas. Reg. §81.18]

(a) **Subjective vs. objective test:** [§212] Thus, initially it appeared that this time period was to be determined with reference to the subjective intent of the transferor. However, the Regulations under the 1954 Code are silent on this point and the Service now undertakes to apply the statutory language literally and ***objectively*** rather than subjectively.

(b) **Court decisions:** [§213] Although at least one decision has specifically approved the Service's objective interpretation [McKeon v. Commissioner, 25 T.C. 697 (1956)] and most cases appear to approve it where the question arises, the particular issue is rarely discussed. Indeed, most cases seem to assume that the requisite time period is present, addressing instead other substantive requirements. [*See, e.g.*, Fry v. Commissioner, 9 T.C. 503 (1947); Prudowski v. Commissioner, 55 T.C. 890 (1971), *aff'd,* 465 F.2d 62 (7th Cir. 1972); *but compare* National Bank of Commerce v. Henslee, 179 F. Supp. 346 (M.D. Tenn. 1959)—where the court apparently adopted a subjective test in a case arising under the 1939 Code and its Regulations]

(c) **Example:** [§214] At age 40 and while in excellent health, D irrevocably transferred property on trust for the benefit of A, but reserved the right to direct the trustee to pay some or all of the income to herself (D) for five years. In the fifth year following the creation of the trust, D is killed in an automobile accident. Even though it does not appear that D ***intended*** to retain a right in the income ***for her life,*** the right to income which she did retain did not, in fact, end before her death; hence applying the Service's objective interpretation, the value of the trust property is included in her estate under section 2036(a)(1).

(d) **Gifts to minors:** [§215] As discussed earlier, there is a reserved "right to income" where the income from transferred property is to be used to fulfill the transferor's legal obligation to support his or her minor children (*see supra,* §168). Since this legal obligation persists only during minority (not for the parent's life) and since most gifts to minors that might serve to discharge the parent's support obligation are likely to be made at a time when it can be anticipated that the parent would survive the child's age of majority, the interpretation of "for a period that does not in fact end before his death" is particularly critical in regard to gifts to minors. And, for the most part, judicial authority appears to support the Service's objective interpretation. [*See* Chrysler v. Commissioner, 44 T.C. 55 (1965), *acq.* 1970-2 C.B. xix, *rev'd on another issue,* 361 F.2d 508 (2d Cir. 1966) *and* Prudowski v. Commissioner, *supra*—both involving gifts under the Uniform Gifts to Minors Act where the parent-donor served as custodian and died before the donees attained majority]

h. **Amount includible:** [§216] As a general rule, the ***entire value*** of the property subject to the retained interest or power is taxable under section 2036; the tax is not limited to the value of the specific interests affected. ***Example:*** D transferred property on trust for A for life, remainder to X, reserving the power to add or substitute other income beneficiaries. Even though D's power affects only the income interest, not that of the owner of the remainder, the full value of the property is taxable in D's estate.

(1) **Retention of right in a portion of the property:** [§217] However, where the retained right relates only to a ***portion*** of the property, ***only that portion is taxed.***

(a) **Example:** Where D transfers property reserving a life interest in the income from ***one-half*** of the property, the value of one-half the property, as of D's death (or the alternate valuation date), is subject to tax.

(b) **Example:** Similarly, where a decedent's right to income is limited (*e.g.*, "$500 a month for life"; or "whatever income is necessary for my support and maintenance"), only that portion of corpus that would be required to produce that amount of income would be taxable to his estate. [Estate of Uhl v. Commissioner, 241 F.2d 867 (7th Cir. 1957)]

1) **Compare:** Where D reserves "as much income as is necessary for my support," the amount is fixed ***objectively***—by reference to the decedent's age, health, standard of living, other sources of income, etc.

(2) **Retained right subject to intervening estate:** [§218] If the retained interest or power relates to possession or income after an intervening estate which cannot be affected by the retained interest or power, the amount taxable is reduced by ***the value of the intervening estate.***

(a) **Example:** D transferred property to A for life, then to himself for life, remainder to X. Should D predecease A and X, the value of the property less the value of A's remaining life estate is taxable in D's estate.

(3) **Retention of power to accumulate income:** [§219] Where D retains the power to direct accumulation of income, and the applicable taxing provision is section 2036 (or 2038, *infra*, §§278 *et seq.*), both the property ***and the accumulated income*** earned therefrom are subject to tax. [United States v. O'Malley, 383 U.S. 627 (1966)]

i. **Relinquishment or transfer of retained interest or power:** [§220] If the decedent divests himself during life of whatever rights or powers he may have retained with respect to transferred property, the estate tax will ordinarily not attach to the property under section 2036.

(1) **Exception—release or transfer within three years of death:** [§221] Under prior law, it was held that section 2035 interacted with section 2036 so that if a taxable interest or power was transferred or released within ***three years of death,*** the entire property remained taxable under section 2036. [*See* Rev. Rul. 56-324, 1956-2 C.B. 999] This result is now specified in section 2035(d), as amended by the 1981 Act. (*See supra,* §115.)

(a) **Note:** As discussed earlier, this rule has been extended to situations where the decedent ***sold*** a retained interest within ***three years of death.*** [*See* Allen v. United States, *supra*, §117]

(b) **And note:** With respect to retained voting rights [I.R.C. §2036(b); *supra*, §§200-201], section 2036(b)(3) specifically provides that the relinquishment of voting rights within three years of death will be treated as a transfer of property by the decedent; *i.e.*, the stock remains taxable under section 2036(b).

6. **Section 2037—Transfers Taking Effect at Death:** [§222] Under section 2037, there is included in the decedent's gross estate the value of any property transferred by him during his lifetime (on trust or otherwise), where (i) the transferee's possession and enjoyment of the property is contingent upon ***surviving*** the decedent-transferor, ***and*** (ii) the decedent-transferor has retained a ***reversionary interest*** in the property ***valued at more than five percent*** of the value of the property at the time of the decedent's death.

a. **Historical background:** [§223] Transfers taking effect at death were also within the contemplation of the tax on lifetime transfers "intended to take effect in possession or enjoyment at or after" the transferor's death under the 1916 Act (*supra*, §121). Section 2037 now specifies the taxability of such transfers (focusing on arrangements often referred to as "*Hallack*-type" transfers, *infra*) and, with the enactment of its predecessor in 1949, the broad and troublesome language of the 1916 Act was eliminated from the Code.

(1) **Review of Supreme Court decisions:** [§224] A survey of the relevant Supreme Court decisions is particularly helpful for a thorough understanding of section 2037.

(a) ***Klein v. United States:*** [§225] In *Klein*, D transferred property to A for life retaining a reversion after A's life estate, but if D predeceased A, then A would take the property in fee. A survived D and the Court held the property taxable in D's estate under the "intended to take effect" language of the 1916 Act. [Klein v. United States, 283 U.S. 231 (1931)]

1) **Rationale:** D retained a reversion after A's life estate, and A was required to survive D in order to secure the property—*i.e.*, until D's death A's interest was held in abeyance. Thus, the Court found a transfer from D to A which would only be effective upon D's death.

(b) ***Helvering v. St. Louis Union Trust Co.:*** [§226] Here D transferred property on trust for A for life, with the proviso that if D outlived A, the property would return to D, but if A outlived D, the remainder would go to X (or, in a companion case, vest in A absolutely). D predeceased the remaindermen, and the transfers were held ***not*** taxable. [Helvering v. St. Louis Union Trust Co., 296 U.S. 39 (1935)]

1) **Rationale:** Although these situations were, as a practical matter, identical to that in *Klein*, the Court found a subtle property law distinction: X (or A) had a vested remainder subject to divestment, and D had a possibility of reverter if A predeceased D (whereas in *Klein*, only a life estate was vested, D having retained a reversion). Consequently, D's death "passed no interest to any of the beneficiaries of the trust, and enlarged none beyond what was conveyed by the indenture. His death simply put an end to what, at best, was a mere possibility of reverter. . . ."

(c) ***Helvering v. Hallock:*** [§227] This decision grew out of a consolidation of three cases, two of which posed facts similar to *St. Louis Union Trust Co.*, and one in which the facts were similar to *Klein*. This time, however, the Supreme Court found no essential difference between the cases and held all the transfers taxable, thereby overruling *St. Louis Union Trust Co.* [Helvering v. Hallock, 309 U.S. 106 (1940)] At the same time, the precise basis for its decision and the rationale for taxing such transfers was left unclear. Specifically:

1) Did the tax attach because the transferor had a reversionary interest, or because the beneficiary's possession or enjoyment was conditioned upon surviving the transferor, or both?

2) Was it necessary that the reversionary interest be expressly reserved or would it be sufficient if it arose by operation of law?

3) Was it sufficient if the reversionary interest was remote and contingent, or must there be some significant possibility of reverter?

(d) ***Spiegel's Estate v. Commissioner:*** [§228] After almost a decade of litigation in the lower courts, the Supreme Court finally answered the questions left open in *Hallock*. [Spiegel's Estate v. Commissioner, 335 U.S. 701 (1949)] Briefly:

1) The reversionary interest is critical, and a condition of survivorship for the beneficiary to take is required (although the Court's decision is not entirely clear on this latter point).

2) It is sufficient if the reversionary interest exists—*i.e.*, contrary to conventional wisdom (which assumed an express reservation was required) it is immaterial whether it is expressly reserved or arises by operation of law.

3) Even a remote reversionary interest is enough for taxation (in fact, the value of D's reversionary interest in *Spiegel's Estate* was less than .004 of the value of the corpus).

(2) **Congressional reaction:** [§229] The broad interpretation given by *Spiegel's Estate* to the taxation of "*Hallock*-type" transfers prompted statutory clarifica-

tion and modification in the Technical Changes Act of 1949. These provisions were further refined in section 2037 of the 1954 Code, the general provisions of which are set forth below in the "introductory analysis."

b. **Introductory analysis:** [§230] For analytical purposes, section 2037 may be viewed as establishing four requirements for taxation.

(1) **Condition of survivorship:** [§231] The decedent's inter vivos transfer of an interest in the property must be such that the transferee can obtain possession or enjoyment of the property ***only by surviving the decedent***. [I.R.C. §2037(a)(1)]

(2) **Reversionary interest:** [§232] Additionally, it must be shown that the decedent retained a reversionary interest in the property. [I.R.C. §2037(a)(2)]

(a) **Note:** With respect to transfers made ***prior to October 8, 1949***, the reversionary interest must be expressly reserved. However, for post-October 7, 1949 transfers, it is sufficient if the reversionary interest arises by operation of law. (Thus, the rule in *Spiegel, supra,* operates prospectively only.)

(3) **De minimis rule:** [§233] Moreover, section 2037 will only apply if the value of decedent's reversionary interest ***exceeds five percent*** of the value of the transferred property immediately before decedent's death. [I.R.C. §2037(a)(2)]

(4) **Power in a third party (the "negative requirement"):** [§234] Finally, the last sentence of section 2037(b) imposes a so-called negative requirement: "Notwithstanding the foregoing, an interest so transferred shall not be included in the decedent's gross estate under this section if possession or enjoyment of the property could have been obtained by any beneficiary during the decedent's life through the exercise of a general power of appointment (as defined in section 2041) which in fact was exercisable immediately before the decedent's death."

(5) **Collateral aspects:** [§235] In addition to the above four basic requirements, three collateral matters should be considered:

(a) ***The requirement of a transfer*** by the decedent;

(b) ***The amount taxable*** under this section; and

(c) ***The relationship of section 2037 to other taxing sections.***

c. **Requirement of a transfer:** [§236] The nature and scope of the transfer requirement under this section is similar to that under section 2036 (*see* discussion *supra,* §§130 *et seq.*). Keep in mind that the property must have been transferred ***by the decedent*** during life. The tax under section 2037 will not reach property transferred by another—even though possession or enjoyment may be dependent upon surviving the decedent and the decedent possesses a "reversionary interest" (*e.g.*, a remainder or a reversion inherited from the actual transferor).

(1) **Limitation—transfer of entire interest outside statute:** [§237] Moreover, a reversionary interest must be "***retained***" by the decedent; *e.g.*, it would be insufficient if the decedent transferred the entire interest in the property and subsequently reacquired a reversionary interest in the form of a remainder from the owner of the remainder.

(2) **Time of the transfer:** [§238] Because this statute operates differently with respect to transfers before October 8, 1949, and those after October 7, 1949, it may be important to determine the time at which the transfer was made. This issue is resolved under the same principles that govern the similar issue under section 2036; *see supra*, §§140-145.

d. **The survivorship requirement:** [§239] It is essential to the operation of section 2037 that a beneficiary's ***possession and enjoyment*** be ***contingent solely*** on ***surviving the transferor.***

(1) **Analytical approach:** In determining whether this requirement is met, it may be helpful to ask the following questions:

(i) Is the interest of any beneficiary ***contingent***?

(ii) If so, is it ***contingent on surviving*** the transferor?

(iii) If so, is it contingent ***solely*** on surviving the transferor—rather than some other person or alternate event?

Additionally, troublesome fact situations might be resolved by asking: "Does it make any difference to a beneficiary whether the transferor lives or dies?"

(2) **Distinguish property law:** [§240] Note that it is a beneficiary's ***possession or enjoyment*** which must be conditioned on surviving the decedent; the statute does not focus upon whether a future interest is technically contingent or vested under property law. Thus, for purposes of section 2037, a survivorship condition may exist in the case of a vested remainder subject to divestment as well as in the case of a contingent remainder, since, in both instances, whether the beneficiary will ever ***possess or enjoy*** the property is held in abeyance.

(a) **Example:** "D to A for life, remainder to D, or, if D is not living at A's death, to X or X's estate." X's interest will vest if D fails to survive A, irrespective of whether X predeceases A and D. However, X cannot ***possess or enjoy*** the property unless she survives D. Hence, the transfer is exposed to section 2037.

(3) **Transferor must be measuring life:** [§241] The fact that the transferee must survive some third person in order to possess or enjoy the property is not

enough to attract the tax. Section 2037 only applies to transfers conditioned upon the transferee surviving the ***transferor***.

(a) **Example:** D transfers property on trust with the income payable to A for life and, upon A's death, remainder to A's surviving children; and if A leaves no surviving children, then to D or to D's estate. Since the remaindermen (A's children) can possess or enjoy the property without surviving D (they need only survive A), the transfer is not taxable under section 2037. (Note, however, that the value of D's reversion is taxed under section 2033; *see supra*, §71.)

(b) **Example:** D transfers property on trust with the income payable to A for life and at A's death, remainder to A's surviving children; and if none of A's children survive, then to D; but if D is then dead, to X. As in the prior example, A's interest and that of A's children is not dependent upon surviving D. But X can only come into possession or enjoyment by outliving D; hence, the value of X's contingent remainder is exposed to the tax in D's estate.

(c) **Example:** D transfers property on trust with the income payable to A for life, remainder to X; but D reserves the power to revoke the trust. Here the ***entire value*** of the property transferred will be taxed under section 2037, since as long as D is alive the interests of both A and X may be divested by exercise of the power of revocation.

(4) **Effect of alternative event:** [§242] Since the beneficiary's possession or enjoyment must be dependent ***solely*** on surviving the transferor, a condition of survival will not support the tax if the beneficiary could take upon the happening of some ***alternative event***. [Treas. Reg. §20.2037-1(b)]

(a) **Example:** D transferred property on trust with directions to accumulate the income from the property until A is fifty years of age and then to distribute the property and any accumulated income to A; but if D died before A reached age fifty, the trust was to terminate at once and the trustee was to distribute the property to A; provided, however, that if A died before attaining age fifty, the trust property was to revert to D or his estate. Here, A's possession or enjoyment of the property, before she attains age fifty, is dependent upon surviving D; however, A will also obtain possession and enjoyment of the property if she lives to age fifty even though D is also alive at that time. Thus, since A's possession or enjoyment is not dependent ***solely*** on surviving D, section 2037 does not apply.

(b) **Compare:** D transferred property on trust to accumulate the income from the property until A was fifty years old and then to distribute the property and accumulated income to A, if D were then dead; but if D were still living when A attained fifty years of age, the trustee was to continue to accumulate the income until D died and then distribute the trust property to A; provided that if A died before reaching fifty years of age, or if A predeceased D, the trust property reverts to D or his estate. Here, section 2037 ***does*** apply; A's possession or enjoyment is contingent on attaining age fifty ***and*** surviving D, whichever occurs ***last.*** Thus, in any event, A must survive D in order to possess and enjoy the property.

(c) **Caution—"unreal" alternative event:** [§243] If the alternative event under which the beneficiary might take is so extreme as to be "unreal," it may be disregarded. [Treas. Reg. §20.2037-1(b)] Thus, if D transfers property on trust with directions to accumulate the income from the trust and to distribute the entire trust property to A "if A survives me or, even if I am then living, at such time as A is elected President of the United States," it is likely that the alternative event upon which A's possession or enjoyment is conditioned will be disregarded and, assuming the reversionary interest requirement is met, the property will be included in D's gross estate under section 2037.

(5) **Expectation that beneficiary must survive not enough:** [§244] Suppose that D, having a life expectancy of five years, transfers property on trust with directions to accumulate the income for thirty years and then to distribute everything to A or her estate. Although it is clear that D intended to defer A's possession or enjoyment until after his (D's) death, the Supreme Court has held that such a transfer is not one "intended to take effect in possession or enjoyment at or after" the transferor's death. [Shukert v. Allen, 273 U.S. 545 (1926)] This case has never been overruled nor modified by statute; hence, neither section 2037 (nor sections 2036 or 2038) will reach this type of transfer.

e. **The reversionary interest requirement:** [§245] In addition to the survivorship requirement, it must appear that the decedent retained a "reversionary interest" in the property.

(1) **What constitutes a "reversionary interest"?** [§246] For purposes of section 2037, a "reversionary interest" ordinarily includes all reversionary interests identified by property law—*i.e.*, reversions, possibilities of reverter, or rights of reentry or powers of termination (*see* Property Summary). However, the term is not limited to reversionary interests in the technical, property law sense. Rather, it encompasses any sort of right or power, vested or contingent, under which there is ***any possibility that the property transferred may return to the transferor, or his estate, or be subject to a power of disposition by the transferor (to himself or any third person)***. [I.R.C. §2037(b)] Thus, powers to revoke or to withdraw, or powers to compel exercise of the trustee's discretion in the transferor's favor (*e.g.*, for the transferor's support) are within the scope of this section. [*See* Valentine v. Commissioner, 54 T.C. 200 (1970)]

(a) **Exception—reversionary interest in income alone:** [§247] It is specifically provided that a mere right to receive or dispose of ***only the income*** from the transferred property does ***not*** constitute a "reversionary interest." [I.R.C. §2037(b); Treas. Reg. §2037-1]

1) **Compare—taxation under section 2036:** [§248] However, such a retained right or power will result in taxation of the property under section 2036. (*See supra,* §§154, 179.)

2) **Rationale:** As already noted, Congress expressly provided that section 2036 would only apply to transfers made after March 3, 1931 (*supra,* §128). Section 2037, however, operates with respect to transfers made before that date. Thus, to assure that transfers wherein a life interest in income or a power to dispose of income was retained would be taxed only if made after March 3, 1931, it was necessary to exclude such transfers from the scope of section 2037.

(b) **Possibility that the property may return—limitations:** [§249] Although "reversionary interest" is defined very broadly, the term is also subject to some well-established limitations:

1) **Technical reversions:** [§250] A grant of alternative contingent remainders is said to create a technical reversion because under the law of future interests some future interest must be vested. However, regardless of such a technical reversion, it is impossible that possession or enjoyment will return to the transferor; therefore, the reversionary interest requirement is not met.

a) **Example:** D transfers property to A for life, remainder to X if X is then living, otherwise to Y. Under property law, X and Y have alternative contingent remainders and there is a technical reversion in D. But, since either X or Y (or Y's estate) necessarily will possess or enjoy the property upon the death of A, D has not retained a reversionary interest, within the meaning of section 2037. (Nor, in this case, is the survivorship requirement met.)

2) **Expectancies:** [§251] In addition, the interest must be more than a mere expectancy. For example, the possibility that the transferor might reacquire the property by inheritance (or by bequest or gift) from the transferee or another is ***not*** a sufficient reversionary interest to render it taxable. [Treas. Reg. §20.2037-1(c)(2)]

3) **Discretionary power in third party:** [§252] The possibility that the property might return to the transferor by reason of a third party's (*e.g.,* the trustee's) authority to distribute all or any portion of the transferred property to the transferor is not taxable as long as the third party's power is ***purely discretionary***. [Estate of Uhl v. Commissioner, *supra,* §217]

a) **Compare—nondiscretionary power:** [§253] But where the transferor may compel the exercise of a third party's discretion in his favor—*e.g.,* where the exercise of the third party's discretion is governed by an enforceable, ascertainable standard—the requisite reversionary interest is present. [Valentine v. Commissioner, *supra*]

(c) **Subject to power of disposition:** [§254] If a power of disposition is retained, the property will be taxed under section 2037. And, it is not necessary that the retained power be a beneficial one (*i.e.*, one that would allow the transferor himself to possess or enjoy the property).

1) **Examples:** Thus, if a settlor of a trust retained a power to designate beneficiaries, to add to or substitute beneficiaries, to shift enjoyment of the property among beneficiaries, or to require that corpus be paid to beneficiaries designated in the settlor's will, the property is taxable in the settlor's estate.

2) **Fiduciary capacity does not affect taxability:** [§255] Moreover, this result under section 2037 is not affected by the fact that the transferor reserved the taxable power in a fiduciary capacity—*i.e.*, designated himself as trustee. But, if the power is one to designate possession or enjoyment of third parties, it must be ***discretionary***. [Estate of Klauber v. Commissioner, 34 T.C. 968 (1960); *and see supra*, §192]

3) **Joint powers:** [§256] Unlike sections 2036 and 2038, section 2037 does not specifically provide that a power of disposition is taxable if it is exercisable "either alone or in conjunction with any person." Thus, it would appear that joint powers are outside the scope of section 2037, particularly if the person whose consent to exercise is required is an adverse party. [*See* Reinecke v. Northern Trust Co., *infra*, §§281-288]

a) **And note:** Quite apart from the language of the statute, a joint power probably would not result in taxation because, in such a case, the value of the reversionary interest could not be determined actuarially—*i.e.*, it is unlikely that actuarial science can determine the probability of the exercise of a discretionary power by a third party. Since the value of the "reversionary interest" would not be ascertainable, it would not meet the requirement that its value be more than five percent of the value of the property. [*See* Estate of Klauber v. Commissioner, *supra; and see infra*, §§261 *et seq.*]

(2) **Express terms vs. operation of law:** [§257] For post-October 7, 1949 transfers, it is immaterial whether the "reversionary interest" arises by the express terms of the instrument or by operation of law. However, for transfers made before October 8, 1949, the reversionary interest must be expressly created by the instrument of transfer.

(a) **Purpose:** The limitation regarding pre-October 8, 1949 transfers is intended to overrule, to this extent, *Spiegel's Estate* (*supra*, §228).

(b) **Express terms of the instrument:** [§258] A reversionary interest arises by the express terms of the instrument not only where it is specifically identified but also, according to the Regulations, where the instrument "contains an express disposition which affirmatively creates a reversionary interest." [Treas. Reg. §20.2037-1(f)(2)]

1) **Example:** D transferred property on trust for A for life, remainder to such of A's children who survive D, remainder in default of such surviving children to D's next of kin. If, under local property law, the limitation to D's next of kin creates a reversion in D, a reversionary interest is deemed reserved under the express terms of the instrument.

2) **Example:** Suppose D conveyed property to A for life, remainder to A's heirs at law "as determined by the present laws of this state," and under the applicable inheritance statute then in force, D was A's only heir at law. If the limitation is construed to be to the heirs at law at the ***time the life tenant dies***, any reversionary interest arises by ***operation of law***, not by the express terms of the instrument; but if the limitation is interpreted as applying to the life tenant's heirs at law at the ***time of the transfer***, and the ***transferor*** is the heir at that time, the reversionary interest would be by the ***express terms*** of the instrument. [Commissioner v. Marshall's Estate, 16 T.C. 918 (1951), *aff'd*, 203 F.2d 534 (3d Cir. 1953)—by designating present law, D effectively incorporated that law in the instrument of transfer and, thus, "affirmatively created a reversionary interest"]

3) **Collateral documents:** [§259] Although the reversionary interest must be expressly reserved for pre-October 8, 1949 transfers, the reservation need not be in the specific instrument of conveyance. A reservation in a collateral document will support taxation under section 2037 if that collateral document is necessarily ***related to the transfer***.

a) **Example:** Assume D transferred property to A for life, remainder to whomever A should appoint by will, remainder in default of appointment to A's children. Assume further that in connection with the transfer D entered into a contract with A where A agreed, in consideration of the transfer of the property to herself, that she (A) would make the testamentary appointment to D if D were then living, remainder passing to contingent appointees (or to the takers in default) if D were dead at the time of A's death. This collateral, enforceable agreement creates a reversionary interest in D arising by the express terms of the instrument. [Gilbert v. Commissioner, 14 T.C. 349 (1950)]

(c) **Operation of law:** [§260] A reversion arises by operation of law where, for instance, D transfers property under circumstances in which a reversion, possibility of reverter, or right of reentry or power of termination would arise under property law (*e.g.*, "D to A for life, remainder to B, providing B survives D"; D has by operation of law retained a reversionary interest which vests if B predeceases D). (*See* Property Summary.)

1) **Transfers voidable by minors:** Likewise, a reversionary interest arises by operation of law where a minor transfers property but under governing law has a right to rescind the transfer (power to revoke) within a reasonable time after attaining majority (*infra*, §343; *and see* Contracts Summary).

f. **De minimis rule—reversionary interest must exceed five percent of property's value:** [§261] The statute expressly provides that a transfer will be taxable only if the reversionary interest retained by the transferor is valued at ***more than five percent*** of the total value of the property transferred. [I.R.C. §2037(a)(2)]

(1) **Time and method of valuation:** [§262] The value of the reversionary interest is determined on the basis of the decedent's life expectancy immediately prior to death. [Treas. Reg. §20.2037-1(c)(3)] For this purpose, actuarial calculations which take into account standard mortality tables are used. [I.R.C. §2037(b); Treas. Reg. §20.2031-10]

(2) **Mortality tables conclusive?** [§263] It is not clear under the statute whether mortality and actuarial principles are the exclusive means for ascertaining value or whether circumstances peculiar to an individual case may be considered. One case has held that where the particular facts and circumstances demonstrate that the decedent's life expectancy, immediately prior to death, was less than that projected in standard mortality tables (*e.g.*, where decedent was suffering from a terminal illness), value can be computed on the basis of the actual facts and standard mortality tables ignored. [Hall v. United States, 353 F.2d 500 (7th Cir. 1965)]

(a) **Service position:** [§264] However, the Service maintains that the valuation question should turn exclusively upon the use of standard mortality tables. [Rev. Rul. 66-307, 1966-2 C.B. 429; *and see* Estate of Roy v. Commissioner, 54 T.C. 1317 (1970)] This appears to be the better view since adherence to the decision in *Hall* would render taxation under section 2037 virtually impossible—*i.e.*, it would be the unusual case in which the facts and circumstances immediately prior to a decedent's death would not indicate a morbid condition, thereby reducing D's life expectancy to a negligible factor; in effect, the statute would only reach cases of sudden or unexpected death. It certainly does not appear that Congress intended to enact such an illusory taxing provision. [*See* Robinson v. United States, 632 F.2d 822 (9th Cir. 1980)—adopts the Service's position and rejects the interpretation in Hall v. United States]

(3) **Five percent of what?** [§265] In determining whether the five percent limitation is met, the value of the reversionary interest is compared to the value of the entire property that would revert to the decedent. [Treas. Reg. §20.2037-1(c)(4)]

(a) **Alternate valuation ignored:** [§266] The property's value as of the decedent's death governs, even though the executor might elect to value the property, for estate tax purposes, at the alternate valuation date, six months after the decedent's death. [Treas. Reg. §2037-1(c)(3); *and see* I.R.C. §2032, *infra*, §§919-921]

(b) **Immaterial that portion of property not subject to tax:** [§267] Moreover, although only a portion of the property is includible in the decedent's gross estate, it is the value of the ***entire property*** to which the reversion relates which is the term for comparison. For example, suppose D transferred property on trust to pay the income to A for life, remainder to X, but if D was alive at A's death, then the property was to revert to D. If D dies before A and X, the value of D's reversion (immediately before death) is compared to the value of the entire trust corpus, even though there is included in D's gross estate only the value of the remainder (total value less the value of A's life estate), since A's interest is not dependent upon survivorship. [*See* Rev. Rul. 76-178, 1976-1 C.B. 273; Treas. Reg. §20.2037-1(c)(4); *and see infra*, §273]

g. **The negative requirement—power of appointment in another:** [§268] Notwithstanding the fact that the survivorship and reversionary interest requirements are met, section 2037 will not apply to a transfer "if possession or enjoyment of the property could have been obtained by any beneficiary during the decedent's life through the exercise of a ***general power of appointment*** (as defined in section 2041) which in fact was exercisable immediately before the decedent's death." [I.R.C. §2037(b)] (A general power of appointment is one that would allow the holder of the power to appoint the property subject to the power to himself, his estate, his creditors, or the creditors of his estate. [I.R.C. §2041(b)(1); *and see infra*, §457])

(1) **Must be a taxable power:** [§269] The reference to section 2041 means that the power must be one that would result in taxation of the property in the holder's estate under section 2041 (*infra*, §§443 *et seq.*).

(2) **Power to appoint to a beneficiary:** [§270] Additionally, the statute requires that the power be of a type that would allow the holder to appoint the property to some beneficiary of the present transfer.

(3) **By whom must the power be held?** [§271] Apparently, the power need not be held by a present beneficiary of the transfer. (However, the grant of a general power to a person might be viewed as making that person a beneficiary of the property even though he is not a beneficiary in the sense of being an income beneficiary or remainder owner.)

(4) **Effect of special powers of appointment:** [§272] Although the grant of a special power to a third person will not automatically preclude taxation (because not a "taxable power"), arguably the existence of such a power will reduce the value of the reversionary interest below the five percent requirement insofar as it cannot be determined actuarially whether a person will or will not exercise a discretionary power. Thus, the existence of a special power of appointment in another may indirectly remove the transfer from the reach of section 2037.

h. **Amount taxable:** [§273] It is not necessarily the entire value of the property transferred that is subject to tax under section 2037. Rather, only the ***value of the interest that is dependent upon survivorship*** is included in the transferor's gross estate; in other words, those interests that are not contingent on surviving the transferor are not taxed under this section. [Treas. Reg. §20.2037-1(e), examples (3) and (4)]

(1) **Example:** D transfers property on trust with directions to pay the income to A for life, remainder to X if D dies before A, but otherwise the property is to revert to D. Only the value of X's remainder interest is taxable in D's estate, because it is the only interest contingent on surviving D. [*See* Rev. Rul. 76-178, 1976-1 C.B. 273]

(2) **Example:** D transfers property on trust with directions to accumulate the income during D's life and upon D's death to distribute the entire property and accumulated income to X; but if X predeceases D, then the property and accumulated income is to be paid to D's estate. If D predeceases X, the entire property must be included in D's estate because of the wording of this gift: X gets the entire property by surviving D, all income having been accumulated.

i. **Relation of section 2037 to other taxing sections:** [§274] It was previously noted that section 2035 (transfers within three years of death) continues to interact with section 2037 to produce a tax under that latter section (*supra*, §§109, 115). Thus, if a transfer is otherwise taxable under section 2037, the decedent cannot avoid the tax by a transfer of the reversionary interest within three years of his death. ***In addition:***

(1) **Section 2033:** [§275] Although a reserved reversionary interest may not be taxable under section 2037 because, *e.g.*, the requisite condition of survivorship is not present or the value of the reversionary interest is less than five percent of the property, section 2033 could still include in the decedent's gross estate the value of the reversionary interest itself (*supra*, §71).

(2) **Section 2036:** [§276] While retention of a reversionary interest in (or power to dispose of) income alone from transferred property will not produce a tax under section 2037, if the transfer occurred after March 3, 1931, the property in which such an interest or power is retained will be taxable under section 2036 (*supra*, §§247 *et seq.*).

(3) **Section 2038:** [§277] A power to revoke, or power to alter or amend, constitutes a reversionary interest or a power to dispose of the property, respectively, and where such powers are retained, a condition of survivorship necessarily exists. Consequently, with respect to these powers, sections 2037 and 2038 overlap. (*See* further discussion *infra,* §343.)

7. **Section 2038—Revocable Transfers:** [§278] Also taxable in the decedent's gross estate is the value of any property that he has transferred during his lifetime, on trust or otherwise, where ***at the date of death*** the transfer was subject to a ***power to alter, amend, revoke or terminate, exercisable by the decedent*** alone or in conjunction with any other person.

a. **Historical development of the tax:** [§279] Many substantive aspects of section 2038 are best explained and analyzed in terms of its historical development.

(1) **Taxation of revocable transfers under early revenue acts:** [§280] Although Congress intended revocable transfers to be taxed under the "intended to take effect in possession and enjoyment" language of the 1916 Act, concern with possible restrictive interpretations by the Supreme Court prompted enactment of a provision specifically taxing revocable transfers as part of the Revenue Act of 1924. The relevant provisions of the 1924 Act are similar to those presently found in paragraph (2) of section 2038(a).

(a) **What about pre-1924 transfers?** [§281] The tax treatment of transfers made prior to the 1924 Act is well illustrated by the decision in *Reinecke v. Northern Trust Co.*, 278 U.S. 339 (1929), wherein the Supreme Court addressed four principal issues (below). That case involved seven trusts, two of which were created prior to the Revenue Act of 1916 and five of which were created in 1919. The decedent died in 1922.

1) **Shifting of enjoyment at death:** [§282] The decedent reserved no beneficial interest in the 1919 trusts, but it was provided that they should terminate and the remainder take effect five years after his death. Even though the trusts were limited to take effect in possession or enjoyment after the decedent's death, the transfers were held not taxable because decedent retained no interest and nothing "passed" from him at his death. Essentially, the Court held that a mere shifting of enjoyment at or after death is insufficient to attract the tax. (This basic rule persists today.)

2) **Administrative powers:** [§283] The decedent also reserved broad administrative powers over the 1919 trusts, *e.g.*, to invest and reinvest trust funds, vote shares of stock owned by the trust, control leases of trust property, and to appoint successor trustees. But the Court said that administrative powers alone will not attract the tax; what is necessary is a power to shift economic enjoyment, and "the shifting of the economic interest . . . was [here] complete as soon as the trust was made."

3) **Power to revoke:** [§284] With respect to the pre-1916 trusts, the decedent reserved a life income interest in and a power to revoke the trusts. The unqualified power to revoke was held to render the trusts taxable, even though they were created prior to the first estate tax.

a) **Constitutionality:** [§285] The Court found the tax constitutional on the theory that a transfer had in fact taken place ***after*** passage of the applicable taxing statute—*i.e.*, the taxable transfer did not occur until the power to revoke lapsed at the decedent's death, so that the statute was not retroactive in effect.

b) **Contemporary application:** [§286] The decision to tax revocable transfers remains in effect today under the present Code: Where an unlimited power to revoke is reserved with respect to a transfer and the power is in existence at the transferor's death, the property is taxable under section 2038.

4) **Power to alter with consent of adverse party:** [§287] The decedent also reserved a power to alter or amend the trusts created in 1919, but the power could only be exercised with the consent of certain beneficiaries, *i.e.*, persons whose interests could be adversely affected by the exercise of the power. The Court held that since the consent of an adverse party was required, for all practical purposes the transfers were complete and thus not taxable under the 1916 Act. (Note that this holding is affected by the 1924 Act; *see* below.)

(b) **Joint powers:** [§288] Under the rule of *Reinecke v. Northern Trust Co.*, a joint power, which is otherwise taxable, will result in a tax ***if*** the co-holder of the power is not an adverse party; but, for ***pre-1924*** transfers, the tax will not attach to the interest of a ***beneficiary*** whose consent is required for the exercise of an otherwise taxable power. [Treas. Reg. §20.2038-1(d)]

1) **Post-1924 transfers—consent of adverse party immaterial:** [§289] The 1924 Act extended the estate tax to transfers wherein the transferor reserved a power to revoke or amend "alone or in conjunction with any person"; and the Supreme Court thereafter held the statute applicable even where the co-holder of the power was an adverse party. [Helvering v. City Bank Farmers Trust Co., 296 U.S. 85 (1935)—"any person" means just that—***any*** person—even a person whose interest might be adversely affected by exercise of the power]

2) **Rescission by consent of all parties:** [§290] But, where the power to revoke, amend, or terminate is exercisable by the decedent and ***all*** the beneficiaries of the trust, and under local law the settlor and the beneficiaries are allowed to rescind the trust by mutual consent,

the transfer is not taxable. *Rationale:* The reservation of such a power adds nothing to the rights already conferred upon the parties by law and thus does not make an otherwise irrevocable trust "revocable" in the tax sense. [Helvering v. Helmholz, 296 U.S. 93 (1935); Treas. Reg. §20.2038-1(a)(2)]

a) **Comment:** This is a very appropriate and practical rule; otherwise, under the law of most states, there could be no such thing as an irrevocable trust for tax purposes.

(2) **Extension of taxing scope by the 1936 Act:** [§291] The provisions of the 1936 Revenue Act relating to revocable transfers (presently embodied in paragraph (1) of section 2038(a)) amended the tax under the 1924 Act (embodied in paragraph (2) of section 2038(a)) as follows: (i) addition of the parenthetical phrase "in whatever capacity exercisable" relating to the decedent's power; (ii) addition of the parenthetical phrase "without regard to whom or from what source the decedent acquired such power" relating, again, to the decedent's power; and (iii) inclusion of the power to "terminate" in the list of taxable powers.

(a) **Source of the power:** [§292] The amendment referring to the source of decedent's power makes clear that for purposes of section 2038 a retained power is not essential; *i.e.*, as long as the power is exercisable by decedent at the date of death, it is immaterial how decedent acquired the power.

1) **Background:** [§293] This addition was prompted by the Supreme Court decision in *White v. Poor*, 296 U.S. 98 (1935). In that case, D created an irrevocable trust, retaining no power or interest, but granting the trustees the power to alter and terminate the trust. Although D originally served as one of the trustees, she later resigned. However, upon the resignation of another trustee, D was reappointed and served as trustee until her death. The Court held the trust property not taxable under the 1924 Act because the power D possessed at death was not reserved but had been acquired by virtue of the action of others in reappointing her as trustee.

2) **Prospective application only:** [§294] Although the amendment overrules *White v. Poor*, it operates prospectively only and thus is limited to transfers made after June 22, 1936. [I.R.C. §2038(a)]

(b) **Capacity in which exercisable:** [§295] **The 1936 Act also makes certain that the statute applies without regard to the "capacity" in which the power is exercisable by the decedent. Thus, even though decedent possessed the power as trustee and was therefore subject to certain fiduciary restraints, the property is includible in her gross estate.**

1) **Purpose:** This issue had not been specifically addressed by the Supreme Court cases dealing with transfers under the 1924 Act. However, the provision was apparently added as a precautionary measure lest the Court find that the capacity in which the power is exercisable bears upon taxation.

2) **Retroactive effect:** [§296] On the other hand, subsequent cases established that the tax would attach even though the decedent's power was exercisable only in a fiduciary capacity. Thus, this amendment is ***not*** limited to prospective application: it is merely declaratory of prior law and therefore reaches transfers made prior to the 1936 Act.

(c) **Power to terminate:** [§297] In *White v. Poor, supra,* the Court had expressed some concern as to whether a power to terminate was the equivalent of a power to alter or amend. To resolve any doubt, the power to terminate was expressly added in the 1936 Act to the list of taxable powers.

1) **Retroactive effect:** [§298] The Supreme Court held in later cases that a power to terminate a trust or to accelerate the remainder is in substance a power to alter or amend. Hence, this provision is also simply declaratory of prior law.

b. **Analytical approach:** [§299] Analysis of the scope of section 2038 focuses on the following issues:

(1) ***Whether the decedent "possesses" the taxable power*** at death or, stated another way, whether the power is ***exercisable by the decedent*** at the date of death.

(2) ***The nature of the taxable powers.***

(3) ***Certain collateral questions*** including:

(a) ***The requirement of a transfer*** by the decedent:

(b) ***The amount taxable;***

(c) ***The effect of a release*** of a taxable power within three years of death: and

(d) ***The relationship of section 2038 to other taxing sections***, in particular section 2036(a)(2).

c. **Requirement of a transfer:** [§300] As in the case of sections 2035 through 2037, a threshold requirement for taxation under section 2038 is that the property must have been transferred by the decedent during her lifetime. The principles governing this issue are identical to those under sections 2036 and 2037 (*see supra,* §§130 *et seq.*)

d. **The power must be exercisable at death:** [§301] The tax is imposed upon transfers "where the enjoyment [of the transferred property] . . . is subject, at the date of the transferor's death, to any change through the exercise of a power by the decedent. . . ." [I.R.C. §2038(a)] Thus, the power must either be "possessed" or "exercisable" by the decedent ***at the time of death***.

(1) **Contingent powers:** [§302] A power that is subject to some contingency before it can be exercised is not a taxable power if: (i) the contingency is not within control of the decedent and (ii) the contingency has not occurred at the time of the decedent's death. [Treas. Reg. §20.2038-1(b); *and see* Jennings v. Smith, 161 F.2d 74 (2d Cir. 1947)]

(a) **Example:** D transferred property on trust with directions to pay the income to A for life, then to B for life, remainder to X. D reserved the right to designate additional income beneficiaries or remaindermen if she (D) survived A. If D predeceases A, no part of the property is taxable under section 2038 since A's death is not within the control of D and the condition did not occur by the time of D's death.

(b) **Compare—section 2036(a)(2): [§303] Such a contingent power will, however, attract the estate tax under section 2036(a)(2) (*see supra*, §182).**

(c) **Exception—ministerial conditions:** [§304] On the other hand, where the exercise of the power is subject only to a ministerial condition—such as the giving of notice or the expiration of a certain period of time before the amendment to the transfer will become effective—taxation is not precluded. However, for purposes of computing the amount includible in the gross estate, the value of the property subject to the power is discounted for the period required to elapse between the date of the decedent's death and the date when the alteration, amendment, revocation, or termination could take effect. [Treas. Reg. §20.2038-1(b)]

(d) **Distinguish—inability or disability preventing exercise:** [§305] A "factual" or legal disability to exercise the power will not affect taxation as long as the power is "possessed" by decedent and is technically "exercisable" by her. Thus, although the decedent may be unable to exercise the power because, *e.g.*, she is not in a position from which she could give the required notice for amendment at the time of death (factual disability), the property will still be included in her gross estate. Similarly, the property will be taxed even though the decedent is incompetent to exercise the power at her death (legal disability). [*See* Round v. Commissioner, 332 F.2d 590 (1st Cir. 1964); Hurd v. Commissioner, 160 F.2d 610 (1st Cir. 1947); Inman v. Commissioner, 18 T.C. 522 (1952), *rev'd on another issue*]

(2) **By whom power exercisable?** [§306] Section 2038 applies only where a taxable power is exercisable by the ***decedent*** or by the ***decedent and another***.

(a) **Joint powers:** [§307] The statute expressly provides that a transfer will be taxed whether the taxable power is exercisable by the decedent ***alone or in conjunction with any other person***. [I.R.C. §2038(a)] It is immaterial that the co-holder may have an adverse interest (*e.g.*, co-holder is a beneficiary; *see supra*, §289). However, recall that the tax will not attach simply because all parties in interest can consent to revocation (*supra*, §290).

(b) **Power exercisable solely by another:** [§308] Unless the ***decedent*** has the right to exercise the power, a transfer subject to such power is not taxable in her estate. This is true even where the power is vested in one who lacks a substantial adverse interest to the decedent, such as a trustee or even a subordinate party (*e.g.*, transferor's spouse). [Commissioner v. Irving Trust Co., 147 F.2d 946 (2d Cir. 1945)]

(3) **Indirect access to the power sufficient:** [§309] But, the decedent need not technically possess the power. As long as the decedent has ***access*** to the power or can ***compel its exercise***, the statute will apply.

(a) **Power to replace trustee:** [§310] Thus, if a trustee is granted a power that in the hands of the decedent would be a taxable power, and the decedent has the right to remove the trustee and appoint a successor trustee, the decedent is deemed to have "access" to the power and therefore to "possess" the power. [Treas. Reg. §20.2038-1(a)(3), *and see supra*, §207]

(b) **Power to compel exercise:** [§311] And, decedent is treated as possessing the power where, although it is technically reposed in a trustee, she can compel exercise of the trustee's discretion (*see supra*, §174).

(4) **Source of the power:** [§312] As noted above, transfers made after June 22, 1936 are subject to the tax whether or not the decedent retained the power; it is sufficient that the power is exercisble by the decedent at her death. (*See supra*, §292.)

(5) **Power of corporate shareholder to modify survivor's benefit held not taxable:** [§313] In *Estate of Tully v. United States,* two fifty percent shareholders caused their corporation to adopt a plan under which the corporation would be required to pay a lump-sum benefit to the surviving spouse of a deceased shareholder. The Court of Claims held that the amount paid to Mr. Tully's widow was not taxable in his estate under section 2038 because any modification of the plan (amendment or alteration) during Mr. Tully's life would require the consent of both Mr. Tully and the other fifty percent shareholder. This result seems incorrect in light of the established rule relating to joint powers (*see supra*, §307). [Estate of Tully v. United States, 528 F.2d 1401 (Ct. Cl. 1976); *but compare* Estate of Levin v. Commissioner, 90 T.C. 723 (1988), *aff'd*, 891 F.2d 281 (3d Cir. 1989)—death benefit paid by a corporation to an eighty percent shareholder's survivor ***was*** included in shareholder-decedent's estate]

e. **Nature of the taxable power:** [§314] Section 2038 enumerates the principal types of powers that render a transfer taxable under this section: powers "to ***alter, amend, revoke, or terminate***." Any of these powers render the transfer taxable; it is immaterial whether the powers are exercisable by will or inter vivos or both; and it is also immaterial whether the power was ever exercised. While such powers occur most frequently with respect to transfers on trust, a nontrust transfer subject to such a power is equally taxable. [Treas. Reg. §20.2038-1(a)]

(1) **General considerations**

(a) **Administrative vs. dispositive or distributive powers:** [§315] To be taxable, the power must be one that can ***affect enjoyment***, *i.e.*, a power to affect the disposition or distribution of the property. A purely administrative power—*e.g.*, power to add to the trust estate or to direct trust investments—which does not affect enjoyment of any beneficial interest will not expose the transfer to the tax. [Central Trust Co. v. United States, 167 F.2d 133 (6th Cir. 1948), *and review, supra*, §§190-198]

(b) **Beneficial power not necessary:** [§316] Clearly, a power that would allow the decedent to beneficially enjoy the property or its income is taxable—*e.g.*, a power to reacquire the property through exercise of a power to revoke, or a power to add or substitute herself as income beneficiary through exercise of a power to amend. However, a beneficial power is not essential for taxation; the decedent's ability to affect the enjoyment of others through exercise of the power is sufficient. [Walter v. United States, 295 F.2d 720 (6th Cir. 1961), *and see supra*, §183]

(c) **Discretionary vs. nondiscretionary powers:** [§317] Only ***discretionary*** powers will render the transfer taxable. Where distributions to others are mandated by the terms of the instrument or are controlled by fixed, external standards, the "power" is not discretionary and is not taxable. [Jennings v. Smith, 161 F.2d 74 (2d Cir. 1947)]

1) **Example—power subject to ascertainable standard:** D declares herself trustee of certain property. Under the terms of the trust, the trustee must pay income to A during A's life and distribute the corpus to X after A's death provided, however, that the trustee may invade the corpus and make distributions to A "to the extent necessary to maintain A in his accustomed manner of living." Since there is a fixed external standard (A's accustomed manner of living), the exercise of the power is nondiscretionary and the transfer is not includible in D's estate. (*See also supra*, §§192-194.)

2) **Compare—vague standards:** [§318] In contrast, a power to invade, "when the circumstances so require," leaves the trustee with too much discretion, and if D had such discretion, the transfer would be taxable. [Hurd v. Commissioner, 160 F.2d 610 (1st Cir. 1947)]

3) **Compare—beneficial power:** [§319] But a fixed, external standard will not prevent taxation where the power is beneficial. Thus, if a trustee is granted power to invade corpus "to the extent necessary to maintain the ***transferor*** in her accustomed manner of living," the transfer is taxable since the transferor can compel exercise of the power in her favor.

(2) **Powers to revoke:** [§320] Any power under which the decedent had the right to repossess herself of the property transferred, directly or indirectly, is a taxable "power to revoke." The form of the power and the manner in which it arises is irrelevant as long as the decedent had beneficial access to the property.

(a) **Right of rescission:** [§321] For example, certain transfers by minors, which are absolute in form, can be rescinded by the minor. This right of recission is a "power to revoke" for purposes of section 2038.

(b) **Right to set aside transfer of community property:** [§322] Likewise, a spouse's power under community property laws to set aside a gift or other improper transfer of his or her share of community property by the other spouse is treated as a power to revoke.

(c) **Power to deal with trust property:** [§323] And, the power to borrow the entire trust corpus without adequate security, or to "repurchase" the corpus for a purely nominal consideration is a taxable power to revoke. [Commonwealth Trust Co. v. Driscoll, 50 F. Supp. 949 (W.D. Pa. 1943), *aff'd*, 137 F.2d 653 (3d Cir. 1943), *cert. denied*, 321 U.S. 764 (1944)]

(3) **Power to terminate:** [§324] A power to end a trust and cause a distribution of trust property before expiration of the term specified in the trust agreement is a taxable power to "terminate."

(a) **Pre-1936 transfers:** [§325] Recall that the addition of the power to terminate under the 1936 Act was not a substantive change, but simply a clarification of preexisting law so that such transfers are taxable even if made before June 22, 1936.

1) **Example—power affecting beneficial interests:** [§326] D established separate trusts for his minor children, each of which was to terminate after fifteen years with distribution of the trust property to the beneficiaries at that time. The trust also provided for gifts over should a child die before the end of the trust term without leaving living descendents. In addition, D reserved a power to terminate the trust and cause immediate distribution to the beneficiary prior to the end of the term. The Supreme Court rejected the argument that the trusts were not taxable because created prior to the 1936 Act. D's power was held to be the equivalent of a power to alter or amend the trusts under the 1924 Act, insofar as exercise of the power would

assure the beneficiary of enjoyment of the property, which otherwise might be shifted to another under the provision for a gift over in the event the child did not survive the fifteen-year term. [Commissioner v. Estate of Holmes, 326 U.S. 480 (1946)]

(b) **Power to affect time and manner of enjoyment:** [§327] Although the power to terminate a trust will often cause a shifting of beneficial enjoyment, this is not required. A power simply to accelerate the time of enjoyment of the trust property is also a taxable power of termination.

1) **Example—termination in favor of existing beneficiaries:** [§328] D established separate trusts for his children under which the corpus and any accumulated income were to be distributed to the beneficiary or the beneficiary's estate after twenty-five years. D reserved a power to direct the termination of the trusts prior to expiration of the stated term. However, no gifts over were provided, so that each beneficiary (or his or her estate) was assured of receiving all of the property and income from his or her separate trust—*i.e.*, exercise of D's power could not shift beneficial enjoyment. The Supreme Court held the trusts taxable in D's estate since the power enabled him to affect the ***time and manner*** of enjoyment of the trust property. [Lober v. United States, 346 U.S. 335 (1953)]

(4) **Power to alter or amend:** [§329] There is no apparent difference between a power to "alter" and a power to "amend" for purposes of section 2038. Both contemplate any discretionary power, the exercise of which will affect the beneficial enjoyment of the property transferred. This includes the power to change the share of income or corpus that a beneficiary will receive, to substitute or add new beneficiaries, to invade corpus for the benefit of an income beneficiary or another, or to invade corpus for the benefit of the remainderman. [Cook v. Commissioner, 66 F.2d 995 (3d Cir. 1933), *cert. denied*, 291 U.S. 660 (1934); Commissioner v. Chase National Bank, 82 F.2d 157 (2d Cir. 1936), *cert. denied,* 299 U.S. 552 (1936)]

(a) **Power to accumulate income:** [§330] The power to direct the accumulation or distribution of income is a taxable power to alter or amend. And this is true even though accumulated income would not be added to corpus (where it would increase the beneficial interest of the owner of the remainder) but must ultimately be distributed to the income beneficiary—since this power would affect the ***time and manner*** of the income beneficiary's enjoyment. [United States v. O'Malley, 383 U.S. 627 (1966)]

(b) **Transfers under Uniform Transfers to Minors Act:** [§331] Property transferred to a minor child under the Uniform Transfers to Minors Act will be included in the donor-parent's estate where the parent serves as custodian since, as custodian, the parent has discretionary power to apply custodial property or income derived therefrom for the benefit of the minor. [Prudowsky v. Commissioner,

55 T.C. 890 (1971)] (Such gifts are also taxable under section 2036: Since application of the fund could inure to the parent's benefit by reducing the obligation to support the minor child, the parent is deemed to retain an interest in the property and its income. *See supra*, §169.)

f. **Amount taxable:** [§332] The amount includible in the decedent's gross estate under section 2038 is the value of the ***interest*** that is subject to the taxable power. Thus, if the decedent retained a taxable power affecting the entire property transferred, its entire value is includible. But, if the exercise of a power would affect only a particular beneficiary's interest, only the value of that interest is taxable in the transferor's estate. [Commissioner v. Bridgeport City Trust Co., 124 F.2d 48 (2d Cir. 1941)]

(1) **Example—distribution of income:** [§333] D transferred property on trust with directions to pay the income to D's three children until the youngest child attained the age of thirty, at which time the trust was to terminate and the corpus was to be distributed to the children (or their estates) equally. D reserved the right to direct how much of the income was to be paid to each child. Since the income interest alone is affected by D's power, section 2038 only taxes the value of the income interest as of the date of D's death.

(a) **Compare—taxation under section 2036:** [§334] However, under section 2036(a)(2), the entire trust property will be included in D's gross estate because of the retained power to designate who shall possess or enjoy the income from the (entire) property (*supra*, §216).

(2) **Distribution of corpus:** [§335] If a decedent has the power to direct invasion of corpus and distribution to the ***owner of the remainder*** (or another), the entire value of the trust property is includible since the power affects not only the interest of the owner of the remainder but also that of the income beneficiary, insofar as it decreases the amount of income that the reduced corpus will produce. If, however, the power is limited to invasion and distribution for the benefit of the ***income beneficiary***, apparently only the value of the remainder interest is taxable since, in any event, the income beneficiary will receive all of the income from the property. [*See* Walter v. United States, 341 F.2d 182 (6th Cir. 1965)]

g. **Relationship between section 2038 and other taxing sections**

(1) **Section 2036(a)(2):** [§336] There is considerable substantive overlap between sections 2038 and 2036(a)(2) in that the comprehension of powers to "designate who shall possess or enjoy the property or the income therefrom" is essentially the same as that of powers to "alter, amend, revoke, or terminate." Indeed, most transfers taxable under section 2038 will be taxable under section 2036. However, at the same time, there are certain differences in the taxing scope of these sections:

(a) **Time of the transfer:** [§337] Section 2036 will not reach transfers made prior to March 3, 1931. However, section 2038 reaches "revocable" transfers whenever made.

(b) **Source of the power:** [§338] Taxation under section 2036 is limited to ***retained*** powers. However, as to transfers made after June 22, 1936, section 2038 will operate without regard to the source of the decedent's power.

(c) **Enjoyment after decedent's death:** [§339] Section 2036 is limited to powers that will affect enjoyment of the income or property during the decedent's lifetime. However, section 2038 applies even though the power will affect enjoyment of interests after the decedent's death.

(d) **Contingent powers:** [§340] Section 2038 will not operate where the decedent's power was subject to a contingency beyond her control and which has not occurred at the time of her death. However, section 2036 will apply in such a case.

(e) **Amount includible:** [§341] Section 2038 only taxes the specific interest that is subject to the taxable power. Section 2036, on the other hand, reaches the entire property to which the retained interest or power relates.

(2) **Section 2035—relinquishment of power within three years of death:** [§342] Section 2038 specifically provides for taxation where a power to alter, amend, revoke, or terminate "is relinquished during the three-year period ending on the decedent's death." And this interaction is also specified in section 2035(d), as amended by the 1981 Act. (*See supra*, §§109, 115.)

(3) **Section 2037:** [§343] Section 2038 also overlaps with the tax on transfers "taking effect at death" under section 2037. For example, a taxable power to revoke, or to alter or amend, would effectively create a condition of survivorship with respect to those beneficiaries whose interests may be affected by the power. Likewise, a power to terminate could create a condition of survivorship where the power would shift enjoyment if exercised. If the decedent also retained a reversionary interest in the property worth more than five percent of its value, section 2037, as well as section 2038 (and section 2036), will apply. (However, where the sections do overlap, inclusion is usually urged under the more straightforward section 2038—or section 2036.)

8. **Section 2039—Annuities:** [§344] There is included in the estate of the decedent the value of amounts receivable by a beneficiary under a contract or agreement where the decedent, during life, was receiving or had a right to receive payments under the contract or agreement.

a. **Background:** [§345] The difficulty encountered in taxing certain employee-survivor benefits under section 2033 has previously been noted (*supra*, §§60-64). Similarly, the taxation of annuity-type survivor benefits under section 2033 and other specific taxing sections was often troublesome. As a result of the difficulty, section 2039 was added to the 1954 Code, providing definitive rules for the taxing of survivor benefits under annuity or annuity-like contacts.

(1) **Taxation of annuities apart from section 2039:** [§346] A review of the application of other taxing provisions to certain types of annuity contracts may be helpful toward an understanding of the basic rationale of section 2039 and its relation to other taxing sections.

(a) **Straight life annuity:** [§347] If the decedent received an annuity during life that terminated on her death, nothing is includible in her estate on account of the annuity—under section 2039 or any other provision of the estate tax—because decedent's interest is extinguished by her death (*see supra*, §68).

(b) **Straight life annuity—benefits payable to another:** [§348] Similarly, if the decedent purchased an annuity for ***another***, ordinarily nothing is included in decedent's estate since she has no interest in the contract. However, if the decedent retained some power with respect to the contract—*e.g.*, the power to change the beneficiary or to cash in the contract—the value of the contract would be taxable under section 2038.

(c) **Refund annuity—payable to decedent's estate:** [§349] If the decedent purchases a refund annuity (*supra*, §69), the amount of any refund payable to her estate is taxable under section 2033 (as property owned at death); but it is not taxable under section 2039 because the refund is not payable to a surviving beneficiary. For example, D purchases a contract calling for a $500 monthly payment to herself for life, but if she dies before receiving back as much as she paid for the annuity, the balance is to be refunded to her estate. If D outlives the refund period so that no refund is owing, nothing is included in her estate; but if a refund is due, that amount is taxable under section 2033 (*supra*, §69).

(d) **Refund annuity—payable to another:** [§350] If the refund is payable to another and the decedent has a right to change the beneficiary designation, the amount of the refund is taxable under section 2038 as a revocable transfer. [Old Colony Trust Co. v. Commissioner, 102 F.2d 380 (1st Cir. 1939)] And, even if the beneficiary cannot be changed, the annuity payment might be taxable under section 2036, on the theory that the decedent essentially reserved a life estate (the annuity) in the property transferred (the premiums which will be refunded). Even so, however, such an annuity is now clearly taxable under section 2039.

(e) **Joint and survivor or self and survivor annuity:** [§351] Joint and survivor annuities are those in which payments are made to the purchaser and another jointly during their lives, with benefits continuing in favor of the survivor during life. Under a self and survivor annuity plan, the primary annuitant receives payments during life, and after death the payments continue to a designated beneficiary. For estate purposes, both types of plans present the same problems.

1) **Possible treatment:** Unless the decedent had a right to change the survivor beneficiary designation [I.R.C. §2038], there are technical difficulties in taxing these survivor's benefits apart from section 2039. Upon her death, the decedent's interest in the contract is extinguished so that she technically has no interest in the survivor's benefits which could be taxed under section 2033. Moreover, since the insurance company's obligation to pay annuity benefits to the survivor may be viewed as a contractual obligation separate from its obligation to make payments to the primary annuitant(s), it is arguable that the decedent has retained no interest in the ***property transferred*** for purposes of section 2036, although some cases suggested that taxation under section 2036 was possible in this case. [*See, e.g.*, Forster v. Sauber, 249 F.2d 379 (7th Cir. 1957)]

2) **Note:** However, survivor's benefits under these types of annuities are now clearly taxable under section 2039.

(2) **Scope of section 2039:** [§352] Although section 2039 is entitled "Annuities," the label is somewhat misleading: As will be seen below, the statute also extends to contractual arrangements that are beyond the typical commercial annuity contract, and, as noted above, certain types of annuity contracts are not taxed under section 2039 but may be taxable under other provisions of the estate tax.

b. **Introductory analysis:** [§353] As originally enacted in the 1954 Code, section 2039 contained the basic substantive provisions exposing survivor's benefits under annuities to the estate tax [I.R.C. §2039(a),(b)], and special rules providing an estate tax exemption for survivor's benefits if the benefits were received under employment-related plans that were "qualified" for special tax treatment under section 401 and following. (*See* Income Tax I Summary.) These special rules relating to qualified plans were modified in 1976 and again in 1981, and were repealed in 1984. Hence, only the basic substantive rules are of concern for decedents dying after 1984.

c. **Nature of the survivor's interest:** [§354] Section 2039(a) taxes "the value of an ***annuity or other payment*** receivable by any beneficiary ***by reason of surviving the decedent*** under any form of ***contract or agreement*** entered into after March 3, 1931 (other than as insurance under policies on the life of the decedent). . . ."

(1) **Annuity or other payment:** [§355] The survivor's benefit need not be in the form of an annuity; any payment or payments, other than as proceeds of life insurance, that become payable to a survivor are taxable in the decedent's estate (if the other requirements are met).

(a) **Exception for life insurance proceeds:** [§356] Where life insurance is part of an annuity-type plan, payments to the survivor that are in the nature of life insurance proceeds are not taxable under section 2039. (However, if the decedent retained "incidents of ownership" in the policy, life insurance payable under an annuity may be taxed in the decedent's estate under section 2042; *see infra,* §§490 *et seq.*)

(b) **Determination of whether benefit is life insurance:** [§357] For federal tax purposes, whether payments are "life insurance proceeds" turns on whether a "***life insurance risk***" exists at the date of the decedent's death. A life insurance risk is present if the reserve value under the contract (premiums paid plus earnings allocated to the cash value of the contract) is less than the proceeds that become payable to the beneficiary upon the death of the primary annuitant (insured). [Treas. Reg. 20.2039-1(d); *and see infra,* §§501 *et seq.*]

1) **Example:** D purchased an annuity contract that provided that when D reached age 65, the insurance company would pay her $300 per month for life and, upon D's death a similar payment would be made to D's designated beneficiary for the beneficiary's life. The contract also provided that should D die before reaching age 65, a lump sum in the amount of $100,000 would be paid to D's designated beneficiary. If D dies before age 65 and if the reserve value of the annuity contract does not equal the $100,000 lump sum benefit (which it normally would not until D is 65), the lump sum benefit is treated as life insurance and is not taxable under section 2039.

2) **All or nothing rule:** [§358] Whether a benefit is life insurance is determined on an all-or-nothing basis. Thus, in the example above, if D died one month before attaining age 65, when the reserve value of the annuity contract was $99,975, the proceeds would be treated as life insurance; it is immaterial that the difference between the reserve value and the amount of the proceeds payable is very small.

(2) **Receivable by reason of surviving the decedent:** [§359] The annuity payable to the beneficiary after the decedent's death must be "by reason of surviving the decedent." If benefits are payable to a beneficiary at a scheduled time or upon the happening of an event, irrespective of whether the decedent is then living or dead, they are not taxable under section 2039, even though the decedent may be dead at the time scheduled for payment. [Treas. Reg. §20.2039-1(b)]

(a) **Need not be solely dependent upon survivorship:** [§360] Although this survivorship requirement is reminiscent of that under section 2037 (*supra,* §239), unlike section 2037, section 2039 does not require that the beneficiary's interest be conditioned ***solely*** on surviving the decedent. If, for example, benefits became payable to the beneficiary upon the death of the decedent or upon the beneficiary attaining age 70, and the decedent dies before the beneficiary reaches age 70, the survivor's benefits are taxable under section 2039. (However, if the primary annuitant is alive when the beneficiary attains age 70, payments thereafter made to the beneficiary are, presumably, not subject to tax under section 2039 because not receivable "by reason of surviving the decedent.")

(b) **Payment need not correspond to decedent's interest:** [§361] Also, there is no requirement that the annuity or other payment to the beneficiary correspond in form or amount to that payable to the decedent under the contract.

(3) **Receivable under a contract or agreement:** [§362] The benefits must be receivable "under any form of contract or agreement entered into after March 3, 1931. . . ."

(a) **Nature of contract:** [§363] The reference to "***any form*** of contract or agreement" makes it clear that taxation under section 2039 is not limited to a formal, commercial annuity. According to the Regulations, section 2039 reaches "any arrangement, understanding, or plan, or any combination of arrangements, understandings or plans arising by reason of the decedent's employment." [Treas. Reg. §20.2039-1(b)(1)]

1) **Private annuities included:** Although the Regulations specifically refer to employment related plans, informal arrangements arising independently of the decedent's employment (*e.g.*, "private annuities") apparently are subject to tax under section 2039.

(b) **The 1931 cut-off date:** [§364] The March 3, 1931 cut-off date is reminiscent of the same cut-off date under section 2036. Presumably, Congress had a reserved life estate analogy in mind in enacting section 2039 and thus felt it appropriate to limit this latter section to the same extent that it limited the taxation of transfers with reserved life estates (*see supra*, §§121 *et seq.*)

1) **What about premium payments after 1931?** [§365] Even though a trust with retained life estate is created before March 3, 1931, section 2036 reaches any ***additions*** to the trust made by the decedent after the 1931 cut-off date (*see supra*, §145). However, it is unclear whether an analogy can be drawn to section 2039; *i.e.*, since section 2039 refers to contracts or agreements ***entered into*** after March 3, 1931, it may be that the statute does not tax premium payments made with respect to annuities entered into prior to the 1931 cut-off date. Neither the Code nor the Regulations indicate when a contract or agreement is "entered into" for purposes of this section.

(c) **Separate contracts do not preclude taxation:** [§366] The rights of the decedent and the survivor need not arise under the same contract or agreement. However, if the benefits are payable under separate contracts, it must appear that they are part of a single, integrated arrangement. [Treas. Reg. §20.2039-1; *and see* below]

d. **Nature of decedent's interest:** [§367] The survivor's benefit is taxable under section 2039(a) "if, under such contract or agreement, an annuity or other payment was payable to the decedent or the decedent possessed the right to receive such annuity or payment either alone or in conjunction with another for his life or for any period not ascertainable without reference to his death or for any period which does not in fact end before his death."

(1) **Decedent's interest in the contract:** [§368] The decedent's interest must be in the contract or agreement under which the survivor's benefits are payable. But, as noted above, section 2039 will tax survivor's benefits even though payable under a contract that is technically separate from the contract under which the decedent was receiving or was entitled to receive payments, ***if*** the separate contracts form an ***integrated plan***.

(a) **Employment related plans:** [§369] Separate arrangements under employment related plans need not be entered into simultaneously or with the intention that they be treated as a single contract. It is sufficient that the plans constitute a single "package" of employment benefits.

1) **Example:** Suppose an employer establishes a pension plan for its employees that will pay a certain amount to retired employees for their lives. Subsequently, the employer establishes a plan that will pay a lump sum to an employee's designated survivor if the employee should die before retirement. Still later, the employer sets up another plan providing for certain payments to a designated survivor if the employee dies after retirement. Under the Regulations, these three plans would be considered part of a single package of employment related benefits and thus would be "integrated." [Treas. Reg. §20.2039-1(b)(2), Example (6); *see also* Estate of Bahen v. United States, 305 F.2d 827 (Ct. Cl. 1962)]

2) **Theory of integration questioned:** [§370] Although it distinguished *Bahen* (*supra*) on the facts, the Second Circuit, in *Schelberg v. Commissioner*, 612 F.2d 25 (2d Cir. 1979), has questioned whether the *Bahen* rule and its extension in later cases is supported by the statutory language and the Committee Reports that accompanied the 1954 Code. *Schelberg* has not been followed and was rejected by a district court considering benefits received by another taxpayer under the same (IBM) employment-related plans. [Looney v. United States, 569 F. Supp. 1569 (M.D. Ga. 1983)]

(b) **Integration of private contracts:** [§371] Although there is little authority on point, it would appear that the concept of integration may be applicable to private contracts. For example, suppose that a decedent purchased a straight-life annuity for himself and then purchased a separate deferred annuity for his spouse with payments under this deferred annuity to begin upon decedent's death. These contracts might be "integrated" and the survivor's benefits under the deferred annuity contract included in the decedent's estate.

(c) **Insurance-annuity "packages":** [§372] Annuity-life insurance arrangements have also been treated as one integrated plan, thus producing a tax under section 2039. For example, where D purchased an annuity-insurance package and assigned the life insurance to another, the Fifth Circuit found the life insurance and annuity contracts to be a single integrated plan, so that the "life insurance" proceeds were includible in D's estate under section 2039. [Montgomery v. Commissioner, 458 F.2d 616 (5th Cir. 1972), *cert. denied,* 409 U.S. 849 (1972)]

1) **Compare—taxation under section 2036:** [§373] However, prior to the *Montgomery* case, the government sought to tax a similar arrangement under section 2036. Its argument rested on the premise that the two contracts were integrated, so that D had in substance transferred a "life insurance" contract to the assignee with a reserved life interest (the annuity). The Supreme Court disagreed: It held that the life insurance and annuity contracts were separate investments; therefore the insurance proceeds were not taxable under section 2036 because D retained no interest in that contract. [Fidelity-Philadelphia Trust Co. v. Smith, 356 U.S. 274 (1958); *and see supra,* §153]

(2) **Annuity or other payment:** [§374] Just as in the case of the survivor's benefit, the interest of the decedent need not be in the form of an annuity; any form of payment will satisfy the requirements of section 2039.

(a) **Exception—salary:** [§375] However, the Tax Court has held that the term "other payment" does not include compensation that the decedent was receiving or was entitled to receive at the time of his death. Rather, the term is "qualitatively limited to post-employment benefits." [Estate of Fusz v. Commissioner, 46 T.C. 214 (1966), *acq.* 1967-2 C.B. 2]

(b) **Compare—retirement benefits disguised as salary:** [§376] However, section 2039 cannot be avoided simply by designating post-employment benefits as continuing compensation. Thus, for example, payments for "consultation services" to be made to a person following withdrawal from full time employment will be scrutinized to determine whether they are in fact compensation for services or merely a disguised form of post-retirement benefit. [*See, e.g.,* Silberman v. United States, 333 F. Supp. 1120 (W.D. Pa. 1971); Rev. Rul. 71-507, 1971-2 C.B. 331; *but cf.* Kramer v. United States, 406 F.2d 1363 (Ct. Cl. 1969)]

(3) **Payable to decedent; right to receive:** [§377] The statutory requirement is met if the decedent was actually receiving payments under the contract or agreement or if he had a right to receive payments in the future. For instance, if the decedent was entitled to receive a pension upon retirement, with a death benefit payable to a designated survivor, and he died before retirement, the survivor's benefit is includible in decedent's estate under section 2039.

(a) **Contingent right:** [§378] The "right to receive payment" has been broadly interpreted, so that the statute may be satisfied even where decedent's right to future payment is subject to a remote contingency.

1) **Example:** D's employer established a plan under which D's survivor would receive certain annuity payments. D was not entitled to receive any payments ***unless*** he became totally and permanently disabled prior to retirement. D died before retirement and had never become disabled. The court held that this contingent right to receive payments in the future was sufficient to meet the "right to receive" requirement of section 2039. [Estate of Bahen v. United States, *supra,* §369; *but cf.* Schelberg v. Commissioner, *supra,* §370]

(b) **Payments terminating prior to death—the gap in section 2039:** [§379] On the other hand, if a decedent has received ***everything*** he is entitled to receive under the contract, benefits payable to the decedent's survivor under the contract are not taxable under section 2039. Thus, suppose the decedent is entitled to receive a lump sum upon retirement and a designated survivor is entitled to receive payments upon decedent's death. If the decedent dies after retirement and after having received the lump sum payment, the survivor's benefit is not taxable under section 2039 since, at death, the decedent was neither ***receiving*** payments nor did he have any ***right*** to receive payments in the future. [Treas. Reg. §20.2039-1(b)(2), Example (5)]

(4) **Joint interests produce tax:** [§380] The decedent's right to receive payments need not be exclusive (as evidenced by the statutory language "either alone or in conjunction with another"). Accordingly, the survivor's benefits are fully taxable to decedent even though lifetime payments are made jointly to the decedent and another.

(5) **Time periods:** [§381] The payments (or right to payments) must persist for decedent's "life or for any period not ascertainable without reference to his death or for any period which does not in fact end before his death." The intendment of these alternative time periods is the same as that for the identical time periods under section 2036 (*supra,* §§208 *et seq.*). Indeed, it is clear under section 2039 that the period "which does not in fact end before his death" is to be applied objectively, rather than subjectively. [*See* Estate of Bahen v. United States, *supra*]

e. **Amount includible:** [§382] The estate tax is imposed upon that value of the survivor's benefit that is proportionate to contributions made by the decedent. [I.R.C. §2039(b)]

(1) **Valuation of survivor's benefits:** [§383] Valuation of the taxable benefit is made as of the date of the decedent's death. If the benefit is in the form of a lump sum payment, the amount of the payment would be the amount of survivor's benefit. But if the benefit is in the form of an annuity or other

deferred payments, the amount of the benefit is the present value of the right to receive these payments, determined actuarially.

(2) **Proportionate inclusion:** [§384] It is not necessarily the entire value of the survivor's benefit that is includible; rather, only the amount that is proportionate to decedent's contributions toward the purchase price of the contract is taxed.

(a) **Determining decedent's contributions—attribution rule:** However, under the general rule of section 2039(b), any contributions to the purchase price made by the decedent's employer are treated as contributions made by the decedent.

(b) **Example:** Assume that the value of the survivor's benefit is $100,000, that the decedent contributed $10,000 of the purchase price, the decedent's employer contributed $60,000, and the survivor contributed $10,000. The decedent and his employer contributed 87.5 percent of the purchase price ($70,000 divided by $80,000). Thus, $87,500 is included in the decedent's estate.

9. **Section 2040—Joint Interests:** [§385] Co-tenancies with a ***"right of survivorship"*** are included in the gross estate of the first joint tenant to die. However, the estate tax consequences may differ radically according to the nature of the ownership interests involved.

a. **Background:** [§386] Because of the peculiar incidents of ownership and property rights that attach to tenancies with a right of survivorship, a special provision is necessary for their taxation. Under technical property law, when the first joint tenant dies, nothing "passes" to the survivor; rather, the decedent's undivided interest is extinguished by death and the survivor "survives" to sole ownership of the property (*see supra*, §40). At the same time, however, it is clear that joint tenancies can be and frequently are used as substitutes for testamentary giving.

(1) **The Revenue Act of 1916:** [§387] The first estate tax Act specifically provided for the taxation of tenancies by the entirety and joint tenancies with right of survivorship. These provisions were virtually identical to those presently found in section 2040(a) of the 1954 Code.

(2) **Husband-and-wife joint tenancies:** [§388] The 1976 Tax Reform Act first provided special rules for husband-and-wife joint tenancies. Modified in the Revenue Act of 1978 and substantially revised in the Revenue Act of 1981, these special rules are now embodied in section 2040(b). (*See infra*, §§421-429.)

b. **Introductory analysis:** [§389] Analysis of the scope of section 2040 may be broken down into five principal elements:

(1) ***Determination of the type of co-tenancies*** to which the section is applicable.

(2) ***The general rule of inclusion*** provided for by section 2040(a).

(3) ***The required nature of the survivor's contribution*** which may allow a portion of the value of joint tenancy property to be excluded from the estate of the first joint tenant to die.

(4) ***The relation of section 2040 to other taxing sections.***

(5) ***Special rules for "qualified joint interests" under section 2040(b).***

c. **Applies only to co-tenancies with right of survivorship:** [§390] Section 2040 reaches those forms of joint ownership having, as one of their incidents, a "right of survivorship"—joint tenancies, tenancies by the entirety, joint bank accounts, etc.

(1) **Taxation of tenancies in common, etc.:** [§391] Accordingly, those forms of co-ownership ***without*** survivorship rights—tenancies in common, community property, etc.—are ***not*** taxable under section 2040. However, the interest of the decedent in such property ***is*** taxable under section 2033 (*supra*, §41).

(2) **Form of joint tenancy:** [§392] The specific form of the joint tenancy—*i.e.*, what it might be called under property law or under a specific mode of title registration—is irrelevant. The critical factor is the ***right of survivorship***, and all forms of co-ownership that have a right of survivorship are subject to section 2040. Thus, in addition to common law joint tenancies or tenancies by the entirety, such forms of co-ownership as joint bank accounts, joint registration of securities or personal property, United States Savings Bonds registered in the name of "D, P.O.D. (payable on death) to X," and joint brokerage accounts are within the scope of section 2040. [*See* Rev. Rul. 69-148, 1969-1 C.B. 226]

d. **General rule of inclusion:** [§393] The estate tax is not limited to the value of the decedent's undivided interest. Rather, it extends to the ***full value*** of the joint tenancy property ***except*** "such part thereof as may be shown to have originally belonged to . . . [the survivor] and never to have been received or acquired by the [survivor] from the decedent for less than an adequate and full consideration in money or money's worth. . . ." [I.R.C. §2040(a); *but see infra*, §§426 *et seq.* in regard to "qualified joint interests"]

(1) **Original consideration or contribution—in general:** [§394] Thus, to the extent the property or a portion thereof originally belonged to the survivor, or to the extent the survivor furnished all or a part of the consideration for its acquisition, the property is not includible in the decedent's estate. However, in order to obtain the exclusion, the taxpayer (estate) has the burden of proving what part of the property (or the consideration therefor) was contributed by the survivor (usually referred to as proof of an "original contribution" by the survivor).

(a) **Proportionate exclusion:** Note that the amount excluded from the decedent's estate is ***not*** the amount that the survivor contributed but, rather, an amount ***proportionate*** to the survivor's contribution.

(b) **Examples**

1) D and X acquired property in joint tenancy for $10,000 and D paid the entire price. At D's death, the property is worth $20,000. The full value of the joint tenancy property is includible in D's estate.

2) Same situation as above, but X made an original contribution of $2,000 to the purchase price of $10,000. Since twenty percent of the consideration was furnished by X ($2,000 divided by $10,000), upon D's death, twenty percent of the value of the property, or $4,000, is excluded from D's estate; eighty percent of the property's value ($8,000 divided by $10,000) is included.

(2) **Joint interests created by another:** [§395] Similarly, where the joint interest was acquired by gift, bequest, devise, or inheritance from a ***third party***, only the value of the fractional interest of the deceased joint tenant is included in the decedent's gross estate. [I.R.C. §2040(a)] In effect, each joint tenant is treated as the original owner of his or her fractional interest in the whole. [Treas. Reg. §20.2040-1(a)(1)]

(3) **Compare—improvements made to joint tenancy property:** [§396] However, if the survivor has paid for improvements on the property after its acquisition, only the ***actual cost*** of the improvements may be excluded from the decedent's gross estate. The apportionment rule is limited to contributions made to the ***creation or acquisition*** of the joint tenancy; it does not apply to improvements. [Estate of Peters v. Commissioner, 386 F.2d 404 (4th Cir. 1967)]

e. **Required nature of the survivor's contribution:** [§397] The critical problem in applying the proportionate exclusion rule is determining whether a portion of the property ***originally belonged to the survivor*** or, where the survivor paid part of the purchase price, whether the consideration furnished by the survivor ***originated with him*** and was not acquired by or received by him, at any time, from the decedent "***for less than an adequate and full consideration in money or money's worth***." [I.R.C. §2040(a)]

(1) **Prior gifts or bequests from third party:** [§398] Any money or property that the survivor acquired from a third party and which is used as consideration for the acquisition of a joint tenancy between the survivor and the decedent is consideration that originates with the survivor; it is not necessary that the survivor "earn" the money or property that he furnishes (although the survivor's earnings or the product thereof will, of course, qualify).

(2) **Prior gifts from decedent:** [§399] In contrast, anything the survivor originally received as a gift from the decedent cannot be claimed as an "original" contribution by the survivor. For example, if D gives separately owned property to X, who then conveys the property back to "D and X as joint tenants with right of survivorship," at D's death, the full value of the property is includible in D's estate since the entire property "originated" with him. [Dimock v. Corwin, 306 U.S. 363 (1939)]

(a) **Compare—consideration furnished:** [§400] On the other hand, although property is received from the decedent, to the extent the survivor paid "full and adequate consideration in money or money's worth" therefor, it will be deemed to originate with the survivor.

1) **Example:** D conveyed property worth $15,000 to X for $5,000. Subsequently, X conveyed the property to "D and X as joint tenants with right of survivorship." Upon D's death, one-third of the value of the property is excludible from D's estate. Although X furnished consideration for the original transfer, he did not pay ***full*** consideration in money or money's worth; thus, to the extent that the original transfer from D to X was a gift (two-thirds), the property originated with D and is includible in D's estate.

(3) **Income from donated property:** [§401] Although property given by the decedent to the survivor remains attributable to the donor, any ***income*** derived from the donated property after the date of the gift belongs to and is attributable to the survivor. Moreover, this rule normally applies even if the income derives from joint tenancy property created by the decedent; one-half of the income belongs to each joint tenant and if the income is used to acquire other joint tenancy property, one-half of the consideration for the acquisition of that joint tenancy is attributable to the survivor.

(a) **Example:** D gives securities to X. Thereafter, X collects and accumulates the dividends and interest and contributes the accumulated income as part of the consideration for the acquisition of joint tenancy realty by D and X. D dies. The income contributed by X is an "original contribution" for purposes of section 2040(a).

(b) **Example:** D pays the entire consideration for the acquisition of an apartment house, taking title in the name of D and X as joint tenants. Accumulated rents from this property are subsequently used to purchase Whiteacre in joint tenancy. D dies. The full value of the apartment house is included in D's estate; however, only one-half of the value of Whiteacre is included in D's estate since one-half of the rents from the apartment house (which were the source of the purchase price) are attributable to X as an original contribution.

(4) **Profits realized from appreciation in value of donated property:** [§402] It is reasonably well accepted now that where one person gives property to another, any profits realized by the donee that are attributable to appreciation

in value of the donated property subsequent to the date of the gift may constitute an original contribution by the donee to the acquisition of joint tenancy property. Note, however, that this rule extends only to profits attributable to ***post-gift appreciation*** in value, not to the taxable gain that the donee may realize upon sale of the donated property. [Harvey v. United States, 185 F.2d 463 (7th Cir. 1950)]

(a) **Example:** D gives securities to X. At the time of the gift, the securities are worth $10,000 and for income tax purposes, D's adjusted basis was $6,000. Subsequently, X sells the securities for $13,000 and contributes the entire proceeds as part of the consideration for the acquisition of joint tenancy real estate with D. X's taxable gain upon the sale of the securities is $7,000 ($13,000 minus $6,000). [*See* I.R.C. §§1001, 1015 *and* Income Tax I Summary] But, since only $3,000 of X's profit is attributable to post-gift appreciation, only $3,000 is treated as an original contribution by X to the acquisition of the joint tenancy property.

(b) **Exception—no exclusion where same property reconveyed in joint tenancy:** [§403] However, according to the Regulations, where the donee reconveys the same property into joint tenancy with the donor, post-gift appreciation may not be attributed to the donee as an original contribution. [Treas. Reg. §20.2040-1(c), Example (4)] Thus, in the example above, if X reconveyed the securities to D and X as joint tenants, and D died before X, the entire value of the securities would be includible in D's estate.

(c) **Exception—reinvestment of joint tenancy property:** [§404] D purchased stock with his own funds and had the stock issued to D and A as joint tenants. Subsequently this stock was sold at a profit and the proceeds were invested in other stock, which was also issued to D and A as joint tenants. Upon D's death, the full value of the "new" stock was included in D's estate; A's one-half of the profit on the sale of the original stock was not accepted as an "original contribution" by A. According to the court, "changing the character of the property but not the character of the ownership will not . . . permit an escape from taxation as joint property. . . ." [Endicott Trust Co. v. United States, 305 F. Supp. 945 (N.D.N.Y. 1969)]

(5) **Assumption of mortgage as original contribution:** [§405] If both joint tenants assume a purchase money mortgage with respect to joint tenancy property, one-half of the mortgage is attributable to each as an original contribution. [Bremer v. Luff, 7 F. Supp. 148 (N.D.N.Y. 1933)]

(a) **Example:** D and X acquire real property in joint tenancy. D pays the entire down payment of $4,000, and both D and X jointly assume a mortgage of $16,000. D dies before any payments are made in amortization of the mortgage principal. In this case, D's contribution is $12,000 ($4,000 down payment plus one-half of the $16,000 mortgage), and X's contribution is $8,000 (one-half of the outstanding mortgage). Thus, forty percent ($8,000 divided by $20,000) is excludible from D's estate.

(b) **Amortization of jointly assumed mortgage:** [§406] As a jointly assumed mortgage is paid off, the proportionate "original contribution" will vary unless both joint tenants contribute equally to the payments. For example, suppose in the above example that before his death, D made payments on the mortgage, reducing the balance to $10,000. D's contribution would be $15,000 (the $4,000 down payment, the $6,000 payments amortizing the mortgage, and one-half of the $10,000 mortgage that remains outstanding); and X's contribution would be $5,000—(one-half of the outstanding mortgage). Hence, only twenty-five percent of the value of the joint tenancy property ($5,000 divided by $20,000) is excludible from D's estate.

(c) **Income from property used to pay off mortgage:** [§407] However, if a jointly assumed mortgage is paid off with ***income*** derived from the property, each joint tenant will be treated as having made equal contributions to the amortization of the mortgage. (*See supra,* §401.) Thus, in the example above, if the income from the jointly held property was used to reduce the mortgage to $10,000 before D dies, forty percent of the value of the joint tenancy property is excludible from D's estate: X's contribution would be in the amount of $3,000 (one-half of the mortgage payments) plus $5,000 (one-half of the balance due), which is forty percent of the acquisition cost.

(6) **Burden of proof:** [§408] As noted earlier, the burden of establishing that consideration originated with the survivor is upon the decedent's estate. [Treas. Reg. §20.2040-1(a)] And, a very strict tracing requirement is insisted upon by the Service and the courts. For example, where both parties made deposits to and withdrawals from a jointly held bank account, the entire account balance was held taxable in the estate of the first to die because it could not be proven that it was not the survivor's deposits that were withdrawn! [Estate of Drazen v. Commissioner, 48 T.C. 1 (1967)]

f. **Relationship of section 2040 to other taxing sections:** [§409] As will be seen by the cases illustrated below, section 2040 does not ordinarily interact with other specific sections of the estate tax; indeed, where it is applicable, it generally ***supersedes*** these other sections.

(1) **Severance of joint tenancy—in general:** [§410] Where a joint tenancy is severed prior to death, section 2040 is inapplicable and the full value of the property is no longer subject to tax in the decedent's estate. However, if the decedent retains an interest as a tenant in common, that interest will be taxed under section 2033.

(2) **No interaction with section 2035:** [§411] Under prior law, property transferred within three years of death was included in the donor's gross estate (*see supra,* §§101 *et seq.*). Nevertheless, it was held that when joint tenancy

property was transferred to a third party within three years of a joint tenant's death, only the undivided interest of the decedent was taxable under section 2035 since it was only this interest that was "transferred." [Sullivan's Estate v. Commissioner, 175 F.2d 657 (9th Cir. 1949)]

(a) **1981 Act:** [§412] As previously discussed (*supra,* §§105 *et seq.*), estate taxation under section 2035 is now limited to: (i) gift taxes paid or payable with respect to gifts made within three years of death, and (ii) the transfer or release of certain interests or powers that would produce taxation under other specific estate tax provisions.

(b) **Section 2040 not specified:** [§413] Since section 2040 is not among the provisions specified for continued interaction with section 2035, no estate tax will attach if joint tenancy property is transferred within three years of a joint tenant's death.

(c) **Application:** [§414] Ten years ago D purchased property and took title in the names of D and A as joint tenants. On his death bed, D conveys his one-half undivided interest to A. Assuming no gift tax liability resulted from this death-bed gift, no portion of the value of the joint tenancy property will be included in D's estate. (Except for the gift, the full value of the property would be subject to the estate tax.)

(3) **Interaction with other sections:** [§415] The interaction (or lack thereof) between section 2040 and other specific taxing sections can be best understood by examining selected cases wherein the courts addressed the issue.

(a) **Joint tenancy transferred on trust:** [§416] In *Horner's Estate v. Commissioner,* 44 B.T.A. 1136 (1941), *aff'd,* 130 F.2d 649 (3d Cir. 1942), D and his wife transferred property held in joint tenancy to a trustee, reserving a life estate and a power to revoke the trust. The transfer was made within three years of (and in contemplation of) D's death, and D had paid the entire consideration for the acquisition of the joint tenancy property. The Tax Court held that the entire value of the property was included in D's estate on the alternative theories that: (i) the reserved life estate and power to revoke deprived the trust of substance and the property should be deemed held by decedent as joint tenancy property; and (ii) the transfer in contemplation of death supported continued taxation of the property under section 2040. The Third Circuit affirmed on the second ground. (Note that this was before the rule in *Sullivan, supra,* was established, and before the special rules for husband-and-wife joint tenancies were introduced into the Code.)

1) **Reserved life estates:** [§417] In *Estate of Borner v. Commissioner,* 25 T.C. 584 (1955), D and his wife transferred joint tenancy property to an irrevocable trust, reserving a life estate. Although the government urged that the full value of the property should be included in D's estate on the first theory of *Horner,* the Tax Court,

relying on the *Sullivan* rationale, found only one-half the property includible. It held that the transfer on trust severed the joint tenancy and since the property was not held in joint tenancy upon death, section 2040 was not applicable. Moreover, since the only interest that D had transferred (reserving a life estate) was the one-half undivided interest that he had as a joint tenant, only that one-half was taxable under section 2036. (Note that this same result would obtain today under the general rule of section 2040(a) ***and*** under the special rules for husband-and-wife joint tenancies.)

2) **Transfers on revocable trusts:** [§418] The Service acquiesced in *Borner* but limited its acquiescence to situations where there was only a reserved life estate. [*See* 1957-2 C.B. 4; Rev. Rul. 57-448, 1957-2 C.B. 618] Where joint tenancy property is transferred to a ***revocable*** trust, the Service still insists on inclusion of the full value of the property [Rev. Rul. 69-577, 1969-2 C.B. 1973]—even though a number of courts, again relying on *Sullivan,* have held that only one-half of the value is taxable in such cases [*see, e.g.*, Glaser v. United States, 306 F.2d 57 (7th Cir. 1962); *but compare* Harris v. United States, 193 F. Supp. 736 (D. Neb. 1961)]. (Note that this same conflict would exist today except in the case of "qualified joint interests" between spouses. In the case of such interests, only the one-half interest of the decedent could be taxed—under section 2038. *See infra,* §§426 *et seq.*)

(b) **Joint tenancy owned at death—which section takes precedence?** [§419] Quite apart from the question of taxing joint tenancy property severed prior to death, the issue has also arisen as to whether another section will apply where property still owned in joint tenancy at death is outside the scope of section 2040.

1) **Creation of joint tenancy with donor:** [§420] The Tax Court addressed this problem in *Koussevitsky v. Commissioner*, 5 T.C. 650 (1945). There D transferred property (which had previously been given to her by A) to herself and A as joint tenants. D predeceased A, but no part of the property could be taxed in her estate under section 2040 since it had originated with the survivor.

a) The government, however, sought to tax one-half of the property on three theories: (i) because D had a right to one-half the income from the joint tenancy property, she had made a transfer reserving a right to income in one-half the property, which was taxable under section 2036; (ii) because A's absolute possession and enjoyment of his one-half interest was conditioned on surviving D, and because D had a "reversionary interest" in that interest by virtue of the right of survivorship which attached to the joint tenancy, the transfer of that one-half interest was taxable under section 2037; and (iii) since D had a power to sever the joint tenancy and possess her one-half interest outright, she had made a revocable transfer of that interest which was taxable under section 2038.

b) But the court rejected the government's theories, essentially holding that where property is owned in joint tenancy at death, section 2040, which is more ***specific*** as to joint tenancy property, takes ***precedence*** over other taxing sections. (*See supra,* §82.)

g. **Special rule for husband-and-wife joint tenancies:** [§421] Section 2040(b) provides a special rule for husband-and-wife joint tenancies. It is applicable to all decedents dying after 1981, without regard to the time the joint tenancy was created.

(1) **Prior law:** [§422] Before 1977, no special rules for spouses existed. And, despite the fact that joint tenancy investments by spouses frequently represented the joint contributions of both spouses, it was usually extremely difficult for the survivor to prove an "original contribution" to the property's acquisition. (*See, e.g., supra,* §408.) A review of some of the authorities will suggest the rationale and motivation for the enactment of section 2040(b).

(a) **Services of a spouse as consideration:** [§423] Although it is clear that an economic value can be placed upon one spouse's services to another spouse or to the family, such services—at least if they are of an ordinary domestic nature—were not deemed to constitute consideration "in money or money's worth" or an "original contribution" to the acquisition of joint tenancy property. [*See, e.g.,* Bushman v. United States, 8 F.Supp. 694 (Ct. Cl. 1934), *cert. denied,* 295 U.S. 756 (1935)]

(b) **Nondomestic services:** [§424] The same result obtained where one spouse rendered gratuitous services in the business of the other spouse. [*See, e.g.,* Rogan v. Kammerdiner, 140 F.2d 569 (9th Cir. 1944)] Of course, if the spouse was paid a ***reasonable salary*** for the services, the earnings would constitute an original contribution on that spouse's part. Or, if the spouse worked in the other spouse's business under a definite ***agreement*** for reimbursement for services by way of an interest in jointly held property, the agreed-upon reimbursement might have been considered an original contribution by that spouse. [*See* Richardson v. Helvering, 80 F.2d 548 (D.C. Cir. 1935)] However, it did not occur to most to formalize the employment arrangement.

(c) **Informal partnerships:** [§425] Taxpayers scored a few victories where the surviving spouse (joint tenant) was able to convince a court that a business in which she materially and continuously participated with the deceased spouse constituted a business partnership and that the partnership profits (to which the survivor was entitled to one-half) were used to acquire the joint tenancy property. [*See* United States v. Neel, 235 F.2d 395 (10th Cir. 1956); Otte v. Commissioner, T.C. No. 76 (1972)] However, the burden of proof was quite difficult to overcome.

(2) **"Qualified joint interests":** [§426] As amended by the 1981 Act, section 2040(b) provides that in the case of a "qualified joint interest" only one-half of the value of the property is includible in the gross estate.

(a) **Definition:** [§427] A "qualified joint interest" is any interest held by a decedent ***and the decedent's spouse*** that is either: (i) a tenancy by the entirety, or (ii) a joint tenancy with right of survivorship, ***but only if the decedent and decedent's spouse are the only joint tenants***. (Note that a tenancy by the entirety can only exist where the only co-tenants are husband and wife. *See* Property Summary.)

(b) **Effect:** [§428] Where a qualified joint interest exists, one-half of the value of the property will be included in the estate of the first to die, without regard to which co-tenant furnished the consideration at the time of the joint tenancy's creation. Thus, if the donor dies first, only one-half of the property's value is included in his estate, whereas under the general rule the entire value would be taxed. But, if the donee dies first, one-half will be included in her estate, even though under the general rule nothing would have been taxed. And, of course, the full value of the property is taxable in the estate of the surviving joint tenant who has survived to sole, fee simple ownership. [I.R.C. §2033]

(c) **Comment:** [§429] Although this special rule responds to some anomalies that attended joint ownership of property by spouses under prior law, it offers dubious relief. The 1981 Act also allows a 100 percent marital deduction, and the joint tenancy property will qualify for this allowance without regard to who dies first, or how much is included in the decedent's estate (*see infra,* §651). Thus, no additional estate tax liability is incurred in any event.

h. **Community property:** [§430] Section 2040 does not apply to community property. However, since community property does represent a form of concurrent ownership, the estate tax aspects are appropriately considered at this point.

(1) **Nature of community property; general application of estate tax:** [§431] In most community property states, each spouse is recognized as having a present, vested one-half interest in all community assets. In turn, on the death of either spouse, only the deceased spouse's one-half of the community property is taxable under section 2033. Thus, in determining the tax status of community property, the extent to which it is "attributable" to the decedent is immaterial. [United States v. Goodyear, 99 F.2d 523 (9th Cir. 1938)]

(a) **Compare—former law:** [§432] At one time, some states held that a ***wife*** had only a power of testamentary disposition over one-half the community property and ***not*** a vested one-half interest therein. In such a case, that one-half interest could not be taxed to her estate under section 2033 (or its predecessor); but it was taxable under section 2041 as a power of appointment if that section was otherwise applicable. [Treas. Reg. §2041-1(b)(1)]

(b) **Form of ownership:** [§433] Note that the form in which property is held is not controlling. An asset may well be "community property" (and taxed as such) even though title is held in some other form of co-tenancy. For example, property acquired with one spouse's earnings during marriage (community property) can be a "community" asset even though title is taken in joint tenancy. [*See* United States v. Goodyear, *supra*]

(2) **Waiver of community interest—the "widow's election":** [§434] A frequent estate planning technique in community property states is for one spouse's will to dispose of the ***entire*** community property—including the other spouse's half—"in trust for (the surviving spouse) for life, remainder to our children." Of course, the decedent has no power of testamentary disposition over the survivor's one-half interest. Therefore, on the decedent's death, the survivor is put to the ***election*** of either accepting the gift under the decedent's will (a life estate in the whole property, but no interest in the remainder) or renouncing the gift, in which case the survivor merely retains her vested one-half interest in the community. [*See* Commissioner v. Siegel, 250 F.2d 339 (9th Cir. 1957)]

(a) **Estate tax consequences:** [§435] If (as is usually the case) the survivor elects the gift under the decedent's will, the survivor is in effect making a ***transfer*** of her interest in the community property to the trust created under the decedent's will. Realistically, however, what the survivor is transferring is a ***remainder*** in her share of the community—retaining a life estate therein—in ***consideration*** for the life estate in the decedent's one-half interest. Note the estate tax consequences:

1) **To decedent's estate:** [§436] First of all, the survivor's election to have her one-half of the community pass under the decedent's will does not enlarge the decedent's estate for estate tax purposes—the survivor's waiver is deemed to be a transfer to the decedent's trust, not to the decedent. Thus, only the decedent's one-half of the community is taxable in the decedent's estate. [Pacific National Bank v. Commissioner, 40 B.T.A. 128 (1939)]

2) **To survivor's estate:** [§437] But the survivor's transfer of her share of the community to the decedent's trust, retaining a life estate, constitutes a transfer with a retained life estate, so that the value of one-half of the property is includible in the survivor's estate under section 2036 when she dies. [Estate of Vardell v. Commissioner, 307 F.2d 688 (5th Cir. 1962)]

a) **Valuation:** [§438] Ordinarily, the full value of property that is transferred with a retained life estate is taxable under section

2036 (*supra*, §216). But here it is recognized that the survivor received consideration for the transfer—*i.e.*, the actuarial value of the life estate in the decedent's one-half of the community. Therefore, only the excess is taxable in the survivor's estate. [Estate of Gregory v. Commissioner, 39 T.C. 1012 (1963)]

3) **Net result:** [§439] The "widow's election" trust effectively avoids double taxation on the decedent's share, which would otherwise result by having the decedent's interest pass to the survivor and then, upon the survivor's death, to their children. And, it reduces the estate tax on the survivor's share by the value of the life estate obtained in the decedent's share.

(b) **Gift tax consequences:** [§440] The survivor's election (*i.e.*, the waiver of her community interest to the trust) also constitutes a taxable gift for gift tax purposes. [Estate of Bressani v. Commissioner, 45 T.C. 373 (1966)]

1) **Valuation:** [§441] Since the survivor retained a life estate in the property, it is recognized that all she has given away is a remainder interest in her one-half of the community; thus, only the value of that remainder is taxable. Moreover, the value of the life estate received by the survivor in the decedent's one-half interest (the "consideration" for the waiver) reduces the value of the remainder interest transferred by the survivor in determining the net value of the gift. [Commissioner v. Siegel, *supra*]

2) **Credit:** [§442] Although the value of the survivor's one-half interest is also taxed in the survivor's estate at death (above), a credit against the estate taxes payable is allowed for the gift tax that was paid in connection with the taxable gift of the remainder (*see infra*, §§1008, 1011, 1024).

10. **Section 2041—Powers of Appointment:** [§443] Under general property law, a "power of appointment" is a power granted by a "donor of the power" to a "donee of the power" by virtue of which the donee of the power may dispose of the property subject to the power even though it is "owned" by another. Under technical property law, the grant of a power of appointment does not give the donee an "interest" in the property subject to the power. At the same time, however, one who enjoys, *e.g.*, a life estate in property and also has a power to appoint the property to whomever she chooses virtually owns that property outright. Consequently, section 2041 includes in the gross estate of the holder of such a power the value of the property subject to the power.

a. **Background:** [§444] The first estate tax (under the 1916 Act) did not specifically tax property subject to a power of appointment. However, this defect was remedied in the Revenue Act of 1918, wherein Congress provided for a tax upon certain powers of appointment. As it turned out, this action was a wise precaution, the Supreme Court having later held that absent a specific provision taxing powers of appointment, the property subject to the power could not be taxed under the estate tax. [United States v. Field, 255 U.S. 257 (1921)]

(1) **Taxation of powers of appointment under the 1918 Act:** [§445] The first provision taxing powers of appointment was limited to ***general powers*** that were ***exercised*** by the decedent. (*See infra,* §§457, 471 for distinction between "general" and "special" powers.)

(a) **Unexercised powers not taxed:** [§446] Recall that the government sought to tax unexercised powers under the predecessor of section 2033, arguing that a person who held a life estate coupled with a general power of appointment in the property was, in effect, the "substantial owner." However, the Supreme Court rejected this assertion. [Helvering v. Safe Deposit & Trust Co., *see supra,* §§80-81]

(2) **The Revenue Act of 1942:** [§447] The Supreme Court's decision in the *Safe Deposit & Trust* case was offset by the passage of the Revenue Act of 1942. Under this Act, powers of appointment created on or before October 21, 1942 (the effective date of the Act) were taxed as before—*i.e.,* the Act operated prospectively only. Powers created after October 21, 1942, however, were taxable whether or not exercised and, indeed, the Act imposed a tax on many special powers of appointment.

(3) **The Powers of Appointment Act of 1951:** [§448] Persuaded that the extensive taxation of post-1942 powers under the 1942 Act was inappropriate, in 1951 Congress limited the tax upon post-1942 powers to ***general*** powers of appointment. Such powers, however, remain taxable whether or not exercised.

(4) **The 1954 Code:** [§449] Section 2041 of the 1954 (and 1986) Code is simply a refinement of the system of taxing powers of appointment adopted in the 1951 Act.

b. **Introductory analysis:** [§450] The treatment of section 2041 may be broken down into four basic issues:

(1) ***Determination of the date of the power's creation***;

(2) ***The nature*** of the taxable power;

(3) ***Special rules relating to preexisting powers***; and

(4) ***Special rules relating to post-1942 powers.***

c. **Date of creation of the power:** [§451] Given the fact that pre- and post-October 21, 1942 powers are taxed differently, it is important to determine when the power was created. In this regard, the rules relating to creation of powers are similar to those relating to the date of a transfer of property (discussed *supra,* §§140-145). Thus:

(1) **Direct transfers:** [§452] Where a power of appointment is granted with respect to property not transferred on trust (an unusual situation today), the power is deemed created on the date it is granted to the donee. And, since powers of appointment are usually granted together with some other interest in the property (such as a life estate), the date of the creation of the power will usually be the same as the date upon which the interest in the property is transferred.

(2) **Transfers on trust:** [§453] Powers of appointment granted with respect to property transferred on trust are deemed created on the same date that the trust came into existence by a transfer of property to the trustee.

(3) **Revocable trusts:** [§454] With respect to revocable trusts, it is uniformly held that the date of creation of the power is the date upon which the property is transferred to the trustee (rather than when the power to revoke lapses or is released). [*See* United States v. Merchant's National Bank, 261 F.2d 570 (5th Cir. 1958); Treas. Reg. §20.2041-1(e)]

(4) **Powers granted under will:** [§455] If the power is created by will, the date of testator's death (when the will "speaks") is the date of the creation of the power. However, section 2041(b)(3) provides a special rule for wills executed on or before October 21, 1942: If the will is not republished after that date and if the testator died before July 1, 1949, the power will be treated as a pre-1942 power.

d. **Nature of the taxable power of appointment:** [§456] Taxation under section 2041 is limited to ***general*** powers of appointment. [I.R.C. §2041(a)]

(1) **Definition of "general power":** [§457] The statute defines a general power of appointment as "a power which is exercisable in favor of the ***decedent, his estate, his creditors,*** or the ***creditors of his estate***. . . ." [I.R.C. §2041(b)(1)] Note that it is not necessary that the decedent be able to appoint the property to all of these objects; a power is general if it ***can*** be exercised ***in favor of any one of them***. And, as long as the decedent could appoint the property to any one of the specified objects, it is immaterial that he might also be able to appoint the property to others.

(a) **Examples:** The power to appoint "to whomever D chooses" is a general power of appointment, as is a power to appoint "to D's children or D's estate." However, a power to appoint to a limited class of persons ***not including*** the decedent, his creditors, his estate, or the creditors of his estate (*e.g.*, "to D's children") is not a general power of appointment.

(b) **Testamentary or lifetime power:** [§458] It is generally sufficient that the power be exercisable either during life or by will; it need not be exercisable both during life and by will.

(c) **Exception for certain powers to consume which are limited by ascertainable standards:** [§459] The statute provides a special exception for "a power to consume, invade, or appropriate property for the benefit of the decedent which is limited by an ascertainable standard relating to health, education, support, or maintenance of the decedent. . . ." Such a limited power is not a general power of appointment even though it enables the decedent to appoint the property to himself or his creditors. [I.R.C. §2041(b)(1)(A)]

(2) **Form of the power:** [§460] For federal tax purposes, it is not necessary that the power be in any particular form. Many rights, powers, and authorities over property are classified as powers of appointment even though they may not be so defined under state property law. For example, powers to withdraw property from a trust, or to consume property (whether held on trust, or otherwise) are powers of appointment since they allow the person who possesses the "power" to obtain beneficial enjoyment of the property.

(a) **Capacity in which exercisable:** [§461] The capacity in which the power is exercisable is immaterial—*e.g.*, the fact that a general power is exercisable by the decedent as trustee will not prevent taxation under section 2041.

(b) **Indirect access to the power:** [§462] Moreover, the power need not technically lie with the decedent. Thus, the decedent will be deemed to possess a general power of appointment if he has authority to compel exercise of a power held by another for his (the decedent's) benefit.

(c) **Contingent powers:** [§463] Since the power must be "exercisable" by the decedent [I.R.C. §2041(b)(1)], it would appear that a contingent power is not taxable if the contingency is beyond the decedent's control and has not occurred at the time of the decedent's death. (*See supra,* §302, discussing contingent powers under section 2038.)

(d) **Administrative powers:** [§464] For purposes of section 2041, the power must be such that decedent can benefit himself, either directly or indirectly (*e.g.*, by appointing to his creditors). Thus, mere powers of management, investment, etc., with respect to the property are not "powers of appointment." (*See* further discussion of administrative powers, *supra*, §§197, 315.)

(e) **Joint powers:** [§465] The treatment of joint powers differs, depending upon whether the power was created before or after October 21, 1942. This is discussed at greater length below in connection with preexisting and post-1942 powers.

(f) **Remainder to decedent's estate:** [§466] Suppose an insured elects a life insurance settlement option under which the insurance company, upon the death of the insured, retains the proceeds of the policy and pays interest thereon to a designated beneficiary for that beneficiary's life, with the proceeds to be paid to the beneficiary's estate upon the beneficiary's death. Does the beneficiary's power to direct distribution of his estate by will make the proceeds includible in his gross estate under section 2041? Two courts addressing the issue have offered conflicting opinions:

1) **Reasoning that any "power" that the deceased beneficiary may have had arose from state law which allowed him to transfer property by will, the Seventh Circuit held the proceeds not taxable under section 2041. [Second National Bank v. Dallman, 209 F.2d 321 (7th Cir. 1954)]**

2) The Fifth Circuit, however, has since held to the contrary, emphasizing that it is the existence of a power freely to direct the transfer of property and not the source of the power that is critical for estate tax purposes. Hence, the court found that when the settlor elected to place the residuum of the insurance proceeds in a position from which the decedent could appoint without restriction, he created a general power of appointment, taxable to the beneficiary under section 2041. [Keeter v. United States, 461 F.2d 714 (5th Cir. 1972)]

   a) *Comment:* The result in *Keeter* represents a realistic interpretation of the scope of section 2041 and thus appears to be the better view.

(3) **Limited to donated powers:** [§467] Section 2041 applies only to powers ***donated*** to the decedent by some third party, not to powers that the decedent ***retained*** or ***reacquired*** in connection with property he formerly owned. Retained or reacquired powers with respect to property may be taxable under some other section, but they are not "powers of appointment" within the scope of section 2041. [*See* I.R.C. §2036(a)(2), *supra*, §§179 *et seq.*; I.R.C. §2038, *supra*, §§278 *et seq.*]

   (a) **Example:** D transferred property on trust for A for life, with the corpus to be distributed to such of A's children as D shall appoint. This power reserved by D is not a taxable power of appointment under section 2041. However, it would be taxable under section 2036(a)(2) or 2038.

   (b) **Compare:** If D had given A the power to determine which children the property would go to after A's death, A's power over the remainder would be a power of appointment. However, the property would not be taxable in A's estate because it is not a ***general*** power (*see* below).

(4) **Direct or indirect benefit:** [§468] A "general power" exists where property may be appointed, ***directly*** or ***indirectly***, for the decedent's benefit.

(a) **Example:** Thus, if D holds a power to appoint property to a trust in which he is a beneficiary, he has a general power of appointment.

(b) **Power to discharge own obligations:** [§469] Moreover, if the holder can utilize the power to discharge his legal obligations, it is deemed exercisable for his benefit and is a general power; in effect, the decedent has the power to appoint to his creditors.

(c) **Power exercisable to support another:** [§470] Similarly, D has a general power where he may exercise a power (or compel its exercise) to use property for the support of a person whom he is legally obligated to support. [*See* Treas. Reg. §20.2041-1(c)(1)]

1) **Note:** This is apparently true even though exercise of the power is limited by an ascertainable standard relating to "health, education, support and maintenance." Thus, although the statute expressly states that a power to withdraw for ***one's own benefit*** is not a general power if its exercise is limited by such a standard (*supra*, §459), an analogous power exercisable in favor of another (whom D has a legal obligation to support) may be treated as a general power of appointment.

(5) **Special powers distinguished:** [§471] A "special power" is any power of appointment that is not a general power, as defined above. For example, a power to appoint property to or among a designated class of persons, ***not including*** the decedent or his estate, etc., is a special power of appointment.

(a) **Not a "taxable power":** [§472] As stated above, the statute only embraces general powers. Hence, property subject solely to a special power is not taxable in the donee's estate under section 2041.

1) **Comment:** The use of special powers of appointment can introduce considerable flexibility in estate planning and it was apparently to allow for this flexibility that Congress limited the estate tax to general powers in the Powers of Appointment Act of 1951.

(b) **Compare—tax treatment under other sections:** [§473] However, note again that section 2041 only applies to donated powers. If the decedent had retained or reacquired a special power of appointment with respect to property formerly owned by him, the property may be included in his gross estate under sections 2036(a)(2) or 2038.

e. **Preexisting powers—special rules:** [§474] A power created on or before October 21, 1942, will produce a tax only if it is ***exercised***. [I.R.C. §2041(a)(1)]

(1) **Exercise by will:** [§475] The exercise of a general power of appointment by will is clearly taxable. [I.R.C. §2041(a)(1)(A)] Moreover, under the law of many states, a decedent's residuary clause will exercise a general power of appointment even though no reference to the power nor intent to exercise it is expressed. In such case, the general power is deemed "exercised" by the decedent's will for federal estate tax purposes.

(2) **Exercise during life:** [§476] On the other hand, if the general power is exercised during the life of the decedent, the property will be included in his estate only if it would have been included under sections 2035 through 2038 had the property subject to the power been transferred by the decedent.

(a) **Example:** If D exercises a general power of appointment within three years of his death, the property subject to the power is included in his gross estate. [I.R.C. §§2041(a)(1)(B), 2035] Or, if D is granted a life estate in property with a general power to appoint the remainder, and four years before his death D exercises the power, the property is includible in his estate. [I.R.C. §§2041(a)(1)(B), 2036] Or, if D appoints the property on trust and reserves the right to revoke the trust, the property is includible in his estate. [I.R.C. §§2041(a)(1)(B), 2038]

(b) **Compare:** In contrast, if D appoints the property more than three years before his death and retains no interest or power with respect to the property, it is ***not*** includible in his gross estate.

(3) **Lapse or release of preexisting powers:** [§477] Since a preexisting power must be exercised to be taxed, a failure to exercise the power, or a lapse or release of the power, will ***not*** cause inclusion of the property in the decedent's gross estate. (But distinguish post-1942 powers, below.)

(4) **Reduction of power and exercise of special power:** [§478] If a preexisting general power was reduced to a special power (*e.g.*, by a partial release) before November 1, 1951, a subsequent exercise of the special power is not deemed to be an exercise of a general power of appointment. [I.R.C. §2041(a)(1)]

(5) **Joint powers:** [§479] A preexisting power granted to the decedent and another, jointly, is ***not*** taxable. [I.R.C. §2041(b)(1)(B)] And, it is immaterial whether the co-holder of the power is an adverse party. (However, note that the result is contra as to post-1942 powers; *see* below.)

f. **Post-1942 powers—special rules:** [§480] Unlike preexisting powers, a power created after October 21, 1942 will be taxed whether exercised ***or unexercised***. In other words, property subject to a post-1942 general power of appointment will be included in the decedent's gross estate if the decedent merely ***possessed*** the general power at the time of his death; the very existence of the power renders the property taxable. [I.R.C. §2041(a)(2)]

(1) **Inability to exercise:** [§481] Since exercise of the power is not crucial, it is immaterial that the decedent was under a legal disability effectively to exercise the power or was otherwise unable to exercise it. Indeed, it has been held that section 2041 will apply even where the decedent was unaware of the power. [Freeman v. Commissioner, 67 T.C. 202 (1976); Alperstein v. Commissioner, 613 F.2d 1213 (4th Cir. 1979); *but cf.* Finley v. United States, 404 F. Supp. 200 (S.D. Fla. 1975)]

(2) **Contingent power:** [§482] However, a power subject to a contingency beyond the decedent's control, which has not occurred at the time of his death, is not "exercisable" at the time of his death and, hence, is not taxable (*supra,* §302).

(3) **Lapse or release:** [§483] The lapse (*i.e.*, failure to exercise within a specified time) or affirmative release of a power is treated as an "exercise" of the power. [I.R.C. §§2041(a)(2), (b)(2)] Accordingly, property subject to a power that lapsed or was released is includible in the decedent's estate if a lifetime exercise of the power would have produced taxation—*i.e.*, if the lapse or release occurs within three years of D's death or under circumstances where property transferred by D would be includible under sections 2036 through 2038 (*see supra,* §471).

(a) **Limitation—lapse of noncumulative powers to withdraw:** [§484] However, where the decedent had a noncumulative power to withdraw funds from a trust annually, a failure to exercise the power in any year or years (lapse of the annual power) is ***not*** treated as the exercise of a general power to the extent of the greater of $5,000 or five percent of the value of the property to which the power relates. [I.R.C. §2041(b)(2)]

1) **Rationale:** This is a relief provision designed to allow a certain flexibility in estate planning.

2) **Example:** A conveys $100,000 on trust for D for life, remainder to X, and grants D a power to compel distribution of the corpus to himself up to $10,000 per year. If D does not exercise the power in any given year, the power lapses for that year. Under the general rules of section 2041, the lapse would be treated as an exercise of the power in favor of the owner of the remainder (X), and the property would be taxed in D's estate because he is deemed to have reserved a life estate in the property "transferred." However, the special exception for lapsed powers limits inclusion in D's estate to the amount by which $10,000 exceeds the greater of $5,000 or five percent of the value of the corpus at the time each annual power lapses.

a) Even so, in the ***year of D's death***, the full amount of the property subject to the power ($10,000) is included. The special rule does not apply to this amount; it is taxed to D's estate not because the power lapsed, but because there was a taxable power to appoint this amount which was in existence at D's death.

(b) **Release of general testamentary power by exercise of lifetime special power:** [§485] If a person is granted both a general testamentary power of appointment and a special lifetime power of appointment, the lifetime exercise of the special power is treated as a release of the general testamentary power. Thus, the property subject to the power is taxed as though there had been a lifetime exercise of a general power (*i.e.*, it is includible if a lifetime exercise of a general power would result in inclusion).

1) **Example:** Suppose D is granted a lifetime income interest in a trust coupled with a general testamentary power over the trust corpus and a lifetime special power over the corpus. If D exercises the special power by appointing the remainder after his life estate, the entire corpus is includible in D's gross estate, on the theory that when he exercised the special power he released the general power by means of a transfer taxable under section 2036 (retained life interest in appointed property).

(4) **Compare—renunciation or disclaimer:** [§486] An unqualified refusal to accept the power in the first place is neither an exercise, lapse, or release of the power—even if the renunciation or disclaimer is made within three years of the death of the disclaimant. [Treas. Reg. §20.2041-3(d)(6)] (As to when the renunciation or disclaimer will be effective for federal estate tax purposes, *see infra,* §§772 *et seq.*)

(5) **Joint powers:** [§487] In contrast to preexisting powers, a power created after October 21, 1942 will be taxed even though exercisable only with the concurrence of another person, ***unless*** the co-holder of the power is the ***donor*** (creator) of the power or a person who has a ***substantial interest in the property*** (adverse party). [I.R.C. §2041(b)(1)(C)(i),(ii)]

(a) **Permissible appointee not adverse party:** [§488] For this purpose, a permissible appointee who possesses no other interest in the property is not deemed to be an adverse party. On the other hand, a person who, ***after the death of the decedent***, would be able to exercise a power of appointment in his own favor (by succeeding to D's power) ***is*** an adverse party. [I.R.C. §2041(b)(1)(C)(ii)]

(b) **Limitation on amount includible where co-holder is a permissible appointee:** [§489] Even though a joint power is taxable where the co-holder is a potential appointee, only a portion of the value of the property subject to the power is included in the decedent's estate. That portion is determined by dividing the value of the property, otherwise includible, by a number equal to the number of permissible appointees (including the decedent). For example, if D had power to appoint property to whomever he chose with the consent of X, and X had no other interest in that property, upon D's death one-half of the value of the property is includible in D's estate (the value of the property divided by two).

11. **Section 2042—Life Insurance:** [§490] Proceeds of life insurance policies on the decedent's life are includible in the gross estate if the proceeds are: (i) payable to (or for the benefit of) decedent's estate; or (ii) payable to any other beneficiary, but only if the decedent possessed "incidents of ownership" in the policy at the time of death.

    a. **Background:** [§491] Life insurance is patently "testamentary" in nature. At the same time, however, since the insured will never receive the proceeds, it is difficult to find that she has an "interest" in the proceeds; and since the premiums paid by the insured bear no necessary relation to the proceeds payable to the beneficiary, it is difficult to find a "transfer" by the insured during life or upon death. For these reasons, taxation under the Revenue Act of 1916, which contained no specific provision taxing life insurance proceeds, was troublesome.

        (1) **The Revenue Act of 1918:** [§492] The deficiency in the first estate tax was remedied with passage of the 1918 Act, expressly providing for the taxation of life insurance to the estate of the insured. The 1918 scheme is similar to the present statute insofar as it divides the taxation of life insurance proceeds into two categories: proceeds payable to the decedent's estate, and proceeds payable to some other beneficiary.

            (a) **Proceeds payable to estate:** [§493] Where payable to the insured's estate, the proceeds of life insurance were fully taxable.

            (b) **Proceeds payable to another:** [§494] Where payable to some beneficiary other than the estate, the 1918 Act imposed a tax on the proceeds if the insurance contract was "taken out by the decedent" on her own life. (It also provided a special $40,000 exemption.)

                1) **"Taken out by the decedent":** [§495] The meaning of this phrase was a source of much confusion. Although it was conceded that the decedent need not have originally applied for the policy, beyond this the interpretations varied.

                    a) The initial Regulations under the 1918 Act maintained that the test was whether the decedent had paid the premiums for the insurance, but subsequently, the Treasury limited taxation to situations where the decedent ***both*** paid the premiums ***and*** possessed incidents of ownership in the policy. Still later, the Regulations were amended to provide that the premium payments and incidents of ownership tests would be applied in the alternative (*i.e.*, either factor would produce taxation).

b) Finally, in 1941, the Regulations returned full cycle and adopted the premium payments standard as the exclusive test for taxability.

(2) **The 1942 Act:** [§496] Responding to the confusion generated by the Regulations, Congress adopted, as part of the 1942 Act, the premium payments and incidents of ownership criteria as ***alternative*** tests for taxability. (In addition, the Act also repealed the $40,000 exemption.)

(3) **The 1954 Code:** [§497] With passage of the 1954 Code, the standard for taxation changed once again. Proceeds payable to beneficiaries other than the estate of the insured are now taxed only if the insured possessed ***incidents of ownership*** in the policy at her death. [I.R.C. §2042(2)]

(a) **Scope of section 2042:** [§498] Note that section 2042 applies only to proceeds from life insurance on the ***decedent's*** life; it has no application to insurance policies on the lives of other persons or to the proceeds therefrom. However, insurance policies owned by a decedent on the lives of others constitute "property owned by the decedent" and so are includible under section 2033. (*See supra,* §48.)

b. **Introductory analysis:** [§499] Analysis of section 2042 raises five principal topics:

(1) ***What constitutes "life insurance"***?

(2) ***The taxation of life insurance payable to the estate.***

(3) ***The taxation of proceeds payable to someone other than the estate***. This is, in fact, the major area of concern and is subdivided into two elements:

(a) The scope of the term "***incidents of ownership***."

(b) The determination of ***whether the decedent possessed incidents of ownership*** at the time of death (which requires analysis of the effect of assignment of incidents of ownership during life).

(4) ***The amount includible***.

(5) ***The taxation of life insurance that is subject to community property laws***.

c. **What constitutes life insurance?** [§500] Neither the Code nor Regulations specifically define life insurance for purposes of section 2042, and the courts have been hesitant to frame a precise and exclusive definition.

(1) **"Life insurance risk" test:** [§501] According to the Supreme Court, the critical issue in determining whether a particular arrangement amounts to "life insurance" is whether that arrangement comprehends a "life insurance risk." In other words, the economic risk of death must be shifted or distributed. [Helvering v. LeGierse, 312 U.S. 531 (1941); *and see supra,* §357]

(2) **Commercial contract not necessary:** [§502] It is not required that the death benefit be payable under a typical life insurance contract purchased from a commercial insurance company. Any arrangement that ***shifts or distributes the economic risk of death*** may be taxable under section 2042. [*See* Treas. Reg. §20.2042-1, stating that section 2042 applies to death benefits "of every description"]

(a) **Examples:** The death benefit payable to the survivor of a member of the New York Stock Exchange has been held to be "life insurance," on the theory that the economic risk of death was distributed among the members of the Exchange who were previously assessed to provide a fund for payment of the benefits. [Commissioner v. Treganowan, 183 F.2d 288 (2d Cir. 1950), *cert. denied*, 340 U.S. 853 (1950)] Similarly, the Regulations identify funeral and death benefits paid by, *e.g.*, fraternal lodges, as "life insurance." [Treas. Reg. §20.2042-1(a)]

(3) **Accidental death policies:** [§503] Moreover, the Supreme Court has refused to limit the term "life insurance" to insurance that covers the ***inevitable*** risk of death. Thus, benefits payable for death by certain accidental causes—whether pursuant to specific accident insurance or double indemnity clauses under regular life insurance (which double the amount of the proceeds payable in the event death should result from accidental causes)—are within the scope of section 2042. [Commissioner v. Estate of Noel, 380 U.S. 678 (1965)—accidental death benefits under "flight insurance" policy purchased by D shortly before fatal air crash includible under section 2042(2); *and see* Rev. Rul. 83-44, 1983-1 C.B. 228—death benefits payable under no-fault automobile insurance policy are "life insurance proceeds" for purposes of §2042]

(4) **Compare—death benefits *not* taxable as life insurance:** [§504] Examples of life insurance-type contracts ***not*** taxable under section 2042 include:

(a) **Life insurance-annuity packages:** *See supra*, §§153, 372.

(b) **Endowment policies or retirement income policies:** [§505] Although such policies may provide death benefits, if they have ***matured*** (*i.e.*, become payable) during the decedent's life, there is no longer any life insurance risk and, hence, the proceeds are not taxable under section 2042 (*see supra*, §§357-358). However, the benefits may be includible under sections 2036, 2038, or 2039. [*See* Seward's Estate v. Commissioner, 164 F.2d 434 (4th Cir. 1947)]

1) **Compare—policies that have not matured:** [§506] On the other hand, if these policies have ***not*** matured, they are taxable as life insurance because the life insurance risk still exists. [Thompson v. Commissioner, 41 B.T.A. 901 (1940)]

d. **Life insurance payable to insured's estate:** [§507] Proceeds of life insurance policies made payable to the insured's estate (or to her executor, administrator, etc.) are fully taxable. [I.R.C. §2042(1)] And this is true regardless of whether the insured paid the premiums or retained any incidents of ownership in the policy.

(1) **Payable "for the benefit of the estate":** [§508] Moreover, proceeds payable to some other beneficiary will be taxed under section 2042(1) if that beneficiary is legally bound to apply the proceeds to ***discharge obligations of the insured's estate***. Thus, if the proceeds are payable to a trustee but the trustee is obliged to remit to the decedent-insured's executor "such amounts as may be necessary to pay death taxes, administration expenses, funeral expenses, etc.," the proceeds will be included in the insured's estate even though she possessed no incidents of ownership in the policy. [Treas. Reg. §20.2042-1(b)(1)]

(2) **Impact of state law:** [§509] In some states, life insurance payable to the insured's estate or executor is not administered and distributed as part of the decedent's estate, but is immediately distributable to certain designated survivors (*e.g.*, the insured's widow or minor children) and is not subject to claims of creditors. In this case, it has been held that the proceeds are payable to beneficiaries ***other than the estate*** and so are ***not*** taxable unless the insured retained incidents of ownership in the policy. [*See* Webster v. Commissioner, 120 F.2d 514 (5th Cir. 1941)]

e. **Life insurance payable to other beneficiaries:** [§510] Insurance benefits payable to named beneficiaries other than the estate, etc., are taxable in the decedent-insured's estate only if the insured possessed ***incidents of ownership*** in the policy at the time of death. [I.R.C. §2042(2)]

(1) **What are "incidents of ownership"?** [§511] Other than certain reversionary interests (below), the Code does not define "incidents of ownership." However, the Regulations and other authorities make it clear that the phrase is not limited to ownership of the contract but extends to any right or interest in the policy whereby the insured has the practical power, directly or indirectly, to ***control the existence of the policy***, to ***rearrange the economic interests therein***, or to ***affect the benefits payable thereunder***. [*See* Treas. Reg. §20.2042-1(c)(2)]

(a) **Examples:** The right to designate or change beneficiaries, even if limited to the designation of contingent beneficiaries, is an incident of ownership, as is the right to borrow against the cash value of the policy, to assign or pledge the policy, or to surrender or cancel the policy. [*See, e.g.*, Nance v. United States, 430 F.2d 662 (9th Cir. 1970); Prichard v. United States, 397 F.2d 60 (5th Cir. 1968); Estate of Selznick v. Commissioner, 15 T.C. 716 (1950), *aff'd*, 195 F.2d 735 (9th Cir. 1952)]

1) **But note:** The right to receive dividends is not an incident of ownership; such right is viewed merely as a reduction of the premium cost. [Old Point National Bank v. Commissioner, 39 B.T.A. 343 (1939)]

(b) **Right to affect time and manner of enjoyment:** [§512] While an early case held that the right to select a settlement option and thus affect the time and manner of a beneficiary's enjoyment of the proceeds was not an incident of ownership [Billings v. Commissioner, 35 B.T.A. 1147 (1937)], the result is contra today. Such right is deemed an incident of ownership. [Estate of Lumpkin v. Commissioner, 474 F.2d 1092 (5th Cir. 1973); *but see* Estate of Skifter v. Commissioner, 468 F.2d 699 (2d Cir. 1972), discussed *infra*, §529]

(c) **Employer group insurance:** [§513] Employer-furnished group term insurance is includible in the employee's estate if the employee possesses any incidents of ownership at death. [Rev. Rul. 69-54, 1969-1 C.B. 221]

1) **Power to terminate employment:** [§514] However, it has been held that an employee's power to affect the cancellation of the employer-owned policy by quitting the job is ***not*** an incident of ownership. [Estate of Lumpkin v. Commissioner, 56 T.C. 815 (1971), *rev'd on another issue*, 474 F.2d 1092 (5th Cir. 1973)] The Service now follows this rule. [Rev. Rul. 72-307, 1972-1 C.B. 307]

2) **Assignment of term insurance:** [§515] Where allowed under state law and the terms of the insurance contract, an assignment by the employee of all incidents of ownership in the contract, including the right to retain the insurance after termination of employment and the right to convert the term insurance into permanent coverage, is effective to remove the proceeds from exposure to the estate tax. [Rev. Rule 69-54; *supra*; Rev. Rul. 72-307, *supra*]

a) **Right to convert if employment terminated:** [§516] A later Ruling held that where an employee assigned incidents of ownership but retained the right to convert the policy upon termination of employment, the proceeds were ***not*** includible in the deceased employee's estate. The power to convert the policy upon termination is ***not*** an incident of ownership because it comprehends a "potentially costly related action"—*i.e.*, the loss of the job. [Rev. Rul. 84-130, 1984-2 C.B. 194]

(d) **Reversionary interests:** [§517] The Code specifically provides that a reversionary interest is an incident of ownership if the value of such interest exceeds five percent of the value of the policy immediately prior to the insured's death. For this purpose, a reversionary interest is any possibility that the policy or its proceeds may return to the decedent or to the estate or be subject to a power of testamentary disposition by her. [I.R.C. §2042(2)]

1) **Example:** Insured transfers the policy on her life to a trust for the benefit of B "provided he survives the settlor-insured." This contingency creates a reversionary interest in the insured and if the value of this interest (computed by actuarial tables just before the decedent-insured's death) is in excess of five percent of the value of the policy, the proceeds are taxable in her estate.

2) **Example:** As part of a divorce settlement, D agrees to maintain a life insurance policy on his life in which his ex-wife is to be named beneficiary until such time as she dies or remarries. Since the ex-wife could marry or die before him, D has a reversionary interest in the policy; hence, it is includible in his gross estate even though D has no power to change the beneficiary or cancel the policy and even though the proceeds are paid to his ex-wife upon his death. [Rev. Rul. 76-113, 1976-1 C.B. 276] (However, the estate can deduct all payments made to purchase or maintain the policy.)

(2) **What constitutes "possession" of incidents of ownership?** [§518] The insured need not have ***retained*** incidents of ownership, as where she owned the policy originally and transferred it to another with a reservation of certain rights. All that is required is that the incidents of ownership be ***possessed*** by the insured at death. For example, where X applies for and at all times is the owner of a policy on D's life, the proceeds are taxable in D's estate if X gave D any incidents of ownership.

(a) **Joint powers taxable:** [§519] The statute specifically provides that the insurance proceeds will be taxed whether the incidents of ownership are exercisable by the insured-decedent "alone or in conjunction with any other person." [I.R.C. §2042(2)] Thus, it is of no consequence that the concurrence of an adverse party may be required. (*See* analogous discussion in connection with section 2038, *supra*, §289.)

(b) **Insurance trusts:** [§520] If a policy is placed on trust, the terms of both the policy and the trust instrument will determine whether the insured possesses incidents of ownership. For example, where a life insurance policy was irrevocably assigned to the trustee of a trust, but the insured possessed the power to alter or amend the trust, the insured was held to possess incidents of ownership in the policy at death. [Estate of Karagheusian v. Commissioner, 23 T.C. 806 (1955)]

(c) **Inability to exercise incidents of ownership:** [§521] The fact that the insured was unable to exercise any right or power with respect to the policy at the time of death is immaterial. Thus, *e.g.*, the proceeds of a flight insurance policy were taxed in the decedent-insured's estate because he reserved the power to change beneficiaries; it was of no effect that he did not have the policy in his possession after boarding the aircraft and so could not have exercised his power to change the beneficiary designation by written endorsement on the policy. [Commissioner v. Estate of Noel, *supra,* §503]

1) **Legal disability:** [§522] Similarly, it is ordinarily deemed immaterial that the insured is incompetent or cannot exercise incidents of ownership because of an agreement with some third party. Whether the insured ***possessed*** any incidents of ownership is determined under the insurance contract itself. [*See* United States v. Rhode Island Hospital Trust Co., 355 F.2d 7 (1st Cir. 1966); Nance v. United States, *supra,* §511]

2) **Economic interest limitation:** [§523] However, in one case, life insurance proceeds were not included in the insured's estate where, although he was technically the owner of the policy, the beneficiary had been irrevocably designated, the policy was within the control of the beneficiary, and the insured had never paid any premiums. *Rationale:* In effect, there had been a full assignment of the policy since not only was the insured unable to exercise any incidents of ownership but, in the court's view, he was precluded from doing so insofar as he had no economic interest in the policy. [Morton v. United States, 457 F.2d 750 (4th Cir. 1972)]

(d) **Business purchase agreements:** [§524] Frequently, the owners of closely held businesses enter into agreements under which the remaining owners or the business entity itself will purchase the interest of a principal who dies. And, oftentimes, these business purchase agreements are funded by insurance—*i.e.*, the life of each principal is insured and upon a principal's death the proceeds of the insurance are collected and paid over to the insured's estate in consideration for the transfer or liquidation of the decedent's interest in the business. However, the tax consequences that attend such arrangements are unclear.

1) **Include insurance but not business interests?** [§525] In *Tompkins v. Commissioner*, 13 T.C. 1054 (1949), a partnership carried life insurance on the life of the principals, payable to itself, in order to fund a partnership liquidation agreement. Upon the death of the insured decedent, the partnership collected the proceeds of the insurance and paid them over to the decedent's estate in complete liquidation of the decedent's partnership interest. The insurance proceeds were held taxable in the decedent-insured's estate since, as a partner, he possessed incidents of ownership in the policy jointly

with the other partners. However, the court refused also to include the value of the partnership interest (under section 2033) since this would in effect result in double taxation.

2) **Include value of interest but not insurance?** [§526] However, in a later case, the Tax Court held that policies transferred by decedent to his partnership were not includible in his estate since he had not retained any incidents of ownership in an individual capacity, but only in his capacity as a partner. [Estate of Knipp v. Commissioner, 25 T.C. 153 (1955), *aff'd on other grounds,* 244 F.2d 436 (4th Cir. 1957), *cert. denied,* 355 U.S. 827 (1957)]

a) **Comment:** The capacity in which incidents of ownership must be exercised is ordinarily immaterial (*see* below). Thus, the best explanation of the *Knipp* case apparently is that the court wished to avoid double taxation—*i.e.*, taxation of the life insurance proceeds owned by the partnership under section 2042, and taxation of the value of the partner's interest (augmented by the insurance proceeds) under section 2033.

(e) **Incidents of ownership held as trustee:** [§527] According to the Regulations, it is of no consequence that incidents of ownership are held as trustee, and this is true whether the insured transferred the policy to the trust or the policy was assigned to the trust by another. [Treas. Reg. §20.2042-1(c)] However, some modification of this general rule has developed as a result of a series of court decisions:

1) **Leading case:** [§528] In *Estate of Fruehauf v. Commissioner,* 427 F.2d 80 (6th Cir. 1970), the insured's wife transferred policies she owned on the life of her husband to a testamentary trust in which the insured was named co-trustee. The court reasoned that, as trustee, the insured possessed incidents of ownership, since by exercising his power of administration and investment he could have cashed in the policy, borrowed against the policy, etc. Hence, the proceeds were includible in his gross estate.

2) **Tax Court distinguishes:** [§529] In *Estate of Skifter v. Commissioner,* 56 T.C. 1190 (1971), *aff'd,* 468 F.2d 699 (2d Cir. 1972), the insured's role as trustee of his wife's testamentary trust—which included policies of insurance on his life—did not support taxation of the proceeds in his estate. The court distinguished *Fruehauf* on the ground that Mr. Skifter had no economic interest in the trust whereas Mr. Fruehauf was one of the trust beneficiaries. The court also reasoned that the decedent's "power" was not reserved and was purely administrative.

3) **Fifth Circuit rejects Tax Court rationale:** [§530] The Fifth Circuit added to the confusion in *Rose v. United States,* 511 F.2d 259

(5th Cir. 1975), where the insured was named as trustee of a trust created by his brother for the benefit of the insured's children and used trust funds to purchase life insurance on his life. Here the insurance proceeds were found taxable in the insured's estate. The court squarely rejected the holding and reasoning in *Skifter*: Section 2042 does not require that the insured have some personal economic interest in the policy; it is sufficient if he could merely affect the time and manner of enjoyment (*supra*). Nor is it necessary that the incidents of ownership be retained (*supra*).

4) **Service ruling:** [§531] Based upon its analysis of the legislative history of section 2042, the Service has adopted a position that strikes a balance between *Fruehauf-Rose* and *Skifter*: A decedent will not be deemed to have incidents of ownership over an insurance policy that is held by a trust if: (i) the decedent's powers are held in a fiduciary capacity as trustee; (ii) the powers cannot be exercised for the decedent's personal benefit; (iii) the decedent did not transfer the policy to the trust; (iv) the decedent did not furnish the consideration for purchasing or maintaining the policy; and (v) the devolution of powers to the decedent was not part of a prearranged plan involving the decedent. [Rev. Rul. 84-179, 1984-2 C.B. 195]

(f) **Policy owned by controlled corporation:** [§532] For many years, the Service has taken the position that proceeds from insurance owned by a corporation that is solely owned by the insured are includible in the insured's estate since the insured indirectly possessed incidents of ownership through an ability to control the corporation. By reason of an amendment to the Regulations, the same result now obtains where the insured, although not sole owner, owns more than fifty percent of the stock of the corporation. [Treas. Reg. §20.2042-1(c)(2)]

f. **Assignment of incidents of ownership:** [§533] If the insured has made a complete and effective inter vivos gift of all ownership and beneficial interest in the insurance policy, retaining ***no incidents of ownership,*** the proceeds are normally not taxable in the estate.

(1) **Exception—where transfer testamentary in effect:** [§534] However, if the transfer has been made under circumstances that would result in its inclusion under sections 2035 through 2038 (*i.e.*, within three years of death (below), reserving a power to revoke the transfer, etc.), the insurance proceeds will be taxed as part of the decedent's estate. [Treas. Reg. §20.2042-1(a)(2); First Trust & Deposit Co. v. Shaughnessy, 134 F.2d 940 (2d Cir. 1943)]

(2) **Continued interaction of sections 2035 and 2041:** [§535] Note that despite the 1981 amendment, which limits the impact of section 2035 (gifts within three years of death), this section continues to interact with section 2041. (*See supra*, §§109, 115.)

(3) **Effect of decedent's payment of premiums:** [§536] If the decedent has divested himself of all incidents of ownership in the policy, his continued payment of premiums should not result in inclusion of the proceeds in his estate. Indeed, as discussed above, the 1954 Code specifically rejected the payment of premiums test.

(a) **Attempt to tax proceeds:** [§537] The Service formerly took the position that, regardless of when or why the policy itself was issued or transferred, premiums paid by the decedent within three years of death were "in contemplation of death," and a ***proportionate part of the proceeds*** was therefore taxable in his estate. [Rev. Rul. 67-463, 1967-2 C.B. 327] However, this position was litigated successfully by taxpayers in a series of cases [*see, e.g.*, First National Bank of Midland v. United States, 423 F.2d 1286 (5th Cir. 1970)], and the Service has since acquiesced in part [Rev. Rul. 71-497, 1971-2 C.B. 429; *but see* §539, below].

(b) **Taxation of premiums:** [§538] Under prior law, the Service continued to seek inclusion in the decedent's gross estate of the actual amount of ***premiums*** paid within three years of death. [Rev. Rul. 71-497, *supra*] It would appear that inclusion of these premiums is prevented by the 1981 amendments to section 2035. (*See supra*, §106.)

(4) **Assignment within three years of death:** [§539] Clearly, if the insured transfers incidents of ownership within three years of death, the proceeds will be taxed in his estate by reason of the interaction between sections 2035 and 2042. (*See supra*, §535.) Moreover, where premiums paid within three years of death constitute the only real "transfer" of economic benefits under the policy, the Service will contend that the entire proceeds are taxable. [Rev. Rul. 71-497, *supra*] This position has been sustained by the courts.

(a) **Example:** The deceased-insured had purchased annual accidental death policies (owned from their inception by his children), and paid each annual premium upon issuance of the policy. The proceeds of the policy in effect at his death were included in the decedent's estate. The court reasoned that "every stick in the bundle of rights constituting the policy" had been created by payment of the premium within three years of the insured's death, and hence it was an effective transfer of the policy within that three-year period. [Bel v. United States, 452 F.2d 683 (5th Cir. 1971)]

(b) **Example:** Similarly, where D, within three years of death, transferred funds to an irrevocable trust with directions to purchase insurance on his life (to be owned by the trust), the entire proceeds were taxable in D's estate, not merely the funds transferred to the trustee. The court's rationale was that the decedent had "beamed" the proceeds to his beneficiaries by the funds transferred within the three-year period. [Detroit Bank & Trust Co. v. United States, 467 F.2d 964

(6th Cir. 1972); *and see* Estate of Schnack v. Commissioner, 848 F.2d 933 (9th Cir. 1988), *quoting* First National Bank of Oregon v. United States, 488 F.2d 575 (9th Cir. 1973)—". . . there is only a formal difference between a decedent first buying a policy, then transferring it to the beneficiary, and the beneficiary purchasing the policy at the urging of the decedent and with the decedent's funds."]

(c) **Rejection of "constructive transfer doctrine" in recent cases:** Where the policy was issued to one other than the insured within three years of the insured's death, recent cases have refused to include the proceeds in the insured's estate even though the insured's funds were used to pay the premiums. [Estate of Leder v. Commissioner, 893 F.2d 237 (10th Cir. 1989); Estate of Headrich v. Commissioner, 93 T.C. 171 (1989)] The rationale of these courts is that the rejection of the "premium payments test" in the 1954 Code precludes inclusion under sections 2041 and 2035(d)(2) unless the policy itself was transferred by the insured within three years of death. (*See supra*, §497.)

(5) **Group term life insurance:** [§540] As noted above, if state law and the insurance contract permit assignment of all incidents of ownership in a group term life policy, and if, in fact, these incidents are assigned more than three years before the insured's death, the proceeds may be excluded from the insured's gross estate. However, since many group term contracts contemplate single year term arrangements which are renewed annually, there was concern that the Service might attack such assignments under the theory of the *Bel* case, *supra*. However, in 1982, the Service ruled that the proceeds of an annually ***renewable*** group term life insurance policy would not be includible in the gross estate of the deceased employee where the decedent had assigned the policy more than three years before death. [Rev. Rul. 82-13, 1982-1 C.B. 132]

g. **Amount includible:** [§541] In general, section 2042 taxes the entire value of the insurance proceeds. Thus, where the proceeds are payable in a lump sum, the lump sum amount is included in the insured's estate.

(1) **Deferred payments under settlement options:** [§542] If the proceeds are payable in installments, the taxable amount is the present fair market value of the installment obligation.

(2) **Payment of premiums by donee:** [§543] However, at least one case has held that where the insured assigns the policy to another within three years of death and the donee thereafter pays all the premiums, only that part of the proceeds proportionate to the premiums paid by the insured prior to the assignment is includible in his estate. In effect, a proportionate ***exclusion*** is allowed based on the premiums paid by the donee. [Silverman v. Commissioner, 61 T.C. 338 (1973)]

(a) **Rationale:** Since premiums were required to keep the face value of the policy intact and since the donee's continued payment of the premiums was a vital part of the consideration necessary to secure full payment on the insurance policy, proportionate exclusion of the proceeds is appropriate: "To hold otherwise would tax the estate on assets greater than that which the decedent transferred." [Silverman v. Commissioner, *supra*]

h. **Life insurance and community property states:** [§544] Where the insurance policy on a decedent's life is purchased with community property funds, it is treated as a community asset—*i.e.*, one in which each spouse is deemed to have an existing, one-half interest (*supra*, §431). And this is true even though the policy itself names the insured as the "sole owner"; the spouse's ownership rights arise by operation of law. [*See* Freedman v. United States, 382 F.2d 742 (5th Cir. 1967)]

(1) **Treatment if insured dies first:** [§545] One-half of the proceeds are taxable in the insured's estate under section 2042, since she is the owner of a one-half interest in the policy. The other half belongs to the surviving spouse as a matter of community property law—even though the insured has named someone else (*e.g.*, a trustee) as beneficiary under the policy. But, if the surviving spouse ***consents*** to payment of the insurance proceeds to the third party beneficiary, the surviving spouse is deemed to have made a ***taxable gift*** of his one-half interest in the proceeds. [Commissioner v. Chase Manhattan Bank, 259 F.2d 231 (5th Cir. 1958)]

(2) **Treatment if spouse dies first:** [§546] The spouse's one-half interest in insurance on the other spouse's life is "property owned by the decedent," taxable under section 2033. However, it is not one-half of the proceeds that would be taxed but, rather, one-half of the present value of the insurance (measured by its replacement cost). [United States v. Stewart, 270 F.2d 894 (9th Cir. 1959)]

(a) **What happens when insured subsequently dies?** [§547] All of the proceeds ***attributable to premiums paid by the insured*** are taxable. Thus, if 80 percent of the insurance premiums were paid with community funds while the uninsured spouse was still alive (40 percent attributable to each spouse), and 20 percent of the premiums are paid by the insured after the spouse's death, 60 percent of the proceeds are taxed in the insured's estate when she later dies. [Scott v. Commissioner, 374 F.2d 154 (9th Cir. 1967)]

(3) **Effect of inter vivos transfer of ownership:** [§548] Different results may follow where the insured has made a valid inter vivos transfer to her spouse of the insured's one-half interest in the insurance on her life (or if the policy had originally been applied for by the spouse, and the insured waived any interest therein).

(a) **On death of insured spouse:** [§549] Nothing is taxable in the insured's estate since she had no incidents of ownership, ***provided*** community funds are not thereafter used for premium payments.

(b) **If spouse predeceases insured:** [§550] Since the spouse owned the policy, the full replacement value of the policy would be included in her estate.

12. **Section 2043—Consideration:** [§551] The estate tax (and the gift tax) reaches ***gratuitous*** transfers only. Accordingly, transfers for "a full and adequate consideration in money or money's worth" are not taxed.

a. **Partial consideration:** [§552] Provision is made, however, for a transaction that is in part a sale and in part gratuitous—*i.e.*, "where property is transferred for less than an adequate and full consideration in money or money's worth, then the amount by which the value of the property exceeded the value of the consideration shall be deemed a gift. . . ." [I.R.C. §2043(a)]

b. **Measure of consideration—"money or money's worth":** [§553] For tax purposes, it is not enough that the consideration be adequate to support a binding contract. Rather, it must be measurable in terms of money or money's worth; *i.e.*, it must constitute the ***economic equivalent*** of the property transferred.

(1) **Examples:** An antenuptial agreement based upon a promise of marriage or upon the actual entering into of a marriage contract, or an agreement not to contest a decedent's will, may constitute adequate consideration for a binding contract. However, since such promises and the performances of such promises cannot be specifically reduced to economic terms, they do not constitute "money's worth" and thus will not insulate transfers pursuant to such contracts from the estate or gift taxes. [Latty v. Commissioner, 62 F.2d 952 (6th Cir. 1933)]

(2) **Rationale—depletion of the estate:** [§554] If the consideration received is the economic equivalent of the property transferred, there is no reduction in the transferor's net worth and thus no reduction of the estate that is subject to the transfer taxes; but where the economic equivalent is not received in exchange, the transferor's estate is depleted, and the transfer is treated as gratuitous in order to prevent avoidance of taxes.

(3) **Form of consideration:** [§555] It is not essential that the consideration be cash as long as it is measurable in economic terms. Thus, in addition to cash and property, services rendered to the transferor that can be translated into economic terms also constitute consideration "in money's worth."

c. **Consideration must move to the decedent:** [§556] It is also essential that the consideration take the form of a benefit to the transferor. Thus, a payment to another in consideration of the transfer, or an economic detriment suffered by the transferee in consideration of the transfer, will not prevent imposition of the transfer taxes.

(1) **Example:** In a leading case, X was the beneficiary of a trust established by her first husband but, under the terms of the trust, she would cease to be a beneficiary upon her remarriage. D proposed to marry X and, in order to

compensate for the economic loss that she would suffer upon marriage, he created a trust for her benefit. Although the Court agreed that the consideration for the transfer included an economic detriment suffered by the transferee (X) that was the economic equivalent of the property transferred, it held that the consideration was inadequate to prevent imposition of the transfer taxes—because the consideration did not move to the transferor. [Commissioner v. Wemyss, 324 U.S. 303 (1945)] Although *Wemyss* is a gift tax case, its theory is equally applicable to the estate tax.

(a) **Rationale:** The "depletion of the estate" theory is also applicable here. Even if the consideration can be expressed in "money or money's worth," unless it moves to the transferor, his estate is depleted by the transfer.

d. **"Business transaction exception":** [§557] Although the absence of donative intent is not critical to the determination of whether a transfer is immune from the transfer taxes, it is not within the legislative intent to impose the tax upon bad bargains. Accordingly, even though the consideration received by the transferor is not the economic equivalent of the property given up, if there is a ***bona fide business reason*** for such a transfer and ***no intent to make a gift***, the transfer is not subject to tax. [Treas. Reg. §25.2512.8—"A sale, exchange or other transfer of property made in the ordinary course of business (a transaction which is bona fide, at arm's length, and free from any donative intent), will be considered as made for an adequate and full consideration in money or money's worth"]

(1) **Example:** Thus, where D sold property for less than its fair market value in order to obtain funds to pay off a third person's debts which he had guaranteed, no part of the transfer was taxed. [McCoy v. Rasquin, 102 F.2d 434 (2d Cir. 1939)]

e. **Private annuities:** [§558] Application of the above rules may be examined in the context of so-called private annuities. Suppose that a parent (P), age 70, owns a piece of property worth $100,000 in which his income tax basis is only $10,000. If P sells the property during life, a $90,000 capital gain will be realized; but if he retains it until he dies it will be taxed as part of his gross estate. However, suppose P transfers the property to his child in return for the child's promise to pay a fixed sum annually for the rest of P's life (a "private annuity").

(1) **Effect—income tax:** [§559] For income tax purposes, the capital gain is deferred over the balance of the annuity. (*See* Income Tax I Summary.)

(2) **Effect—estate tax:** [§560] For estate tax purposes, the "private annuity" may be regarded as a bona fide transfer for consideration, so that the property is no longer taxable in P's estate upon his death. However, one must be cautious that the form of the annuity does not suggest a transfer with the reservation of a life estate; if the parent retains some "string" on the property (such as a mortgage to secure the promise to pay) and if the "annuity" payments are tied to the income produced by the property, the transfer might be included in the parent's gross estate under section 2036 (*see supra*, §175).

(3) **Effect—gift tax:** [§561] If the value of the property transferred exceeds the value of the annuity, the excess is subject to the gift tax. [Rev. Rul. 69-74, 1969-1 C.B. 43]

f. **Release of marital rights:** [§562] Section 2043(b)(1) expressly states that ". . . a relinquishment or promised relinquishment of dower or curtesy, or of a statutory estate in lieu of dower or curtesy, or of other marital rights in the decedent's property or estate, shall ***not*** be considered to any extent a consideration in 'money or money's worth.' " This is, of course, a logical corollary to section 2034, which includes in the decedent's estate the value of all interests possessed by the surviving spouse under laws relating to dower, curtesy, or a statutory forced share (*supra*, §§94 *et seq.*). Thus, section 2043(b) precludes decedents from circumventing section 2034 by contracting to transfer property in consideration of the spouse's release of marital rights.

(1) **Contrast support rights:** [§563] However, it has been held that the "other marital rights" under section 2043(b) refer only to post-death rights in the decedent's estate that are analogous to dower, curtesy, or statutory forced shares. Accordingly, the release of a spouse's right to be ***supported*** by the other spouse may be deemed adequate consideration for transfer tax purposes. [Rev. Rul. 68-379, 1968-2 C.B. 414]

(a) **Comment:** Of course, whether or not a spouse's support rights can effectively be released during life may be questionable. And, even if such a release is possible, the valuation of such support rights may be troublesome; the taxpayer has the burden of proving the value of the consideration. [*See* United States v. Past, 347 F.2d 7 (9th Cir. 1965)]

(2) **Involuntary transfer:** [§564] Moreover, a transfer in discharge of marital rights that is part of a ***divorce settlement*** and is incorporated into the decree of divorce is not a taxable transfer. [Estate of Watson v. Commissioner, 20 T.C. 386 (1953); Harris v. Commissioner, 340 U.S. 106 (1950)—gift taxes] This rule has also been extended by statute to divorce settlements excluded from the gift tax under section 2516. [I.R.C. §2043(b)(2); *see infra*, §813]

(3) **Compare—community property:** [§565] The relinquishment or other disposition of community property is always sufficient consideration for a transfer of property of equivalent value, since each spouse has an existing, vested one-half interest in the community assets (*supra*, §431).

(4) **Transfers between other co-tenants:** [§566] Similarly, transfers of property between co-tenants (holding title as joint tenants or tenants in common) is a transfer for adequate consideration. [Sullivan's Estate v. Commissioner, 175 F.2d 657 (9th Cir. 1949)]

13. **Section 2044—Certain Marital Deduction Property:** [§567] The 1981 Revenue Act amended the estate and gift tax marital deduction provisions to allow that

the value of property in which the decedent's (or donor's) spouse was granted a life estate might, under certain circumstances, qualify for the marital deduction. (*See infra*, §§697 *et seq.*) Under general rules of the estate tax, this property would not be included in the spouse's estate upon death. (*See supra*, §68.) In order to prevent such property from being excluded from ***both*** spouse's estates—the transferor's because of the deduction and the donee's because of the operation of general estate tax rules—the Act introduced this section 2044, which requires, in effect, that property that qualifies for the marital deduction under the new allowance be included in the donee spouse's estate upon death. [I.R.C. §2044(a), (b)(1)] However, this special estate tax inclusion does not apply if the spouse disposed of the granted life estate before death under circumstances where a gift tax would attach under new section 2519—*i.e.*, where the property had already been exposed to the unified transfer taxes applicable to the spouse. [I.R.C. §2044(b)(2); *and see infra*, §758]

14. **Section 2045—Prior Interests:** [§568] This section provides, essentially, that an interest in property or powers with respect to property that result in inclusion of the property in the gross estate under the estate tax provisions (previously reviewed) will, except as otherwise specifically provided, produce that result without regard to when the particular transfer, interest, right, or power was made, created, exercised, etc.

    a. **Example—joint interests:** [§569] Thus, for example, a joint tenancy created prior to the first estate tax will be taxed in the estate of the first to die under section 2040(a) since that section contains no limitation regarding the date of the joint tenancy's creation. [*See* United States v. Jacobs, 306 U.S. 363 (1939)]

    b. **Compare—transfers with retained life estate:** [§570] However, where the decedent transferred property reserving a life estate prior to March 3, 1931, no estate tax will attach under section 2036 since that section is specifically limited to transfers made on or after March 3, 1931. [I.R.C. §2036(c)]

15. **Section 2046—Disclaimers:** [§571] A disclaimer or renunciation—*i.e.*, an unqualified refusal to accept a transfer of property—is not a "transfer" for estate or gift tax purposes, even though other persons may acquire an interest in the property as a result of the disclaimer. However, prior to 1977, the effectiveness of a disclaimer or renunciation depended on state law, and because state laws vary, this produced a lack of uniformity in the imposition of the transfer taxes.

    a. **Uniform rule under Tax Reform Act:** [§572] As part of the Tax Reform Act of 1976, Congress enacted section 2518, under the gift tax, which purports to establish a uniform rule as to when a disclaimer or renunciation will be effective for federal tax purposes (*i.e.*, when a disclaimer will not be treated as a "transfer"). Section 2045 incorporates the rule of section 2518 for estate tax purposes. Because the new federal disclaimer rule is closely related to certain substantive aspects of the gift tax, disclaimers are fully discussed in connection with the gift tax. (*See infra*, §§770 *et seq.*)

B. DEDUCTIONS

1. **Introductory Analysis:** [§573] Four deductions are allowed under the estate tax:

   (i) ***Certain expenses of and claims against the estate*** [I.R.C. §2053];

   (ii) ***Certain losses*** incurred during the period of administration [I.R.C. §2054];

   (iii) ***Certain transfers to charity*** [I.R.C. §2055]; and

   (iv) The ***marital deduction*** [I.R.C. §2056].

   Of these four deductions, the marital deduction is of principal importance in estate planning and is also the most complex.

2. **Section 2053—Expenses, Indebtedness, and Taxes:** [§574] A deduction is allowed for various types of expenses incurred or paid by the estate and for various types of claims against the estate, including debts and taxes owed by the decedent. Specifically, subsection (a) lists four categories of deductible items: (i) ***funeral*** expenses; (ii) ***administration*** expenses; (iii) ***claims against the estate;*** and (iv) "***unpaid mortgages*** on, or any indebtedness in respect of, property where the value of the deceased's interest therein, undiminished by such mortgage or indebtedness, is included in the value of the gross estate. . . ."

   a. **Expenses of administering nonprobate assets:** [§575] A further deduction is authorized under subsection (b) of section 2053 for expenses related to the administration of property that is not part of the decedent's probate estate but which is included in the gross estate for federal estate tax purposes—*i.e.*, property taxable under sections 2035 through 2042.

      (1) **Scope of deduction:** [§576] These expenses are deductible "to the same extent that such expenses would be allowable as a deduction . . . if such property were [administered as part of the probate estate]. . . ." Thus, the nature of the deductible expenses must be similar to those allowable under subsection (a)—*i.e.*, those occasioned by the decedent's death and incurred in settling the decedent's interest in the property or vesting good title to the property in the beneficiaries. [Treas. Reg. §20.2053-8(b)]

         (a) **And note:** The rules relating to deductions of, *e.g.*, executor's and attorney's fees and miscellaneous administration expenses "are applied in determining the extent to which trustee's commissions, attorney's and accountant's fees and miscellaneous administration fees are allowed in connection with the administration of property [outside the probate estate]." [Treas. Reg. §20.2053-8(c)]

      (2) **Time limitation:** [§577] However, such expenses are only deductible if paid before expiration of the statute of limitations relating to the estate tax return, normally three years after the date upon which the return is filed. [I.R.C. §2053(b)]

b. **Funeral expenses:** [§578] Such expenses include the amounts actually spent to inter (or cremate) the deceased, as well as reasonable amounts paid for a tombstone, monument or mausoleum, or for a burial lot (for the decedent or the family), and reasonable expenditures for future care of the lot. Also included is the cost of transporting the body to the place of burial. [Treas. Reg. §20.2053-2]

(1) **Limited to amounts actually expended:** [§579] Unlike the deduction for administration expenses, where reasonable estimates of such expenses are deductible (*see* below), the deduction for funeral expenses is limited to amounts ***actually paid*** before the estate tax return is filed. [Treas. Reg. §20.2053-2]

(2) **Limitation under community property law:** [§580] If the community property law of the state imposes a charge for funeral expenses upon the entire community, not merely the property interests of the decedent, only one-half of the funeral expenses are deductible. [Rev. Rul. 70-156, 1970-1 C.B. 190; Rev. Rul. 71-168, 1971-1 C.B. 271]

c. **Administration expenses:** [§581] This deduction is limited to expenses that are ***actually and necessarily incurred*** in the administration of the decedent's estate (*i.e.*, in the collection of assets, payment of debts, and distribution of property to the persons entitled thereto). [Treas. Reg. §20.2053-3(a)] The Regulations divide administration expenses into: (i) executor's commissions; (ii) attorney's fees; and (iii) miscellaneous expenses.

(1) **Executor's commissions:** [§582] Executor's fees may be deducted if they have been paid or it is expected that they will be paid but no deduction may be taken if commissions are not anticipated. [Treas. Reg. §20.2053-3(b)(1)]

(a) **Limited to estate administration:** [§583] The deduction only extends to fees relating to administration of the decedent's ***estate***; it cannot be taken for fees associated with services that are in the nature of trust administration.

1) **Note:** Fees of a trustee under a revocable inter vivos trust that relate to services normally performed by an executor (collection of assets, payments of debts and distribution to beneficiaries) are deductible. [Commissioner v. Bronson, 32 F.2d 112 (8th Cir. 1929)] But a testamentary trustee's fees relating to trust investment and administration are not deductible; and this limitation also extends to situations where the decedent's executor unduly deferred distribution of the estate and undertook to perform services in the nature of a trustee's duties.

2) **And note:** Likewise, expenses incurred for the benefit of heirs or legatees that are not essential to the proper settlement of the estate are not deductible as administration expenses. [Treas. Reg. §20.2053-3(b)(1)]

(b) **Reasonable estimates allowed:** [§584] Administration of the estate will normally extend beyond the time at which the estate tax return must be filed (nine months after decedent's death). To accommodate for this, the Regulations allow a deduction for a reasonable estimate of the fees to be paid the executor. [Treas. Reg. §20.2053-3(b)(1)]

(2) **Attorney's fees:** [§585] Attorney's fees relating to legal counsel to the executor, the collection or settlement of claims against the estate, and litigation expenses, including litigating estate tax deficiencies, are deductible. However, legal services incurred in protecting the interests of a particular beneficiary, rather than for the benefit of the estate as a whole, are not deductible. And, again, reasonable estimates of attorney's fees that will be paid are deductible. [Treas. Reg. §20.2053-3(c)]

(3) **Miscellaneous expenses of administration:** [§586] In addition to executor's commissions and attorney's fees, various other administration costs are deductible—*e.g.*, court costs, accountant's fees, appraiser's fees, costs of storing or maintaining the property of the estate, and the cost of selling estate assets where such sales are necessary for payment of debts, etc., or for the orderly distribution of the estate. [Treas. Reg. §20.2053-3(d)]

d. **Claims against the estate:** [§587] Debts and other claims asserted against the estate are deductible if they represent personal obligations of the decedent that existed at the time of death. [Treas. Reg. §20.2053-4]

(1) **Must be legally enforceable:** [§588] However, no deduction is allowed unless the claim was legally enforceable against the decedent ***and*** is legally enforceable against the decedent's estate. Thus, for example, claims on which the statute of limitations has run cannot be deducted, nor can claims that are filed with the executor after the time allowed by state law. [Treas. Reg. §20.2053-4; *but cf.* Russell v. United States, 260 F. Supp. 493 (N.D. Ill. 1966)—allowing deduction for a claim filed and paid after the nonclaim period; *and see* Rev. Rul. 75-24, 1975-1 C.B. 306—allowing deduction of an unfiled claim settled with the consent of all beneficiaries]

(2) **Liabilities created by law:** [§589] Claims arising as a result of the decedent's torts, court ordered support claims, certain tax claims, etc., are deductible. [*See* Harris v. Commissioner, 340 U.S. 106 (1950)]

(3) **Contingent claims:** [§590] No deduction is allowed if it appears that the claim may never be paid by the decedent's estate. Thus, claims on which the decedent was only secondarily or contingently liable (*e.g.*, as a guarantor) are not deductible unless it is shown that the person primarily liable has defaulted so that the decedent's liability has become fixed and immediate. [DuVal's Estate v. Commissioner, 152 F.2d 103 (9th Cir. 1945)]

(4) **Tax claims:** [§591] The decedent's liability for income taxes, gift taxes, and property taxes, etc., that accrued prior to death are deductible as claims against the estate. [Treas. Reg. §20.2053-6]

(a) **Compare—taxes accruing after death:** [§592] However, taxes that accrue after the decedent's death cannot be deducted. [I.R.C. §2053(c)(1)(B)] Accordingly, estate or inheritance taxes are generally not deductible since they accrue ***at*** the decedent's death, and not ***before.***

(b) **Special rule for certain death taxes:** [§593] Section 2053(d) allows the executor to elect to deduct certain state death taxes imposed upon charitable transfers and foreign death taxes imposed upon property that is also included in the decedent's gross estate for federal estate tax purposes. However, if such an election is made, the estate must forego the credit allowed for these taxes. [*See* I.R.C. §§2011, 2014]

(5) **Contractual claims:** [§594] If the claim is "founded on a promise or agreement" (*i.e.*, a contractual claim), it must be supported by "adequate and full consideration in money or money's worth." [I.R.C. §2053(c)(1)(A)]

(a) **Rationale:** Otherwise, the decedent could diminish the taxable estate by creating "obligations" against herself as gifts.

(b) **Marital rights as consideration:** [§595] For this purpose, the relinquishment of marital rights is ***not*** deemed a consideration "in money or money's worth." [I.R.C. §2053(e)] The rationale for this limitation is similar to that of section 2043(b), which generally denies that the release of marital rights is sufficient consideration to immunize a transfer from the transfer taxes (*supra*, §562).

(c) **Special exception for charitable pledges:** [§596] However, the decedent's promise or agreement to make a charitable contribution is deductible as a claim despite the fact that the pledge was gratuitous, but only to the extent that a bequest to the charity would be allowed as a charitable deduction under section 2055 (*infra*, §§612 *et seq.*). [I.R.C. §2053(c)(1)(A)]

(6) **Community debts:** [§597] Since only the decedent's half of community property assets are taxable in his gross estate, only half of the community debts are deductible.

e. **Unpaid mortgages:** [§598] The amount of any mortgage, trust deed, or other lien against property included in the decedent's gross estate is deductible if the full value of the property, unreduced by the amount of the lien, is included in the decedent's estate. [I.R.C. §2053(a)(4)]

(1) **Application—decedent personally liable:** [§599] If the decedent is personally liable on the mortgage note, etc., the full value of the property is includible in his estate, and then a deduction is allowed under section 2053. [Treas. Reg. §20.2053-7] Consequently, the estate can deduct the full amount of the liability even though it might exceed the value of the encumbered property.

(2) **Application—decedent not personally liable:** [§600] In contrast, where the decedent is not personally liable on the mortgage, only the ***net value*** of the property (value less amount of encumbrance) is included in the decedent's estate and, hence, no deduction is allowed. [Treas. Reg. §20.2053-7] Thus, if the encumbrance exceeded the value of the property, nothing would be includible or deductible.

f. **Special limitations on deductions:** [§601] In addition to the limitations relating to specific types of expenses (above), the statute imposes three special limitations:

(1) **Allowable under local law:** [§602] Claims and expenses related to the probate assets are deductible only if they are "allowable by the laws of the jurisdiction . . . under which the estate is being administered." [I.R.C. §2053(a)]

(a) **Determination of when allowable:** [§603] State law governs whether a particular claim or expense is "allowable." [Treas. Reg. §20.2053-1(a)(1)] However, the fact that the state probate court allows (or disallows) a particular claim or item of expense is not necessarily dispositive. Rather, under the rule of *Commissioner v. Estate of Bosch* (*supra,* §91), the federal courts, in resolving the estate tax issue, are not bound by lower state court decisions but may ***independently*** determine whether or not a claim is allowable under the governing state law. [*See* First National Bank v. United States, 422 F.2d 1385 (10th Cir. 1970)]

(b) **Nonprobate assets:** [§604] This limitation is not reiterated as to expenses relating to nonprobate assets. [*See* I.R.C. §2053(b)] However, since such deductible expenses must be of a nature similar to those expenses that are allowed as deductions to the probate estate, it can be inferred that they must also be allowable under state law. [*See* Rev. Rul. 68-611, 1968-2 C.B. 410]

(2) **Insolvent estate:** [§605] Generally, expenses and claims against the decedent's probate estate are deductible only to the extent of the value of the assets in the probate estate. If such expenses and claims exceed the value of the probate assets, the excess may be deducted (and the deduction applied against the value of the non-probate assets included in the decedent's gross estate) ***only if*** these excess claims are actually paid before the date for filing of the estate tax return. [I.R.C. §2053(c)(2); Treas. Reg. §20.2053-1(c)] Expenses and claims relating to non-probate assets (but which are included in the decedent's gross estate) are not subject to this limitation; such expenses and claims are deductible as long as they are paid before the statute of limitations for reassessment of tax expires. (*See supra,* §577.)

(3) **No double deductions:** [§606] Most administration expenses and claims deductible under section 2053 could also be taken as deductions on the estate's ***income tax return*** under section 212. However, both deductions are not

ordinarily allowed—the executor must ***elect*** whether to claim the deductions against the estate's income ***or*** against the gross estate. [I.R.C. §642(g)]

(a) **Exception—"income in respect of decedent":** [§607] However, if the gross estate includes "income in respect of a decedent" (*e.g.*, income earned prior to death but not payable until after the date of death), the expenses paid by the estate attributable to such income (*e.g.*, business expenses, interest, taxes, etc.) are allowable ***both*** as deductions for income tax purposes and as claims against the estate for estate tax purposes. [Treas. Reg. §1.642(g)-2]

(b) **Selling expenses:** [§608] Prior to 1976, expenses incurred in selling estate property were deductible under section 2053 even though they were also applied to offset the taxable gain realized upon the sale. The theory was that section 642(g) was limited, by its terms, to expenses that were ***"deductible"*** for both income and estate tax purposes, and did not extend to nondeductible capital expenditures even though such expenditures operated to reduce the amount of taxable gain realized. [Commissioner v. Estate of Bray, 46 T.C. 577 (1966), *aff'd*, 396 F.2d 452 (6th Cir. 1968)] However, the 1976 Tax Reform Act eliminated the opportunity for such a double "deduction." As amended, section 642(g) now requires that the executor elect to apply such expenses against the gross estate or against the taxable gain realized on the sale of the property.

3. **Section 2054—Deductions for Losses:** [§609] Although generally captioned "losses," the deduction under section 2053 is limited to ***casualty or theft losses*** that are ***not*** compensated for by insurance or otherwise.

   a. **No double deduction:** [§610] Such losses may be deductible against the estate's income tax return under section 165 as well as against the gross estate under section 2054. However, as with deductions for expenses and claims (above), the executor must elect whether to deduct casualty or theft losses against the estate's income ***or*** from the gross estate—again, double deductions are disallowed. [I.R.C. §642(g)]

   b. **Other losses:** [§611] Losses incurred upon the sale of property during the course of administration may be deducted (or may offset gains) for income tax purposes, but they are ***not*** deductible for estate tax purposes.

4. **Section 2055—The Charitable Deduction:** [§612] Section 2055 allows a deduction for the value of all property transferred by the decedent for specified public, religious, educational, or other charitable purposes.

   a. **Charitable object:** [§613] Note that not all inter vivos gifts or charitable bequests qualify: The gift must be to an organization operated ***exclusively*** for a ***recognized religious, scientific, literary, educational,*** or ***other charitable*** purpose. [I.R.C. §2055(a); *and see* Treas. Reg. §20.2055-1(a)]

b. **Property transferred inter vivos:** [§614] Deductions are available not only with respect to transfers under the decedent's will, but also for any inter vivos transfers made by the decedent to the extent that they are taxable in her gross estate. [*See* Treas. Reg. §20.2055-1(a)]

(1) **Example:** If D transferred a remainder interest in her personal residence to a charity, reserving a life estate, the value of the residence would be included in D's gross estate but that same amount would be allowed as a deduction under section 2055. The effect is to wash out any tax on inter vivos transfers to charity.

(2) **Special rules for powers of appointment:** [§615] Similarly, if the property is included in a decedent's gross estate under section 2041 (relating to powers of appointment), the appointment of the property to a charity is treated as a transfer and therefore qualifies for the charitable deduction. [I.R.C. §2055(b)]

c. **Limitations on deductible amount:** [§616] The amount of the deduction is limited to the value of the property that is transferred to the charity. [I.R.C. §2055(a)] Further, two special limitations apply:

(1) ***The amount of the deduction cannot exceed the value of the transferred property*** that is included in the decedent's gross estate. [I.R.C. §2055(b)]

(2) ***And, if the property transferred to the charity is burdened with an obligation to pay any death taxes*** imposed upon the decedent's estate, the charitable deduction will be reduced by the amount of such taxes, since the outstanding obligation also reduces the amount that actually passes to the charity. [I.R.C. §2055(c)]

(a) ***This reduction of the deductible amount may operate to increase the amount of death taxes,*** certainly federal estate taxes and possibly state inheritance taxes. And, to the extent that the increased death taxes burden the charitable bequest, the deduction is further reduced, with a further increase in death taxes, and so on, and so on!

d. **Split interest gifts:** [§617] Interests in the same property may be given to both a charitable and noncharitable object ("split interest gifts"), *e.g.*, a life interest to an individual with the remainder to a charity ("charitable remainder gifts") or a term of years to a charity followed by a remainder to an individual ("charitable lead gifts"). In either case, the charitable deduction is generally limited to the value of the interest actually transferred to the charity. [I.R.C. §2055(a)]

(1) **Prior law:** [§618] Prior to the Tax Reform Act of 1969, a deduction was allowed for the value of the remainder interest (or lead interest) as long as the gift was ***unconditional*** and ***certain to vest*** sometime. If these factors were established, the amount of the gift was deemed ascertainable. [Treas. Reg. §20.2055-2(a)]

(a) **Power to invade:** [§619] However, if a trustee of a charitable remainder trust had the power to invade or distribute corpus to the individual income beneficiary, the charitable deduction was disallowed (the amount of the charitable remainder deemed unascertainable), ***unless*** the power was limited by an external standard ***and*** the possibility of its exercise was minimal. [Treas. Reg. §20.2055-2(b); Ithaca Trust Co. v. United States, 279 U.S. 151 (1929)]

(b) **Conditional gift:** [§620] And, if the charitable remainder was subject to any contingency, the deduction was disallowed unless the contingency was "so remote as to be negligible." [Treas. Reg. §20.2055-2(b); Commissioner v. Estate of Sternberger, 348 U.S. 187 (1955); Rev. Rul. 59-143, 1959-1 C.B. 243]

(2) **Present law:** [§621] Under the Tax Reform Act of 1969, charitable remainder or charitable lead gifts are deductible only if the split interest gift is made in certain designated forms:

(a) **Form required:** [§622] The statute requires that the gift be in the form of an ***"annuity trust,"*** a ***"unitrust,"*** or a ***"pooled income fund."*** [I.R.C. §2055(e)]

1) **Annuity trust:** [§623] This is a trust in which the trustee is required to distribute annually to the noncharitable beneficiary a specified sum that is at least five percent of the original value of the trust assets. [I.R.C. §664(d)]

2) **Unitrusts:** [§624] Under a "unitrust," the trustee must distribute annually a sum that is either a fixed percentage (at least five percent) of the trust estate (determined annually) or the entire trust income, whichever is less. [I.R.C. §664(d)]

3) **Pooled income fund:** [§625] This is a trust where a public charity is trustee, and several donors contribute property to the trust, each reserving for himself or herself a life estate in a proportionate share of the combined property. The public charity must have an irrevocable remainder. [I.R.C. §642(c)]

(b) **Limitations:** [§626] Even if an annuity trust or unitrust otherwise qualifies, no deduction is allowed if another, noncharitable remainder precedes the charitable remainder; or the income interest is for a term of years (rather than a life estate), and the term exceeds twenty years. [I.R.C. §664(d)]

(c) **Exceptions:** [§627] The special forms required by the 1969 Act do not apply to certain split interest gifts. [I.R.C. §§2055(e)(2), 170(f)(3)(B)] The principal types of split interests excepted are:

1) ***An undivided interest in the property***—*e.g.*, a tenancy in common;

2) ***A remainder interest in a personal residence*** or a farm following a ***legal life estate***.

5. **Section 2056—The Marital Deduction:** [§628] A deduction is also allowed for property that passes to the surviving spouse upon the decedent's death. Formerly, the maximum allowable deduction was fifty percent of the adjusted gross estate; however, with passage of the 1981 Revenue Act a deduction is allowed for ***all property*** passing to the spouse—*i.e.*, a 100 percent deduction.

a. **Background:** [§629] Prior to the allowance of the marital deduction, decedents' estates in community property jurisdictions enjoyed a singular advantage: Since one-half of the property was already "vested" in the surviving spouse, only the decedent's half was taxable on death (*supra,* §431). The marital deduction was enacted in 1948 for the purpose of securing approximately equal estate tax treatment of decedents' estates in community property and non-community property jurisdictions.

(1) **Impact on substantive requirements:** [§630] This focus upon equalizing the treatment of residents of common law and community property states shaped the substantive requirements of the deduction.

(a) **Quantitative limitation:** [§631] Since one-half of the community property was effectively excluded from the gross estate of a community property state resident decedent, a ***quantitative*** limitation (fifty percent of the adjusted gross estate) was imposed upon the amount of separate property that could be "excluded" from tax by means of the marital deduction. Also, since community property enjoyed this "exclusion" ipso facto, the one-half of community property that ***was*** included in the decedent's estate could not be taken into account in determining the fifty percent ceiling.

(b) **Qualitative limitation:** [§632] Since the one-half interest in community property owned by the surviving spouse was owned outright, and this would be includible in her estate when the survivor died, the Code provided a ***qualitative*** limitation on the type of interests that would qualify for the deduction. Essentially it was required that in order to be deductible to the decedent, the interest passing to the survivor must be of a type that was potentially includible in the survivor's estate upon her death.

(2) **Should marital transfers be taxed at all?** [§633] In a very real sense, transfers of property between spouses represent little more than a shifting of marital wealth within a single community of economic interest. Thus, whether such transfers should be taxed at all is an important policy question.

(a) **Comment:** As noted above, this question was not a paramount consideration in the 1948 allowance of the marital deduction; rather, parity between common law and community property jurisdictions was the primary concern.

(b) **Compare—1981 Act:** Over the years, however, the policy question was addressed by commentators and "law reform" groups, and occasionally by committees of Congress. It received a generally sympathetic hearing in connection with the formulation of the Tax Reform Act of 1976, but a full 100 percent deduction did not emerge in that Act because of concern with anticipated revenue losses it would occasion. However, the substantial tax reductions proposed (and enacted) in the 1981 Act persuaded Congress to answer the policy question in the affirmative, despite the (relatively insignificant) revenue loss that the 100 percent marital deduction would produce.

b. **General scope of the deduction:** [§634] Section 2056(a) allows a deduction in an "amount equal to the value of any interest in property which passes or has passed from the decedent to his surviving spouse. . . ."

(1) **Value of property passing to surviving spouse:** [§635] The marital deduction is limited to the ***net*** value of the property interests passing to the surviving spouse.

(a) **Encumbrances:** [§636] Thus, if the property bequeathed to the surviving spouse is subject to a mortgage or other encumbrance that is not released by a payment from the estate, the value of the property for purposes of the marital deduction is reduced by the amount of the encumbrance. [I.R.C. §2056(b)(4)(B)]

(b) **Death taxes:** [§637] Similarly, the value of the interest passing to the surviving spouse must be reduced by any federal estate or other death taxes payable by the spouse or payable out of the interest passing to her. [I.R.C. §2056(b)(4)(A)]

1) **Note:** If the marital portion is reduced by death taxes, a circular computation may result: The maximum marital deduction that was used to compute the federal estate taxes in the first instance is reduced by those taxes; the reduction of the marital deduction then increases the estate taxes payable which, in turn, reduces the amount of the marital deduction—and so forth.

(c) **Conditional bequests:** [§638] Moreover, the marital deduction is limited to property that the surviving spouse receives ***unconditionally.*** Consequently, if the decedent's will requires the surviving spouse to relinquish some right or property in order to take under the will, only the excess of the value of the property received under the will over what the spouse was required to relinquish is deductible. [United States v. Stapf, 375 U.S. 118 (1963)]

(2) **Maximum allowed:** [§639] As noted above, there is no longer any quantitative limitation upon the marital deductions. The value of ***all*** property passing to the surviving spouse is deductible—as long as it meets the ***qualitative*** requirements. (*See* below, §§641 *et seq.*)

(3) **Effect of community property:** [§640] Nor is there any further differential treatment of community property for purposes of the marital deduction. A bequest of a decedent's one-half interest in community property to the surviving spouse qualifies for the marital deduction to the same extent as a bequest of separate property.

c. **Overview of requirements for marital deductions:** [§641] There are five basic requirements for allowance of the marital deduction.

(1) **Citizens and residents only:** [§642] The decedent must have been a citizen or resident of the United States. This derives from the fact that the marital deduction only applies to taxes imposed under section 2001—*i.e.*, the estate tax imposed upon citizens or residents. [I.R.C. §2056(a)]

(2) **Inclusion in gross estate:** [§643] The property passing to the surviving spouse must have been included in the decedent's gross estate. [I.R.C. §2056(a)] This is a logical limitation: The estate should not receive a deduction with respect to a transfer of property that was never subject to the estate tax in the first place.

(3) **Surviving spouse:** [§644] The decedent must have been married at the time of death, and the spouse must survive the decedent.

(a) **"Spouse":** [§645] Whether the recipient was in fact the decedent's spouse is determined by state law. [Rev. Rul. 67-442, 1967-2 C.B. 65]

(b) **"Survived":** [§646] And, in determining whether the spouse survived the decedent, the presumptions (or reversal of the presumptions) under the Uniform Simultaneous Death Act are taken into account. [Treas. Reg. §20.2056(e)-2(e)]

(4) **Passing requirement:** [§647] An interest in property must have "passed" from the decedent to the surviving spouse—by will, by operation of law, or otherwise (*see* below).

(5) **The interest must be a "deductible interest":** [§648] Discussed in detail below.

d. **Requirement of property "passing" to surviving spouse:** [§649] The marital deduction is ***not*** limited to property passing from the decedent to the surviving spouse by way of will or intestacy. Rather, the "passing" requirement includes just about all situations where the surviving spouse acquired property from the decedent to the extent such property is included in the decedent's gross estate. [I.R.C. §2056(c)]

(1) **Marital shares:** [§650] Thus, interests acquired as dower, curtesy, or a statutory forced share are deemed to "pass" from the decedent to the surviving spouse. [I.R.C. §2056(c)(3)] (However, in order to be deductible, the interest must also be a "deductible interest"; *see infra,* §675.)

(2) **Inter vivos transfers:** [§651] Also, inter vivos transfers made to a spouse and which are includible under sections 2035 through 2038 (reserved life estates, etc.) "pass" to the surviving spouse for purposes of the marital deduction. [I.R.C. §2056(c)(4)]

(a) **Other includible interests:** Likewise, joint interests, appointed property, and life insurance received by the surviving spouse are deductible if and to the extent they are included in the decedent's gross estate. [I.R.C. §§2056(c)(5)-(7); *and see* I.R.C. §§2039-2042]

(3) **Will contest:** [§652] Moreover, any interest that a surviving spouse receives pursuant to a settlement or compromise of a will contest "passes" to that spouse, provided that such settlement resulted from a "bona fide recognition of enforceable rights of the surviving spouse in the decedent's estate." [Treas. Reg. §20.2056(e)-2(d)(2); *and see* Estate of Brandon v. Commissioner, 91 T.C. 829 (1988)]

(4) **Effect of disclaimers:** [§653] Under prior law, if within nine months of the decedent's death any other beneficiary disclaimed an interest in the decedent's estate and the surviving spouse became entitled to that interest (under the decedent's will or by intestacy), such an interest was deemed to "pass" to the surviving spouse. On the other hand, property disclaimed ***by the surviving spouse*** did ***not*** "pass" to that spouse. The subsection of section 2056 that specified this rule was repealed by the 1976 Act. However, it appears that the disclaimer rules of section 2518 (incorporated in the estate tax by section 2046) secure the same results. (*See supra,* §571, *and infra,* §770.)

e. **The interest must be a "deductible" interest:** [§654] Only ***deductible*** interests that pass to the surviving spouse qualify for the marital deduction. In general, there are four types of ***nondeductible*** interests:

(1) **Interest not included in gross estate:** [§655] As noted above, the deduction is limited to interests that are subject to tax in the decedent's gross estate. Thus, *e.g.,* property received by the surviving spouse upon exercise of a nontaxable, special power of appointment does not qualify for the marital deduction.

(2) **Interests deductible under section 2053:** [§656] Interests passing to the surviving spouse but which are properly deductible under section 2053 (*supra*) may not also be taken as a marital deduction. For example, payments from the estate in satisfaction of a bona fide loan that the spouse had made to the decedent, or fees the spouse receives for services as executor of the decedent's estate, are only deductible under section 2053. [Treas. Reg. §20.2056(a)-2(d)(2)]

(3) **Losses:** [§657] Similarly, if property passing to a surviving spouse is subject to a casualty or theft loss during the course of administration, the value of that property does not qualify for the marital deduction to the extent that a deduction for the loss was claimed under section 2054. [Treas. Reg. §20.2056(a)-2(b)(3)]

(4) **Nondeductible terminable interests:** [§658] The disallowance of any deduction for certain "terminable interests" is one of the principal and most complex limitations on the marital deduction and is discussed in detail below.

f. **The "nondeductible terminable interest" rule:** [§659] No deduction is allowed for certain "terminable interests" that pass to the surviving spouse, *i.e.*, interests that will terminate or fail upon lapse of time or the happening of some event. [I.R.C. §2056(b)]

(1) **Rationale:** In community property states, the surviving spouse's share of the community assets passes to her in fee (*i.e.*, absolutely) and will ordinarily be taxable in her estate when she dies (*see supra*, §431). Since the marital deduction was designed to approximate the estate tax treatment between spouses in community property and common law jurisdictions, it was deemed inappropriate to allow the deduction for interests that would be extinguished prior to or upon the death of the surviving spouse and thus would not be taxed in that spouse's estate. (*See supra*, §630.) In other words, to allow a deduction for a terminable interest would permit complete estate tax avoidance (*i.e.*, the interest would neither be taxed in the decedent's estate nor in the surviving spouse's estate), and this was not the purpose of the marital deduction. Nor is it presently the purpose of the marital deduction, despite the 100 percent deduction of the 1981 Act; while transfers within the marital community are freed of tax, succession from the marital community is the proper subject of the tax.

(2) **What is a "terminable interest"?** [§660] The statute defines a terminable interest as one where "on the lapse of time, on the occurrence of an event or contingency, or on the failure of an event or contingency to occur, an interest passing to the surviving spouse will terminate or fail. . . ." [I.R.C. §2056(b)(1)] Examples include a life estate, a term for years, or a defeasible fee.

(3) **Caution—not all terminable interests are nondeductible:** [§661] It is important to keep in mind that a terminable interest is only outside the scope of the marital deduction if it is ***nondeductible***. Two types of terminable interests that are nondeductible are specified in the Code:

(a) **Interests passing to third party:** [§662] The first type of nondeductible terminable interest is one in which an interest in the same property in which the terminable interest passed to the surviving spouse also passes or has passed (for less than an adequate and full consideration in money or money's worth) from the decedent to a person other than the surviving spouse (or the estate of such spouse)—if such third person may possess or enjoy the property ***after*** the surviving spouse's interest terminates. [I.R.C. §2056(b)(1)(A),(B)]

1) **Example:** D bequeaths Blackacre "to A (my wife) for life, remainder to my children." Such a bequest meets each of the conditions for nondeductible terminable interests: A's interest terminates at her death, after which D's children will enjoy the property by virtue of the interest that they were given by D.

(b) **Executor required to acquire terminable interests:** [§663] Secondly, a terminable interest that the decedent has directed his executor or trustee to purchase for the surviving spouse will not qualify for the marital deduction—*e.g.*, D directs his executor to use a certain amount of property from the estate to purchase an annuity for the life of the surviving spouse. [Treas. Reg. §20.2056(b)-1(g), Example (7)]

(c) **Application**

1) **Contingent gifts:** [§664] A bequest to a surviving spouse that will terminate upon her death or remarriage (with a gift over to a third party) is a nondeductible terminable interest. [Estate of Cunha v. Commissioner, 279 F.2d 292 (9th Cir. 1960)] Similarly, a bequest to the surviving spouse upon a condition precedent that she survive some designated event is a nondeductible terminable interest. [United States v. Mappes, 318 F.2d 508 (10th Cir. 1963)] But note the "survivorship exception," *infra,* §676.

2) **Contractual wills:** [§665] Where the spouses had an agreement that all property was to go to the surviving spouse and then to their children, the survivor is treated as if she acquired a life estate, with remainder to the children. In other words, even though the bequest to the surviving spouse is outright in form, if she is bound by an agreement to pass ownership to the children, the marital deduction cannot be taken when the first spouse dies.

a) Similarly, ***joint and mutual wills*** (contractual in nature) pass nondeductible terminable interests to the survivor. [Estate of Siegel v. Commissioner, 67 T.C. 662 (1977)] However, to the extent that property passes to the survivor ***outside*** a joint and mutual will (*e.g.*, property held in joint tenancy), a marital deduction may be allowed. [Awtry v. Commissioner, 221 F.2d 749 (8th Cir. 1955)]

3) **Dower and curtesy, etc.:** [§666] Similarly, the surviving spouse might receive a nondeductible terminable interest under laws relating to dower, curtesy, or a statutory forced share. In such cases, no deduction is allowed. For example, under common law dower, the surviving widow is entitled to a life estate in one-third of the real property owned by her deceased husband; the life estate is a nondeductible terminable interest and does not qualify for the marital deduction. [Treas. Reg. §20.2056(e)-2(c)]

(d) **Limitation—nature of the interest actually received governs:** [§667] The issue of deductibility turns on the nature of the interest ***actually acquired*** by the surviving spouse, not that which could have been acquired. For example, if the surviving spouse was left an outright bequest but elected to take common law dower, no marital deduction would be allowed (above). Conversely, if the surviving spouse was bequeathed a life estate, but elected to renounce the will and take a statutory forced share in one-third of the estate's assets (outright), a marital deduction would be available.

1) **And note:** Further, where state law provides for common law dower but also affords the surviving spouse an election to take ***"commuted dower"***—*i.e.*, a cash amount equal to the value of a life estate in one-third of the realty—the cash received outright under such an election qualifies for the marital deduction. [United States v. Hiles, 318 F.2d 56 (5th Cir. 1963); Rev. Rul. 72-7, 1972-1 C.B. 308]

(e) **Special rules for support allowances:** [§668] Practically every state has provision in its probate law for payment of a support allowance to a widow or widower out of the deceased spouse's probate estate. Whether the money so paid qualifies for the marital deduction depends upon the nature of the allowance:

1) ***The time for determining whether such payments are "terminable"*** is the date of the decedent's death—not the date when the allowance is ordered by the probate court. [Jackson v. United States, 376 U.S. 503 (1964)]

2) ***If local law provides the surviving spouse a fixed and indefeasible right*** to a specific sum of money or a fixed percentage of the decedent's estate for support during the period of probate administration, the payments will qualify for the marital deduction.

3) ***However, if (as is far more typical) the spouse has no vested rights*** to such payments at the time of the decedent's death

but merely acquires a right to payments if and when ordered by the probate court, the payments are deemed terminable on the theory that the survivor would get no allowance if she died or remarried before it is granted. [Jackson v. United States, *supra*]

a) *But note:* Two cases have held that the fact the surviving spouse must petition the court for the allowance will not preclude the marital deduction. [Estate of Green v. United States, 441 F.2d 303 (6th Cir. 1971); Estate of Watson v. Commissioner, 94 T.C. 262 (1990)] "To hold that an interest is terminable only because legal procedures are invoked to enforce an interest which is otherwise vested at the date of the husband's death, is to hold that all elective rights, such as the widow's allowance and the statutory interest in lieu of dower, are disqualified as marital deductions." [Watson *quoting* Green]

4) ***If the allowance is for an indefinite period*** (no fixed amount) ***or is dependent upon the spouse surviving*** throughout the period of allowance, it is also a terminable interest and does not qualify for the deduction. [Estate of Cunha v. Commissioner, *supra*, §664]

(f) **Interest in unidentified assets:** [§669] The terminable interest rule applies not only to nondeductible interests passing directly to a surviving spouse, but also where the estate contains a terminable interest that could be used to satisfy the marital bequest (*e.g.*, W bequeaths H one-third of the residue of her estate and the residue contains a terminable interest). Moreover, this is true whether or not the executor in fact distributes the terminable interest to the surviving spouse. In such cases, the amount of the marital deduction is reduced by the full value of the nondeductible terminable interest that could be so used. [I.R.C. §2056(b)(2)]

(g) **Compare—deductible terminable interests:** [§670] In contrast, a number of interests, although technically terminable, are deductible—*i.e.*, outside the two classes of nondeductible terminable interests discussed above:

1) **Wasting assets:** [§671] For example, a bequest of an automobile to the surviving spouse would qualify for the marital deduction even though the auto is likely to become valueless after a few years; no other person acquires an interest in the property.

2) **Property with limited life:** [§672] Similarly, a bequest, *e.g.*, of a patent, which will expire after a certain period of time, is deductible.

3) **Bonds, notes, etc.:** [§673] Moreover, the statute specifically provides that an interest shall not be considered terminable merely because it is the ownership of a bond, note, or similar contractual obligation, the discharge of which would not have the effect of an annuity for life or for a term. [I.R.C. §2056(b)(1)]

4) **Estate trusts:** [§674] An estate trust is one in which the surviving spouse is made sole beneficiary during life with the corpus to be distributed to that spouse's estate upon death. Since no one other than the surviving spouse or his estate acquires an interest in the property passing from the decedent, the interest passing to the surviving spouse is deductible.

g. **Exceptions to the "terminable interest" rule:** [§675] There are five situations in which an interest although technically classifiable as a "nondeductible terminable interest" will nonetheless qualify for the marital deduction:

(1) **Survivorship exception:** [§676] As noted above, bequests to a spouse conditioned upon surviving a period of time after the death of the decedent or surviving some event that would occur after the death of the decedent are nondeductible terminable interests. However, the Code recognizes a limited exception where the condition is restricted to surviving the decedent for a period of not more than ***six months*** ("to A, provided she survives for five months after my death"), ***or*** not dying from a ***common disaster*** ("provided that she does not perish in the same disaster in which I lose my life"). Where these limited contingencies are used, the interest granted to the survivor is deductible—provided, of course, that the surviving spouse in fact outlives the prescribed period, or does not perish as a result of such common disaster. [I.R.C. §2056(b)(3)]

(a) **Contingency must necessarily occur within six months:** [§677] It is not enough that the event upon which survivorship is conditioned (other than death by common disaster) might ***possibly*** occur within the six-month period. For example, a bequest conditioned upon surviving distribution of the decedent's estate ("to my husband if living at the time of distribution of my estate") is ordinarily not considered to be within the statutory survivorship exception, even though distribution might conceivably occur within the six-month period; the fact that the distribution could occur after the six-month period removes this type of bequest from the statutory exception—even if the distribution is in fact made within the six-month period. [Hanson v. Vinal, 413 F.2d 882 (8th Cir. 1969)]

(b) **Compare—immediate vesting:** [§678] However, it has been held that such a bequest is deductible if, under local property law, the interest is deemed to vest in the surviving spouse immediately upon the decedent's death. [*See* Kellar v. Kasper, 138 F. Supp. 738 (D.S.D. 1956); Kasper v. Kellar, 217 F.2d 744 (8th Cir. 1954)]

(2) **Life estate with power of appointment exception (marital deduction trust):** [§679] A transfer in which the surviving spouse is to receive all the income from the property during her life (or all the income from a specific portion of the property) ***and*** is granted an unqualified power to appoint the property (or a specific portion thereof) to herself or her estate will qualify for the marital deduction. [I.R.C. §2056(b)(5)] This provision forms the basis for the widely used marital deduction trust.

(a) **Income requirement:** [§680] To invoke this exception, it is essential that the surviving spouse be entitled to ***all*** of the income from the property or a portion thereof payable at least annually. If the trustee has any power to accumulate or withhold income beyond the period of administration (below), the trust will not qualify ***unless*** the survivor is granted an unlimited power to demand that the income be distributed. [Treas. Reg. §20.2056(b)-5(f)(8)]

1) **The specific portion rule:** [§681] If the spouse is entitled, *e.g.*, to one-half of the income from the trust (or her power of appointment over the corpus is limited to one-half of the corpus), a deduction will be allowed under the "specific portion rule"; however, the amount of the deduction will be restricted to one-half of the value of the property transferred on trust. [Treas. Reg. §20.2056(b)-5(b)]

a) **Application:** It is the ***lowest*** portion or fraction to which the spouse is entitled that determines the deductible amount. Thus, if the survivor was bequeathed one-half of the income and a power to appoint one-quarter of the corpus, the deduction would be limited to one-quarter of the value of the property transferred.

b) **Fractional vs. dollar amount:** [§682] Originally, the Service required that the specific portion be expressed as a fraction or percentage of the total trust income or corpus and that if it was limited to a fixed amount the marital deduction could not be taken. However, the Service lost in litigation and now the specific portion rule will operate even where the power or right to income is restricted to a dollar amount.

1/ **Example:** Where the surviving spouse is entitled to receive $10,000 of the income per year, and has a power to appoint the entire property, the amount of the deduction will be the amount necessary to produce $10,000 each year, or the entire value of the property, whichever is less. [Gelb v. Commissioner, 298 F.2d 544 (2d Cir. 1962); Northeastern Pennsylvania National Bank & Trust Co. v. United States, 387 U.S. 213 (1967)]

2) **Income during administration of estate:** [§683] The Regulations provide that the income requirement is met even though the executor is authorized to accumulate income from the marital portion during the period of administration, as long as the executor cannot delay settlement of the estate beyond a reasonable period of time. [Treas. Reg. §20.2056(b)-5(f)(9)]

3) **Effect of administrative powers:** [§684] Additionally, normal administrative powers conferred on a trustee—*e.g.*, to apportion receipts and expenses between income and corpus, etc.—do not disqualify the trust for marital deduction purposes. [Rev. Rul. 69-56, 1969-1 C.B. 224]

4) **Compare—powers to withhold income are disqualifying:** [§685] A direction to the trustee to distribute income for ". . . care and support in the style and manner of living to which [the spouse] . . . has become accustomed . . ." does not meet the income requirement. [Wisely v. United States, 993 F.2d 660 (4th Cir. 1990)]

(b) **Power of appointment requirement:** [§686] It is also crucial that the surviving spouse have the power to appoint the property to herself or her estate, and this power must be exercisable by the survivor alone and in all events. Moreover, no other person may have the power to appoint the property away from the surviving spouse. [I.R.C. §2056(b)(5)]

1) **Nature of the power:** [§687] Although the required power is frequently referred to as a "general power," it is more specific than a "general power of appointment." In other words, under section 2041 it is sufficient if a person has a power to appoint to herself, her creditors, her estate, or the creditors of her estate; but, for purposes of section 2056, the power must be exercisable in favor of ***oneself or one's estate.***

2) **Lifetime or testamentary power:** [§688] However, as with a section 2041 power, it is sufficient that the power be exercisable ***either*** during life or by will; it need not be exercisable both during life and by will.

3) **Ability to exercise:** [§689] It is generally immaterial whether the surviving spouse is capable of exercising the power; *i.e.*, the survivor's incompetence will not preclude allowance of the marital deduction. [Rev. Rul. 55-518, 1955-2 C.B. 384; *but cf.* Stockdick v. Phinney, 16 A.F.T.R.2d 6202 (1965)]

4) **Formalities:** [§690] Moreover, limitations of a formal nature—*e.g.*, requiring that the holder make specific reference to the power, etc.—will not disqualify an interest. [Treas. Reg. §2056(d)-5(g)(4)]

5) **Powers to consume:** [§691] Although an unlimited power to withdraw the trust corpus is a sufficient power to appoint to oneself, it has often been held that powers to consume are not enough to qualify the interest since such a power is limited to withdrawals for one's own needs, whereas the power required under the statute must be one that is freely exercisable for any purpose. [*See* Estate of Pipe v. Commissioner, 241 F.2d 210 (2d Cir. 1957), *cert. denied,* 355 U.S. 814 (1957); Commissioner v. Ellis, 252 F.2d 109 (3d Cir. 1958)]

6) **Joint powers:** [§692] The statute specifies that the requisite power be exercisable by the surviving spouse ***alone;*** thus, no marital deduction is allowed if the power is a joint power.

7) **Contingent powers:** [§693] In addition, the power must be exercisable by the surviving spouse "in all events." Accordingly, any condition or limitation upon its exercise will disqualify the interest. Indeed, it has been held that even though the competence of the surviving spouse is immaterial (above), where the power of appointment has been granted in such a way that it is to cease if the survivor becomes incompetent or a guardian or conservator is appointed for her, the power is not exercisable "in all events," and no marital deduction is allowed. [Starrett v. Commissioner, 223 F.2d 163 (1st Cir. 1955)]

8) **No power in a third party:** [§694] It is equally essential that no person have the power to appoint property away from the surviving spouse. However, a third party's power to appoint property ***to*** the surviving spouse is not fatal to the marital deduction. [Treas. Reg. §2056(b)-5(j)] And, the Regulations permit a third party power to appoint trust property as long as the power is not "in opposition" to that of the surviving spouse. [Treas. Reg. §20.2056(b)-(5)(j)]

   a) **Example:** Where H gives W a life interest in income and a general testamentary power of appointment, the marital deduction is allowed even though a third party can appoint the property after W's death in the event that W has not exercised her power.

(3) **Insurance settlement exception:** [§695] Certain interests passing to a surviving spouse in the proceeds of life insurance, endowment and annuity contracts held by the insurer are not considered terminable where conditions similar to the life estate with power of appointment exception are satisfied.

(a) **Example:** Thus, if the surviving spouse has a right to all interest or installment payments with respect to the insurance proceeds (or to a specific portion of such payments) during her life, ***and*** has an unqualified power to appoint the entire residue (or a specific portion of the proceeds) to herself or her estate, the marital deduction is available. [I.R.C. §2056(b)(6)]

(b) **Contrast—balance payable to third party:** [§696] But if, on the death of the surviving spouse, remaining unpaid benefits are payable to another, the entire amount is a nondeductible terminable interest. Thus, where a settlement option provided for an annuity to be paid to the surviving spouse with 120 payments guaranteed, and further provided that any balance should be paid to another, no part of the proceeds qualified for the marital deduction—not even the part related to the surviving spouse's life expectancy. [Meyer v. United States, 364 U.S. 410 (1960)]

(4) **Exception for "qualified terminable interest property":** [§697] The Revenue Act of 1981 introduced a fourth exception to the nondeductible terminable interest rule. Section 2056(b)(7) allows the marital deduction in the case of "qualified terminable interest property." [I.R.C. §2056(b)(7)(A)] (Very quickly, this type of interest became known by the acronym "***Q-tip.***")

(a) **Definitions:** [§698] Critical definitions are: (i) "qualified terminable interest property," and (ii) the surviving spouse's "qualifying income interest."

1) **"Qualified terminable interest property":** [§699] Q-tip is defined as property (or an interest therein [I.R.C. §2056(b)(7)(B)(iii)]) that ***passes*** from the decedent, in which the ***surviving spouse*** has a ***qualifying income interest for life,*** and with respect to which the decedent's executor makes an ***election*** to have the property qualify as a Q-tip interest. [I.R.C. §2056(b)(7)(B)(i)]

2) **"Qualifying income interest":** [§700] The surviving spouse has a "qualifying income interest for life" if the surviving spouse is entitled to ***all of the income*** from the property (or a specific portion thereof [I.R.C. §2056(b)(7)(B)(iv)]), payable at least annually, and ***no*** person ***has a power to appoint*** any part of the property ***to anyone other than the surviving spouse, except*** that the surviving spouse (or some other person) may be granted a power of appointment if this power is exercisable only at or after the surviving spouse's death [I.R.C. §2056(b)(7)(B)(ii)].

(b) **Election:** [§701] An affirmative election by the decedent's executor is a substantive requirement for allowance of the deduction. It must be made on the estate tax return (for the decedent) filed by the executor and, once made, the election is irrevocable. [I.R.C. §2056(b)(7)(B)(v)]

(c) **The "passing" requirement:** [§702] This is the same as the general passing requirement of section 2056(a). (*See supra*, §649.)

(d) **The "income" requirement:** [§703] This is the same as the income requirement under the life estate with power of appointment exception—including the "specific portion rule." [*See supra*, §§680, 681; *and see* Estate of Nicholson v. Commissioner, 94 T.C. 666 (1990)—as in Wisely v. United States, *supra*, §685, the court in Nicholson, a Q-tip case, held that the marital deduction was disallowed where the trustee was directed to pay income to the spouse ". . . as she may from time to time require to maintain her usual and customary standard of living. . . ."]

(e) **Power of appointment:** [§704] No person (***including*** the surviving spouse) may have a power to appoint the property away from the surviving spouse under the Q-tip exception. [*See* Estate of Bowling v. Commissioner, 93 T.C. 286 (1989)—no Q-tip deduction where the trustee could invade the corpus of the trust for the "emergency needs" of ***any*** beneficiary]

1) **Compare:** However, another person ***may*** be granted a power to appoint the property ***to*** the surviving spouse. And, the surviving spouse may be granted a limited (non-"general") power to consume. *But note:* If the surviving spouse was granted a general power of withdrawal, the marital deduction would be allowed under the life estate with power of appointment exception (*see supra*, §§679, 686 *et seq.*).

2) **Note:** The surviving spouse may be granted a special testamentary power of appointment. Again, note that if the surviving spouse's testamentary power is a "general" power, the marital deduction would be allowed under the life estate with power of appointment exception (*see supra*, §686).

3) **And note:** Some other party may be granted a power to appoint the property (special or general) as long as the power may not be exercised until the surviving spouse's death. [I.R.C. §2056(b)(7)(B)(ii) (last sentence); *and see supra*, §694]

(f) **Effects of election:** [§705] The initial effect of the election is to allow the Q-tip interest to qualify for the marital deduction in the decedent's estate. The ultimate effect is to expose the surviving spouse to transfer taxes, even though she possesses only a limited interest in the property.

1) **Property taxed in survivor's estate:** [§706] Upon the death of the surviving spouse, the Q-tip property will be included in her gross estate. [I.R.C. §2044] *Note:* It is the value of the entire property, not just the spouse's income interest, that is subject to the estate tax. (*See supra*, §567). *But also note:* The estate is entitled to reimbursement from the recipient of the

property (owner of the remainder) for the estate taxes attributable to the Q-tip property's inclusion. [I.R.C. §2207(A)(a); *and see infra*, §1036]

2) **Property subject to gift taxes:** [§707] If the surviving spouse makes a lifetime transfer of her income interests in the Q-tip property, the full value of the property (not just the value of the income interest) will be treated as a taxable gift by the surviving spouse. [I.R.C. §2519; *and see infra*, §758]

(g) **Partial elections permitted:** [§708] The election is not an "all or nothing" option; the executor may elect to qualify all ***or any portion*** of the Q-tip property. Moreover, the executor may make a partial election in the form of a formula, *e.g.*, qualifying "so much of the property as may be necessary to reduce the federal estate tax liability to $0, after taking into account all other allowable deductions and credits. . . ." [Letter Ruling 8301050, September 30, 1982]

(5) **Exception for certain charitable remainder trusts:** [§709] The 1981 Act also introduced a special exception for qualified charitable remainder trusts. A marital deduction will be allowed for the value of the ***income interest*** passing to a surviving spouse if she is the only noncharitable beneficiary of a trust that qualifies as a charitable remainder annuity trust or unitrust. [I.R.C. §2056(b)(8); *and see supra*, §§623-624]

h. **Disallowance of marital deduction under Revenue Procedure 64-19:** [§710] Under this Procedure, an amount that might otherwise qualify for the marital deduction will not be allowed where certain conditions appear.

(1) **Requirements:** [§711] The Procedure lists four facts that must coexist for disallowance of the marital deduction:

(a) **Pecuniary bequest:** The bequest to the surviving spouse is a pecuniary bequest—*i.e.*, either in the form of a specific amount or determined under a marital deduction formula clause;

(b) **Distribution in kind:** The decedent's executor is authorized to distribute assets in kind to satisfy the pecuniary bequest;

(c) **Select assets:** The executor is authorized to select among assets for purposes of making the distribution in kind; and

(d) **Estate tax values:** The executor is directed to use estate tax values in effecting distribution.

(2) **Rationale:** Although the estate value of assets is fixed as of the date of the decedent's death (or at the alternate valuation date), the actual value of the assets may increase or decrease prior to distribution. Where

the conditions for application of the Procedure exist, the executor might be able to satisfy the surviving spouse's bequest by selecting assets with a lower distribution date value than their estate tax value and at the same time distribute other (appreciated) assets to other beneficiaries. Such a power would undermine the essential purposes and requirements of the marital deduction insofar as it might support a deduction in excess of the amount that the surviving spouse actually received (so that less property will be taxed in her estate) and, in effect, amount to a power in another (the executor) to appoint property away from the surviving spouse. It is to eliminate this potential abuse that the Procedure was promulgated.

(3) **Exceptions:** [§712] There are two principal exceptions to the "no-deduction" rule of the Procedure:

(a) **Discretion limited:** [§713] If applicable state law or the governing instrument limits the potential abuse, the marital deduction will be allowed. This will occur where:

1) ***The executor must distribute assets whose value is at least equal*** to the amount of the marital deduction, ***or***

2) ***The executor is required to take into account the relative appreciation and depreciation*** in the value of all the assets available for distribution and to make distribution equitably between the marital portion and the nonmarital portion.

(b) **Pre-1964 wills:** [§714] An exception is also made for wills executed before October 1, 1964, the date of the Revenue Procedure's promulgation. With respect to such wills, the marital deduction will be allowed if the executor and the surviving spouse enter into and file an agreement that the executor will make distribution to the surviving spouse in accordance with the guidelines set out above. Note that this exception applies only if the pre-October 1, 1964, will has not been reexecuted or republished (by codicil or otherwise) on or after October 1, 1964.

i. **Estate planning technique—"equalization clauses":** [§715] Where both spouses have independent wealth, it may be preferable not to take the maximum marital deduction but, rather, leave only that amount of property to the survivor that will increase the estate to the point where it is equal to the estate of the first to die. To secure this equalization, the will may contain a formula clause, *e.g.*, "I give to my spouse only so much of my property which, when added to the value of the property owned by my spouse, will make her estate equal in value to that of my estate." (*Note:* Clause is oversimplified for clarity.)

(1) **Service challenges equalization clauses:** [§716] In *Estate of Smith v. Commissioner*, 66 T.C. 415 (1976), *aff'd*, 565 F.2d 455 (7th Cir. 1977), the Service disallowed the marital deduction in the case of such an equalization

clause. Its position was, essentially, that since the executor could value both estates (for purposes of equalization) either at the date of the decedent's death or at the alternate valuation date allowed by section 2032(b) (six months after death), the executor in effect possessed a power to appoint property away from the surviving spouse, and thus, the interest passing to the surviving spouse was a nondeductible terminable interest. [I.R.C. §2056(b)(1)(A), (B); *and see* I.R.C. §2056(b)(5)]

(a) **Example:** Suppose D's estate had a date of death value of $700,000 and the surviving spouse's estate was $500,000 on that date. And, suppose D's estate value remained constant but the surviving spouse's estate increased to $600,000 by the alternate valuation date. By electing the alternate valuation date, the executor would reduce the amount passing to the surviving spouse from $100,000 ($700,000 − [($700,000 + $500,000) ÷ 2]) to $50,000 ($700,000 − [($700,000 + $600,000) ÷ 2]).

(2) **Court approval of clauses:** The Tax Court and appellate court rejected the Service's theory. Both courts reasoned that the value of the surviving spouse's interest was ***determinable*** under the equalization formula as of the date of the decedent's death, even though it could not be ***determined*** until the executor elected date-of-death or alternate valuation date values. And, this election was one granted by the estate tax law. [I.R.C. §2032(b)] Thus, the statutory election did not create a terminable interest or a "power" to appoint property away from the spouse, any more than it would do so in the case of any formula bequest. [Estate of Smith v. Commissioner, *supra*; *and see* Estate of Meeske v. Commissioner, 72 T.C. 73 (1979); Estate of Laurin v. Commissioner, T.C. Mem. No. 145 (1979), *aff'd*, 645 F.2d 8 (6th Cir. 1981)]

(3) **Service acceptance:** [§717] The Service has agreed to follow the case law and allows the marital deduction for property passing under an equalization clause even though the executor has the option of valuing the survivor's estate, for equalization purposes, at the alternate valuation date. [Rev. Rul. 82-23, 1982—1 C.B. 139]

j. **Disallowance of marital deduction where surviving spouse is not a U.S. citizen:** [§718] No marital deduction is allowed if the surviving spouse is not a citizen of the United States, even though the decedent is a citizen. [I.R.C. §2056(d)(1)]

(1) **Rationale:** The underlying rationale of the marital deduction is that the interest passing to the surviving spouse must be potentially includible in her estate at death (*see supra*, §632). However, if the surviving spouse is not a citizen, there is a possibility that the property could escape taxation because the property of a nonresident alien is subject to the federal estate tax only if it is located in the United States. Thus, if the surviving spouse is not residing in the United States at her death, some or all of the property passing to her from her deceased spouse would escape estate taxes. To

avoid this risk, the Code does not allow the marital deduction for property passing to a noncitizen surviving spouse.

(2) **Exception:** [§719] The marital deduction will be allowed to the estate of the citizen spouse if the otherwise qualifying interest passes to a "qualified domestic trust." [I.R.C. §2056(d)(2)]

(a) **Qualified domestic trust:** [§720] A qualified domestic trust is defined as a trust: (i) that requires at least ***one trustee to be a citizen*** or domestic corporation; (ii) that provides that no distribution may be made from the trust ***unless the citizen-trustee withholds the tax*** imposed by section 2056A; (iii) with respect to which the ***citizen-decedent's executor elects to have the trust qualify*** as a qualified domestic trust; and (iv) that otherwise ***meets requirements*** established by the Treasury Department. [I.R.C. §2056A(a)]

(b) **Tax imposed:** [§721] Under section 2056A(b), a tax is imposed on any and all distributions from a qualified domestic trust ***except*** distributions of income and distributions ". . . to the surviving spouse on account of hardship." [I.R.C. §2056A(b)(1)(A), (b)(3)] Also, a tax is imposed on the value of any property remaining in the trust on the date of the surviving spouse's death. [I.R.C. §2056A(b)(1)(B)]

(c) **Amount of tax:** [§722] The tax is that amount by which the citizen-decedent's estate tax would have been increased if the amount taxable (the amount of the distribution or amount remaining on trust at the surviving spouse's death) had been included as part of the citizen-decedent's taxable estate. And, for this purpose, any previous taxable distributions from the qualified domestic trust must be taken into account. [I.R.C. §2056A(b)(2)(A)]

III. SUBSTANTIVE ASPECTS OF THE GIFT TAX

chapter approach

The gift tax is imposed upon "taxable gifts." [I.R.C. §§2501, 2502] This is defined as the total amount of gifts made during the calendar year less allowable deductions. [I.R.C. §2503(a)] Thus, to determine gift tax liability, you need to determine:

1. **"Gifts":** What transfers are treated as "gifts" for purposes of the gift tax?

2. **Any allowable deductions:** Are there any allowable gift tax deductions?

Note that as a matter of terminology, the first issue is commonly referred to as what transfers are "taxable gifts," even though, as mentioned, this phrase technically refers to the ***total amount of gifts less allowable deductions.***

A. TAXABLE GIFTS

1. **Introductory Analysis:** [§723] Unlike the estate tax—where a number of specific Code sections define the types of property and types of transfers that are subject to the tax—the subject matter of the gift tax is, for the most part, simply but broadly defined as "the transfer of property by gift." [I.R.C. §§2501, 2511] Accordingly, the primary focus must be upon the authorities that have interpreted this broad statement of the tax base. At the same time, however, chapter 12 of the Code (the gift tax) does contain certain specific provisions relating to taxable gifts which must also be examined.

    a. **Special statutes:** [§724] Sections 2514 through 2519 set forth the gift tax "rules" governing certain transactions: the exercise, release, or lapse of powers of appointment [I.R.C. §2514]; certain transfers pursuant to property settlements [I.R.C. §2516]; the treatment of disclaimers [I.R.C. §2518]; and the disposition of life estates in "qualified terminable interest property" for which a marital deduction was previously allowed [I.R.C. §2519].

    (1) **The annual exclusion:** [§725] In addition, subsections (b) and (c) of section 2503 allow, subject to specified limitations, an exclusion of $10,000 for gifts made to any donee during a calendar year.

    (2) **Provision for split gifts:** [§726] And, section 2513 allows spouses to treat gifts made to third parties as though each spouse had transferred one-half of the property, without regard to who the actual transferor was.

    b. **Elements of a taxable gift:** [§727] The gift tax attaches to "the transfer of property by gift . . . by any individual. . . ." [I.R.C. §2501(a)(1)] Section 2511(a) elaborates upon this principle by adding that the tax "shall apply whether the transfer is in trust or otherwise, whether the gift is direct or indirect, and whether the property is real or personal, tangible or intangible. . . ." For purposes of analysis, these concepts may be best understood by considering the four basic elements of a taxable gift:

(1) ***The identity and capacity*** of the donor and donee;

(2) ***The subject matter*** of the gift;

(3) ***The sufficiency of the transfer*** that will attract the tax; and

(4) ***The lack of adequate consideration***—which is the principal touchstone of a "gift" for gift tax purposes.

2. **Donor and Donee:** [§728] The tax is imposed only on gifts made "by any individual." [I.R.C. §2501(a)(1)]

a. **Donor:** [§729] Since the statute addresses gifts by "individuals," it might appear that the gift tax cannot be imposed upon an entity—*e.g.*, a partnership or corporation—that has made a gratuitous transfer. However, the Regulations take the position that a gift by an entity is taxable to the persons who have a beneficial interest in the entity. Thus, a gift made by a partnership is taxable to the partners in proportion to their partnership interest; and a corporate gift is taxable to the shareholders in proportion to their financial equity. [Treas. Reg. §25.2511-1(h)]

(1) **Beneficial owner:** [§730] The transfer must be made by a person who owns a ***beneficial interest*** in the property transferred. Thus, a trustee whose only interest in the property is the legal title he holds in a fiduciary capacity does not make a "gift" when he distributes property from the trust. [Treas. Reg. §25.2511-1(g)(1)] And this is true whether the distribution is required or is pursuant to a discretionary power granted to the trustee. (Note, however, that a different result may obtain if the trustee is also a beneficiary of the trust and the discretionary power is deemed to be a power of appointment. *See infra,* §§768-769.)

(2) **Nonresident aliens:** [§731] Nonresident aliens are subject to the tax only upon gifts of property located in the United States. [I.R.C. §2511(a)] Moreover, transfers of ***intangible*** property by nonresident aliens are not subject to the gift tax at all. [I.R.C. §2501(a)(2)]

(a) **Exception for certain expatriates:** [§732] However, transfers of intangible property by certain expatriate citizens whose loss of United States citizenship was principally for the purpose of avoiding United States taxes are subject to the gift tax. And, in this regard, shares of stock of United States corporations or the debt obligations of the United States or a United States person are deemed to be property situated within the United States. [I.R.C. §§2501(a)(3), 2511(b)]

(3) **Competency of donor:** [§733] Gifts that would be completely void under local law (*e.g.*, transfer by a person declared mentally incompetent) are not taxable gifts. In addition, a gift that is voidable at the option of the donor (*e.g.*, gift by a minor) is treated as a revocable transfer, which is not a taxable gift. The ultimate issue here is whether there has been a completed transfer. [Treas. Reg. §25.2511-2] (*See infra*, §§779 *et seq.*)

(4) **Identity of donor:** [§734] The gift tax is imposed upon the ***actual*** owner and transferor of the property, not upon one who is merely a nominal tranferor.

(a) **Example—indirect gifts:** The statute expressly provides for the taxation of indirect as well as direct gifts. [I.R.C. §2511(a)] Thus, if A transfers property to B on condition that B transfer the property to C, A is the actual transferor of the property to C. Or, if A transfers $20,000 to B on the condition that B transfer $10,000 to C, A has made a gift of $10,000 each to B and C. [Treas. Reg. §25.2511-1(h)]

(b) **Example—reciprocal trusts:** Similarly, as in the case of the estate tax, the substance rather than the form of reciprocal or crossed-trusts determines the identity of the transferor. (*See supra*, §§136-139.) Thus, if A transfers $100,000 on trust for B's children, and in consideration therefor B creates a similar trust for A's children, A and B will each be treated as having made an indirect gift to their own children. [Commissioner v. Warner, 127 F.2d 913 (9th Cir. 1942)]

(5) **Agents of the donor:** [§735] A gratuitous transfer made by an agent or legal representative of the owner of the property is a taxable gift by the owner if the agent or representative has the authority to make such a transfer. [*See* Commissioner v. Greene, 119 F.2d 383 (9th Cir.), *cert. denied*, 341 U.S. 641 (1941)—gratuitous transfer of incompetent's property by legal representative pursuant to court order; Estate of Bronston v. Commissioner, 56 T.C. Mem. 550 (1988)—power of attorney held broad enough to authorize gifts by attorney-in-fact]

b. **Donee:** [§736] Although a gift is taxable only if made ***"by"*** an individual (above), the statute does not require that the ***donee*** be an individual. Note, however, that a gift to an entity is treated as a gift to the individuals who own beneficial interests in the entity.

(1) **Beneficial owners**

(a) **Transfers to a trust:** [§737] A gratuitous transfer to a trust is not treated as a single gift to the trustee but, rather, as a gift to the several trust beneficiaries. The value of each beneficiary's interest, determined actuarially, is the amount of the gift to each of them. [Helvering v. Hutchings, 312 U.S. 393 (1941)]

(b) **Gifts to corporations or partnerships:** [§738] Likewise, a gift to a corporation has been held to be a gift to the individual shareholders of the corporation, the value of the separate gifts being proportionate to the interests of the shareholders. [Heringer v. Commissioner, 235 F.2d 149 (9th Cir.), *cert. denied*, 352 U.S. 927 (1956)] And, the same rule applies in the case of gifts to a partnership.

(2) **Identity of the donee:** [§739] There is no requirement that the donee be identified or ascertained. Thus, a gratuitous transfer to an unascertained person or to persons not yet in being ("to my grandchildren") is a taxable gift. [Robinette v. Helvering, 318 U.S. 184 (1943)]

3. **Subject Matter of the Gift:** [§740] The gift tax is imposed upon transfers of ***property***. [I.R.C. §2501(a)(1)]

a. **Property—in general:** [§741] For purposes of the gift tax, property is defined broadly and in the most comprehensive sense to include ***any type*** of interest "real or personal, tangible or intangible." [I.R.C. §2511(a)]

(1) **Equitable interests:** [§742] The transfer of equitable interests as well as legal interests is subject to the gift tax. Thus, the transfer by a trust beneficiary of her interest in the trust (if alienable) is a taxable gift of the interest. [Treas. Reg. §25.2511-1(f)]

(2) **Future interests:** [§743] Similarly, gifts of future interests (remainders, reversions, etc.) as well as present interests may be the subject matter of taxable gifts. [Treas. Reg. §25.2511-1(f)]

(3) **Contingent interests:** [§744] Moreover, as long as the gift is otherwise complete, the fact that the transferred interest is subject to a condition precedent, or may be divested upon the happening of a condition subsequent, does not prevent imposition of the tax.

(a) **Valuation:** [§745] Contingent interests are valued actuarially. For example, if the gift is contingent on survivorship, actuarial valuation is made on the basis of standard mortality tables. If the condition is one that does not permit actuarial valuation, or if the value of the interest is not otherwise ascertainable, the interest will be assigned a value of zero. [*See* Robinette v. Helvering, *supra*]

(b) **Compare—contingency within donor's control:** [§746] Note, however, that if the condition is within the donor's voluntary control, the transfer would be merely tentative or revocable, and since the gift is incomplete, no gift tax would attach. (*See* discussion of complete vs. incomplete transfers, *infra*, §§779 *et seq.*)

(c) **Public policy limitation—the *Procter* dilemma:** [§747] An interesting problem is presented where a gift is conditioned so as to make it "void, if ever held subject to the gift tax," thus producing the dilemma that the transfer would be complete (and taxable) if no gift tax is imposed, but incomplete (and nontaxable) if a gift tax is imposed. However, when this issue arose in *Commissioner v. Procter*, 142 F.2d 824 (4th Cir.), *cert. denied*, 323 U.S. 756 (1944), the court circumvented the problem by holding such a condition void as contrary to public policy. [*See also* Rev. Rul. 86-41, 1986-1 C.B. 300]

b. **Types of property subject to tax:** [§748] Special attention should be given to the taxation of certain types of property:

(1) **Foreign real estate:** [§749] A gift of real property located outside of the United States is a taxable gift if made by a ***United States citizen or resident.*** [I.R.C. §2501(a)(1)] (Recall that nonresident aliens are subject to the gift tax only on transfers of property located in the United States. [I.R.C. §2511(a)])

(2) **Tax-exempt securities:** [§750] The fact that various government bonds and other securities are declared "exempt from taxes" does not affect the taxability of a gift of such securities since the gift tax is a tax upon the ***transfer*** of property, not upon the property itself (*supra*, §11). [*See* Blodgett v. Holden, 275 U.S. 142 (1927); Treas. Reg. §25.2511-1(a); *and see* United States v. Wells Fargo Bank, 485 U.S. 351 (1988)]

(3) **Debts**

(a) **Checks and notes:** [§751] A gratuitous transfer of the donor's own note or check is not taxable until the donee cashes the check or collects the note, because until then it is merely an unenforceable indebtedness of the donor, unsupported by consideration. [Rev. Rul. 67-396, 1967-2 C.B. 351] But a gift of a ***third party's*** note or check would be a taxable transfer of property—a chose in action. [Rev. Rul. 84-25, 1984-1 C.B. 191]

(b) **Payment of another's debt:** [§752] The payment of the debts of another is as much a gift as actually giving the money to the debtor and, hence, is taxable accordingly.

(c) **Forgiveness of indebtedness:** [§753] Similarly, the forgiveness of a debt, with the intent to make a gift to the debtor, is a taxable gift to the debtor. [Treas. Reg. §25.2511-1(a)] However, one who forgives a debt in a bona fide business transaction (*e.g.*, as a compromise of a dispute, etc.) does not make a taxable gift; *see infra*, §§807 *et seq*.

(4) **Promise to make a transfer in the future:** [§754] The assumption of a legal obligation to transfer property at some time in the future is treated as a ***present*** gift of property. The value of the gift is the present discounted value of the right to receive the amount of property that the donor is

obliged to transfer at the future date. [Rev. Rul. 69-347, 1969-1 C.B. 227] (Note that this principle applies to a promise supported by adequate ***contractual*** consideration but not to a promise for consideration that prevents the transfer from being a taxable gift. *See infra*, §§801 *et seq.*)

(5) **Gifts of income:** [§755] The gratuitous transfer of a right to receive income from property is a taxable gift. For example, if A creates a trust to pay the income from the trust principal to B for ten years, there is a gift by A to B of the right to receive ten years' income. The value of the gift is the present discounted value of the right to receive the income payments, determined under tables prescribed by the Regulations. [*See* Treas. Reg. §25-2512-5, Table B]

(6) **Life insurance:** [§756] One who transfers a life insurance policy to another, or purchases a life insurance policy for another, makes a taxable gift of the value of the insurance contract (its cost or replacement value). [Treas. Reg. §25.2512-6] Moreover, if the donor thereafter pays the annual premiums on the policy, each premium payment is also a taxable gift. [Commissioner v. Boeing, 123 F.2d 86 (9th Cir. 1941)]

(7) **Annuities:** [§757] Similarly, the gratuitous transfer or purchase of an annuity is a taxable gift. And, the irrevocable designation of a beneficiary (primary or survivor) is a taxable gift of the value of the benefits, determined actuarially. [Treas. Reg. §25.2511-2(f)]

(8) **Disposition of life estate in marital deduction ("Q-tip") property:** [§758] For purposes of the estate ***and*** gift taxes, the 1981 Act permits certain "qualified terminable interest property" to qualify for the marital deduction to the donor or to the decedent's estate. (*See supra*, §§697 *et seq., and infra*, §§901 *et seq.*) Recall that despite the fact that the spouse only has a life estate in such property, the full value of the property will be included in his estate if the spouse dies while still enjoying the life interest. (*See supra*, §706.) Similarly, if the spouse disposes of the life interest during his lifetime, the spouse will be treated as having made a gift of the ***full value of the property*** to which the interest relates, not just the life interest itself. [I.R.C. §2519] (*But note:* The spouse is entitled to reimbursement from the recipient for the gift taxes imposed. [I.R.C. §2207A(b); *see infra*, §1036])

c. **Performance of personal services:** [§759] Although the gratuitous performance of services for another may constitute a "transfer" of a valuable economic benefit, a "gift" of services is not subject to the gift tax. [*See* Rev. Rul. 56-472, 1956-2 C.B. 21]

(1) **Rationale—no estate tax avoidance:** The theory is that a gift of services, unlike a gift of property, does not deplete the donor's estate and thus is not within the essential purpose of the gift tax. In other words, to prevent avoidance of the estate tax, the gift tax attaches to transfers that reduce or ***deplete*** the donor's estate; however, the transfer taxes do not require a person to ***augment*** her estate by charging for services rendered. (*See supra*, §554.)

(2) **Compare—third party payment for services rendered:** [§760] On the other hand, if one pays for services rendered by a third party to another, the payment may constitute an indirect gift to the recipient of the services and, thus, be a taxable gift. [Treas. Reg. §25.2511-1(h)(3)]

d. **Right to use property:** [§761] Although an economic benefit can be conferred by allowing another to use premises rent free or by lending money to another without charging interest, the authorities had generally held that such arrangements did not result in a taxable gift. The rationale was similar to that of gratuitous personal services: In neither case had the estate been depleted; rather, the donor had simply not undertaken to augment her estate by charging rent or interest. [*See* Johnson v. United States, 254 F. Supp. 73 (N.D. Tex. 1966); Crown v. Commissioner, 67 T.C. 1060 (1977), *non. acq.* 1978-1 C.B. 2, *aff'd*, 42 A.F.T.R.2d 6503 (1978)]

(1) **Supreme Court view—taxable gift:** [§762] The United States Supreme Court has held that an ***interest free loan*** by parents to their son and to a closely held family corporation constituted taxable gifts to the extent of the reasonable value of the use of the money lent. [Dickman v. Commissioner, 465 U.S. 330 (1984)] The Court reasoned that the "no obligation to augment one's estate" argument "misses the mark" in this instance. While it is true that one is not obliged to put one's property to productive use, when one "chooses not to waste the use value of money . . ., but instead transfers the use to someone else," a taxable event has occurred.

(a) **Demand loans:** According to the Supreme Court, the fact that the loan is a demand loan may affect the value of the gift, but does not gainsay that there has been a taxable gift.

(b) **Application:** The *Dickman* case appears to be applicable to the gratuitous, ***rent free use*** of tangible property as well as the interest free use of money.

e. **Lapsing rights:** [§763] Prior to 1990, tax free transfers of significant economic benefits were possible where a transferor transferred an interest in property by gift, retained valuable rights with respect to the property, and then permitted or caused these rights to lapse, thus effectively shifting the value of these rights to the original donee. Under the 1990 Act, these lapsing rights are considered gifts (or transfers includible in the gross estate if such rights lapse at the death of the original donor). [I.R.C. §2704]

(1) **Example:** Parent owns all the stock of a corporation. Parent transfers 40 percent of the stock to her child, but retaining voting control of the corporation through the 60 percent stock ownership that was not given away. Subsequently, Parent causes the corporation to issue nonvoting stock in exchange for her voting stock. The effect is that the child-donee now possesses 100 percent of the voting power, and this shift of control

enhances the value of the child's stock and decreases the value of the parent's. Despite the clear economic benefit conferred upon the child by the parent, prior law did not tax this transaction as a gift because the right to vote stock, albeit a significant factor in valuation, was not, itself, treated as "property." [*See* Estate of Harrison v. Commissioner, 52 T.C. Mem. 1306 (1987)] Section 2704 of new Chapter 14 now treats such lapsing rights as a gift. (*See infra,* §§959 *et seq.*, for discussion of this and related provisions of new Chapter 14.)

4. **Sufficiency of Transfer:** [§764] The third principal element of a taxable gift is that there be "a ***transfer*** of property." [I.R.C. §2501(a)(1)]

   a. **Form of transfer:** [§765] The transfer need not be in any particular form. Any type of transaction by which property rights are passed to or conferred upon another is regarded as a "transfer" for gift tax purposes. [Treas. Reg. §25.2511-1(a)]

      (1) **Indirect gifts:** [§766] Thus, as previously mentioned, indirect as well as direct transfers are subject to the gift tax (*supra,* §734).

      (2) **Delivery and donative intent:** [§767] Although under general property law, delivery and donative intent are critical elements of a gift, neither is technically necessary for federal gift tax purposes. [*See* Treas. Reg. §25.2511-1(g)(1)] At the same time, however, since a gratuitous transfer would not be effective under property law where these elements are absent, they do bear upon the sufficiency of the transfer for gift tax purposes. This is another illustration of how local law, although not determinative of the federal tax question, affects the tax issue insofar as it establishes the property rights upon which the federal taxes focus. (*See supra,* §§85 *et seq.*)

         (a) **Compare:** As will be seen, there are many instances in which the gift tax will attach even in the clear absence of donative intent because of the lack of adequate consideration for gift tax purposes (*infra,* §801).

      (3) **Powers of appointment:** [§768] Under technical property law, the exercise or nonexercise of a power of appointment is not a "transfer" by the holder of the power to the appointees or takers in default; rather, the property is deemed to pass from the original donor of the power. Thus, just as with the estate tax (*supra,* §§443 *et seq.*), a special statute is required to reach property subject to a power of appointment.

         (a) **Gift tax parallels estate tax:** Section 2514 of the gift tax is virtually identical in language, scope, and thrust to section 2041 of the estate tax. Thus:

            1) ***Only general powers*** of appointment are subject to the gift tax. [I.R.C. §2514(a), (b)] The definition of a general power for gift tax purposes is the same as that for estate tax purposes. [I.R.C. §2514(c); *and see supra,* §457]

2) ***Different rules apply to preexisting and post-1942 powers***, just as in the case of the estate tax. With respect to preexisting powers, only the exercise of the general power will attract the tax. [I.R.C. §2514(a)] But, general powers created after October 21, 1942 are subject to the gift tax upon their exercise ***or release***. [I.R.C. §2514(b)]

3) ***And, the lapse of a noncumulative annual power*** is exempt from the gift tax to the extent of $5,000 or five percent of the value of the property out of which the power could be satisfied. [I.R.C. §2514(e); *and compare supra*, §484]

(b) **Essential difference:** [§769] Section 2514 is part of the gift tax and thus addresses the lifetime ***exercise*** of a power that effectively transfers the property subject to the power to another (or, with respect to post-1942 powers, the release or lapse of the power that effectively shifts the property interests). On the other hand, section 2041 is part of the estate tax and focuses on the exercise of a power by will or, if exercised during life, an exercise that would subject the property to the estate tax under sections 2035 through 2038, and, in the case of post-1942 powers, the existence of the power at the date of a decedent's death.

1) **Comment:** Thus, section 2514 is concerned with a lifetime shifting of interests in property, which is analogous to making a gift; section 2041 is concerned with the testamentary-type shifting of enjoyment of the property subject to a general power.

(4) **Disclaimers:** [§770] A disclaimer (or renunciation) is an unqualified refusal to accept a transfer of property. As discussed under the estate tax (*supra*, §571), although other persons may acquire an interest in the property as a result of the disclaimer, an effective disclaimer is ***not a "transfer."*** *Rationale:* No property interest was ever acquired by the disclaimant and, thus, no interest passes from the disclaimant to another. [Treas. Reg. §25.2511-1(c)]

(a) **Prior law:** [§771] Despite the fact that an effective disclaimer has never been regarded as a "transfer" for estate or gift tax purposes, the effectiveness of the disclaimer, and thus the issue of whether there was a transfer, formerly turned upon state law. But, the laws of the several states are not uniform as to the time and circumstances in which an effective disclaimer might be made.

1) **Example:** Many states hold that a bequest can be disclaimed but that an intestate share cannot; some states allow partial disclaimers while others do not, and in many states it is unclear whether one can partially disclaim an interest in property; and, some states authorize the disclaimer of a future interest at the time the interest would vest in possession while others insist that a future interest must be disclaimed at the time it is created.

2) **Comment:** Further, state disclaimer statutes deal primarily with probate property and hence fail to address many interests in property that are subject to the estate or gift taxes; *e.g.*, there may be no effective way for a life insurance beneficiary to disclaim the proceeds upon the death of the insured.

(b) **Rule under the 1976 Tax Reform Act:** [§772] Out of concern for establishing a uniform rule governing disclaimers, section 2518 was promulgated as part of the 1976 Tax Reform Act. This rule does not, of course, preempt state property law; it simply establishes a federal rule as to when a disclaimer of property will be effective ***for federal gift and estate tax purposes.***

1) **Requirements:** [§773] Section 2518(b) lists four requirements for a ***"qualified disclaimer"***:

a) The disclaimer must be in ***writing.*** [I.R.C. §2518(b)(1)]

b) It must be ***received by the donor*** (or the donor's estate) ***within nine months*** of the date of the transfer creating the interest (or within nine months of the day on which the donee attains age 21). [I.R.C. §2518(b)(2)]

c) The donee must ***not have accepted*** the interest or any of its benefits. [I.R.C. §2518(b)(3)]

d) As a result of the refusal to accept property, the interest must ***pass to a person other than the disclaimant without any direction*** on the part of the disclaimant. [I.R.C. §2518(b)(4)] (Under the 1978 Act, this subsection was amended to provide that a disclaimer will be a "qualified disclaimer," even though as a result of the disclaimer an interest passes to the disclaiming spouse of the decedent. The purpose of this amendment is to allow a surviving spouse to disclaim, *e.g.*, an absolute bequest, but take a life estate under the nonmarital portion of the will.)

2) **Comments**

a) **Future interests:** [§774] The requirement that the disclaimer be filed within nine months of the date upon which the transfer creating the interest is made (subsection (b)1)b), *supra*) forecloses the opportunity to defer a disclaimer of a future interest (even a contingent future interest) until the interest would vest in possession, or until the person who will possess the interest can be identified and the value of the interest can be ascertained. This is contrary to the statutory trends of most states (and the rule of the Uniform Probate Code), and effectively overrules a number of cases which, for federal tax purposes, allowed deferral of the disclaimer. [*See* Uniform Probate Code §2-801; Keinath v. Commissioner, 480 F.2d 57 (8th Cir. 1973)]

b) **Partial disclaimers:** [§775] Initially, there was concern that the requirement that a person not accept "the interest or ***any*** of its benefits" (subsection (b)1)c), *supra,* §773) might prevent a partial disclaimer for federal tax purposes—even though such a partial disclaimer was valid under the local law. However, it has been ruled that, subject to certain limitations, partial disclaimers are valid for federal tax purposes. [*See* Treas. Reg. §2518-3(a); Ltr. Rul. 7913119]

c) **Independence from state law:** [§776] The requirement that the interest pass to a person other than the disclaimant without any direction on the part of the disclaimant was interpreted to prevent an effective disclaimer under section 2518 where the disclaimer was ineffective under local law. [*See* Ltr. Rul. 7937011] The theory was that if the disclaimer was ineffective under local law the interest vested in the disclaimant, and thus the transfer to some other person was a result of the voluntary "direction" of the disclaimant (subsection (b)1)d)—*see supra,* §773).

1/ **Congressional intent:** [§777] This ruling may have been a literally accurate interpretation of the language of subsection (b)1)d), but it also undermined the stated intent of Congress to provide a uniform rule which would operate independently of state law (*supra*).

2/ **1981 amendment:** [§778] Congress responded in 1981 with an amendment which allows that a disclaimer will be effective for federal tax purposes, even though technically invalid under state law, if the disclaimant has otherwise met requirements of subsections (b)1)b) and c)—disclaimer within nine months and no acceptance of interest—and if a written transfer of the property is made (within the nine-month period) to those persons who would have received the property had the disclaimer in fact been valid. [I.R.C. §2518(c)(3)] The intent of this provision is to allow the federal statute to operate independently of state law if the disclaimant "effectuates" the intended disclaimer by transferring the property to the proper persons.

b. **Complete vs. incomplete transfer:** [§779] One of the essential elements of a taxable gift is that the transfer be ***complete.*** Thus, to the extent that some interest in the property is retained, there is no gift of that interest—even though there may be a taxable gift of other interests in the property. And, to the extent that the donor has retained powers with respect to the disposition of the property, the gift may be incomplete and not taxable. [*See* Treas. Reg. §25.2511-2]

(1) **Categories of incomplete transfers:** [§780] For purposes of analysis, there are three general categories of incomplete transfers:

(a) **Retained interests:** [§781] An interest retained in transferred property is not taxable because it has not been "transferred." Accordingly, the amount of the taxable gift is the value of the property less the value of the retained interest. [Smith v. Shaughnessy, 318 U.S. 176 (1943)]

(b) **Revocable transfers:** [§782] In *Burnet v. Guggenheim*, 288 U.S. 280 (1933), the Supreme Court held that the creation of a trust that was revocable by the settlor without the concurrence of anyone having a substantial adverse interest in the trust was incomplete and nontaxable. And, this is true whether the power to revoke is expressly reserved or arises by operation of the law (*e.g.*, a transfer by a minor where local law grants the minor a power to rescind within a reasonable time after attaining majority; or a state law that makes all trusts revocable where the settlor has not expressly made them irrevocable).

(c) **Power to alter or amend:** [§783] Subsequently, the Supreme Court went beyond the *Guggenheim* case and held that the settlor's reservation of the mere power to change the beneficiaries under the trust made the transfer "incomplete" and nontaxable, even though the settlor retained no power to revoke the trust or to make himself a beneficiary. [Sanford's Estate v. Commissioner, 308 U.S. 39 (1939)]

(2) **The nature of retained powers that may render a gift incomplete**

(a) **Similarities to estate tax:** [§784] In a number of ways, the types of retained powers that will render a transfer incomplete (and nontaxable) for gift tax purposes are similar to those powers to revoke or alter or amend that will render a lifetime transfer incomplete (***and taxable***) for estate tax purposes. Thus:

1) **Power must affect beneficial enjoyment:** [§785] As with the estate tax, the power must be one that ***affects beneficial enjoyment***. Thus, a purely administrative power will not render the gift incomplete. [Du Pont v. Commissioner, 2 T.C. 246 (1943); *and see supra*, §316]

2) **Capacity in which exercisable:** [§786] The capacity in which the power is held is immaterial; *e.g.*, the gift is incomplete where a power to alter or amend beneficial enjoyment is held by the settlor as trustee. [*See* Treas. Reg. §25.2511-2; *and see supra*, §295]

3) **Discretionary vs. nondiscretionary powers:** [§787] But, in order for the gift to be incomplete, the power must be ***discretionary***. A mandatory direction to make certain distributions to third parties is not a discretionary power, nor is a power that is governed by ascertainable external standards. [*See* Treas. Reg. §25.2511-2(g); *and see supra*, §317]

4) **Access to the power:** [§788] A discretionary power held by a ***third party*** does ***not*** render the gift incomplete. However, the gift would be incomplete if the settlor retained the right to compel exercise of the power by the trustee or to remove the trustee and appoint a successor trustee. [*See* Treas. Reg. §25.2511-2(b); *and see supra*, §§309-311]

(b) **Differences from estate tax:** [§789] However, there are also some substantial differences between the estate tax law and the gift tax law.

1) **Power to affect time or manner of enjoyment:** [§790] A gift is complete for gift tax purposes (although not for estate tax purposes) even though the settlor has retained power to affect the time and manner of enjoyment of the property by the designated beneficiaries. [Treas. Reg. §25.2511-2(d); *compare supra*, §327]

2) **Contingent powers:** [§791] Moreover, for purposes of the gift tax, the fact that exercise of the reserved power is contingent upon the happening of an event beyond the grantor's control will not render the gift incomplete. To this extent, gift tax law is similar to the treatment under section 2038 but differs from the estate tax treatment under section 2036. [*Cf.* Griswold v. Commissioner, 3 T.C. 909 (1944); Rev. Rul. 54-537, 1954-2 C.B. 316; *and compare supra*, §§182, 302]

3) **Joint powers:** [§792] And, unlike the result under sections 2036 and 2038 of the estate tax, a transfer that can be altered or revoked by the settlor only with the consent of a person possessing a ***"substantial adverse interest"*** is a complete transfer and a taxable gift. However, if the co-holder of the power does not possess a substantial adverse interest, the gift is incomplete. [*See* Treas. Reg. §25.2511-2(e); Higgins v. Commissioner, 129 F.2d 237 (1st Cir. 1942); *and compare supra*, §§184, 289]

a) **Persons with a "substantial adverse interest":** [§793] Ordinarily, the beneficiaries of the trust as well as their successors in interest are deemed to have the requisite adverse interest. The trustee, on the other hand, does not have a substantial adverse interest.

1/ **Compare—duty to support beneficiary:** [§794] The cases are split as to whether those under a legal duty to support the beneficiary (but who are not themselves beneficiaries—*e.g.*, parent, guardian) have a substantial adverse interest. [*See* Fleischmann v. Commissioner, 40 B.T.A. 672 (1939); Commissioner v. Prouty, 115 F.2d 331 (1st Cir. 1940)]

b) **Amount taxable:** [§795] As indicated above, to the extent that the settlor can alter or amend the trust without the concurrence of an adverse party, the gift is incomplete. Accordingly, only the ***value of the adverse party's interest*** is subject to the gift tax.

1/ **Example:** If A transfers property on trust reserving a right to alter or amend the trust with the consent of the life income beneficiary (B), the value of the life income interest is a taxable gift; but the value of the remainder interest is treated as an incomplete and nontaxable transfer since B has no interest adverse to the exercise of a power to revoke the remainder. [*See* Camp v. Commissioner, 195 F.2d 999 (1st Cir. 1952)]

(3) **Payments made under an incomplete trust:** [§796] Although the reservation of a power to alter or revoke may render a transfer on trust "incomplete" and nontaxable at the time of its creation, any distributions of income (or corpus) ***actually made*** to the beneficiaries under such a trust are taxable gifts to the beneficiaries at the time of the distribution. [Treas. Reg. §25.2511-2(f); Commissioner v. Warner, 127 F.2d 913 (9th Cir. 1942)]

(4) **Relinquishment of powers:** [§797] A gift that is incomplete because of powers retained by the settlor becomes complete—and taxable—if she subsequently relinquishes the power, or her right to exercise it terminates. For example, if A reserves power to revoke a trust "until ten years from the date this trust is created," the gift is complete and becomes taxable upon expiration of the ten-year period (unless previously revoked). [Treas. Reg. §25.2511-2(f)]

c. **Correlation with estate tax:** [§798] As previously discussed, the principal purpose of the gift tax is to prevent avoidance of the estate tax. Accordingly, practically any transfer for less than a full consideration that is not taxed under the estate tax will be taxed under the gift tax. But, as the above analysis indicates, many transfers that are taxable under the estate tax are also taxable gifts.

(1) **Estate tax credit:** [§799] Prior to 1977, this double taxation was remedied by the allowance of a credit against the estate tax for any gift taxes that were paid with respect to a transfer that was subsequently included in the donor's gross estate. [I.R.C. §2012; *and see infra*, §1024]

(2) **Relief under unified tax system:** [§800] The computational mechanics of the new unified transfer tax system (introduced by the 1976 Tax Reform Act) prevent double taxation by authorizing a deduction from estate tax liability for any gift taxes payable with respect to post-1976 transfers. [I.R.C. §2001(b); *and see infra*, §1011]

5. **Lack of Consideration:** [§801] For federal gift tax purposes, a "gift" is defined under section 2512(b) in terms of the type of consideration that will ***prevent*** a transfer from being treated as gratuitous. The requisite consideration is the same as that under the estate tax—*i.e.*, "adequate and full consideration in money or money's worth." Thus, a transfer is a taxable gift to the extent that this consideration is absent. [Treas. Reg. §25.2512-8]

a. **"Money or money's worth":** [§802] The nature of the consideration required for gift tax purposes is virtually identical to that required under the estate tax (*supra*, §§551 *et seq.*).

(1) **Monetary terms:** [§803] Thus, consideration that would support a simple contract may not be sufficient; rather, it must be measurable in ***monetary terms.*** [Treas. Reg. §25.2512-8]

(2) **More than mere detriment:** [§804] And, even though expressible in monetary terms, the consideration must ***move to the transferor.*** A mere detriment to the transferee will not prevent a transfer from falling within the gift tax. [Commissioner v. Wemyss, 324 U.S. 303 (1945)]

b. **Effect of partial consideration:** [§805] Section 2512(b) makes it clear that where some consideration is paid (but not "full" consideration) only the excess of the value of the property transferred over the consideration received by the transferor is subject to the gift tax.

c. **Marital rights as consideration:** [§806] Although the gift tax provisions do not specifically preclude the release of dower, curtesy, or other marital rights as "consideration," the Supreme Court has held that the gift and estate tax should be read in pari materia (*i.e.*, construed together) in this regard. Consequently, the Court has read into the gift tax the rule of section 2043(b), which states that the release of such rights is not to be treated as consideration "in money's worth." [Merrill v. Fahs, 324 U.S. 308 (1945); *and see supra*, §562]

d. **"Business transaction exception":** [§807] As with the estate tax (*supra*, §557), Congress did not intend to tax business motivated transfers as gifts, even where made for less than an "adequate and full consideration in money or money's worth." Consequently, transfers that are a product of bona fide, arm's length negotiations and which are free from donative intent are not taxable gifts, regardless of the adequacy of consideration. [Treas. Reg. §25.2512-8]

(1) **Examples:** Thus, if it appears that the transferor was motivated by economic considerations, the transfer will not be taxed as a gift—*e.g.*, employee bo-

nuses, "gifts" to customers or suppliers, sales below market value of property due to necessity, or merely a bad business bargain. [*See, e.g.*, Anderson v. Commissioner, 8 T.C. 706 (1947); Rev. Rul. 68-558, 1968-2 C.B. 415]

(2) **Settlement of bona fide disputes:** [§808] Similarly, amounts paid in settlement of a bona fide dispute are not taxable gifts. And, this rule has been extended in some cases to the settlement of a will contest. [Estate of Friedman v. Commissioner, 40 T.C. 714 (1963)]

(3) **Family transactions:** [§809] The fact that the parties to a transfer are related does not preclude arm's length business negotiations. However, the Service and the courts closely scrutinize transfers between family members so as to assure that the transaction is not a disguised gift. [*See* Rev. Rul. 73-61, 1973-1 C.B. 408; Giannini v. Commissioner, 2 T.C. 1160 (1943), *aff'd*, 148 F.2d 285 (9th Cir. 1945), *cert. denied*, 326 U.S. 730 (1945)] (In regard to divorce settlements, *see* below.)

(4) **Political contributions:** [§810] Against the Service's continued objection, it was held that contributions to political parties or candidates were not "gifts" for gift tax purposes. [*See* Stern v. United States, *supra*; Carson v. Commissioner, 641 F.2d 864 (10th Cir. 1981)] The controversy was resolved by Congress in 1974—section 2501(a)(5) exempts all transfers to political organizations made after May 7, 1974.

e. **Involuntary transfers:** [§811] It is generally said that the gift tax only reaches ***voluntary*** transfers. Certainly, if a person "transfers" property to another at gunpoint it would be absurd to impose a gift tax, even though the avoidance of injury or death, which prompted the transfer, might not be measurable in economic terms.

(1) **Divorce settlements:** [§812] The issue of "involuntary transfers" is most frequently raised in connection with property settlements incident to a divorce. In *Harris v. Commissioner*, 340 U.S. 106 (1950), the leading case in the area, it was held that a transfer of property pursuant to a property settlement agreement entered into between spouses was not subject to the gift tax where the agreement was incorporated in the divorce decree and the court had the power to modify the agreement. The Supreme Court's theory was that the transfer resulted not from the voluntary agreement, but by virtue of the divorce court's decree, and therefore was involuntary.

(2) **Statutory exception for certain property settlement and support agreements:** [§813] However, since the scope of *Harris* is not entirely clear, section 2516 was enacted to provide specific statutory relief. Under this section, any transfer made pursuant to a written agreement between spouses in settlement of marital property rights ***or*** to provide a reasonable allowance for ***support*** of minor children is ***not taxable*** under the gift tax, ***provided*** that a divorce actually occurs within a three-year period beginning one year before the agreement is executed.

(a) **No requirement of court approval:** [§814] Note that it is ***not*** necessary that the court approve the property settlement or support agreement, and the fairness or adequacy of the exchange is immaterial.

(b) **Compare—no divorce:** [§815] If a divorce does not occur within the three-year period, then the general gift tax rules relating to consideration are applied. [Treas. Reg. §25.2516-1]

(c) **Obligation of support:** [§816] Apart from section 2516, a transfer and satisfaction of one spouse's obligation to support the other spouse is not a taxable gift; *i.e.*, the discharge of a valid support obligation owed by the transferor to the transferee is consideration measurable in money's worth (*supra*, §563). [Rev. Rul. 68-379, 1968-2 C.B. 414]

(d) **Divorce after three-year period:** [§817] Also, it would appear that the *Harris* rule may still be applied even where section 2516 is inapplicable (*e.g.*, where the divorce does not occur within the three-year period).

f. **Widow's election in community property states as taxable gift:** [§818] As discussed under the estate tax (*supra*, §434), a frequent estate planning device in community property states is for one spouse's will to dispose of the entire community property (both the share of the testator and the spouse) "to my spouse for life, remainder to my children." Since the surviving spouse has a vested one-half interest in the community assets, such a disposition of her share would be invalid without her consent, but often she consents in order to carry out the mutually agreed upon testamentary scheme.

(1) **Effect of survivor's consent:** [§819] If the surviving spouse consents to the distribution under the decedent's will, she is held to have made a taxable gift to the owners of the remainder (children). The gift is the excess in value of the remainder in the survivor's one-half interest in the community property over the value of the life estate in the decedent's community property which the survivor takes under the decedent's will. [Commissioner v. Siegel, 250 F.2d 339 (9th Cir. 1957)]

(2) **Effect of election to take against will:** [§820] However, a surviving spouse who elects to take her share of the community property against the terms of the decedent's will, normally takes nothing under the will. And, there are no gift tax consequences; the election is not a renunciation of a bequest.

6. **Treatment of Concurrent Interests in Property**

a. **Creation of concurrent interests:** [§821] For the most part, the general rules of the gift tax are applicable to the creation of concurrent interests in property (*i.e.*, a tenancy in common, a joint tenancy, or a tenancy by the entirety). And, the gift tax law closely tracks property law in regard to the nature of the co-tenants' interests.

(1) **General rule:** [§822] Where property is acquired and title is taken in a form of co-tenancy, there is a taxable gift to the extent that the value of the undivided interest acquired by one co-tenant exceeds what that party contributed to the purchase price.

(a) **Examples:** If A purchases property for $10,000 and takes title in the name of A and B as co-tenants (either a tenancy in common or a joint tenancy), the value of B's one-half undivided interest ($5,000) is a taxable gift from A to B. Or, if B contributed $2,000 to the purchase price, there would be a taxable gift of $3,000 from A to B (the value of B's one-half undivided interest less the consideration which B provided).

(b) **Relevance of "original consideration" under the gift tax:** [§823] In determining the amount of any taxable gift upon the creation of a joint tenancy, general principles of property law are followed. For instance, suppose in the example above, that A had previously given $2,000 to B, and B then contributed the $2,000 to the acquisition of the joint tenancy property. The taxable gift from A to B is still $3,000; it is irrelevant that the consideration paid by B "originated" with A. In the contemplation of property law (and hence the gift tax law), the $2,000 previously received by B as a gift ***belongs*** to B, and A is not taxed again on this amount when the joint tenancy is acquired.

(2) **Exception for certain "revocable" joint interests:** [§824] There is no taxable gift upon the creation of a ***joint bank account*** because there is not a "completed transfer"—*i.e.*, the depositor may withdraw the money deposited (revoke the transfer) at any time without any obligation to account to the other joint tenant.

(a) **Compare:** However, a taxable gift will occur if the "donee" joint tenant withdraws funds from the account for her own use. [Treas. Reg. §25.2511-1(b)(4)]

(b) **And note:** This rule is also applicable to other forms of "revocable" joint tenancies—*e.g.*, United States Savings Bonds acquired in a form of co-ownership with right of survivorship, and certain joint brokerage accounts where the securities are held in the broker's "street name" and the donor joint tenant has a right to direct investments and distributions without the consent of the other joint tenant. [Rev. Rul. 68-269, 1968-1 C.B. 399; Rev. Rul. 69-148, 1969-1 C.B. 226]

(3) **Prior law—exception for real property acquired by spouses:** [§825] Until 1981, section 2515 provided that the creation of a tenancy by the entirety or a joint tenancy between spouses in ***real property*** would ***not*** be treated as a taxable gift to any extent unless the donor spouse ***elected*** to treat it as such by filing a gift tax return at the time the co-tenancy was created. (Note that section 2515 was not enacted until 1954 and operated prospectively. Hence, intra-spousal co-tenancies in real property created prior to 1954 were taxed under the general gift tax rules.)

(a) **Present treatment:** [§826] The unlimited (100 percent) marital deduction allowed by the 1981 Act rendered this special exception unnecessary (*see infra*, §§906 *et seq*.). And, consequently, it was repealed. Thus, the creation of such joint tenancies after 1981 may constitute taxable gifts under the general rule (*see supra*, §822), but any gift is completely offset by the marital deduction.

(b) **Relevance of prior law:** [§827] The applicable law is that which is in effect at the time of the transfer. Thus, joint tenancies created prior to 1982 (or 1954) are subject to the prior gift tax rules.

b. **Termination of concurrent interests:** [§828] Again, the gift tax law generally tracks local property law with respect to the nature of each co-tenant's property interest and any "transfer" effected by the severance or termination of a co-tenancy.

(1) **Severance or partition of co-tenancy—general rules:** [§829] Since each co-tenant owns an undivided interest in the property, the severance or partition of a joint tenancy (or tenancy in common) is not a "transfer" if each co-tenant receives a proportionate share of the property. In other words, there is only a taxable gift where one of the co-tenants receives more than a proportionate share.

(a) **Example:** A acquired property and took title in the name of A and B as joint tenants (or as tenants in common), reporting a taxable gift upon creation of the co-tenancy. Subsequently, A and B agreed to a partition and each received one-half of the property outright. This latter transaction is not a taxable gift.

(b) **Compare:** [§830] However, suppose in the above example that A and B agreed that the property should be solely owned by A, and B quitclaimed her one-half undivided interest to A. This would result in a taxable gift of one-half of the value of the property (at the time of the transfer) from B to A.

(c) **Sale of property held in co-tenancy:** [§831] The same basic rules are applied where co-tenants sell the property to a third party: If each co-tenant receives a proportionate share of the proceeds of sale, there is no taxable gift; but if one of the co-tenants receives more than the proportionate share, the "excess" is a taxable gift from the other co-tenant.

(d) **Transfer by gift:** [§832] The gratuitous transfer by one co-tenant of her undivided interest to a third party is a taxable gift to the third party. Likewise, where both co-tenants join to transfer the property to a third party, each makes a taxable gift of his or her undivided interest.

(2) **Special rules where creation of a joint tenancy was not a taxable gift:** [§833] The gift tax law does ***not*** follow property law principles of ownership and transfer where a joint tenancy in real property created

by spouses was not treated as a taxable gift under former section 2515 (above). [*See* Treas. Reg. §25.2515-3]

(a) **Transfers between joint tenants:** [§834] If the donee-spouse quitclaims his interest back to the donor joint tenant, there is no taxable gift; for gift tax purposes, the creation of the joint tenancy is treated, in a sense, as a tentative or incomplete transfer so that a taxable transfer does not occur when the tentative gift is reversed (just as there is no taxable gift upon the creation or revocation of a revocable trust). However, if the ***donor-spouse*** quitclaims her interest to the donee-spouse, the joint tenancy is severed, the allowance of former section 2515 is abrogated, and at this time the donor is treated as transferring the ***entire*** property to the donee.

(b) **Severance of joint tenancy:** [§835] If the spouses agree to convert the joint tenancy into a tenancy in common, the severance of the joint tenancy abrogates the allowance of former section 2515 (which is only applicable to joint tenancies or tenancies by the entirety, above) and the donor-spouse is thereby deemed to have made a taxable gift of her one-half undivided interest to the donee-spouse.

(c) **Sale of joint tenancy:** [§836] The above rules are applicable by analogy to the sale of joint tenancy property. If the donor-spouse receives the entire proceeds of the sale there is no taxable gift, just as there is no taxable gift if the donee-spouse quitclaims his interest back to the donor. However, if the donee-spouse receives any part of the consideration, there is a taxable gift of that amount from the donor to the donee.

(d) **Present relevance of these special rules:** [§837] It appears that these special rules continue to define the gift tax consequences where a joint tenancy was created between 1954 and 1982 and former section 2515 operated to prevent the creation from being treated as a taxable gift. However, after applying these rules to determine the extent of any current ***gift***, the 100 percent marital deduction will preclude any ***tax*** on account of gifts made by one spouse to the other.

c. **Income from jointly held property:** [§838] The general and special rules of the gift tax, outlined above, are applicable by analogy to the gift tax consequences of receipt of income from joint tenancy property.

(1) **Where creation of joint tenancy was a taxable gift:** [§839] In this case, each joint tenant is deemed to own an undivided interest in property for federal gift tax purposes as well as under local property law. Thus, where each joint tenant receives the proportionate share of income from the property to which each is entitled under local law, there is no taxable gift. But, if one joint tenant receives more than the proportionate share of income, there is a gift of the "excess" from the other joint tenant.

(2) **Where creation was not treated as a taxable gift:** [§840] If an intraspousal joint tenancy in real property was not treated as a taxable gift under former section 2515, it appears that the rules with respect to income from incomplete transfers would apply (*see supra*, §796). Accordingly, if the donor-spouse receives all the income there is no taxable gift from the other spouse. However, if the spouses divide the income equally, the one-half received by the donee-spouse is a taxable gift from the donor-spouse. (Note that these rules technically appear to continue to operate for purposes of determining the amount of any "gift"; but the 100 percent marital deduction would preclude any tax. *See supra*, §837.)

7. **The Annual Exclusion:** [§841] Once the total value of all gifts made during the year has been determined, the allowable annual exclusion must be deducted to arrive at "gross gifts." However, although the $10,000 annual exclusion of section 2503(b) operates like a deduction, it is an exclusion: If a gift does not exceed $10,000, no gift tax return need be filed at all; and, the gift tax deductions are applied after the annual exclusion against "gross gifts." [I.R.C. §§6019(a), 2524]

a. **Amount of exclusion:** [§842] The first $10,000 of gifts—other than gifts of "future interests"—given by a donor to any single donee in any calendar year is excluded in the computation of the donor's taxable gifts. [I.R.C. §2503(b)]

(1) ***If the donor's gift to any particular donee is less than $10,000***, the balance of the exclusion is lost; there is no carry-over to other donees or to any other years.

(2) ***Conversely, if a gift is over $10,000,*** only the excess is taxable.

b. **Effect—optimum availability for tax-free gifts:** [§843] Since the exclusion is an ***annual*** amount ***per donee***, a taxpayer can give away, tax-free, a substantial amount of her estate each year by simply dividing her gifts into amounts of under $10,000 each and giving them to a large number of donees. There is no limit on the number of exclusions which a donor can utilize in any year. (*See also* discussion of gift splitting, *infra*, §§869-874.)

c. **Identity of donees:** [§844] Because the annual exclusion is allowed on a ***per donee*** basis, the identity (and number) of donees must be ascertained. (But note that the donees need not be identified for a gift to be complete and taxable; *see supra*, §739]

(1) **Gifts on trust:** [§845] Recall that where a gift is made to a trust having several beneficiaries, the beneficiaries, not the trustee, are the real donees of the gift. Thus, the donor is entitled to an annual exclusion for each beneficiary's interest, so long as the interest is a "present" interest. [Helvering v. Hutchings, 312 U.S. 393 (1941); *and see* below]

(2) **Discretionary distributees:** [§846] If distributions (of income or corpus) are to be made in the trustee's discretion, the actual donees cannot, for purposes of

the annual exclusion, be identified, and, hence, no annual exclusion would be allowed. And, this is true even though the trustee's discretion is governed by an ascertainable standard. [Van Den Wymelenberg v. United States, 272 F. Supp. 571 (E.D. Wis. 1967), *and see infra,* §862]

d. **Exclusion not allowed for gifts of "future interests":** [§847] No exclusion is allowed in the case of a gift of a "future interest in property."[I.R.C. §2503(b)]

(1) **What is a "future interest"?** [§848] For purposes of the annual exclusion a future interest is either:

(a) ***Any interest or estate,*** whether vested or contingent, that is ***limited*** to commence in use, possession, or enjoyment at a ***future date***, or

(b) ***Any interest or estate,*** whether vested or contingent, that is ***subject to the will of some other person.*** [Treas. Reg. §25.2503-3]

(2) **Examples of "present" and "future" interests:** [§849] It can be deduced from the above definition that the term "future" interest is not necessarily limited to future interests as determined under property law. Thus, for example:

(a) **Reversions, remainders, possibilities of reverter, etc.:** [§850] Whether vested or contingent, these are clearly "future" interests. [United States v. Pelzer, 312 U.S. 399 (1941)]

(b) **Life estates:** [§851] A life estate is ordinarily a "present" interest. But where it is limited to commence at some time in the future (even one year from the date of the gift), or at the will of another, it is a "future" interest. [*See* Fondren v. Commissioner, 324 U.S. 18 (1945)]

(c) **Right to income from a trust:** [§852] A life income interest under an existing trust is a "present" interest, even though the actual distribution of income will occur annually. The value of this interest is the present value of the right to receive income over the term of the interest (for life or a term of years), determined actuarially. [*See* Treas. Reg. §25.2512-6]

1) **Compare—discretionary distributions:** [§853] However, if the trustee has discretion concerning the distribution of income to the beneficiary, the interest is a "future" interest for which no annual exclusion is allowed.

2) **Right to corpus:** [§854] Where the life income beneficiary is also to receive distributions of corpus (whether upon termination of the trust or at the discretion of the trustee), her income interest is a "present" interest, but any right to corpus is a "future" interest. [Fondren v. Commissioner, *supra*]

a) **Compare—third party distributions:** [§855] On the other hand, if the trustee has discretion to distribute corpus for the benefit of ***another***, the income beneficiary's interest is a ***"future"*** interest since her right to income is dependent upon the will of the trustee—*i.e.*, by distributing corpus to the third party the trustee can reduce or eliminate the amount of income payable to the income beneficiary.

(d) **Contract rights:** [§856] The Regulations specifically provide that gifts of bonds or rights under executory contracts are gifts of "present" interests, even though redemption of the bonds or payment under the contracts will take place in the future: it is the contract right itself which constitutes the subject matter of the gift. Likewise, a gift of insurance or annuity contracts is a present interest. [Treas. Reg. §20.2503-3(a)]

(3) **Exception—special rule for certain minor's trusts:** [§857] An outright gift to a minor, like an outright gift to an adult, is a gift of a present interest even though state law may require the appointment of a guardian to take charge of the property. (Similarly, an outright gift to a custodian under the Uniform Transfers to Minors Act is a gift of a present interest.) However, it is usually preferred to make gifts to minors on trust with discretionary distributions of income—*i.e.*, allowing the trustee to distribute such income (or corpus) as may be necessary for the minor's support but to accumulate any income not needed for support for ultimate distribution at a more mature age. Prior to 1954, no annual exclusion would be allowed for such discretionary trusts, the gift being of a "future" interest under the general rules of section 2503(b). In order to permit prudent planning of trusts for minors without loss of the annual exclusion, section 2503(c) was promulgated under the 1954 Code.

(a) **Requirements:** [§858] An annual exclusion for property transferred to a trust for a minor is authorized if at all times the property and the income therefrom ***may*** be expended for the benefit of the minor before he attains age 21, ***as long as*** the property and any accumulated income will be distributed to the minor at age 21 or, if the child dies before attaining age 21, to his estate or appointee (under a general power granted to the minor). A gift over to another upon the minor's death before age 21 in default of the exercise of the required power of appointment is permitted. [I.R.C. §2503(c)]

1) **Income interest may qualify separately:** [§859] Although a literal reading of section 2503(c) suggests that the trust must terminate when the minor reaches age 21 and that the corpus as well as any accumulated income must be distributed to the minor at that time, it has been held that the income interest alone may qualify for the exclusion if it meets the section 2503(c) requirements—*i.e.*, if that income is to be used for the benefit of the minor, and any accumulations are to be distributed to him at age 21 (or to his estate or appointee, etc.). [Commissioner v. Herr, 303 F.2d 780 (3d Cir.

1962)] Thus, under the rule of the *Herr* case, distribution of the principal may be deferred beyond age 21.

2) **Power to require distribution of accumulated income:** [§860] The property (or income interest) will also qualify for the annual exclusion under section 2503(c) even though the trust instrument provides for continuation of the trust beyond age 21, ***as long as*** the minor is granted a power to require distribution of the property (or accumulated income) upon attaining age 21 and this power persists until the time specified for mandatory distribution. [Heidrich v. Commissioner, 55 T.C. 746 (1971)]

e. **Exclusion not allowed if value of present interest not "ascertainable":** [§861] Closely related to the requirement that the gift not be a future interest is the requirement that the value of the present interest be "ascertainable." [Treas. Reg. §25.2503(c)] Essentially, this means that there must be no ***condition*** or ***power*** that could operate to impair or destroy the gift. [Geller v. Commissioner, 9 T.C. 484 (1947)] *Application:*

(1) **Discretionary power in trustee:** [§862] As previously seen, if a trustee is given discretionary power to accumulate or distribute income, the income interest is a future interest (because subject to the will of another). [*See* Prejean v. Commissioner, 354 F.2d 995 (5th Cir. 1966)] (But recall the statutory exception for certain minor's trusts, above.) Likewise, if the trustee is given power to sell assets and apportion ("sprinkle") proceeds among several beneficiaries, the income interests are future interests. [Van Den Wymelenberg v. United States, *supra;* Rev. Rul. 55-303, 1955-1 C.B. 471] And in both cases, the income interests have no ascertainable value because the trustee's power could impair or destroy beneficial enjoyment.

(2) **Conditional gifts:** [§863] Even though an interest (on trust or otherwise) is "vested," if it can be divested upon the happening of some condition and the probability of the condition occurring cannot be determined actuarially, the interest has ***no ascertainable value*** and no annual exclusion would be allowed. For example, if property were transferred on trust with income to be paid "to A for life or until A remarries," the income interest would not qualify for the annual exclusion.

(3) **Unproductive property:** [§864] Sometimes it is impossible to ascertain the value of a gift because of the nature of the gift itself. For example, if A transfers stock on trust with directions to pay the income to C, the income interest is a present interest. But, if the stock is in a closely held corporation that has never paid dividends and seems unlikely to do so in the future, and if the trustee is directed to retain the shares (*i.e.*, is precluded from making the property "productive"), there is no way of ascertaining the present value of the income interest and, hence, no annual exclusion would be allowed. [*See* Stark v. United States, 477 F.2d 131 (8th Cir. 1973)]

8. **Exclusion for Certain Transfers for Educational or Medical Expenses:** [§865] The 1981 Act amended section 2503 to allow an ***unlimited*** exclusion for payments made to an institution or person furnishing education or medical services to another person. [I.R.C. §2503(e)] The person receiving the educational or medical services need not be related to the donor.

   a. **Limitations—education:** [§866] The exclusion is limited to ***tuition*** paid to a ***qualified educational organization*** (described in section 170(b)(1)(A)(ii)) for the ***education or training*** of an individual. [I.R.C. §2503(e)(2)(A)] According to the Committee Reports, the exclusion is permitted for either full-time or part-time students, but is limited to direct tuition cost (*i.e.*, no exclusion for books, supplies, dormitory fees, etc.).

   b. **Limitations—medical services:** [§867] The payments must be made directly to the person or institution that provides the medical care; *i.e.*, reimbursements to the patient do not qualify. Moreover, the exclusion is limited to costs or expenses for medical services defined in section 213—*i.e.*, for diagnosis, care, mitigation, treatment, or prevention of disease, etc. (*See* Income Tax I Summary.) Also, according to the Committee Reports, no exclusion is allowed for amounts that are reimbursed by insurance; *i.e.*, if the patient receives insurance reimbursement, the donor's payments are not excluded.

   c. **Does not preempt other gift tax rules relating to support:** [§868] Payments in discharge of the transferor's legal obligation to support another are not taxable gifts. (*See supra*, §§563, 816.) According to the Committee Reports, the statutory exclusion of section 2503(e) "does not . . . change the law that there is no gift if a person paying the medical expenses or tuition is under an obligation under local law to provide such items to the recipient."

9. **Gift Splitting Between Spouses**

   a. **Automatic for community property:** [§869] Since each spouse in community property states has a vested one-half interest in the community assets, a gift of such property is treated as a gift by ***each*** spouse of his or her one-half interest. Thus, the gift is "split," and one-half of the value of the property is exposed to the separate graduated rates applicable to each spouse. Moreover, each spouse is entitled to a separate, annual exclusion, thereby enabling the spouses to jointly give a total of $20,000 tax-free each year to each donee.

   b. **Special provision for gifts of separate property:** [§870] Secton 2513, enacted in 1948, allows for the same tax advantage when the separate property of one spouse is transferred by gift (whether or not the spouse resides in a community property or common law state).

      (1) **General rule:** [§871] Where a gift of separate property is made by a married person, the spouses may, by mutual consent, elect to treat the gift as having been made one-half by each spouse. If such consent is signified (on the gift tax return(s) timely filed by the spouse(s)), the effect is to expose one-half of the value of the donated property to the graduated rates of each spouse and to allow each spouse to claim his or her own annual exclusion.

(2) **Limitations:** [§872] However, the spouses must be married when the gift is made, and the consent must be applied to ***all*** gifts made by each spouse during the calendar year in question. [Treas. Reg. §25.2513-1]

(3) **Exception for gifts to spouse:** [§873] Note also that gift splitting is allowed only for gifts by a spouse to a ***third party;*** the statute does not reach gifts made between spouses. Moreover, section 2513 will not apply if the donor grants his or her spouse a ***general power of appointment*** with respect to the property transferred. [I.R.C. §2513(a)(1); *and see* Treas. Reg. §25.2513-1(b)(3),(4)] Thus, if A transfers property on trust for X for life, remainder to Y, but grants her (A's) spouse, S, a power to appoint the property to whomever S wishes, the gift may not be "split."

(4) **Impact upon estate tax:** [§874] For purposes of determining the amount included in the gross estate, the provisions of section 2513 are inapplicable. Thus, if A released a power to revoke a revocable trust within three years of death, the full value of that property would be included in A's estate even though A's spouse consented to "split" the gift.

B. DEDUCTIONS

1. **Introductory Analysis:** [§875] Once the amount of "gross gifts" has been determined, there are two possible gift tax deductions that may be taken in arriving at "net" or "taxable gifts," within the meaning of section 2503(a): (i) the ***charitable deduction*** [I.R.C. §2522]; and (ii) the ***marital deduction*** [I.R.C. §2523].

2. **Former Specific Exemption:** [§876] Prior to the 1976 Tax Reform Act, a United States citizen or resident was allowed a single, lifetime exemption of $30,000. [*See* former I.R.C. §2521] Unlike the annual exclusion, the specific exemption did not operate on an annual basis, but was a single, lifetime deductible amount. The taxpayer could use as much or as little of the exemption as he wished in one year, and the balance would be available as a deduction in subsequent years. (Of course, once the $30,000 limit was reached, no further exemption was allowed.)

a. **Repeal of specific exemption:** [§877] The 1976 Reform Act abolished the $30,000 exemption for all transfers made after December 31, 1976, substituting in its place the "unified credit" (discussed *infra,* §§994 *et seq.*).

b. **Present relevance of specific exemption:** [§878] For gifts made prior to January 1, 1977, the specific exemption remains applicable in determining the amount of taxable gifts. And, since pre-1977 taxable gifts must be cumulated with post-1976 gifts to determine the marginal rates of tax at which these latter gifts are exposed (*see infra,* §991), the allowance of the specific exemption for pre-1977 gifts is of continuing importance. Further, if any portion of the specific exemption was applied as a deduction against gifts made between September 9, 1976 and December 31, 1976, the amount of the allowable unified credit will be reduced (*see infra,* §999).

3. **The Charitable Deduction:** [§879] A United States ***citizen or resident*** is allowed an ***unlimited*** deduction for the ***full value*** of all property transferred to a public, religious, charitable, scientific, literary, or educational institution that meets the tests specified in the statute. [I.R.C. §2522]

   a. **Nonresident aliens:** [§880] However, a nonresident alien's right to this deduction is limited. Basically, it is allowed only where the charitable donee, if a corporation, is a domestic corporation; and, if a trust, foundation, etc., where such gifts are to be used within the United States exclusively for charitable purposes. [I.R.C. §2522(b)]

   b. **Requirements:** [§881] The requirements for allowance of the gift tax charitable deduction are virtually identical to those of the estate tax charitable deduction, *supra*, §§612 *et seq*. Thus:

      (1) **Donee must be a "charitable object":** [§882] Only gifts to certain types of identified organizations for certain identified charitable purposes qualify for the deduction. [I.R.C. §2522(a); *and compare* I.R.C. §2055(a), *supra*, §613]

      (2) **Limitations on amount:** [§883] The amount of the deduction is limited to the value of the property transferred to the charity. [I.R.C. §2522(a)] Additionally, in determining the amount of the charitable gift, any allowable annual exclusion related to the gift must be taken into account. [I.R.C. §§2524, 2503(b)]

         (a) **Example:** If $25,000 was given outright to a charity, the amount of the gross gift would be $15,000—the value of the gift less the $10,000 annual exclusion; and the amount of the charitable deduction would be limited to $15,000. Otherwise, of course, there would be a "double deduction" with respect to $10,000.

   c. **Split interest gifts:** [§884] Just as in the case of the estate tax, the gift of a remainder to a charity after an intervening (noncharitable) life estate or term of years (*i.e.*, a "charitable remainder gift"), or the gift of a term of years to a charity followed by a remainder to a noncharitable object (*i.e.*, a "charitable lead gift") must be made in certain specified forms to qualify for the deduction. (*See supra*, §§621-627.)

      (1) **Specified forms:** [§885] Such split interest gifts must be in the form of an "annuity trust," a "unitrust," or a "pooled income fund." [I.R.C. §2522(c)(2)]

      (2) **Exceptions:** [§886] However, these specific forms are not required in the case of an undivided interest in property, or a remainder interest in a personal residence or a farm. [I.R.C. §2522(c)(2)]

4. **The Marital Deduction: [§887] In computing "net gifts," a deduction is also allowed for the value of any property transferred by the taxpayer to the taxpayer's spouse. [I.R.C. §2523]**

a. **Background:** [§888] As in the case of the estate tax marital deduction, the gift tax marital deduction was enacted in 1948 to give residents of noncommunity property states "tax-splitting" advantages similar to those enjoyed by spouses who reside in community property states. But, as in the case of the estate tax, the underlying rationale for the allowance is now to exempt all intraspousal transfers from tax, which is accomplished by allowing a 100 percent deduction for gifts by one spouse to another. *(See supra,* §§628-633.)

b. **Requirements:** [§889] The gift tax marital deduction is governed generally by the same rules and concepts as the estate tax marital deduction. Indeed, the differences that do exist are because of the practical context in which the transfer is made, not because of any underlying theoretical difference; *i.e.*, the gift tax marital deduction applies to transfers made by a living donor, whereas the estate tax marital deduction is applicable to a deceased spouse's estate.

(1) **Citizens and residents only:** [§890] The donor must be a citizen or resident of the United States. [I.R.C. §2523(a)(1)]

(2) **For spouse:** [§891] The donee must be the spouse of the donor ***at the time the gift is made.*** [I.R.C. §2523(a)(1)]

(3) **The interest must be a "deductible interest":** [§892] For purposes of the gift tax, any completed gift to the donor's spouse will be a gift of a deductible interest, unless it is a nondeductible terminable interest (below).

(a) **Community property:** [§893] Under prior law, a gift of the donor's interest in community property was not a gift of a deductible interest. *Rationale:* The spouses had already enjoyed transfer tax relief in connection with community property since at the time the community property was acquired each spouse obtained a vested one-half interest in the property without any transfer tax exposure. [*See* former I.R.C. §2523(f), repealed effective December 31, 1981] With the advent of the 100 percent marital deduction, however, community property qualifies as a "deductible interest" to the same extent as separate property.

(4) **The "nondeductible terminable interest rule" under the gift tax:** [§894] The basic rules, definitions, and rationale of the nondeductible terminable interest rule under the gift tax are the same as under the estate tax. [I.R.C. §2523(b)-(e)] *(See supra,* §§659 *et seq.)*

(a) **Definition of terminable interest:** [§895] As in the case of the estate tax, a terminable interest is defined as one where "on the lapse of time, on the occurrence of an event or contingency, or on the failure of an event or contingency to occur, such interest transferred to the spouse will terminate or fail. . . ." [I.R.C. §2523(b); *and see supra,* §660]

(b) **Nondeductible terminable interests:** [§896] In addition to the situation where an interest in the same property was transferred by the donor to a third party (the ownership of which would allow the third party to possess or enjoy the property after the interest of the donee-spouse terminates), a terminable interest will be nondeductible for gift tax purposes where:

1) ***The donor retains*** an interest that would allow him to possess or enjoy any part of the property after the donee-spouse's interest terminates [I.R.C. §2523(b)(1)]; or

2) ***The donor*** immediately after the transfer ***has the power to appoint an interest*** in the property "which he can exercise in such a manner that the appointee may possess or enjoy any part of such property after such termination. . . ." [I.R.C. §2523(b)(2)] It ***does not*** matter whether this retained power is exercisable by the donor alone or in conjunction with ***any*** person, or that the power cannot be exercised until after the lapse of some time period or only upon the occurrence or nonoccurrence of some event or contingency.

(c) **Joint interests:** [§897] Notwithstanding the basic definition of a nondeductible terminable interest for gift tax purposes, it is specifically provided that the creation or transfer of an undivided interest to the donee-spouse as joint tenant with right of survivorship with the donor is a deductible interest, despite the fact that the donor possesses an interest in the property (as a joint tenant) and the donor-spouse could survive to the donee-spouse's undivided one-half interest by outliving the donee. [I.R.C. §2523(d)]

1) **Rationale:** The donee-spouse does possess a present one-half undivided interest in the property (analogous to a life estate) and, in the case of a joint tenancy, could sever the joint tenancy, thereby extinguishing the right of survivorship (analogous to a power to appoint the property to herself).

2) **But note:** Even though a tenant by the entirety may not have a power of severance, this "exception" also applies to tenancies by the entirety. [I.R.C. §2523(d)]

(d) **Interest in unidentified assets:** [§898] As in the case of the estate tax, the terminable interest rule under the gift tax also applies where the interest of the surviving spouse is in an unidentified group of assets that contains a nondeductible terminable interest that could be used to "fund" the gift to the spouse. [I.R.C. §2523(c); *and see supra*, §669] Such a situation would exist, for example, if a group of assets (including nondeductible terminable interests) are transferred to a trustee with directions to allocate a certain portion or amount to the spouse with the balance to be allocated to others, and the trustee is given discretion as to what assets to allocate to the separate portions.

(5) **Exceptions to the terminable interest rule:** [§899] Unlike the estate tax, the gift tax contains an exception neither for survivorship nor for insurance proceeds. The reason for this omission is obvious: In the case of the gift tax, the donor is alive so that conditions of survivorship and selection of insurance settlement options are not particularly relevant. At the same time, however, the gift tax marital deduction provides a special exception for joint interests between donor and donee (noted above), which is not contained in and is obviously irrelevant to the estate tax.

(a) **Life estate with power of appointment exception:** [§900] But the gift tax does allow for the same "life estate with the power of appointment" exception that is recognized under the estate tax (*supra*, §§679 *et seq.*). [I.R.C. §2523(e)] Accordingly, an interest transferred to one's spouse will qualify for the gift tax marital deduction if:

1) ***The donee-spouse is entitled to all of the income*** (or to a specific portion thereof) ***for life,*** payable at least annually;

2) ***The donee-spouse has a power to appoint the interest*** (or a specific portion thereof) ***to herself, or to her estate*** (during life or by will, or both);

3) ***The power is exercisable by the donee-spouse alone and in all events;*** and

4) ***No other person has a power to appoint*** the interest to ***any person other than the donee-spouse.***

(b) **Exception for "Q-tip" interests:** [§901] Also, the gift tax now allows a deduction for "qualified terminable interest property" given to one's spouse. [I.R.C. §2523(f)] This exception to the nondeductible terminable interest rule likewise tracks the Q-tip exception under the estate tax (*supra*, §§697 *et seq.*).

1) **Requirements:** [§902] Property transferred to one's spouse will qualify for the gift tax marital deduction if:

a) The donee-spouse is granted a "qualifying income interest for life"—defined (by cross reference) identically to the "qualifying income interest" under the estate tax (*supra*, §§698-700), and

b) An election is made to have this exception apply. [*See* I.R.C. §2523(f)(2),(3)]

2) **Election:** [§903] The required election is made by the donor on the gift tax return for the calendar year in which the interest was transferred. Once made, the election is irrevocable. [I.R.C. §2523(f)(4)]

3) **Effect—property ultimately taxed to donee:** [§904] As previously discussed, Q-tip property will be subject to estate taxes in the estate of the donee or, if the life interest is disposed of before death, as a taxable gift made by the donee-spouse. (*See supra*, §§707, 758.)

(c) **Exception for certain charitable remainder trusts: [§905] Finally, the gift tax now allows a deduction, coordinate with that allowed under the estate tax (*see supra*, §709), for the value of the income interest given to one's spouse in a qualified charitable remainder annuity trust or unitrust. [I.R.C. §2523(g); *see supra*, §§623, 624]**

c. **Maximum allowed**

(1) **Present law:** [§906] The gift tax marital deduction is allowed for the full value (100 percent) of the property transferred to the donee-spouse, subject to two limitations:

(a) **Net value:** [§907] If the property is subject to an encumbrance, or if the donee incurs some obligation as a condition of receiving the gift, the deduction is limited to the ***net*** value of the property—*i.e.*, its value less the amount of the encumbrance or obligation. (*Compare supra*, §§635 *et seq*.)

(b) **Annual exclusion:** [§908] The allowable marital deduction must be reduced by the amount of any allowable annual exclusion. [I.R.C. §2524; *compare supra*, §883]

(2) **Prior law:** [§909] For gifts made before 1982, prior law will continue to determine the amount of any allowable gift tax marital deduction and, hence, the amount of the taxable gift—for purposes of delinquent (or unfiled) gift tax returns ***and*** for purposes of determining the amount of "adjusted taxable gifts" on the donor-decedent's estate tax return. (*See infra*, §1010.) Thus the allowances of prior law remain relevant.

(a) **Pre-1977 gifts:** [§910] Prior to the 1976 Tax Reform Act, the maximum gift tax marital deduction was one-half of the value of the deductible interest given by one spouse to the other (***before*** taking the annual exclusion—then $3,000).

1) **Example:** For instance, suppose A gave her spouse $100,000 in 1975. The marital deduction which A could claim was $50,000—one-half of the value of the gift. And, an additional $3,000 would be excluded under section 2503(b). Thus, the amount of the taxable gift would be $47,000.

2) **Limitation—"gross gift" ceiling:** [§911] However, the maximum marital deduction could not exceed the amount of the "gross gift." [I.R.C. §2524] For example, if the amount given was $5,000, fifty percent of the value of the gift would be $2,500; but the marital

deduction would be limited to $2,000 since, after application of the annual exclusion, the gross gift is only $2,000.

(b) **Gifts made in 1977 through 1981:** [§912] The 1976 Tax Reform Act liberalized the gift tax marital deduction to a certain extent. Under this Act, the first $100,000 of cumulative gifts given to a spouse after December 31, 1976 was entirely tax free; the second $100,000 of cumulative gifts was fully taxable (after the annual exclusion); and the former fifty percent-of-value limitation applied with respect to cumulative gifts in excess of $200,000. [I.R.C. §2523(a)]

1) **Example:** W gave her spouse, H, $150,000 in 1977. The amount of the marital deduction would be $100,000. The first $100,000 of the gift was fully deductible and the excess ($47,000 after application of the annual exclusion) was fully taxable. If W then gave H $100,000 in 1978, W could claim a marital deduction of $23,500: The first $53,000 of the gift was fully taxable; and one-half of the cumulative gifts in excess of $200,000 ($47,000) was deductible.

IV. VALUATION

chapter approach

Although, as a practical matter, valuation problems and controversies absorb a great deal of professional time, you will probably see this issue only peripherally in your estate and gift tax course or exam; the primary emphasis is on the substantive law of the transfer tax system. However, you would be well-advised to review this general overview of valuation problems, the relevant legal authorities that address valuation questions, and the basic methods, as such knowledge will prove helpful to a basic understanding of the federal estate and gift tax system.

A. INTRODUCTORY COMMENTS

1. **Valuation of Estates and Gifts:** [§913] Both the estate and gift taxes are measured by the "fair market value" of the property transferred. Thus, the valuation questions under each of the transfer taxes are essentially the same. However, certain special rules (*e.g.*, concerning the valuation date and the property subject to tax) apply separately and sometimes differently for estate and gift tax purposes.

2. **Valuation Issues Addressed:** [§914] As with most estate and gift tax courses, this Summary addresses three categories of valuation issues:

   a. ***Rules of law*** relating to valuation under the estate and gift taxes.

   b. An introduction to ***valuation methods***.

   c. A review of the valuation of ***certain specific types of property***.

B. RULES OF LAW RELATING TO VALUATION [§915]

While valuation is essentially a factual determination, there are certain rules of law that must also be considered.

1. **Valuation Date:** [§916] As a general proposition, it is the value of the property ***at the date of the transfer*** that is critical.

   a. **Gift tax:** [§917] A taxable gift is valued for gift tax purposes as of the date the gift is made. Thus, the issue is dependent upon the substantive rules relating to when a gratuitous transfer is complete (*see supra*, §§779 *et seq.*). [I.R.C. §2512(a); Goodman v. Commissioner, 156 F.2d 218 (2d Cir. 1946)]

   b. **Estate tax:** [§918] The estate tax attaches at the instant of death. Consequently, the value of the assets included in the decedent's estate is their fair market value ***immediately after*** death, not the instant before death. [*See, e.g.*, Goodman v. Granger, 243 F.2d 264 (3d Cir. 1957)—executory contracts which had only a speculative value until decedent died, but which acquired a fixed value upon his death were included in the decedent's estate at the fixed value]

(1) **Alternate valuation date:** [§919] Under section 2032 of the Code, the executor or administrator of the estate is given an election to value the estate assets either at the date of the decedent's death or at the "alternate valuation date." If the alternate date is elected, all assets included in the gross estate are valued as of ***six months after*** the decedent's death, ***except*** that any assets sold, distributed, exchanged or otherwise disposed of during the six months following death are valued as of the date of their sale, distribution, etc. [Treas. Reg. §20.2032-1(a)]

(a) **Purpose:** [§920] The alternate valuation date is made available for the purpose of minimizing the danger of an untoward tax burden or even complete confiscation of estates due to a sudden decline in market value of the decedent's assets following death. In fact, the predecessor of section 2032 was enacted during the "Great Depression" when many estates were faced with just such a situation.

(b) **Limitation—valuation changed solely by lapse of time disregarded:** [§921] Since the purpose of section 2032 is to protect against sudden declines in value, it does not apply to changes in value (declines) attributable solely to lapse of time. For example, the value of a patent, an annuity, or a life estate on the life of another, etc., naturally diminishes with lapse of time because its "life" is thereby shortened. However, such changes are disregarded; *i.e.*, even though the decedent's executor has elected the alternate valuation date, these assets are valued as of the date of decedent's death. [Treas. Reg. §20.2032-1(a)(3)]

(c) **Procedure—election made on estate tax return:** [§922] The executor's election to value the assets at the alternate valuation date must be made on the estate tax return. Moreover, once made, the election is irrevocable and affects ***all*** assets except as indicated above; *i.e.*, the executor cannot elect on an item by item basis. [Treas. Reg. §20.2032-1(b)]

(2) **Valuation of assets transferred inter vivos but included in decedent's estate:** [§923] Assets included in the decedent's estate under sections 2035 through 2038 (because, *e.g.*, of a retained life estate, etc.) are valued on the basis of their value at the ***date of the decedent's death*** (or alternate valuation date)—***not*** their value at the time of transfer.

(a) **Gifts of cash or property:** [§924] Thus, as a general rule, it is the value of the ***actual property transferred,*** as of the date of the donor's death, that is included in the gross estate. The fact that the donee may have sold, exchanged, replaced, or consumed the donated property is irrelevant.

(b) **Gifts on trust:** [§925] However, if the property was transferred on trust, the value of the trust ***principal*** is included in the decedent's estate, even though this may consist of property other than that which was originally transferred.

(c) **Improvements made by donee:** [§926] If the donee improves the property with his own funds, the value of the improvements is excluded in determining the includible amount.

(d) **Income from donated property:** [§927] Where property is taxed under sections 2036 through 2038, income that is ***accumulated*** and added to the principal of the gift ***is*** included in the gross estate, provided the taxable interest or power extends to this accumulated income as well as to the principal. However, income that is ***distributed*** is not included. [United States v. O'Malley, 383 U.S. 627 (1966)]

2. **Fair Market Value:** [§928] As mentioned above, the "fair market value" of the property measures the gift and estate taxes. This is generally defined as the price that a willing buyer and a willing seller would arrive at after arm's length bargaining where there is no compulsion to buy or to sell and where both parties are aware of all relevant facts.

a. **Determination of fair market value:** [§929] The taxpayer (donor or estate) has the burden of proof; *i.e.*, the Service's determination of fair market value is presumed correct until proved erroneous by the taxpayer.

(1) **Valuation statements by I.R.S.:** [§930] The 1976 Tax Reform Act requires that, upon request of the taxpayer, the Service furnish a written statement explaining any determination or proposed determination of the value of the property. The statement must (i) explain the basis of the valuation, (ii) set forth any computation, and (iii) include a copy of any expert appraisal. However, the method employed in arriving at the valuation is not binding on the Service. [I.R.C. §7517]

b. **Special use valuation for estate tax purposes:** [§931] Under section 2032A (enacted as part of the 1976 Tax Reform Act), farmland and real property used in connection with other closely held businesses may be valued in the decedent-owner's estate at less than its fair market value.

(1) **Background:** [§932] The statute was promulgated out of recognition that it is often unreasonable to tax such land at its fair market value. Basically, the price that farmland can command on the market frequently exceeds the value that would be economically justified on the basis of the income it produces. Accordingly, the estate tax burden imposed upon the land's inflated value might often force the estate to sell the land to pay the taxes, thereby depriving succeeding generations of the opportunity to continue the "family farm." Further, a sale might have the effect of removing the land from agricultural use where it is purchased at its speculative value by developers. Section 2032A

was adopted to provide relief where the farmland has been and will remain in agricultural production in which family members of the decedent will be actively engaged.

(a) **Expanded to trade or business:** [§933] Although this relief was initially extended to benefit farmland, it was ultimately extended to real property devoted to "use in a trade or business other than . . . [that] of farming." [I.R.C. §2032A(b)(2)(B)] Such other trade or business must, apparently, be a ***"closely held business,"*** as defined in section 6166(b), since section 2032A(g) directs the Treasury to promulgate Regulations as to the application of section 2032A to "an interest in a closely held business (within the meaning of paragraph (1) of section 6166(b))." (*See infra,* §1059 for discussion of closely held business interests.)

(2) **Special valuation in lieu of "fair market value":** [§934] If certain requirements are met (below), special methods of valuation may be used which take into account the earning power of the land, as farmland, rather than its speculative, inflated "market value." [*See* I.R.C. §2032A(a)]

(a) **Limitation:** At present, the decrease in value for estate tax purposes cannot exceed $750,000. [I.R.C. §2032A(a)(2)]

(b) **Valuation methods**

1) ***Farmland*** may be valued by dividing the net average annual gross cash rental for comparable land (gross cash rental or "net share rental," less real estate taxes) by the average annual effective interest rate for all new federal land bank loans. [I.R.C. §2032A(e)(7)] (The preceding five calendar years are used to obtain the averages.)

2) ***Real property used in other closely held businesses*** (or farmland, if the special farm method is not applicable) may be valued by various methods which rely principally upon a capitalization of earnings and which may produce a value lower than the land's speculative value. [I.R.C. §2032A(e)(8)]

(3) **Basic requirements:** [§935] Essentially, six requirements must be met in order for the estate to invoke the special use valuation:

(a) **U.S. decedent and property:** The decedent must have been a citizen or resident of the United States, and the real property must be located in the United States. [I.R.C. §2032A(a)(1)(A), (b)(1)]

(b) **Farm:** At the date of the decedent's death, the land must have been devoted to use as a farm for farming purposes (or to some other closely held trade or business use). [I.R.C. §2032A(b)(1), (2)]

(c) **Adjusted value:** Fifty percent or more of the adjusted value of the gross estate must consist of the adjusted value of property (real or personal) that was being so used, ***and*** twenty-five percent or more of the adjusted value of the gross estate must consist of the adjusted value of ***real property*** that was being so used. [I.R.C. §2032A(b)(1), (3)]

1) **Note:** "Adjusted value" for these purposes means the value of the property (or the gross estate) determined without reference to the special use value of section 2032A, ***reduced*** by any mortgage liability relating to the property (or gross estate). [I.R.C. §2032A(b)(3)]

2) **And note:** For purposes of determining the applicability of the fifty percent-twenty-five percent tests, the surviving spouse's community property interest in the farmland may be taken into account. [I.R.C. §2032A(e)(10)]

3) **Gifts made within three years of death:** Although outright gifts made within three years of death are no longer included in the donor-decedent's gross estate (*see supra*, §106), they are taken into account for purposes of the fifty percent-twenty-five percent tests. [I.R.C. §2035(d)] The purpose of this provision is to prevent persons from obtaining special valuation for real property by "death bed" gifts of nonqualifying property.

(d) **"Qualified heir":** The qualified property must pass from the decedent to a "qualified heir"—*i.e.*, a member of the decedent's family related in direct line or the immediate collateral line. [I.R.C. §2032A(b)(1), (e)(1), (2)]

1) ***Under section 2032A(e)(9)***, property will be deemed to have "passed" to a qualified heir where it is distributed to the heir in satisfaction of a pecuniary bequest.

2) ***The 1978 Act amended section 2032A(b)*** to make it clear that only such qualifying property as actually passes to a qualified heir may be used in determining the applicability of the fifty percent-twenty-five percent tests (above).

(e) **Use of property:** The property must have been owned by the decedent or a member of decedent's family and used as a farm (or in another closely held business) for five of the eight years immediately preceding the decedent's death, and the decedent or member of his family must have "materially participated in its operation." [I.R.C. §2032A(b)(1)(C)] Note that liberalized "material participation" rules applicable to retired or disabled persons and to surviving spouses were added by the 1981 Act. [*See* I.R.C. §2032A(b)(4), (5)]

(f) **Election of special use valuation:** The executor must elect the special use valuation, and all persons who acquire an interest in the property must consent to this election and assume personal liability for the potential "additional estate tax" (below). [I.R.C. §2032A(a)(1), (d)]

(4) **Additional tax imposed upon termination of qualified use:** [§936] Unless the land continues to be owned by a qualified heir and continues to be used for farming (or other closely held business use) in which a member of the decedent's family materially participates, the estate tax that was saved as a result of electing the special use valuation will become due and payable. [I.R.C. §2032A(c); *and see* special "material participation" rules for retired or disabled persons and for surviving spouses—I.R.C. §2032A(b)(4), (5)]

(a) **Liability:** However, liability for the "additional estate tax" is imposed upon the qualified heir; *i.e.*, the decedent's estate does not remain liable for this potential recapture of the estate taxes saved. [I.R.C. §2032A(c)(5)]

(b) **And note:** Continued ownership and use is required for a ***ten-year period***. [I.R.C. §2032A(c)(1)]

c. **Special valuation rules designed to limit "estate tax freezes":** [§937] During the decades of the 1970's and 1980's, planners employed a number of sophisticated devices to "freeze" the value of property expected to appreciate in value and to give away the anticipated appreciation in value free of gift or estate tax liability.

(1) **Example:** A owns all of the stock of M Corp. M Corp. is presently valued at $1 million. It is a prospering business and it is expected that M Corp. will at least double in value before A dies. A undertakes to "freeze" the present value of her ownership interest by recapitalizing the corporation and giving away the residual equity represented by the common stock. Specifically, A surrenders all of her stock to the corporation and receives, in return, 10,000 shares of voting preferred stock and 1,000 shares of voting common stock. The preferred stock has a par value and liquidation preference of $100 per share (aggregate book value of $1 million); the common stock has a nominal stated value of $.001 per share (aggregate book value of $1). A then gives all the common stock to her children. By these transactions, A intends to give all the residual equity and all future appreciation in value of the business to her children (at a minimal present gift tax cost), retain the present financial worth and voting control of the corporation during her life, and limit the estate tax value of her retained interest (in the form of the preferred stock) to about $1 million.

(2) **Effect:** The government found it difficult to limit the gift and estate tax avoidance potential of these types of "freeze" devices. It could successfully assert that the fair market value of the preferred stock might be less than its book value and, hence, that the value of the common stock,

for gift tax purposes, was greater than $1 (in the above example). [*See* Rev. Rul. 83-120, 1983-2 C.B. 170] This, however, did not prevent a tax-free gift of a substantial share of the future appreciation in value of the business. The government had less success in urging that the preferred stock should be valued at more than its book value for estate tax purposes. [*See* Estate of Salsbury v. Commissioner, 34 T.C. Mem. 1441 (1975)]

(3) **Legislative intervention:** [§938] Congress enacted section 2036(c) of the Code in 1987, then extended its scope in 1988. Section 2036(c) was a ***substantive estate tax inclusion*** section. It included in the gross estate the value of an interest in property transferred by a decedent during life if the decedent had retained an interest in the same property in the form of a ***management interest*** (voting rights) ***or financial interest*** (interest in the income stream of a business). It would apply to the estate tax freeze example set out above by including in A's gross estate the value of the common stock A gave to her children, thus preventing a gift of the appreciation in value.

(a) **Objections to section 2036(c):** The scope of section 2036(c) was extremely broad; it extended well beyond the typical estate tax freeze device of the above example. And, its provisions were extraordinarily complex. These aspects of the statute, taken individually, were very troublesome; taken together, they created a series of traps for taxpayers.

(b) **Repeal of section 2036(c):** Persuaded that section 2036(c) represented a case of legislative "over-kill," Congress repealed this provision ***retroactively*** in 1990. In its place, Congress enacted new Chapter 14. [I.R.C. §§2701-2704]

(4) **Chapter 14 valuation:** [§939] New Chapter 14 approaches the estate tax freeze problem as essentially a gift tax ***valuation issue***. Its general rules do not contemplate substantive amendments to the basic gift and estate tax inclusion rules.

(a) **Transactions affected:** [§940] Four types of situations are affected by Chapter 14:

1) Transfers of ***interests in corporations or partnerships*** [I.R.C. §2701];

2) Transfers of ***interests in trusts*** [I.R.C. §2702];

3) Valuation of ***property subject to certain rights and restrictions*** [I.R.C. §2703]; and

4) Treatment of certain ***lapsing rights and restrictions*** [I.R.C. §2704].

(b) **Transfer of interests in corporations or partnerships:** [§941] In general, section 2701 applies if a person transfers an interest in a corporation or partnership ***to or for the benefit of a family member*** (defined in section 2701(e)(1)), ***and*** the transferor or an "applicable family member" (defined in section 2701(e)(2)) ***retains an interest*** in the same corporation or partnership. [I.R.C. §2701(a)(1)]

1) **General exceptions to the application of section 2701:** [§942] There are three general situations where section 2701 will ***not*** apply:

a) Where ***market quotations*** are readily available for the transferred stock or the retained interest. [I.R.C. §2701(a)(1), (2)(A)]

b) Where there is only ***one class*** of interest or, if two classes, the classes of interest differ only as to voting rights. [I.R.C. §2701(a)(2)(B), (C)]

c) Where there is a ***proportionate transfer*** of all classes of interest. [I.R.C. §2701(a)(2)(C)]

2) **Valuation rules:** [§943] In general, the value of the interest transferred will be its fair market value, determined under usual valuation rules, but subject to the following special rules.

a) **Zero value rule for retained interests:** [§944] The transferred interest is valued by a "subtraction method," *i.e.*, the (proportionate) fair market value of the entire enterprise less the value of the retained interest. And, if the retained interest is an "applicable retained interest" it will be assigned a value of ***zero***. [I.R.C. §2701(a)(1), (3)(A)] The effect is to expose to the gift tax the entire (proportionate) value of the business with no reduction for the theoretical value of the retained interest.

1/ ***"Applicable retained interest"*** is defined in section 2701(b)(1) as a "distribution right" or a "liquidation, put, call or conversion right." These rights, in turn, are defined as:

a/ ***Distribution right*** is any right to receive distributions from a corporation with respect to its stock or from a partnership with respect to a partnership interest. [I.R.C. §2701(c)(1)(A)] b/ ***Liquidation, etc. right*** includes such rights or similar rights ***that affect the value of the transferred interest***. [I.R.C. §2701(c)(2)(A)]

2/ **Exceptions:** [§945] The statute contains a number of special exceptions. Those of most general applicability are:

a/ **Control:** The zero value rule will not apply to a distribution right unless the transferor (or applicable family member) holds at least fifty percent of the value or voting power of the entity immediately before the transfer. [I.R.C. §2701(b)(1)(A), (2)]

b/ **Qualified payments:** Nor does the zero value rule generally apply to distribution rights in the form of "qualified payments," defined as a fixed amount (or rate) payable on a periodic basis under a cumulative preferred stock or similar partnership interest. [I.R.C. §2701(a)(3)(A), (c)(3)(A)]

c/ **Junior equity:** Similarly, distribution rights with respect to a ***retained junior equity interest*** are not subject to the zero value rule. [I.R.C. §2701(c)(1)(B)] For this purpose, "junior equity" means common stock or an analogous subordinate interest in a partnership. [I.R.C. §2701(a)(4)(B)]

d/ **Fixed rights:** A liquidation, etc. right which must be exercised at a ***specific time and in a specific manner*** is also excepted. [I.R.C. §2701(c)(2)(B)]

b) **Minimum value rule:** [§946] If a "junior equity interest" is transferred, the proportionate value of the interest must be determined by valuing all junior equity interests at not less than ten percent of the total value of all equity interests in the entity, ***plus*** the total amount of any indebtedness of the entity to the transferor or to an applicable family member. [I.R.C. §2701(a)(4)(A)] The effect of this is to assure some value for gift tax purposes even where the zero value rule for retained interests is not applicable.

3) **Valuation of retained interest upon death of transferor:** [§947] Section 2701 affects valuation for gift tax purposes. If the retained interest of the transferor was subject

to the zero value rule, but is valued in the gross estate at its fair market value, some "double taxation" would occur.

a) **Adjustments to avoid double taxation mandated by statute:** Section 2701(e)(6) proposes to avoid this result by requiring the promulgation of Regulations which allow ". . . appropriate adjustments . . . for purposes of . . . [the estate, gift, and generation-skipping tax] to reflect the increase in the amount of the prior taxable gift made by the transferor. . . ."

b) **Adjustments allowed by Regulations:** The most recent Proposed Regulation provides that in computing the estate tax, the retained interest will be included at its fair market value, ***but*** the decedent's "adjusted taxable gifts" are to be reduced by the ***lesser*** of the amounts by which the decedent's taxable gifts were increased by reason of section 2701 ***or*** the difference between the value of the retained interest for estate tax purposes and the value assigned to that interest under section 2701 at the time of the initial transfer. [*See* Prop. Treas. Reg. 25.2701-5(b)]

4) **Illustration:** [§948] The effect of new section 2701 may be illustrated with respect to the example set out *supra*, §937. Assume for purposes of this illustration that the anticipated increase in the value of the corporation is realized; *i.e.*, the entire corporation is worth $2 million when A dies.

a) If A's "distribution rights" (dividends on preferred stock) are not fixed and cumulative ("qualified payments") or her liquidation right is not a "fixed right," her retained rights (all the preferred stock) will be valued at zero, and the gift of all common stock to her child will be valued at $1 million—the entire present value of the corporation.

b) If the dividends payable on the preferred stock retained ***are*** "qualified payments" and the liquidation provisions are "fixed rights," the zero value rule will not apply, ***but*** the value of the common stock must be assigned a value of at least $100,000 (10% of $1 million). Assuming that the valuation of the common stock, taking into account its junior equity status, minority discount, and lack of marketability, would be $40,000, the "minimum value rule" of section 2701(a)(4) will nevertheless produce a taxable gift of $100,000.

c) Upon A's death the preferred stock will be included in her estate under section 2033. Assuming that its fair market value, taking into account the liquidation preference and a premium for control, is determined to be $1.1 million, it will be included at that value. However, to avoid "double taxation," adjustments of A's "adjusted taxable gifts" are permitted:

1/ If the zero value rule applied to the lifetime gift of the common stock, A's adjusted taxable gifts would be reduced by $960,000—the lesser of the value of the includible preferred stock and the amount by which her lifetime gift was increased by virtue of the application of the zero value rule (assuming, as in b), above, that the common stock would have been valued at $40,000 apart from section 2701).

2/ Assuming that the minimum value rule applied, A's adjusted taxable gifts would be reduced by $60,000.

5) **Comment:** [§949] Note that although section 2701 clearly prevents undervaluation of the lifetime gift (indeed, it may produce overvaluation in some instances), it does not eliminate the opportunity to "freeze" estate tax values nor the opportunity to give away a significant amount of the anticipated appreciation in value.

(c) **Transfers of interests in trusts:** [§950] Retained interest gifts on trust were also deemed to provide a context for both the tax-free transfer of appreciation in value and for undervaluation of the interest transferred during life.

1) **Example:** D transfers real property valued at $100x to a trust for the benefit of his children. The property generates a modest income of about $6x per year (presently six percent of value); the property is held primarily for appreciation in value. D retains a right to income from the trust for a period of ten years. Using the then current ten percent tables prescribed for the valuation of term interests, the value of D's reserved ten-year term is approximately $62x, and the taxable gift of the remainder would be valued at $38x. However if the actual six percent return was used for valuation, D's retained interest would be valued at approximately $44x, and the value of the taxable gift would be $56x. Moreover, if D lives more than ten years, the remainderman will succeed to the then appreciated property with no further gift tax, and no inclusion in D's gross estate under section 2036.

2) **GRITs, GRATs, and GRUTs—section 2702:** [§951] Under section 2702, a "grantor retained income trust" (GRIT) will

be valued at zero for purposes of determining the value of the taxable gift of the remainder. [I.R.C. §2702(a)(1), (a)(2)(A)]

a) **Qualified interests—valued at greater than zero:** A value will be assigned to the grantor's retained interest only if it is a "qualified interest." [I.R.C. §2702(a)(2)(B)] There are two general types of qualified interests:

1/ **GRAT:** An interest that consists of a right to receive a ***fixed amount***, payable at least annually, is a GRAT "grantor retained annuity trust." [I.R.C. §2702(b)(1)]

2/ **GRUT:** An interest that consists of a right to receive a ***fixed percentage*** of the fair market value of the trust property, determined annually, is a GRUT "grantor retained unitrust." [I.R.C. §2702(b)(2)]

3) **Applies to term interests as well as remainders:** [§952] If one gives a term interest but retains a remainder, the remainder will be valued at zero unless the remainder is "noncontingent," and the term interests are in the form of either GRATs or GRUTs. [I.R.C. §2702(b)(3)]

4) **Exceptions:** [§953] The section 2702 zero value rule does not apply to:

a) **Transfers to nonfamily members:** Section 2702 only applies to the transfer of remainder interests to family members of the transferor, and only if the retained interest is held by the transferor or an applicable family member. [I.R.C. §2702(a)(1)]

b) **Incomplete gifts:** Gifts that are "incomplete" for gift tax purposes are logically excepted—and also specifically excepted by the statute. [I.R.C. §2702(a)(3)(A)(i), (B); *and see supra*, §§779 *et seq*., for discussion of incomplete gifts]

c) **Personal residence:** The zero value rule does not apply to the transfer of an interest in property that is to be used as a personal residence by the persons holding the term interests. [I.R.C. §2702(a)(3)(A)(ii)]

5) **Comments:** [§954] Again, this section does not prevent gifts of anticipated appreciation in value. But it does prevent undervaluation of the lifetime gift, and increases the real cost (present gift tax) of making the gift of anticipated (speculative) appreciation.

(d) **Property subject to restrictions:** [§955] Various types of burdens on property must be taken into account in valuing the property and may reduce its "fair market value." For example, restrictions on the transfer of property, options to buy for less than fair market value, or rights to use property for less than a fair rental value decrease the investment value and fair market value of the burdened property.

1) **Gift tax avoidance:** [§956] Congress was apparently concerned that real or colorable restrictions might be used to reduce the fair market value of property for gift tax purposes. Thus, section 2703 mandates that such restrictions are to be ***disregarded*** for purposes of the estate, gift, and generation-skipping taxes. [I.R.C. §2703(a)]

2) **Exception—bona fide business agreements:** [§957] This rule, however, does not apply to any option, agreement, right, or restriction that meets three statutory requirements set out in section 2703(b):

a) The option, etc., is a ***bona fide business arrangement***;

b) It is ". . . not a device to transfer . . . property to members of the decedent's family for ***less than full and adequate consideration*** in money or money's worth"; and

c) ". . .[I]ts terms are ***comparable to*** similar arrangements entered into by persons in an ***arm's length transaction***."

3) **Comments:** [§958] Although transactions between nonfamily members are not specifically excluded, the limitation of section 2703(b)(2)—not a device to make a disguised gift to family members—may effectively limit the broad language of section 2703(a) to intrafamily arrangements.

a) **And note:** Business purchase ("buy-sell") agreements represent the principal area for options coupled with restrictions on transfer. As noted below, section 2703 elaborates, but does not seem to substantially change, the valuation rules relating to such agreements which were previously developed by administrative rules and regulations and by court decisions. (*See infra*, §977.)

(e) **Lapsing rights and restrictions:** [§959] Under prior law, tax free transfers of significant economic benefits were possible where a transferor transferred an interest in property by gift, retained valuable rights with respect to the property, and then permitted or caused these rights to lapse, thus effectively shifting the value of these rights to the original donee.

1) **Example—right to vote stock:** Parent owns all the stock of a corporation. Parent transfers forty percent of the stock to her child retaining, however, voting control through the sixty percent stock ownership not given away. Subsequently, Parent causes or permits the voting power of the retained stock to lapse. Following the lapse, child-donee would possess 100 percent of the voting power, and this shift of control enhances the value of the child's stock while decreasing the value of the parent's. (*See supra*, §§200, 763.)

2) **Prior law:** [§960] Prior to 1990, the gift and estate tax was unable to reach this gratuitous shift of economic benefits because of the difficulty in finding that there was a ***transfer of property***. (*See supra*, §§200, 763.)

3) **Taxable transfers under section 2704:** [§961] Unlike the other provisions of new Chapter 14, which prescribe special ***valuation*** rules, section 2704 provides that the lapse of any voting or liquidation right in a corporation or partnership shall be treated as a ***transfer by gift*** or as a transfer ***includible in the decedent's gross estate***. [I.R.C. §2704(a)(1)]

   a) **Operative limitation—control:** [§962] A lapse of such a right is treated as a transfer (above) only if the individual holding the right immediately before the lapse and members of that individual's family (both before and after the lapse) ***control*** the corporation or partnership. [I.R.C. §2704(a)(2)] Control is defined as ownership of fifty percent or more of the voting power or value of the stock of a corporation, or fifty percent or more of the capital or profits interest in a partnership. [I.R.C. §§2704(c)(1), 2701(b)(2)]

      1/ **Implicit limitation—family owned entities:** The transfer treatment is limited to the shifting of economic benefits resulting from the lapse within family units (as defined in section 2704(c)(1) and (2)).

   b) **Amount of the transfer:** [§963] The taxable amount is the difference between the value of the interest retained immediately prior to the lapse and its value immediately after the lapse. And, for this purpose, the fact that the interest may be subject to lapsing rights is to be disregarded. [I.R.C. §§2704(a)(2); 2704(b)(1), (2)]

   c) **Exception for certain restrictions on liquidation:** [§964] Commercially reasonable restrictions imposed by an unrelated party in connection with a financing transaction and restrictions imposed by any federal or state law are disregarded in valuing any transfer. [I.R.C. §2704(b)]

4) **Comment:** [§965] This section eliminates a tax avoidance device without, apparently, undue distortion of traditional valuation rules.

C. VALUATION METHODS [§966]

There are, essentially, three general methods of valuation commonly used: (i) appraisal based upon known ***prices paid in the market***; (ii) ***actuarial valuation***; and (iii) an estimate of the market or investment value of property based upon a ***capitalization of the earnings*** of the property.

1. **Market Price Method**

   a. **Reference to identical property:** [§967] Where free market prices of identical property are known, the price at which that property is sold on the relevant valuation date is the best indication of fair market value. Valuation by reference to known market prices is most common in the case of listed securities regularly traded on an exchange.

   b. **Reference to comparable sales:** [§968] Where free market prices for identical property are not available, appraisal may be based upon "comparable sales," *i.e.*, known market prices of similar property. Valuation using comparable sales is most common in the case of real property appraisals.

2. **Actuarial Valuation:** [§969] The value of life estates, remainders, terms for years, annuities, etc., is based upon actuarial tables prescribed by the Regulations. [Treas. Reg. §§20.2031-10(f); 25.2512-9(f)]

3. **Capitalization of Earnings Method:** [§970] The market value of property may also be estimated by capitalizing the known earnings derived from the property. The economic theory underlying this method is that the value of property (what a person would pay for the property) is a function of the income that can be produced by the property. Although this is a rather sophisticated technique, it may be fairly simply described:

   (i) ***The anticipated earnings are determined on the basis of historical earnings.*** Usually the average earnings over the three to five years immediately preceding the valuation date are used.

   (ii) ***An educated guess*** is then made (from the appraiser's experience, reference to comparable businesses, etc.) as to the ***return on investment that a prudent investor would expect*** (or require) for the particular property involved, taking into account the stability of the investment, risks involved, etc.

   (iii) ***The estimated earning potential of the property is then capitalized*** using the guesstimated rate of return. The result of this computation is the estimated fair market value.

a. **Example:** If it is determined that the income to be derived from the property is $10,000 per year and that a prudent investor would require a ten percent return on investment for the type of property involved, the fair market value, under a capitalization of earnings method, would be $100,000 ($10,000 x 10).

D. VALUATION OF SOME SPECIFIC ITEMS

1. **Real Property:** [§971] As noted above, the fair market value of real property is usually established by appraisals employing a comparable sales method of valuation. Local assessed valuations cannot be used, except where they are shown to represent fair market value throughout the community. [Garstin v. United States, 352 F.2d 537 (Ct. Cl. 1965)]

    a. **"Highest and best use" standard:** [§972] As a general rule, the appraisal must take into account the "highest and best use" of the property (*i.e.*, the most economically productive use possible), even though the property was not being so used by the decedent (*e.g.*, decedent maintained his home on a lot zoned for commercial use).

2. **Stocks and Bonds**

    a. **Listed securities:** [§973] If the security is listed on an exchange or is regularly sold "over-the-counter," the fair market value is the mean between the highest and lowest selling price on the valuation date or the nearest trading date. If there are no sales on the valuation date for securities traded "over-the-counter," reference is made to the average of bid and asked prices to ascertain fair market value.

        (1) **"Blockage rule":** [§974] Securities that constitute a large block of stock or bonds of a particular corporation may be valued at less than market value on the theory that the sale of such a large block would depress the market price obtainable. [Treas. Reg. §20.2031-2(e)] (However, this rule will not be applied by the Service for purposes of valuing stock transferred by inter vivos gift.)

        (2) **Control premium:** [§975] On the other hand, where stock owned by the decedent represents effective ***control*** of a corporation, it may be valued at an amount ***greater*** than the "market price," on the theory that a person would pay more for a controlling block of stock than for an individual share.

    b. **Unlisted securities—closely held stocks, family corporations, etc.:** [§976] Unlisted securities are valued by considering all recent sales thereof, corporate net worth, earning capacity, etc. Although capitalization of earnings is frequently used to value such securities, all relevant factors must be considered: book value, earning power, general economic outlook, goodwill, reliance on decedent's services, etc. [Treas. Reg. §§20.2031-3; 25.2512-3; O'Malley v. Ames, 197 F.2d 256 (8th Cir. 1952); Rev. Rul. 59-60, 1959-1 C.B. 237]

        (1) **Effect of buy-sell agreement:** [§977] Traditionally, the price established in a buy-sell agreement (whereby the decedent agreed to sell her interest

at death to another) has been accepted as the value of the decedent's interest as long as the agreement was bona fide (negotiated at arm's length) and binding on the decedent both during her life and upon her death. [Treas. Reg. §20.2031-2(h); Brodrick v. Gore, 224 F.2d 892 (10th Cir. 1955)] The new "anti-freeze" valuation rules continue to recognize this effect of bona fide business arrangements, but also specify that the agreement must not be ". . . a device to transfer . . . property to members of the decedent's family for less than a full and adequate consideration . . .," and that the terms of the agreement must be ". . . comparable to similar arrangements entered into by persons in an arm's length transaction." [I.R.C. §2703(b); *and see supra*, §§955 *et seq.*]

c. **Mutual fund shares:** [§978] Formerly, the Service maintained that mutual fund shares should be valued at their "asking price"—the price for which they could have been purchased on the valuation date—even though the "asking price" is inflated by a sales commission or "load" and, as a practical matter, such shares can only be sold back to the fund at a determined redemption price which does not include the sales "load" and is, thus, less than the asking price. [*See* Treas. Reg. §20.2031-8(b)] However, in 1973 the Supreme Court rejected this position, holding that such shares should be valued at their "net asset value"—*i.e.*, the asking price less any sales commission or "load." [United States v. Cartwright, 411 U.S. 546 (1973)]

d. **Bonds, notes, evidences of indebtedness:** [§979] Such obligations are valued at their face value (unpaid principal) plus accrued interest, unless evidence is introduced to justify a discount (*e.g.*, an interest rate considerably below that regularly being charged). [Treas. Reg. §§20.2031-4; 25.2512-4]

3. **Life Estates, Annuities, Remainders, Reversionary Interests, etc.:** [§980] Annuities issued by a company regularly selling annuity contracts are valued by reference to the present cost of purchasing a similar contract from the company. [Treas. Reg. §§20.2031-8; 25.2512-6] All other annuities, life estates, reversions, and other future interests are valued under "present worth tables" prescribed by the Regulations, which are based upon standard mortality tables. [*See* Treas. Reg. §§20.2031-7; 25.2512-5]

V. COMPUTATION OF TAX

chapter approach

As with the valuation issues in the previous chapter, it is not very likely that your law school exam will place a great deal of emphasis upon tax computations. However, a basic familiarity with the manner in which the gift and estate taxes are computed will aid your understanding of the operation of the transfer taxes. Moreover, since the unified gift and estate tax system introduced by the Tax Reform Act of 1976 is, essentially, a computational rather than a substantive unification, familiarity with the tax computations is necessary for an understanding of the unified tax system.

This chapter first considers the procedure and rationale of the ***gift tax*** computation, including application of the unified credit. Then, attention is focused on ***estate tax*** computations, in connection with which the special credits against the estate tax allowed by sections 2011 through 2014 are discussed.

A. GIFT TAX COMPUTATIONS

1. **Overview:** [§981] The first three elements of the gift tax computation, whereby one arrives at "net" or "taxable" gifts [I.R.C. §2503], were previously discussed in connection with the substantive aspects of the gift tax. (*See supra,* §§723 *et seq.*) The remaining five elements of the computation—encompassing application of the rates of tax to taxable gifts and allowance of the gift tax unified credit—are specified in sections 2502, 2504, and 2505.

   a. **Computational procedure:** [§982] The gift tax liability for any calendar year is computed as follows:

      (1) ***Determine the amount of gifts*** made during the calendar year.

      (2) ***Deduct the annual exclusion*** with respect to present interest gifts made to the donee(s) to arrive at "gross gifts."

      (3) ***Deduct any allowable charitable and marital deductions*** to arrive at "net" or "taxable" gifts.

      (4) ***Add to the total value of the taxable (net) gifts for the current year*** the total amount of all taxable (net) gifts made ***in all prior*** calendar periods (*i.e.*, calendar quarters or years, depending upon the law applicable at the time of the prior gift). [I.R.C. §2502(a)(1); *and see* I.R.C. §2504(a), (b)]

      (5) ***Apply the rate schedule set out in section 2001(c)*** to the ***sum of total taxable gifts***—current taxable gifts plus all prior taxable gifts. [I.R.C. §2502(a)(1)]

(6) ***Apply the rate schedule of section 2001(c)*** to the total of taxable gifts for ***prior*** quarters and years. [I.R.C. §2502(a)(2)]

(7) ***Subtract the "tentative tax"*** computed with respect to prior taxable gifts (step 6) from the tentative tax computed with respect to all taxable gifts made by the donor (step 5). [I.R.C. §2502(a)]

(8) ***From this result*** (which represents the tax upon current taxable gifts at marginal rates of tax determined with reference to prior as well as current taxable gifts) ***subtract any allowable gift tax unified credit***. [I.R.C. §2505] The balance is the tax liability for the current calendar quarter.

b. **Brief elaboration:** [§983] Some "definitional" aspects of the computational elements should be noted.

(1) **Prior taxable gifts:** [§984] With one exception, the taxable gifts for prior calendar quarters or years are determined in accordance with the law applicable at the time the gift was made. [I.R.C. §2504] Thus, it is the law in effect ***at the time of the actual transfer***, not the present law, that governs whether a transfer was a "gift," the amount of any exclusion allowed in arriving at "gross gifts," and the amount of allowable deductions.

(a) **Application**

1) **Annuities:** [§985] Between 1954 and 1986, the transfer of annuities under qualified plans was at least partially excluded from the gift tax. [I.R.C. §2517—*repealed* in 1986] Such gifts made during this period would, to the extent former section 2517 applied, be exempt and are not included among prior taxable gifts.

2) **Marital deduction:** [§986] Prior to 1948, no marital deduction was allowed; thus, the full value of property transferred to a spouse prior to 1948 would be taken into account in determining prior taxable gifts. And, before 1982, transfers to a spouse were not fully deductible. (*See supra,* §§909 *et seq.*) Thus for gifts made between 1948 and 1982, any taxable (nondeductible) portions of the gift would enter into the determination of prior taxable gifts.

3) **Annual exclusion:** [§987] Further, prior to 1982, the amount of the annual exclusion was $3,000 ($4,000 between 1938 and 1943, and $5,000 between 1932 and 1938); and the amount of the exclusion allowable at the time the transfer was made determines the "gross gift" (and "taxable gift").

(b) **Exception—the specific exemption:** [§988] However, for purposes of determining prior taxable gifts, the deduction for the specific exemption (allowed for gifts prior to 1977) is limited to $30,000, even though an exemption of $40,000 was allowed between 1936 and 1942 ($50,000 between 1932 and 1935). [I.R.C. §2504(a)(3)]

(2) **Rates of tax:** [§989] The rates of tax to be applied in arriving at the tentative tax upon current gifts ***and*** the tentative tax upon prior taxable gifts are the rates ***currently*** specified in section 2001(c), ***without regard*** to the fact that different rates may actually have been used in computing tax liability with respect to prior taxable gifts. [I.R.C. §2502(a)]

2. **Unified Tax Rate Schedule:** [§990] Prior to 1977, gift taxes were computed in accordance with a special tax rate schedule applicable only to the gift tax. However, with passage of the Tax Reform Act of 1976, effective for transfers made after December 31, 1976, the same rate schedule is now applied to both lifetime and testamentary transfers. As originally enacted in 1976, the unified rate schedule was graduated from 18 percent (upon gifts up to $10,000) to 70 percent (upon gifts in excess of $5,000,000). The 1981 Act phased in a reduction of ***top-bracket*** rates to a maximum of 50 percent. The phase-in of the top bracket rates was, however, modified and extended by subsequent Revenue Acts. Under present law, the top bracket of 50 percent for taxable estates in excess of $2,500,000 applies to estates of decedents dying in 1993 and thereafter. [I.R.C. §2001(c)(2)(D)] However, the rates used in computing the tentative tax must be increased by five percent in the case of estates valued between $10,000,000 and $21,040,000 (or $18,340,000 after 1992). [I.R.C. §2001(c)(3)] This latter augmentation of rates for mega-estates is designed to reduce and ultimately eliminate the benefit of the graduated rates and the unified credit for these estates.

3. **Cumulative Nature of Tax:** [§991] As noted above, the tax rates applicable to current gifts are determined not only by the amount of gifts made during the calendar quarter but also with regard to ***all prior gifts*** made by the donor since the enactment of the gift tax in 1932. In other words, the gift tax rates are ***cumulative***.

   a. **Cumulation of pre-1977 gifts:** [§992] Again, note that the unified tax rates are applied not only with respect to all gifts made after 1976 but also, for purposes of computing the current tax liability, with respect to gifts made prior to 1977. (*Compare* unified estate taxes, *infra*, §1010.)

   b. **Effect of cumulation:** [§993] However, this does not mean that a gift tax is paid over and over again! The tentative tax computed with respect to all taxable gifts is reduced by the tentative tax applicable to prior taxable gifts and, thus, there is no multiple taxation. What the cumulation of taxable gifts does, essentially, is to expose current taxable gifts to ***higher marginal rates*** of tax, because the value of the current gifts are "placed on top of" the amount of all prior taxable gifts.

4. **Unified Gift Tax Credit:** [§994] The 1976 Tax Reform Act introduced a gift tax credit (applied directly against tax liability) in place of the former $30,000 specific exemption (which operated as a deduction). [I.R.C. §2505] This gift tax credit operates in tandem with the unified estate tax credit (*infra*, §1014) to provide, in effect, a ***single credit*** against transfer taxes, whether the transfers were made during life or upon death.

a. **Amount of credit:** [§995] As initially enacted, the unified credit was phased in over a five-year period (1977 through 1981) from $30,000 (in 1977) to $47,000 (by 1981). The 1981 Act substantially increased the amount of the unified credit; by 1987, a credit in the amount of $192,800 may be claimed. [I.R.C. §2505]

(1) **Exemption equivalent:** [§996] The exemption equivalent of a $192,800 credit is $600,000. Thus, the unified credit effectively eliminates any transfer taxes upon taxable transfers (lifetime and/or testamentary) of up to this amount.

(2) **Five-year phase-in of initial credit:** [§997] There was a five-year phase-in of the unified credit for gifts made after 1976 and before 1981. The amount of the credit during this phase-in period, and the exemption equivalent represented thereby, was as follows:

Year	Credit	Exemption Equivalent
1977	$30,000	$126,667
1978	$34,000	$134,000
1979	$38,000	$147,333
1980	$42,000	$161,563
1981	$47,000	$175,625

(3) **Six-year phase-in of credit allowed by 1981 Act:** [§998] For gifts made in 1982 and thereafter, there was a six-year phase-in of the augmented unified credit, as follows:

Year	Credit	Exemption Equivalent
1982	$62,800	$225,000
1983	79,300	275,000
1984	96,300	325,000
1985	121,800	400,000
1986	155,800	500,000
1987	192,800	600,000

(4) **Effect of pre-1977 gifts:** [§999] With one exception, the amount of the unified gift tax credit is ***not*** affected by the amount of pre-1977 gifts or by the

fact that the donor utilized the full $30,000 exemption allowed under prior law.

(a) **Exception:** The one exception pertains to gifts made between September 8, and December 31, 1976: If any portion of the $30,000 specific exemption, then allowable, was applied as a deduction against these gifts, the amount of the unified credit available for post-1976 transfers is reduced by twenty percent of that portion of the specific exemption that was so utilized. [I.R.C. §2505(b)]

(b) **Example:** If a taxpayer made a present interest gift of $15,000 in December 1976 and applied $12,000 of an allowable specific exemption against the $12,000 "gross gift" (after the $3,000 annual exclusion then applicable), the amount of the unified credit available to the taxpayer after 1976 will be reduced by $2,400 ($12,000 x 20%).

b. **Limitation—unified credit must be claimed or forfeited:** [§1000] The statute expressly states that the amount of the unified credit available for current gifts must be reduced by the sum of any amounts ***allowable*** as a credit for prior gifts. [I.R.C. §2505(a)] Thus, unlike the $30,000 specific exemption which would not be reduced or lost merely because it was not claimed as a deduction against prior gifts, the unified gift tax credit must be applied against the tax liability produced by post-1976 gifts in the order of time in which they are made and, if not so applied, the amount of the credit that could have been claimed for preceding calendar years is forfeited.

c. **Relationship to estate tax:** [§1001] Because the unified gift and estate tax credits are set forth under separate sections of the Code, it may appear that they operate consecutively. However, the computational mechanics of the estate tax assure that only a single, unified credit will be allowed against lifetime and testamentary transfers (*see infra*, §§1008, 1015).

5. **Example of Gift Tax Computation:** [§1002] Assume that in 1975, D made a gift of $133,000 to X against which D claimed the $3,000 annual exclusion and the $30,000 specific exemption. The taxable gift was therefore $100,000, upon which D paid a gift tax of $15,525 (under prior rates). Assume further that in 1982, D makes a gift of $250,000 to Y, and in 1990, D makes a gift of $500,000 to Z.

a. **Illustrative computation:** Based upon the above hypothetical facts, D's gift tax liability for 1982 and 1990 would be computed as follows:

(1) D's 1982 gift tax liability would be $14,800:

Amount of gift [§§2501, 2511]	$250,000
Less: annual exclusion [§2503(b)]	10,000
Taxable gift	240,000
Add: prior taxable gifts	100,000
Total taxable gifts	$340,000

Tentative tax ($70,800 + 34% of $90,000) [§2001(c)]	$101,400
Less: tentative tax on prior gift of $100,000 (use unified rates)	23,800
Tax	77,600
Less: unified credit (1982 limit) [§2505]	62,800
Gift tax liability	$ 14,800

(2) And D's 1990 gift tax liability would be $87,100:

Amount of gift	$500,000
Less: annual exclusion	10,000
Taxable gift	490,000
Add: prior taxable gifts	340,000
Total taxable gifts	$830,000
Tentative tax ($248,300 + 39% of $80,000)	$279,500
Less: tentative tax on prior gifts of $340,000	101,400
Tax	178,100
Less: unified credit (1990 limit less credit previously allowable: $192,800-$62,800)	130,000
Gift tax liability	$ 48,100

B. ESTATE TAX COMPUTATIONS

1. **Background:** [§1003] Prior to the 1976 Tax Reform Act, the estate tax liability was determined separately, without regard to whether the decedent had made taxable gifts during life. This allowed for substantial aggregate transfer tax savings where a person was willing and able to make completed gifts during life which would not be exposed to the estate tax. The advantages were threefold: (i) the donor would utilize the separate gift tax exclusions and specific exemption as well as the former $60,000 exemption under the estate tax; (ii) the prior gift tax rates were set at 75 percent of the estate tax rate within the same brackets; and (iii) property not given away during life received a "new start" through the separate graduated estate tax rates rather than being exposed to marginal rates of tax determined "on top of" previous lifetime gratuitous transfers.

   a. **Pre-1977 estate tax computations:** [§1004] From the value of the gross estate, allowable deductions were subtracted to arrive at the taxable estate. The separate estate tax rate schedule was then applied to the taxable estate to arrive at the estate tax. Finally, where applicable, the estate tax could be reduced by certain credits against tax allowed under sections 2011 through 2014. The result was the estate tax liability.

   b. **Post-1976 estate tax computations:** [§1005] The 1976 Act retained the same basic procedure but made several important changes designed to equalize the tax treatment of gratuitous transfers, whether testamentary or inter vivos. The present computations undertake to produce essentially the same aggregate tax results whether the property is transferred during life or upon death.

(1) **Application:** A unified rate schedule applies for ***both*** estate and gift taxes, ***and*** the aggregate amount of taxable gifts made by the decedent after 1976 (other than gifts included in the gross estate under sections 2035 through 2038) is ***added*** to the taxable estate to form the relevant estate tax base. Then, as with the cumulative gift tax computation, the tentative tax—computed by applying the unified rate schedule to aggregate gratuitous transfers—is reduced by the gift taxes payable with respect to gifts included in the estate tax base.

(2) **Remaining advantages of lifetime gifts:** [§1006] Although the unified system reduces the transfer tax savings that can be produced by making lifetime gifts, it does not eliminate the advantages altogether.

(a) **Example:** The gift tax annual exclusion of $10,000 per year per donee is still allowed. Thus, by making annual gifts to multiple donees (and splitting these gifts with one's spouse) considerable amounts of property can be transferred with no transfer tax exposure.

(b) **Example:** The gift tax is based upon the value of the property at the date of the gift. Hence, if the gift is complete (not subject to the estate tax), all appreciation in value of the transferred property between the date of gift and date of death "passes" to the donee with no transfer tax exposure.

2. **Overview:** [§1007] The "taxable estate" (gross estate less allowable deductions) is determined in accordance with the rules previously discussed in connection with the substantive aspects of the estate tax (*supra*, §§26 *et seq.*). The remaining elements of the present, cumulative estate tax computation are analogous to (but differ somewhat from) the cumulative gift tax computation (*compare supra*, §§983 *et seq.*).

a. **Computational procedure:** [§1008] The present estate tax computation may be divided into seven steps:

(1) ***First, determine the value of the gross estate.***

(2) ***From the gross estate, any allowable deductions*** are subtracted. The result is the taxable estate.

(3) ***The amount of "adjusted taxable gifts" (below) is then added*** to the amount of the taxable estate. [I.R.C. §2001(b)(1)] The result is the base for the "tentative estate tax."

(4) ***The "tentative estate tax"*** is then ascertained by applying a unified rate schedule to the estate tax base. [I.R.C. §2001(b),(c)]

(5) ***From the tentative estate tax, there is subtracted the aggregate amount of "tax payable"*** under the gift tax with respect to gifts made by the decedent after December 31, 1976. [I.R.C. §2001(b)(2)] The result is the estate tax.

(6) ***The estate tax thus computed is then reduced by the amount of the estate tax unified credit.*** [I.R.C. §2010]

(7) ***And finally, any applicable credits*** under sections 2011 through 2014 are subtracted. The result is the estate tax liability.

b. **Applicable definitions:** [§1009] Certain definitions and special aspects of the computational mechanics should be noted.

(1) **"Adjusted taxable gifts":** [§1010] This is defined as the total amount of taxable gifts made by the decedent ***after*** December 31, 1976, ***except*** gifts that are includible in the decedent's gross estate—*i.e.*, gifts that comprise part of the "taxable estate." [I.R.C. §2001(b)]

(a) **Example:** In arriving at the total amount of taxable gifts, the annual exclusion is taken into account. For example, if a present interest gift of $25,000 was made in 1990 against which an annual exclusion ($10,000) was applied, $15,000 would be deemed part of "adjusted taxable gifts."

(b) **Note:** "Adjusted taxable gifts" is ***limited*** to gifts made ***after*** the effective date of the Tax Reform Act (after December 31, 1976). (Contrast this with the cumulative gift tax computation, which takes into account all taxable gifts made by the taxpayer, *supra*, §991.)

(c) **Compare:** In the case of "split gifts" (*supra*, §871), the estate of each spouse would treat the one-half of each split gift attributed to the spouse as an "adjusted taxable gift" made by that spouse, ***except*** that where the full value of the gift is included in the ***gross estate*** of the ***actual donor*** under section 2035 (transfers within three years of death), ***no portion*** of the gift will be included in the ***consenting spouse's*** estate tax computation as an adjusted taxable gift. [I.R.C. §2001(e)]

(2) **"Tax payable":** [§1011] The gift "tax payable" which will reduce the tentative tax computed on the entire estate tax base includes those gift taxes payable with respect to ***all*** gifts made ***after December 31, 1976***—*i.e.*, gifts included in the gross estate (and thus the taxable estate), as well as "adjusted taxable gifts." It does not include gift taxes paid or payable with respect to pre-1977 gifts since these gifts do not form any part of the estate tax base. [I.R.C. §2001(b)(2); *and see infra*, §1024, concerning the credit for gift taxes with respect to pre-1977 gifts that are included in the decedent's gross estate]

(3) **Adjustment for gift tax paid by spouse:** [§1012] If the decedent's spouse consented to split a gift (*supra*, §§869-874) which is thereafter included in full

in the decedent's gross estate (since the decedent was the actual donor), the tentative tax is reduced by the ***entire*** amount of the gift tax payable with respect to the gift—*i.e.*, the gift tax imposed upon the decedent's spouse as well as that imposed upon the decedent. [I.R.C. §2001(d)]

3. **Rates of Tax:** [§1013] For purposes of determining the "tentative estate tax" and the "tax payable" (with respect to prior gifts made by the decedent), the unified graduated rates of section 2001(c), ***as in effect at the decedent's death***, are applied. [I.R.C. §2001(b)]

4. **Unified Estate Tax Credit:** [§1014] The unified estate tax credit is identical in amount (and phase-in) to the unified gift tax credit; *see supra*, §§994-998. [I.R.C. §2010; *and compare* I.R.C. §2505]

   a. **No double credit:** [§1015] Although the unified gift and estate tax credits are separately applied under two different sections of the Code, the computational mechanics of the estate tax assure that there is only a ***single, unified credit***. Because the gift "tax payable" (which serves as a type of credit against the tentative estate tax) will have been reduced by any unified gift tax credit allowed or allowable against gift taxes, the use of the unified gift tax credit is effectively factored out at this point of the estate tax computation and, thus, must be reintroduced by application of the unified estate tax credit against the tentative estate tax liability.

   b. **Reduction of credit for certain pre-1977 gifts:** [§1016] Just as in the case of the unified gift tax credit, the deduction of the former $30,000 gift tax specific exemption against pre-1977 taxable gifts does not generally affect the allowance of the unified credit with respect to post-1976 gift or estate tax liability. However, if the specific exemption was applied against gifts made between September 8, 1976, and December 31, 1976, the amount of the allowable unified credit is reduced by twenty percent of the amount of the exemption so used (*supra*, §999).

5. **Other Credits Allowed Against Estate Tax:** [§1017] In addition to the unified estate tax credit, the Code authorizes four other credits against the estate tax:

   a. **Credit for state death taxes paid:** [§1018] Under section 2011, a credit is allowed for inheritance, legacy, estate, and succession taxes actually paid to any state of the United States (or territory or the District of Columbia).

      (1) **Limitations:** [§1019] The state death tax credit is subject to three principal limitations:

         (a) **Property taxable in estate:** [§1020] A credit is not allowed for state death taxes paid on property that is not included in the decedent's gross estate for federal estate tax purposes; *i.e.,* the credit is limited to property subject to both federal and state death taxes. [I.R.C. §2011(a)]

(b) **Amount of credit**

1) **Percentage of "adjusted taxable estate":** [§1021] The total credit that can be claimed is limited to certain amounts depending on the size of the federal "adjusted taxable estate." These limits are specified in a table set out in subsection (b) of section 2011. In general, no credit is permitted where the adjusted taxable estate is under $40,000; for taxable estates in excess of this amount, the maximum credit is established as a percentage of the adjusted taxable estate ranging from 0.8 percent to 16 percent.

a) The term "adjusted taxable estate" means the decedent's taxable estate (*supra*) ***minus*** $60,000. [I.R.C. §2011(b) (last sentence)]

2) **"Tax less unified credit" ceiling:** [§1022] Note that the credit for state death taxes cannot exceed the amount of the estate tax reduced by the unified credit (above). [I.R.C. §2011(f)]

(c) **Time of payment:** [§1023] Generally, the credit is allowed if the state death taxes are actually paid within a period of four years following the filing of the estate tax return, and credit therefor against the federal estate tax must be claimed within the same four-year period. [I.R.C. §2011(c)]

b. **Credit for certain pre-1977 gift taxes paid:** [§1024] As previously noted, in order to prevent "double" taxes, a credit was allowed for gift taxes paid on gifts that were also included in the donor's gross estate. [I.R.C. §2012(a)-(d)] This credit may still be claimed with respect to pre-1977 gifts. However, the credit is inapplicable to gifts made after 1976 since the reduction of the tentative estate tax by the gift "tax payable" under section 2001(b)(2) accomplishes this same result. [I.R.C. §2012(e)]

c. **Credit for taxes paid on prior estate—property previously taxed to another:** [§1025] Section 2013 authorizes a credit for the estate tax imposed upon other estates with respect to property that passed from such other estates to the decedent and which is included in the latter decedent's gross estate. This credit was enacted to relieve against repeated estate taxation, in quick succession, of property passing from one decedent to another. The following rules are applicable:

(1) ***A credit*** is allowed for the federal tax actually paid on any property passing to the decedent during her lifetime from the estate of some prior decedent. (The credit is available as to property passing from one spouse to another, but only to the extent that the property did ***not*** qualify for the marital deduction.)

(2) ***It is not required*** that the same property that the present decedent received from the prior decedent be a part of her estate. All that need appear is that some property subject to a prior estate tax was received by the decedent, even if the decedent has consumed, sold or otherwise disposed of that property.

(3) ***The amount of the credit*** depends upon the interval between deaths. If the first decedent died within two years of the death of the present decedent, 100 percent of the estate tax paid in the first decedent's estate is allowable; 80 percent if within four years; 60 percent if within six years; 40 percent if within eight years; and 20 percent if within ten years.

(4) ***One other limitation*** is imposed—the credit cannot be more than the estate tax savings if the previously taxed property were entirely excluded from the decedent's estate. This is to account for situations where property has fallen steeply in value since the date of the first decedent's death.

d. **Foreign tax credit:** [§1026] Recall that both foreign real and personal property may be included in the estate of a United States citizen (*supra*, §23). Since such property is usually also taxed by the country in which it is located, the decedent's estate may be subject to double taxation. To avoid this, section 2014 allows a credit against the United States estate tax for the amount of any foreign death taxes payable with respect to property situated in a foreign country and included in the decedent's gross estate for federal tax purposes.

(1) **Executor's election:** As seen earlier, the executor may elect to claim certain foreign death taxes as a deduction in computing the decedent's taxable estate in lieu of applying these taxes as a credit (*supra*, §593).

(2) **Credit pursuant to treaty:** In addition to the foreign tax credit, the United States has treaties with several foreign nations providing reciprocal recognition and credits for death duties paid. Where death taxes are paid to a country with which such a treaty is in effect, the estate may claim the larger of the statutory credit or the treaty credit.

6. **Example of Estate Tax Computation:** [§1027] Assume the same facts set out *supra*, §1002. In addition, assume that D (in that example) dies in 1992, leaving a taxable estate of $2,000,000.

a. **Illustrative computation:** D's estate tax liability would be $906,800, computed as follows:

Taxable estate	$2,000,000
Add: adjusted taxable gifts (post-1976 gifts only) [§2001(b)(1)]	730,000
Base for tentative tax	$2,730,000
Tentative tax ($1,025,800 + 53% of $230,000) [§2001(c)(2)(D)]	$1,147,700
Less: gift taxes payable (only post-1976 gifts): ($155,800 + 37% of $230,000 ***less*** allowable credit) [§2001(b)(2)]	48,100
Tax	1,099,600
Less: unified credit [§2010]	192,800
Estate tax liability	$ 906,800

VI. RETURNS AND PAYMENT OF TAX

chapter approach

This chapter considers some of the basic rules relating to the filing of returns and the payment of transfer taxes and also introduces some special provisions relating to installment payment of estate taxes. While this material comprises only a very minor portion of most estate and gift tax courses, a review of the basic rules is appropriate for you to have a systematic understanding of the transfer tax schemes.

A. GIFT TAX

1. **Returns:** [§1028] A gift tax return must be filed for any calendar year in which a gift is made. [I.R.C. §6019]

   a. **Exceptions:** [§1029] A gift tax return need not be filed if the only transfers made during the year are fully exempt from tax or are nontaxable because of the 100 percent marital deduction. [I.R.C. §6019(a)] Specifically that would be:

      (1) ***If no gift exceeds the $10,000 annual exclusion*** for present interest gifts under section 2503(b) (*see supra*, §§841 *et seq.*).

      (2) ***Gifts for certain educational or medical expenses*** that are exempt under section 2503(e) (*see supra*, §865).

      (3) ***Gifts that qualify for the gift tax marital deduction*** under section 2523 (*see supra*, §§887 *et seq.*).

   b. **Time for filing:** [§1030] Gift tax returns must be filed on or before the fifteenth day of April following the close of the calendar year in which a gift is made. [I.R.C. §6075(b)]

      (1) **Extensions of time:** [§1031] However, extensions of up to six months may be granted upon application. [I.R.C. §6081]

      (2) **Special rules:** [§1032] If a donor is granted an extension of time to file an ***income tax return*** for the calendar year in which a gift was made, this extension will ***also apply*** to any ***gift tax return*** to be filed. [I.R.C. §6075(b)(2)] Also, if a donor dies within the calendar year in which a gift was made, the gift tax return may be filed (by the executor) on or before the time required for the filing of the donor-decedent's estate tax return (*infra*, §1047). [I.R.C. §6075(b)(3)]

c. **Responsibility for filing:** [§1033] The ***donor*** is required to file the gift tax return. [I.R.C. §6019(a)] (If deceased, the donor's executor files the return.)

2. **Payment of Tax:** [§1034] The donor is primarily liable for payment of the gift tax. [I.R.C. §2502(c)]

a. **Transferee liability:** [§1035] If the donor fails to pay the tax, the government has a lien on the donated property to the extent of the tax due, and also has the right to hold the ***donee*** liable (transferee liability) for the unpaid gift tax, to the extent of the value of the property received by the donee. [I.R.C. §6324(b)]

b. **Reimbursement where "Q-tip" property transferred:** [§1036] If a donee-spouse incurs gift tax liability on account of a transfer of the donee-spouse's life interest in "qualified terminable interest property" (*see supra*, §758), the donee-spouse is entitled to be reimbursed by the recipient of the property for the gift taxes attributable to this transfer. [I.R.C. §2207A(b)]

c. **Time for payment:** [§1037] Payment of the tax is due at the same time that the return must be filed (above) and should accompany the return. [I.R.C. §6151(a)]

(1) **Extensions of time:** [§1038] Extensions of time for payment may be granted for up to six months upon application. [I.R.C. §6161] However, the grant of such an extension does not waive the government's right to interest upon the unpaid tax from the due date.

3. **Special Rules for Split Gifts:** [§1039] There is no reason for a husband and wife to "split" a gift under section 2513 unless the value of the gift would require a return to be filed—*i.e.*, where the gift is of a future interest to which the annual exclusion does not apply, or the value of a present interest gift exceeds $10,000.

a. **Filing requirement:** [§1040] If the gift of a future interest is split, both spouses must file a return reporting one-half of the value of the property. In the case of a present interest gift, the actual donor must file a return if the gift exceeds $10,000; the consenting spouse need not file a return unless the one-half of the value of the gift that is attributed to that spouse itself exceeds $10,000.

(1) **Note:** If the consenting spouse is not obliged to file a return, his consent to split the gift will be indicated on the return filed by the actual donor. Otherwise, the consent is indicated on the consenting spouse's return (although apparently it is sufficient if the consent is indicated on the return filed by the actual donor).

b. **Liability for tax:** [§1041] Both spouses are jointly and severally liable for payment of the gift tax on split gifts. [I.R.C. §2513(d)] Note, however, that if the actual donor pays the entire tax (or the consenting spouse pays the entire tax), this payment of the other spouse's "share" is not a taxable gift to the other spouse. [Treas. Reg. §25.2511-1(d)]

B. ESTATE TAX

1. **Returns:** [§1042] The executor of the decedent's estate is responsible for the filing of the estate tax return. [I.R.C. §6018(a)]

    a. **Who is the executor:** [§1043] For estate tax purposes, the term "executor" means "the executor or administrator of the decedent, or, if there is no executor or administrator appointed, qualified, and acting within the United States, then any person in actual or constructive possession of any property of the decedent." [I.R.C. §2203]

    b. **Returns by beneficiaries:** [§1044] If the executor is unable to file a complete return with respect to some portion of the gross estate, he must identify that portion of the estate and provide the name of the persons holding legal title or a beneficial interest in the property. The government may then require those persons to file a return as to that part of the estate. [I.R.C. §6018(b)]

    c. **Limitation—filing amount:** [§1045] A return is required only if the amount of the ***gross estate*** exceeds certain specified amounts. [I.R.C. §6018(a)(1), (3)] These filing amounts track the "exemption equivalent" of the unified credit (*supra*, §998). Since 1987, the filing amount has been $600,000.

    d. **Nonresident aliens:** [§1046] A return is required for estates of nonresident aliens if that part of the gross estate that is situated in the United States exceeds $60,000. [I.R.C. §6018(a)(2)]

    e. **Time for filing:** [§1047] The return must be filed no later than nine months after the date of the decedent's death. [I.R.C. §6075(a)]

        (1) **Extensions of time:** [§1048] However, extensions of time for up to six months may be granted upon application. [I.R.C. §6081(a)]

2. **Payment of Estate Tax:** [§1049] The executor is also primarily responsible for payment of the estate tax. [I.R.C. §6151(a)]

    a. **Personal liability:** [§1050] Moreover, the executor is personally liable for payment of the tax until he has been discharged from liability upon application to the Service. [I.R.C. §2204]

    b. **Estate's right to reimbursement in certain instances:** [§1051] Sections 2206 and 2207 entitle the executor to recover from the beneficiary of life insurance proceeds and from a person who takes property in which the decedent had a taxable power of appointment the proportionate share of the estate tax that was payable because of inclusion of the life insurance proceeds or property subject to the power in the decedent's gross estate.

    c. **Reimbursement where estate includes "Q-tip" property:** [§1052] Where a decedent's (surviving spouse's) estate includes "qualified terminable interest property" (*see supra*, §§697, 704-705), the executor (unless otherwise directed by the decedent's will) is entitled to recover from the recipient of the property the attributable estate taxes. [I.R.C. §2207A(a)]

d. **Lien for taxes; transferee liability:** [§1053] If the estate tax is not paid when due, those persons who hold legal or beneficial interests in property that was included in the gross estate are liable for the payment of the estate tax to the extent of the value of the property. [I.R.C. §6324(a)(2)] In addition, the government has a lien on all the estate assets to secure payment of the tax and may institute proceedings to foreclose the lien. [I.R.C. §6324(a)(1)]

e. **Time for payment:** [§1054] Payment of the estate tax is due at the same time that the estate tax return must be filed—nine months after the decedent's death. [I.R.C. §6151(a)]

(1) **Extensions of time for payment**

(a) **Upon showing of cause:** [§1055] Extensions of time for payment may be granted, upon a showing of reasonable cause, for periods of up to ten years from the date upon which the payment is otherwise due. [I.R.C. §6161(a)(2)] However, as with gift tax payments, the granting of such an extension does not preclude the running of interest.

(b) **Extensions of time for reversionary or remainder interests:** [§1056] Further, if the estate of the decedent includes a reversionary interest or a remainder interest in property, the executor may elect to postpone the payment of tax with respect to such interests until six months after the termination of the precedent interest or interests in the property. [I.R.C. §6163]

(c) **Installment payments allowed in certain situations:** [§1057] Where an estate is substantially composed of an interest in a ***"closely held business"*** (which might have to be liquidated to pay the estate tax at the due date), the Code authorizes payment of the estate tax liability related to the closely held business interest in installments. [I.R.C. §6166]

1) **Five-year deferral; ten yearly installment payments:** [§1058] Under section 6166, the executor may elect to defer payment of the estate tax attributable to a closely held business interest for up to five years, and then pay the tax in up to ten equal annual installments. [I.R.C. §6166(a)]

2) **Requirements:** [§1059] There are essentially two requirements for this relief:

a) The interest must be an interest in a ***"closely held business,"*** which is defined for this purpose as a sole proprietorship or a twenty percent or greater interest in a partnership or corporation (or a lesser interest if the partnership had fifteen partners or less, or the corporation had fifteen shareholders or less). [I.R.C. §6166(b)(1)]

b) **The *value*** of the closely held business interest must exceed thirty-five percent of the adjusted gross estate. [I.R.C. §6166(a)]

3) **Disqualification—acceleration:** [§1060] However, provision is made for acceleration of installments upon default or the disposition or withdrawal of more than fifty percent in value of the business interest. [I.R.C. §6166(g)]

f. **Apportionment of tax:** [§1061] The estate tax is imposed upon the estate as a whole, not upon any particular property or asset therein. In the absence of a contrary direction in the decedent's will or in local statutes, the burden of the estate tax follows the general order of abatement prescribed by the state statute; typically, this would require payment of tax first from property that passes by intestacy, then from the residuary estate, then general legacies, and, finally, specific bequests.

VII. TAX ON GENERATION-SKIPPING TRANSFERS

chapter approach

As we have seen, life estates and other interests that were granted to a decedent and which ***terminate*** on the decedent's death are not subject to the estate tax (*supra,* §37). And where a person is granted a ***special*** power of appointment, the exercise or nonexercise of the power is not subject to either the estate or gift taxes (*supra*, §§472, 768). Further, a person may be a permissible distributee or appointee of property and have access to (and enjoyment of) the property for support, etc., during life without estate tax exposure upon death (*supra*, §42). These limitations upon the scope of the estate and gift taxes created opportunities for considerable tax avoidance and, in turn, led to the enactment of Chapter 13, the "Generation-Skipping Transfer Tax."

For purposes of analysis of generation-skipping transfer tax provisions, you should determine:

1. ***The transfers to which the tax applies;*** and

2. ***The amount of the transfer***, *i.e.*, the tax base.

And, although unlikely to be found in your exam questions, you should also review the sections on computation of the tax and the filing of returns and payment of the tax found at the end of this chapter.

A. BACKGROUND AND INTRODUCTION

1. **Prior Law:** [§1062] Prior to 1976, so-called generation-skipping transfers were a popular estate and tax planning device. By granting successive life estates to succeeding generations—frequently coupled with powers in the trustee to distribute corpus for support, etc., powers to withdraw up to $5,000 or five percent of corpus annually, and special powers to appoint all or a portion of the property during life or upon death—succeeding generations could be afforded significant enjoyment of the property transferred without transfer tax exposure; *i.e.*, the shifting of enjoyment from one generation to a succeeding generation would not attract the gift or estate taxes.

    a. **Example:** D conveys property on trust for his son, B, for life, and upon B's death to B's daughter, M, for her life, and upon M's death to M's surviving children. Under prior law, there was no estate tax payable on the death of B or M, because their interests terminated on their deaths.

    b. **Note:** The only effective legal limitation upon the use of such generation-skipping transfers was the Rule Against Perpetuities. But, despite the Rule, it was frequently possible to "skip" two and sometimes three generations before an outright distribution would be required.

c. **Comment:** While the use of such generation-skipping transfers was theoretically available to everyone, in practice the device was most valuable to, and was used most often by, the very wealthy (since multi-generational trusts are economically feasible only where significant wealth is involved and since wealthier families could enjoy the greatest tax savings).

2. **Overview of the Tax under the 1976 Act:** [§1063] The generation-skipping transfer tax was promulgated to close this gaping loophole in the federal transfer tax system and to eliminate the special advantage enjoyed by the "super rich." The taxing provisions are contained in Chapter 13 of the Code.

   a. **Transfer tax:** [§1064] Like the estate and the gift taxes, this new tax was a ***transfer*** tax. It applied only when a "generation-skipping" transfer occurred.

   b. **Separate transfer tax:** [§1065] However, the tax did not amend or modify the substantive law of the estate and gift tax systems. Rather, it was an entirely separate transfer tax.

   c. **Correlation with estate and gift tax:** [§1066] Nevertheless, the tax was closely related, technically and conceptually, to the estate and gift tax.

      (1) **Approximated same tax results:** [§1067] It was designed to achieve the same tax result in the case of generation-skipping transfers as would occur if the property were transmitted outright, by gift or bequest, through succeeding generations.

      (2) **Method:** [§1068] Not only was the unified estate and gift tax schedule applied, but the tax was imposed upon the value of the generation-skipping transfer as if the transfer had been made by an ancestor to a descendant (by gift or bequest)—*i.e.*, the value of the transfer was cumulated with the taxable gifts and/or taxable estate of the ancestor.

3. **Objections to the 1976 Act:** [§1069] As originally enacted, the generation-skipping transfer tax (GST) embodied a number of complex provisions which were perceived as major defects from the viewpoint of practical administration of the tax. Consequently, Congress continually deferred the effective date for the application of this tax. The principal objections were:

   a. **Computational complexity:** Tying the amount of the GST to the gift and estate taxes of the ancestor, including the cumulative taxable gifts and the taxable estate of the ancestor, was unduly complicated.

   b. **Gaps in coverage:** The 1976 GST only addressed generation-skipping through the use of successive interests in a trust or trust equivalent. It did not take into account generation-skipping by the super rich using outright gifts ("direct skips") to multiple successive generations.

4. **Repeal and Replacement in 1986:** [§1070] As part of the 1986 Tax Reform Act, Congress repealed the 1976 GST, and replaced it with a new generation-skipping transfer tax.

   a. **Retroactive repeal:** [§1071] The 1976 provisions were repealed retroactively. As a result, any generation-skipping transfers that occurred prior to the effective date of the 1986 Act's GST ***are not subject to the GST.***

   b. **1986 GST:** [§1072] The GST of the 1986 Act is essentially the same in all substantive respects to its predecessor, with two notable exceptions:

      (1) **Simplified computations:** [§1073] The present GST imposes a flat rate of tax upon generation-skipping transfers. The computational complexities of the 1976 Act, which tied the rate of tax to the ancestor's cumulative gift and estate taxes, are eliminated.

      (2) **Direct skips also taxed:** [§1074] So-called direct skips are now subject to the GST.

B. TRANSFERS TO WHICH THE TAX APPLIES [§1075]

The GST is imposed upon "every generation-skipping transfer." [I.R.C. §2601] Such transfers include: (i) "taxable distributions"; (ii) "taxable terminations"; and (iii) "direct skips." [I.R.C. §2611]

1. **Basic Definitions:** [§1076] Definitions of the three categories of generation-skipping transfers are contained in I.R.C. section 2612.

   a. **"Taxable distribution":** [§1077] This is defined as any distribution from a trust to a "skip person," except a distribution that would be considered a "taxable termination" or a "direct skip." [I.R.C. §2612(b)]

   b. **"Taxable termination":** [§1078] This means any termination (by death, lapse of time, release of a power, or otherwise) of an interest in property held in a trust, except where a "non-skip person" has an interest in the property immediately after the termination, ***or*** if no distribution may thereafter be made by the trust to a skip person. [I.R.C. §2612(a)]

   c. **"Direct skip":** [§1079] This is a transfer that is subject to the gift or estate taxes but which is made to a skip person. [I.R.C. §2612(c)]

2. **Subsidiary Definitions:** [§1080] To understand the basic definitions, one must understand the special meaning of the terms used in these definitions.

   a. **"Trust":** [§1081] For purposes of the GST, a "trust" refers not only to an actual trust but also to "***any arrangement*** (other than an estate) which . . . has substantially the same effect as a trust." [I.R.C. §2652(b)(1)] Thus, successive legal life estates would be treated in the same manner as successive income interests in a trust.

b. **"Interest in property":** [§1082] A person has an interest in the property held by a trust if she has a right to receive distributions of income or principal from the trust, ***including permissible*** (discretionary) ***distributions***, but ***excluding*** distributions that cannot be made until some time in the future. [I.R.C. §2652(c)]

c. **"Skip person" and "non-skip person":** [§1083] A "skip person" is a person assigned to a generation that is two or more generations below that of the transferor. [I.R.C. §2613(a)(1)] A "non-skip person" is a person who is not a skip person. [I.R.C. §2613(b)]

(1) **Skip person can include trust:** [§1084] A trust will be treated as a skip person if all interests in the trust are held by skip persons, or if no person holds a present interest in the trust but all future distributions from the trust must be made to skip persons (*i.e.*, no non-skip person may receive any future distributions). [I.R.C. §2613(a)(2)]

(2) **Generation assignments:** [§1085] The starting point for assignment of persons to generations is the "transferor."

(a) **"Transferor":** [§1086] For purposes of the GST, the "transferor" is the decedent or the donor, depending upon whether the trust or direct skip is initiated by bequest or lifetime gift. [I.R.C. §2652(a)]

(b) **Family generations:** [§1087] Generations are ordinarily determined along family lines. For instance, the transferor and the transferor's siblings would be in the same generation. Any of their children (including adopted children) would be assigned to the first younger generation. Grandchildren would be assigned to the next younger generation, and so forth. [I.R.C. §2651(b)] Spouses of transferors or of lineal descendants of transferors are assigned to the same generation as the other spouse. [I.R.C. §2651(c)]

(c) **Nonfamily generations:** [§1088] The generation assignment of nonfamily members is determined by comparing their ages to that of the transferor. A person born within 12½ years of the date of the transferor's birth is assigned to the transferor's generation; persons born more than 12½ years but less than 37½ years from the date of the transferor's birth are assigned to the first younger generation; and each succeeding 25 years defines new generations. [I.R.C. §2651(d)]

(d) **Entities:** [§1089] If any entity—estate, trust, partnership, or corporation—has an interest in the property, the individuals having a beneficial interest in the entity are treated as having an interest in the property, and are assigned to generations according to the above rules. [I.R.C. §2651(e)]

3. **General Exceptions:** [§1090] Exceptions are contained in section 2611(b). The two exceptions of general applicability are:

   a. **Excluded under gift tax:** [§1091] If the transfer would be excluded under section 2503(e) of the gift tax (tranfers for educational or medical expenses), it is not taxable under the GST. [I.R.C. §2611(b)(1)]

   b. **No tax avoidance:** [§1092] The GST does not apply to any transfer to the extent that: (i) the property was subject to a prior generation-skipping tax; (ii) the prior taxable transfer was to a transferee assigned to a generation the same as or lower than that of the present transferee; and (iii) the transfer does not have the effect of avoiding the generation-skipping tax. [I.R.C. §2611(b)(2)]

4. **Special Exception for Direct Skips:** [§1093] A transfer to the grandchild of the transferor (direct skip) is not subject to the GST if the transferor's child who is the parent of the grandchild is dead. [I.R.C. §2612(c)(2)]

5. **Example—Taxable Distribution:** [§1094] During life, D created a trust directing the trustee to pay the income of the trust to D's child, C. The trustee is also authorized to pay such amounts of corpus to any of C's children as may be necessary for their health, education, support, and maintenance. This year the trustee pays $12,000 to X University for tuition for G, a child of C. Under the general rules of the GST, this distribution for G's benefit would be a taxable distribution. However, the exception for educational expenses may apply (*see supra*, §1091).

6. **Example—Taxable Termination:** [§1095] Assume the same trust as above. The trust provides that upon the death of C, the trust corpus is to be divided into as many shares as there are surviving children of C and, thereafter, the income of each share is to be distributed to the appropriate child of C. Upon C's death, there will be a taxable termination of C's interest.

7. **Example—Direct Skip:** [§1096] D's will bequeaths the residue of her estate to her grandchild, G. This is a direct skip. Moreover, it is subject to the GST even though the property is subject to the estate tax in D's estate. It will be subject to the special "grandchild" exception for direct skips only if D's child who was the parent of G is dead. (*See supra*, §1093).

C. AMOUNT TAXABLE [§1097]

The amount taxable depends on the type of generation-skipping transfer. [I.R.C. §2602(1)]

1. **Taxable Distributions:** [§1098] The base for the GST in the case of a taxable distribution is the value of the property ***received*** by the transferee, ***reduced by*** any expenses incurred by the transferee in connection with the determination or collection of the GST tax. [I.R.C. §2621(a)]

a. **Payment of GST tax—special rule:** [§1099] If the trust pays the GST tax for the recipient of a taxable distribution, the amount of the GST tax so paid is considered a taxable distribution. [I.R.C. §2621(b)]

2. **Taxable Terminations:** [§1100] The taxable amount is the value of all property that was the subject of the taxable termination, ***reduced by*** expenses of a nature that would be allowable as estate tax deductions under section 2053(b). [I.R.C. §2622; *and see supra*, §574]

3. **Direct Skips:** [§1101] The GST is imposed on the value of the property received by the transferee. [I.R.C. §2623]

4. **Valuation Rules:** [§1102] The value of the property is its fair market value ***at the time of the generation-skipping transfer,*** reduced by any consideration provided by the transferee. [I.R.C. §2624(a), (d)]

   a. **Time of transfer:** [§1103] In the case of a taxable distribution or a direct skip produced by a lifetime gift, the time of the transfer is the date of the distribution or gift. In the case of a direct skip produced by bequest from a decedent, the time of the transfer is the date of the decedent's death. In the case of a taxable termination, the time of the transfer is the date of the termination—the date of death of the holder of the prior interest if death is the cause of the taxable termination. [I.R.C. §2624(a)]

   b. **Alternate valuation date:** [§1104] Where a direct skip or a taxable termination occurs as a result of death, special rules allow use of the alternate valuation date. [I.R.C. §2624(b), (c); *and see supra*, §919]

5. **GST Exemption:** [§1105] Section 2631 allows a $1 million GST exemption which may be allocated by a transferor (or her executor) to any property transferred by the transferor. [*See* I.R.C. §2632—special allocation rules]

   a. **Not an exclusion:** [§1106] Note that the GST exemption does not operate as an exclusion or deduction. Rather, it is used in the tax computation to determine the effective rate at which a generation-skipping transfer will be taxed. (*See infra*, §1109.)

D. COMPUTATION OF TAX [§1107]

The amount of the GST is the taxable amount (above) multiplied by the "applicable rate." [I.R.C. §2602]

1. **Applicable Rate of Tax:** [§1108] This is the ***maximum federal estate tax rate*** in effect on the date of the generation-skipping transfer, multiplied by the "***inclusion ratio***" with respect to the transfer. [I.R.C. §2641]

2. **Inclusion Ratio:** [§1109] This is a fraction arrived at by subtracting a known fraction from 1. The known fraction will have, as its numerator, the amount of the GST exclusion allocated to the trust (or direct skip property) and, as its

denominator, the value of all the property transferred to the trust (or transferred in the direct skip) less any federal estate or death taxes actually paid from the property (and any charitable deduction allowed with respect to the property). [I.R.C. §2642]

3. **Example:** [§1110] D bequeathed the residue of her estate to a trust, with directions to pay all the income from the trust to her niece N, and upon N's death, to distribute the trust corpus to the children of N. The residue of D's estate was $3,000,000. The residuary trust's share of D's federal and state death taxes (which it paid from the property it received) was $1,000,000. D's executor allocated the $1,000,000 GST exemption to this residuary trust. Upon N's death, the value of the property held by the trust is $2,500,000.

    a. ***The value*** of the property that is subject to the taxable termination occurring at N's death is $2,500,000—the fair market value at the time of the termination. (*See supra*, §1100.)

    b. ***The inclusion ratio*** is 1 minus $1,000,000 (allocable GST exemption) over $2,000,000 ($3,000,000 transferred to the trust less the $1,000,000 death taxes paid by the trust); *i.e.*, 1 minus ½ = ½.

    c. ***The applicable rate,*** then, is .50 (maximum federal estate tax rate after 1992) multiplied by ½ or .25.

    d. ***And the GST tax*** is, then, .25 multiplied by $2,500,000 (the taxable amount—*see* above) or $625,000.

E. PAYMENT OF TAX [§1111]

The person liable for the GST tax depends upon the type of generation-skipping transfer.

1. **Taxable Distributions:** [§1112] The transferee, *i.e.*, the person who receives the distribution, is liable to pay the tax. [I.R.C. §2603(a)(1)]

2. **Taxable Terminations:** [§1113] The trustee is liable for the tax. [I.R.C. §2603(a)(2)] For arrangements that are not formal trusts, "trustee" means the person in actual or constructive possession of the property that is the subject of the arrangement. [I.R.C. §2652(b)(2)]

3. **Direct Skips:** [§1114] The transferor pays the tax. [I.R.C. §2603(a)(3)]

REVIEW QUESTIONS

FILL IN ANSWER

1. Clare, a U.S. citizen, owns a villa on the French Riviera. If France imposes an estate tax upon this property, it would not be included in Clare's gross estate. True or false? ________

2. Xenia devises Blackacre to her son Roland for life, remainder to Roland's children. Upon Roland's death, the value of his interest in Blackacre is includible in his gross estate. True or false? ________

3. Prior to her death, A instituted an action for personal injuries against C. A died while the action was still pending. Is the tort claim includible in A's gross estate? ________

4. Owen is the owner of an insurance policy on the life of Tad. If Owen predeceases Tad, are the proceeds of the policy includible in Owen's gross estate? ________

5. For a number of years, D served as trustee of a trust established by his father for the benefit of various other family members. Upon D's death, should the corpus of the trust be included in D's gross estate? ________

6. A judgment by the highest state court on the nature or extent of a decedent's interest in property is binding for federal estate tax purposes. True or false? ________

7. At the time of his death, Herbert owned corporate stock worth $200,000. Under applicable state law, Herbert's spouse, Wanda, has dower rights in the stock. The value of the stock in Herbert's gross estate is therefore less than $200,000. True or false? ________

   a. Would the result be different if Wanda had a community property interest in the stock? ________

8. D transferred $100,000 in cash by gift in December 1990, and died in July 1992. Is the value of this property includible in D's gross estate? ________

9. Same facts as in Question 8, above, except that D transferred a life insurance policy on his own life. Assuming that the face amount of the policy was $100,000 but the replacement value was only $35,000, D's executor should include $35,000 in D's gross estate on account of this gift. True or false? ________

10. D gave her daughter a painting worth $500,000 in February 1990, and paid a gift tax of $155,800. D died in July 1992. With respect to this gift, D's executor should include $155,800 in D's gross estate. True or false? ________

11. In 1977, D transferred certain property on trust but reserved the power to revoke the trust. In 1990, D released the power to revoke the trust. D died in February 1992. Assuming that the value of the property transferred by D in 1977 was $200,000, that it was worth $800,000 when D released the power in 1990, and that it was worth $850,000 when D died in 1992, $800,000 should be included in D's gross estate. True or false? ________

12. A established a trust to pay the income to his brother, B, for life, remainder to B's children. B established a similar trust to pay the income to A for life, remainder to A's children. Is the corpus of the trust established by B includible in A's gross estate? ________

    a. Would the result be the same if B's trust was to pay the income to C for life, remainder to C's children? ________

13. D transfers the residence he owns to his wife, W, but continues to occupy the residence with W until his death. Is this sufficient to show a transfer with retained interest under section 2036? ________

14. Dee establishes a trust for the support of her minor child. If Dee dies before the child reaches the age of majority, is the trust corpus includible in Dee's estate? ________

15. The trustee of a trust created by X is empowered to apply the income or corpus of the trust as needed for X's support during her life. None of the income or corpus is ever paid to X. Is the trust corpus includible in X's estate at her death? ________

16. Potter transfers property on trust, with all right to trust income to Peter for life. Potter retains the power to designate a new income beneficiary in the event of Peter's death. If Potter predeceases Peter, is the trust corpus includible in Potter's estate? ________

17. T established a trust, retaining the power to direct that the trust income be accumulated rather than distributed to a life beneficiary. Should the trust corpus be included in T's gross estate? ________

    a. Would the result be different if T never exercised his power under the trust? ________

18. If Minerva names herself as trustee of a trust under which all trust income must be paid to Irving during his life, the trust corpus is includible in Minerva's gross estate. True or false? ________

19. Sam transfers certain property to Quincy in trust, retaining a right to income from the trust "except such income as may accrue during the last year of my life." Is the trust corpus includible in Sam's gross estate? ________

20. D grants a life estate in certain property to C, retaining a secondary life estate in the same property. Is the full value of the property includible in D's gross estate? ________

21. Same facts as in Question 11, above. However, assume that the $850,000 corpus of the trust at D's death included $150,000 of ***income*** which the trustee had accumulated and added to corpus. For estate tax purposes, this accumulated income should ***not*** be included in D's gross estate since D never "transferred" the income. True or false? ________

22. Professor Ipsi Dixit states, "A person may always avoid taxation by transferring or releasing any retained, taxable power or interest." Is she correct? ________

23. Larry transfers property "to Cary for life, remainder to Mary unless I am alive at the time of Cary's death." If the reversionary interest retained by Larry is worth more than five percent of the value of the property at the time of Larry's death, is the property includible in his gross estate? ________

24. H transfers property "to L for life, remainder to N if N is alive at L's death, but otherwise the property is to revert to me." Is the value of the property includible in H's gross estate? ________

25. A retained power to direct the trustee to pay income to the transferor does not fall within the scope of section 2037. True or false? ________

26. Assume the same transfer of property described in Question 23, above. If Larry also granted Harry the power to appoint the property free of trust to Cary, would the property be includible in Larry's gross estate under section 2037? ________

27. P transfers property "to Q for life, remainder to R unless I am alive when Q dies." Only the value of the remainder interest is taxable to P's estate under section 2037. True or false? ________

28. R transfers certain property to Q, retaining a power to terminate the transfer in the event of T's death. If R predeceases T, is the property taxable to R's estate under section 2038? ________

29. T transfers certain property to P, retaining a power to revoke the transfer; however, such power must be exercised jointly by T and S. If S has a beneficial interest in the property adverse to that of T, is the transfer subject to tax under section 2038? ________

30. Nick transfers property on trust, appointing Frieda as trustee with the power to change the named beneficiaries of the trust income. Nick retains the right to call for Frieda's resignation and appoint a successor trustee. Will the trust property be included in Nick's gross estate? ________

31. X created a trust in 1986 which empowered the trustee to sprinkle income among a number of beneficiaries. X retained no power with respect to the trust but was subsequently appointed trustee. Will the trust corpus be included in X's estate under section 2038? ________

32. For a tax to attach under section 2038, must the transferor have some beneficial interest in the transferred property? ________

33. Maud transfers property on trust to pay the income to Harold for twenty years and then to distribute the entire corpus to Harold. If Maud retains the power to terminate the trust and cause the corpus to go to Harold prior to the end of the twenty-year term, is the trust corpus includible in Maud's gross estate? ________

34. A straight life annuity is not includible in the annuitant's gross estate at death. True or false? ________

35. To be taxable under section 2039, the benefit to the surviving beneficiary must be the same basic type of annuity as that paid to the decedent-annuitant. True or false? ________

36. X has only a contingent right to receive payments under an annuity contract purchased by his employer. The contingency is not within X's control, nor does it occur prior to his death. Are the annuity payments payable to another person after X's death includible in X's gross estate? ________

37. The interest of a joint tenant in jointly-held property may be includible in the tenant's gross estate. True or false? ________

38. Sandy and Mandy hold property as tenants in common. If Mandy dies, is it permissible to include only one-half the value of the property in her gross estate? ________

39. Frick and his brother, Frack, acquire property in joint tenancy with a right of survivorship. Frick pays $60,000 of the $100,000 purchase price, and Frack pays the remaining $40,000. Upon Frick's death, his estate should include the full value of the joint property, less $40,000. True or false? ________

40. A devises property to B and C as joint tenants with a right of survivorship. Should the full value of the joint tenancy property be included in B's gross estate if she predeceases C? ________

41. X gives her son, Y, $50,000. Y subsequently contributes this money as his part of the purchase price for property acquired by X and Y as joint tenants. If X predeceases Y, is the full value of the joint tenancy property includible in X's gross estate? ________

42. Would the result in Question 41 be the same if X gave Y a $50,000 certificate of deposit, and Y contributed the income earned thereon as his share of the purchase price? ________

43. The assumption of a purchase money mortgage by both joint tenants is treated as an original contribution by each joint tenant of one-half the amount of the mortgage. True or false? ________

44. Dark pays the full purchase price for property acquired by Dark and his sister, Mindy, as joint tenants. Dark then gives his interest in the property to Cindy, an unrelated friend. If Dark dies two years later, the full value of the property is includible in his estate. True or false? ________

45. With reference to questions dealing with joint tenancies, above, would the answers be ***different*** if: ________

a. In Question 39, Frick and Frack were husband and wife? ________

b. In Question 41, X and Y are husband and wife? ________

46. **A beneficiary's power to withdraw principal from a trust makes the trust corpus includible in her gross estate. True or false?** ________

47. Pea creates a trust naming Bea as trustee and giving her a life interest in the income therefrom. The trustee is given the power to invade principal for the benefit of the life beneficiary. Is the trust corpus includible in Bea's estate under section 2041? ________

48. P transfers certain property on trust, reserving a general power to change the beneficiaries and trustee thereunder. Does section 2041 require that the trust corpus be included in P's gross estate? ________

49. W is the trustee of a trust giving her a power to appoint beneficiaries thereunder. If W completely exercises this power inter vivos, is the property which comprised the trust corpus includible in her estate under section 2041? ________

50. **Post-1942 powers that must be exercised jointly with another person may still be considered general powers under section 2041. True or false?** ________

51. D carries a medical policy which pays $10,000 if D should die from any of several specified ailments. Are such benefits includible in D's gross estate? ________

52. X is an employee of Z Corporation. The Corporation carries a policy on X's life, with benefits payable to X's executor. X pays no premiums on the policy and has no other incidents of ownership. Are the policy benefits includible in her gross estate? ________

a. Would the result be the same if X's sister, Y, were the named beneficiary of the policy? ________

53. Tiny is insured under his employer's group life insurance policy. If Tiny can cancel the insurance by quitting his job, should the benefits thereunder be included in his estate? ________

54. A reversionary interest in a life insurance policy or its proceeds makes the proceeds taxable to the holder's gross estate. True or false? ________

55. Under the terms of his life insurance policy, B (the insured) may change the beneficiaries only by written endorsement on the policy. B never changes the beneficiaries and is not in actual possession of the policy for several years prior to his death. Will B be deemed to have had an incident of ownership in the policy at the time of his death? ________

56. **Potsy, the insured under a life insurance policy, transfers all interests and rights under the policy to his brother, Ronald, in 1991. If Potsy dies in 1993, are the policy proceeds includible in his estate?** ________

a. Would the result be the same if the policy had been purchased by Potsy with community property funds? ________

57. Professor Res Ipsa tells his class, "A transfer will not be included in the decedent's estate if it was made for consideration that would support an enforceable contract." Is this an accurate statement? ________

58. D's will bequeathed a substantial sum of money outright to B, an infant. At the request of B's guardian, D's executor (E) and A, the attorney for D's estate, arrange for the creation of a trust to hold and manage the bequest until B attains majority. Are the fees charged by E and A for this service deductible from D's gross estate? ________

59. Prior to their marriage, Henry and Wilma entered into a valid antenuptial agreement under which, in consideration of marriage and Wilma's release of any marital inheritance rights in Henry's estate, Henry agreed to leave Wilma $100,000 in his will. After Henry's death, his executor paid $100,000 to Wilma. Can this amount be deducted for federal estate tax purposes? ________

60. At the time of his death D, a cash basis proprietor, owed salaries to certain of his employees and rent on his business property. After D's death, D's executor paid these claims. The payments are deductible against the gross estate ***and*** against the estate's taxable income. True or false? ________

61. P's executor sells certain property in the estate at a loss. Is the loss deductible under section 2054? ________

62. In his will, X bequeaths $20,000 to Acme Watch Company for the sole purpose of establishing a scholarship fund for the children of Acme employees. Is the bequest deductible from X's estate as a charitable contribution? ________

63. Generally, the gift of a remainder interest to a charity is not deductible unless made in the form of a special, qualifying interest. True or false? ________

64. The maximum estate tax marital deduction is fifty percent of the decedent's adjusted gross estate. True or false? ________

65. Two weeks before his death in April 1992, H gave twenty percent of his cash assets to his spouse, W, as an inter vivos gift. Does this property "pass" to W for estate tax marital deduction purposes? ________

66. During his life, Duke purchases a straight life annuity for his spouse, Bertha, payments on which are to begin upon Duke's death. If the annuity is included in Duke's gross estate, is its value deductible as a section 2056 marital deduction? ________

67. Shortly after H's death, W petitions the local probate court for an allowance for her support during probate. The court reviews W's petition and determines that an award of $500 per month from H's estate is appropriate. Do these monies qualify for the marital deduction? ________

68. In his will, H bequeaths his rights in an exclusive patent to his spouse, W. Will this be considered a terminable interest not deductible under section 2056? ________

a. Would the result be different if the bequest is also conditioned upon W's surviving H by three months? ________

69. W's will bequeaths certain property on trust with directions to pay the income to H, her surviving spouse, for life, and upon his death to pay the corpus to H's estate. Is W's bequest deductible under section 2056? ________

a. Suppose W's bequest provides that H may direct the trustee to pay all or a portion of the trust income to other persons. Will this affect deductibility of the bequest under section 2056? ________

70. D's will left the entire residue of her estate to T, as trustee, with directions to pay all the income from the trust to A (D's husband) for his life and, upon A's death to pay over the entire corpus of the trust to their (D and A's) children in such proportions as A might designate in his will or, if D did not exercise this power, to their children equally. Will the marital deduction be allowed for this bequest? ________

71. No marital deduction is allowed for federal estate tax purposes if the surviving spouse is a nonresident alien. True or false? ________

72. A makes a gift of $50,000 to B, on the condition that B give $20,000 to C. Will this be treated as a single taxable gift from A to B? ________

73. T places certain property on trust, income and principal to be given to "my first nephew, upon the date of his fifteenth birthday." Is this a taxable gift? ________

74. A and B, an elderly married couple, are both independently wealthy. Harry Bond, a "financial consultant," advises them to leave all their property to each other in the form of a "Q-tip" interest. He says that this will avoid all estate taxes in the estate of the first to die (because of the 100 percent estate tax marital deduction) and eliminate most transfer taxes to the survivor since the survivor can give his or her interest in the "Q-tip" away and only be taxed on the value of the life estate which is transferred. Is Harry right? ________

75. Attorney X gratuitously prepares a will for Y. Has X made a taxable gift? ________

76. T exercises a special power of appointment under a trust in favor of S. Will this be treated as a taxable gift to S? ________

77. Leonard transfers certain property on trust, naming Iantha as beneficiary thereunder. If Leonard can redesignate the trust beneficiary, has he made a taxable gift? ________

a. Would the result be different if the power to change beneficiaries was held by Catherine as trustee? ________

78. If a transfer involves partial consideration but is otherwise a taxable gift, the value thereof for gift tax purposes is the fair market value of the property in question. True or false? ________

79. Horatio agrees to pay his spouse, Wilona, $50,000 in exchange for Wilona's agreement to release her marital dower rights. Will the $50,000 transfer be treated as a taxable gift? ________

80. Sady, a traveling salesperson, gives a number of her best customers wristwatches as Christmas gifts. Are these transfers subject to the federal gift tax? ________

81. D purchases certain securities and has them registered in the names of D and E as joint tenants with right of survivorship. Has D made a gift of any interest in the securities? ________

82. A purchases Blackacre with his own funds but takes title to the property in joint tenancy with his wife, W. Has H made a taxable gift to W? ________

a. Should A file a gift tax return? ________

83. During 1987, P made gifts of $5,000 to R and $15,000 to S. Are these gifts fully excludible from gift tax? ________

84. The 1976 Tax Reform Act eliminated all incentives to make inter vivos (as opposed to testamentary) gifts. True or false? ________

85. A transfers certain property on trust with the income to B for life, then to C for life, remainder to D. Is the annual exclusion available for the life estate gifts to B and C? ________

86. A creates a trust, with income to E for life according to his needs, and the remainder to F. Would the transfers to both E and F be denied the annual exclusion? ________

87. The "nondeductible terminable interest rule" of the gift tax marital deduction is identical to that under the estate tax. True or false? ________

88. The alternate valuation date for assessing the assets of the gross estate is available only where the assets have declined in value less than fifty percent since the date of death. True or false? ________

89. Mickey dies, leaving as part of his gross estate a life estate based upon the life of Minnie, his surviving spouse. Will election of the alternate valuation date produce a lower includible value for this asset? ________

90. T's estate includes a farm which is located near a developing "industrial park." T bequeathed the farm to his son, R. Assuming that all the requirements of section 2032A (special farm use valuation) are met, the value of the farm in its possible use as an industrial site may be disregarded. True or false? ________

91. All gifts made by a decedent must be added to his taxable estate to determine the appropriate tax base. True or false? ________

92. The 1976 Act provided a separate "unified" gift tax credit for gifts made after 1976. True or false? ________

93. There is a limit on the credit allowed against federal estate taxes for state death taxes paid. True or false? ________

94. The donor is primarily responsible for payment of the gift tax on donative transfers. True or false? ________

95. B is the beneficiary of certain life insurance proceeds which are includible in D's gross estate. Once the proceeds are paid to B, is he primarily responsible for paying the federal estate taxes attributable thereto? ________

96. In Question 95, can D's executor recover payment of the pro rata estate tax from B? ________

97. X creates a trust for his brother, W, for life, then to X's nephew Y for life and upon his death to W's son, Z. Is this trust subject to the tax on generation-skipping transfers? ________

98. A conveys property on trust to his son, B, for life, then B's daughter, C, for life, remainder to C's issue. Is there a generation-skipping termination upon B's death? ________

99. P conveys municipal bonds to R, his daughter-in-law, as custodian for S and T, the children of R and P's son Q. Is this a generation-skipping transfer? ________

100. X conveys certain property in trust to his nephew, Q, for life, then to Q's children, O and N, for life, remainder to the issue of O and N. Upon Q's death, the value of the life estates of O and N is subject to the tax on generation-skipping transfers. True or false? ________

a. O and N are personally liable for any tax due on the trust property at Q's death. True or false? ________

ANSWERS TO REVIEW QUESTIONS

1. **FALSE** The property would be included in her gross estate since Clare is a U.S. citizen. However, the French tax could be credited against the federal estate tax payable. [§§23, 1026]

2. **FALSE** An interest in property that is extinguished by the death of the holder, such as a life estate, is not transferable at death and hence is not taxable under section 2033. [§§37, 68]

3. **YES** Claims in litigation are property rights includible regardless of their contingent nature (although their value may be minimal—or even zero—depending upon how speculative the potential amount of recovery may be). [§§47, 72]

4. **NO** Only the value of the policy (*i.e.*, its replacement cost) is includible in the policy owner's estate where he or she dies before the insured. [§§48-49]

5. **NO** Where title to property is held solely as trustee for others, there is no beneficial interest in the property—and hence it is not included in the trustee's gross estate. [§74]

6. **TRUE** Except where the property or interest is based on federal law, an opinion by the highest state court is determinative. [§§91-93]

7. **FALSE** Section 2034 requires that the ***full value*** of decedent's property be included in the gross estate, regardless of the spouse's marital interests therein. [§95]

   a. **YES** In this case, Wanda ***owned*** a present one-half interest in the stock at Herbert's death, and this would ***not*** be includible in Herbert's gross estate. [§98]

8. **NO** By virtue of the 1981 Act amendment of section 2035, the estate tax no longer attaches to outright gifts made within three years of death. [§§105-106]

9. **FALSE** Although section 2035 no longer taxes outright gifts made within three years of the donor's death, it continues to interact with other specific taxing provisions, including section 2042 which deals with life insurance. Under section 2042, it is the proceeds (face amount) of the life insurance which is included in the insured's estate if he or she possesses "incidents of ownership" in the policy at death. And, the interaction of section 2035 with section 2042 will produce the same result where incidents of ownership are transferred within three years of death. Thus, $100,000 is includible. [§§107, 114-115, 534-535]

10. **TRUE** The value of the property given by D to her daughter (within three years of her death) is not included in D's estate. (*See* Answer 8, above.) ***But note:*** The gift tax paid with respect to gifts made within three years of death continues to be includible under the "gross-up" rule. [§§110-111]

11. **FALSE** Section 2035 continues to interact with section 2038 ("revocable transfers") so as to produce the same estate tax result that would obtain if a power to revoke was exercisable by the decedent at the time of his death. Property included in a decedent's gross estate is valued as of the date of the decedent's death (or at the alternate valuation date—six months after death). And, this rule is applicable to transfers included under section 2038 (and section 2035). Thus, it is not the value of the property at the time of the transfer ($200,000 in 1977), or its value when D released

the power to revoke ($800,000 in 1990), but its value at D's death ($850,000) that is the includible amount. [§§107, 115, 342, 923]

12. **YES** This is a typical reciprocal trust situation; A and B will each be deemed to have retained a life estate in the trust established by the other (making it taxable to their respective estates). [§§135-136]

a. **NO** In order to be "reciprocal," cross-trusts must have equivalent economic effect. Here, however, A has ***no*** life estate interest in either trust; therefore, B's trust is not includible in A's gross estate. [§§137-139]

13. **NO** ***Joint*** occupancy of a residence by husband and wife subsequent to a transfer is not enough to show the implied retention of an interest subject to section 2036. [§§157-159]

14. **YES** There is a retained right to income where the transferred property (or income therefrom) is used to discharge the transferor's legal obligations, such as child support. And where decedent-transferor dies before her child attains majority, there is a retention of the right for a period which does not in fact end before her death. [§§168-169, 215]

15. **YES** X is deemed to have retained a sufficient right to income, since the trustee's discretion was governed by an ascertainable standard (support) enforceable by X. [§§172, 174]

16. **YES** The fact that a retained power is contingent (and never exercised) does not prevent the transfer from being taxable under section 2036. [§182]

17. **YES** This makes the trust taxable under section 2036(a)(2), since the power can be exercised to increase the size of the remainder interest (*i.e.*, trust corpus). [§187]

a. **NO** The mere ***retention*** of the power makes the corpus taxable under section 2036(a)(2). [§187]

18. **FALSE** To result in a taxable transfer, the power retained must be ***discretionary.*** Here, Minerva is required to pay all income to Irving, so the trust would not be taxable in Minerva's estate. [§192]

19. **YES** The retained right to income for a period ascertainable only with reference to the transferor's death brings the property within section 2036. [§210]

20. **NO** Although the retained secondary life estate causes the property to be included in D's estate, it will be included at its full value ***less*** the value of C's prior life estate. [§§218, 156]

21. **FALSE** Where the taxable power (here, a power to revoke under section 2038) extends to post-gift accumulated income, the accumulated income as well as the original corpus (and its appreciation in value) is includible. [§§219, 335]

22. **NO** While taxation is avoided if the transfer or relinquishment is made more than three years before death, transfers ***within*** three years of death would be taxable under section 2035. [§§220-221]

23. **YES** This is a typical example of a taxable transfer under section 2037. [§§222 *et seq.*]

24.	**NO**	N need not survive the transferor, H; he need merely survive the life tenant, L. Hence, the survivorship requirement of section 2037 is not satisfied, and the transfer is not taxable. [§241]
25.	**TRUE**	Such a right to income is not a "reversionary interest" subject to section 2037. (However, it may well be taxable under section 2036.) [§§247-248]
26.	**PROBABLY NOT**	The power granted to Harry would probably preclude a valuation of the reversionary interest retained by Larry. If so, it will be assigned a value of zero—which is less than the five percent necessary for a taxable transfer under section 2037. [§272]
27.	**TRUE**	Q's life estate is not affected by whether P lives or dies. [§273]
28.	**NO**	The transfer is not taxable under section 2038 where a retained power to terminate is subject to a contingency outside the transferor's control ***and*** which does not occur prior to the transferor's death. [§302]
29.	**YES**	If the retained power is otherwise taxable, the fact that it can be exercised only with the consent of a person having an adverse interest will not affect taxability under section 2038. [§307]
30.	**YES**	Retention of such power is sufficient access to the taxable power (to change beneficiaries) and therefore results in inclusion in Nick's gross estate. [§§309-310]
31.	**YES**	To be a taxable transfer under section 2038, the power need not be retained. It is sufficient that the transferor possessed it at the time of her death—whatever the source. [§312]
32.	**NO**	It is sufficient if the transferor retains a power to affect the beneficial enjoyment of others. [§316]
33.	**YES**	The power to accelerate the remainder (by terminating the trust) is sufficient for taxation under section 2038—even though Harold is the sole beneficiary under the trust. [§§327-328]
34.	**TRUE**	Section 2039 applies to annuity benefits payable on account of the decedent's death—*i.e.*, survivorship annuities. Since all benefits under a straight life annuity terminate at the annuitant's death, there is no inclusion in the annuitant's gross estate. [§347]
35.	**FALSE**	There is no requirement that the payment to the beneficiary correspond in form or amount to that payable to decedent. [§355]
36.	**YES**	Since the annuity was purchased by his employer, it is considered a contribution by X and is therefore includible in its entirety. The fact that the decedent's right to payment did not mature during his lifetime, or that X had no control over the contingency in question, is immaterial. [§378]
37.	**TRUE**	While the interest terminates at death, and thus is not taxable under section 2033, it may still be included in the deceased tenant's gross estate under section 2040. [§§385 *et seq.*]
38.	**YES**	"Full value" taxation under section 2040 applies only to those forms of joint ownership having rights of survivorship. It does not apply to tenancies in common. [§§390-391]

39. **FALSE** The amount included in Frick's estate is the value of the property ***proportionate*** to the amount of his original contribution—here, sixty percent of the present value. [§§393-394]

40. **NO** Where the joint tenancy is created by a third party, only the one-half undivided interest of the joint tenant who dies first is included in that tenant's gross estate. [§395]

41. **YES** Property that originates with the decedent joint tenant cannot be claimed as a "contribution" by the survivor. [§§397, 399]

42. **NO** ***Income*** derived from donated property is treated as having originated with the contributor. Hence, only the proportionate share of the property attributable to X's contribution would be included in her estate. [§401]

43. **TRUE** One-half the mortgage is attributed to each as an original contribution. [§405]

44. **FALSE** Section 2040 does not apply where the joint tenancy is severed prior to death—even where the transfer severing the tenancy is made within three years of death. Moreover, since section 2035 no longer taxes outright gifts made within three years of death, ***nothing*** will be included in Dark's estate on account of this property; neither section 2040 nor section 2035 operates here. [§§410-411, 105-106]

45.a. **NO** Same answer, but different rationale. In the case of interspousal joint tenancies ("qualified joint interests"), the relative consideration furnished is irrelevant. In any case, one-half of the value of the property is included in the estate of the first to die. [§§426 *et seq.*]

b. **YES** The amount and source of any consideration furnished by the spouses is irrelevant in the case of "qualified joint interests." One-half is included in the gross estate of the first to die in all cases. [§426]

46. **TRUE** This is considered a "power of appointment" under section 2041. [§§443, 456-457, 460]

47. **DEPENDS** Bea's power to invade principal would be a general power of appointment ***unless*** limited by an "ascertainable standard" relating to decedent's health, support, etc. Thus, if Bea's power were limited to her "maintenance and support," for example, the corpus would not be taxable in Bea's estate under section 2041. [§459]

48. **NO** Section 2041 applies only to powers granted to the decedent by a ***third party***. It does not cover reserved powers (although these may be taxable under sections 2036 or 2038). [§467]

49. **POSSIBLY** If W's exercise of the power was such that it would have been a taxable transfer under sections 2035 through 2038, it falls within section 2041. [§§476, 483]

50. **TRUE** A general power exists unless the co-holder is either the donor of the power or a person who has a substantial interest in the property (*i.e.*, an "adverse party"). [§487]

51. **YES** This type of death benefit is also considered "life insurance" under section 2042. [§§501-506]

52. **YES** As long as the benefits are payable to X's executor or estate, they are includible in her gross estate regardless of whether X had any incidents of ownership in the policy. [§507]

a. **NO** Where the beneficiary is someone other than decedent's estate, executor, etc., policy benefits are includible only if decedent had some incident of ownership in the policy. [§510]

53. **NO** This "power" is not considered an incident of ownership in the policy. [§514]

54. **DEPENDS** The value of the reversionary interest must exceed five percent of the value of the policy before it is a sufficient "incident of ownership" to come within section 2042. [§517]

55. **YES** The ***right*** to change beneficiaries is an incident of ownership under section 2042 even if the right is not—and as a practical matter could not—be exercised by the insured. [§521]

56. **YES** Section 2035 interacts with section 2042. Thus the transfer of incidents of ownership within three years of death is ineffective to prevent inclusion in the gross estate. [§§534-535]

a. **NO** Here, Potsy's spouse owns an undivided one-half interest in the policy. Thus, assuming Potsy predeceases his spouse, only fifty percent of the proceeds would be taxable to his estate (assuming all premiums were paid with community funds). [§§544-546]

57. **NO** The consideration must be measurable in ***money or money's worth***. Thus, certain noneconomic consideration that would support a contract (promise to marry, etc.) would ***not*** prevent estate tax exposure. [§§551, 553]

58. **NO** Deductibility of expenses depends upon their ***purpose.*** Where, as here, the purpose is to protect a beneficiary, the expenses are ***not*** deductible. [§§581-583]

59. **NO** A claim founded upon a promise or agreement must be supported by "full and adequate consideration in money or money's worth" to be deductible. And section 2053(e) specifically provides that the release of marital rights is not adequate consideration for this purpose. [§§594-595]

60. **TRUE** These are items of "deductions in respect of a decedent" which may be deducted both from the gross estate ***and*** estate income. [§607]

61. **NO** Deductions under section 2054 are limited to casualty and theft losses not otherwise compensated for. Mere diminutions in value are not deductible thereunder. [§§609, 611]

62. **NO** To qualify under section 2055, the bequest must be made to an organization operated exclusively for a recognized charitable purpose. [§613]

63. **TRUE** Under the Tax Reform Act of 1969, charitable remainders are deductible only if the trust involved qualifies as an "annuity trust," "unitrust," or "pooled income fund" (or where the income beneficiary is also a charity). [§§621-622]

64. **FALSE** The 1981 Act abolished all "quantitative" limitations on the marital deduction. The full value of qualifying property which passes to the surviving spouse is now deductible (100 percent deduction). [§§632-633, 639]

65. **NO** Inter vivos transfers to a spouse which are includible in the decedent's gross estate under sections 2035 through 2038 are deemed to "pass" to the surviving spouse for

marital deduction purposes. However, since outright gifts are no longer includible, even when made within three years of death, no estate tax marital deduction is allowable here. [§§651, 643, 105, 106]

66. **YES** The annuity was not purchased by Duke's executor but by Duke himself; and since no interest therein passes to a third person, it comes within section 2056. [§663]

67. **PROBABLY NOT** The facts indicate that W's right to this award is not vested under local law but is discretionary with the court. It is therefore deemed a terminable interest not deductible under section 2056. [§668]

68. **NO** The value of the patent is deductible, provided no interest has passed from H to a third person which would allow that person to possess the patent after termination of W's interest therein. [§§670, 672]

a. **NO** While a survivorship condition would otherwise make the bequest a nondeductible terminable interest, there is a statutory exception where the period of survivorship is not more than six months. [§676]

69. **YES** H and his estate are considered the same person. Hence, no interest in the trust passes to one other than the surviving spouse and the bequest is properly part of the marital deduction. [§674]

a. **NO** Since it is the surviving spouse, H, who has the power to direct income to others, the bequest still qualifies for the marital deduction (*i.e.*, as a marital deduction trust). [§§679-680, 694]

70. **POSSIBLY** Since A's power is not a "general power," the bequest cannot qualify under the life estate with power of appointment exception. But it appears to meet the requirements for the "Q-tip" exception. Thus, if D's executor elects to have the interest qualify, the marital deduction is allowable. [§§686-687, 696 *et seq.*]

71. **FALSE** The marital deduction may be allowed for a bequest to a noncitizen spouse (whether a resident or nonresident alien) if the decedent is a U.S. citizen and the otherwise qualifying bequest is to a "qualified domestic trust." [§§718-719]

72. **NO** C is a "third party beneficiary"; the transfer is treated as a direct gift of $30,000 to B and an indirect gift of $20,000 from A to C (both of which are taxable). [§734]

73. **YES** The donee need not be identified (or ascertained) at the time of transfer in order to create a taxable gift. [§739]

74. **PARTLY** The 100 percent marital deduction will eliminate taxes to the estate of the first to die. But the gift of the life interest in the "Q-tip" property is treated as a gift of the entire property, not just the life interest. [§758]

75. **NO** A gift of personal services is not taxable, since the services would not otherwise be includible in X's estate. [§759]

76. **NO** Only the exercise of a ***general*** power of appointment is a taxable gift. [§768]

77. **NO** The settlor's power to change beneficiaries is sufficient to make the transfer incomplete and hence nontaxable. [§783]

a. **YES** This would be treated as a complete transfer and a taxable gift. [§788]

78. **FALSE** The value is computed as the fair market value ***less*** the amount of consideration received by the transferor. [§805]

79. **YES** Wilona's release of dower rights is insufficient consideration for Horatio's payment. [§806]

80. **PROBABLY NOT** Sady's gifts should come within the "business transaction exception." [§807]

81. **YES** In creating a joint tenancy and supplying all the consideration therefor, D has made a gift of one-half the value of the securities to E. [§822]

82. **YES, BUT . . .** The creation of the joint tenancy constitutes a gift of an undivided one-half interest from H to W. However, there will be no tax liability since the 100 percent marital deduction completely offsets the value of the gift. [§§825-826]

a. **NO** No gift tax return is required where the marital deduction eliminates any tax liability. [§1029]

83. **NO** The $5,000 gift to R is excludible; but only $10,000 of the gift to S is excluded. [§842]

84. **FALSE** While most incentives were removed by requiring that inter vivos gifts be included in decedent's estate tax base and by instituting identical gift and estate tax rates and credits, the annual exclusion for inter vivos gifts (now $10,000) still remains in effect. [§843]

85. **NO** The exclusion is available for the gift to B, since it is a present interest. However, the gift to C is a future interest which does not qualify for the exclusion. [§§847, 851]

86. **YES** E's present interest is not "ascertainable," since the trustee has ***discretion*** to distribute to E according to his needs. F's gift is a future interest and thus not excludible. [§§847, 850, 853]

87. **FALSE** While the rules (and their exceptions) are essentially the same in substance and purpose under both transfer taxes, specific applications are not identical because of the different context in which the rules operate—*i.e.*, the estate tax rules operate in the case of property passing from a decedent to a surviving spouse, whereas the gift tax rules operate in the case of lifetime gifts. [§§894 *et seq.*]

88. **FALSE** The alternate valuation date may be elected in any case. [§919]

89. **NO** Any decrease in value in the life estate after Mickey's death would probably be attributable solely to lapse of time; and such decreases must be ***disregarded.*** [§921]

90. **FALSE** Since the special use value allowed by section 2032A may not reduce the "actual" value by more than $750,000, the actual fair market value, which must take into account the "highest and best use" of the land, is still relevant. [§934]

91. **FALSE** Only "adjusted taxable gifts"—*i.e.*, taxable gifts ***made after*** 1976 ***other than*** those includible in the decedent's gross estate—are added. [§§1008, 1010]

92. **TRUE** However, this credit can effectively be used only once. [§1015]

93. **TRUE** The state taxes must be on property included in the gross estate; and the adjusted gross estate must be at least $40,000 (with ceilings imposed for taxable estates exceeding this amount). [§§1018-1021]

94.	**TRUE**	However, the donee can be held liable if the donor fails to pay (to the extent of the value of the property she receives). [§§1034-1035]
95.	**NO**	The executor of the estate remains primarily responsible for paying all federal estate taxes on D's estate. [§1049]
96.	**YES**	This is one of the three situations in which the executor may enforce payment of part of the estate tax from outside the estate. [§1051]
97.	**NO**	No beneficiary is a "skip person"; *i.e.*, none would be assigned to a generation two or more generations below that of X, the transferor. [§§1064, 1083-1085]
98.	**YES**	This is a generation-skipping trust; and B's death constitutes a "taxable termination" thereunder. [§§1078, 1083]
99.	**DEPENDS**	This gift is a "direct skip" to P's grandchildren. However, if P's son Q is dead, it is excluded from tax under the GST. [§§1079, 1093]
100.	**FALSE**	The entire trust property (not merely the succeeding life estates) is subject to the tax. [§1100]
a.	**FALSE**	Since Q's death results in a taxable termination rather than a taxable distribution, the ***trustee*** is liable for the tax. [§1113]

SAMPLE EXAM QUESTION I

Baron purchased Blackacre, taking title in his name and that of Bernard, his brother, as joint tenants. If Bernard predeceases Baron, will anything be included in Bernard's gross estate under the federal estate tax because of his interest in Blackacre?

SAMPLE EXAM QUESTION II

In 1972, Dent purchased unimproved land for $50,000. He took title in the names of "Dent and Wendy [his wife] as joint tenants with right of survivorship." Early in 1992 Dent learned that he had incurable cancer. He consulted with his attorney regarding his will and estate plan. Assuming the following transactions are undertaken upon the advice of counsel and that Dent died in September 1992, what are the federal gift and estate tax consequences to Dent and Dent's estate?

(a) Dent and Wendy deeded one-half of the property "to Dent" and one-half "to Wendy."

(b) Dent and Wendy deeded the entire property "to Wendy."

SAMPLE EXAM QUESTION III

D transferred property to T in trust for A for life, remainder to X and his heirs. D provided that she should have the power to revoke the trust if she outlived A. D died survived by A and X. At the time of her death, D's chance of outliving A was one in ten. Is the trust property taxable to D's estate under the federal estate tax?

SAMPLE EXAM QUESTION IV

Ten years ago, D transferred $1,000,000 in stocks and bonds to T in trust for his three children, A, B, and C. D retained no interest or power with respect to the trust but provided that his wife, W, should have the power to alter or amend the trust in any way she saw fit, except that she could not make herself beneficiary of the trust, directly or indirectly. W was in Europe when D created the trust. Upon her return, D told W what he had done. He informed her that he had given her power to alter or amend the trust so that if any one of their children entered into an unfortunate marriage they could protect the trust property against the child's undesirable spouse. He explained to W that he had given her the power instead of reserving it for himself so that he could keep the property out of his estate for federal estate tax purposes. W was so much impressed by D's explanation of the trust that she promptly transferred $1,000,000 in stocks and bonds to T upon a similar trust for A, B, and C. Under this trust, W gave D the power to alter or amend the trust in any way he saw fit except that he could not make himself beneficiary of the trust. D and W were both killed in an automobile accident this year.

(a) Will either trust be taxed to D's estate under the federal estate tax?

(b) Will either trust be taxed to W's estate under the federal estate tax?

SAMPLE EXAM QUESTION V

In 1975, D insured his life for $500,000. In 1985, D irrevocably assigned the policy to A, completely divesting himself of all incidents of ownership in the policy. However, D paid all the premiums on the policy until his death this year. Is the insurance taxable to D's estate under the federal estate tax?

SAMPLE EXAM QUESTION VI

During her life, Dolores gratuitously deeded Whiteacre to her son, Samuel, in fee, reserving a term for twenty years which in her will she left to her husband, Wilbur.

(a) Does the interest in Whiteacre that Dolores devised to Wilbur qualify for the marital deduction?

(b) How would the answer be affected if instead of giving the remainder in Whiteacre to Samuel, Dolores sold it to him for $50,000, its fair market value?

SAMPLE EXAM QUESTION VII

D bequeathed $200,000 worth of stocks and bonds to T in trust with directions to accumulate the income from the trust property during the life of his wife, W, or to distribute the income to W as T in his discretion saw fit, and at W's death to pay over the principal of the trust and any accumulated income to W's estate. Does this bequest qualify for the marital deduction?

SAMPLE EXAM QUESTION VIII

In 1980, A transferred $1,000,000 in trust for B during the life of A, remainder to C if C survived A, and if C did not survive A, then to A or his estate. A died this year survived by C. At the date of his death, his chances of outliving C were one in ten. To what extent, if at all, is the transfer subject to:

(a) The gift tax?

(b) The estate tax?

SAMPLE EXAM QUESTION IX

A transferred $500,000 to T in trust to pay the income to C for life, remainder to D. A retained the power to change the beneficiaries under this trust with the consent of D. This year the trustee paid C $25,000 income from the trust. What are the gift tax consequences of the creation of the trust? Of the payment of the income from the trust to C?

ANSWER TO SAMPLE EXAM QUESTION I

No. This problem raises the question of the relation between section 2033 and other taxing provisions of the estate tax. Under section 2040, which deals explicitly with joint estates, Bernard's interest in Blackacre is not taxable to his estate because the surviving joint tenant, Baron, contributed the entire consideration for the property. Nor may Bernard's interest in the property be taxed under section 2033, even though, in substance, Bernard owned one-half of the property in fee at his death. Since section 2040 is a specific section covering the taxation of joint estates, joint estates are excluded from the tax imposed by section 2033.

ANSWER TO SAMPLE EXAM QUESTION II

(a) Dent probably would be treated as having made a gift of one-half of the value of the property to Wendy in 1992, but the 100 percent marital deduction would preclude any gift tax liability and eliminate any requirement to file a gift tax return. For estate tax purposes, one-half of the property's value is includible in Dent's gross estate.

(b) Dent probably would be treated as having made a gift of the entire property to Wendy but, again, the 100 percent marital deduction would preclude tax liability and any reporting requirement. For estate tax purposes, no part of the value of the property is includible in Dent's gross estate.

Prior to 1982 (and after 1954), the creation of a joint tenancy in real property between husband and wife was not treated as a taxable gift unless the "donor" spouse elected to so treat it. Assuming no election was filed, Dent would be theoretically treated, for gift tax purposes, as the sole owner of the property, *i.e.*, as if no gift was ever made to Wendy. Thus, when the joint tenancy was severed in 1992 by the creation of a tenancy in common (part (a) of the question), Dent made a completed gift of a one-half undivided interest in the property to Wendy; or when the property was transferred to Wendy as sole owner (part (b) of the question), Dent made a completed gift of the entire property to Wendy. However, since these "gifts" occurred after 1981, the 100 percent gift tax marital deduction introduced by the 1981 Act completely offsets the amount of the gift and precludes any gift tax liability. Moreover, since no gift tax return need be filed where the 100 percent deduction completely offsets the amount of the "gross gift," there is no need to report these transactions.

Prior to 1982, transfers within three years of death were included in the transferor's gross estate. Although the 1981 Act eliminated estate tax exposure in the case of "outright gifts," it preserved the interaction of section 2035 with certain of the specific taxing sections of the Code—*i.e.*, sections 2036, 2037, 2038, and 2042. However, under prior law, section 2035 was held ***not*** to interact with section 2040, and this ***lack*** of interaction is preserved since section 2035(d), as amended, fails to identify section 2040 as a provision with which section 2035 will interact. Thus:

In part (a), the "transfer" of the one-half undivided interest to Wendy is not subject to the estate tax under section 2035 (or section 2040), but the one-half interest that Dent owned at death is includible in his gross estate—under section 2033. Note, however, that this transfer did not really change the estate tax result since Dent died in 1992, at which time the new rules relating to "qualified joint interests" under section 2040(b) would require inclusion of only one-half of the value of the property anyway.

In part (b), the "transfer" of the entire interest to Wendy precludes any inclusion in Dent's estate. Under the rationale of prior cases, section 2040 is inoperative since no joint tenancy existed at Dent's death. And, since this was an "outright" gift, section 2035, as amended, is inoperative. Finally, since Dent did not own any interest in the property at death, nothing can be included under section 2033.

ANSWER TO SAMPLE EXAM QUESTION III

Yes. Except for the value of A's life estate, the property is taxable in D's gross estate.

There are two possible theories under which the trust property might be exposed to the estate tax upon D's death: (1) as a revocable transfer under section 2038; and (2) as a transfer taking effect at death under section 2037. Section 2038 does ***not*** apply where, as here, the transferor's power to revoke is contingent upon an event beyond the transferor's control and the contingency has not occurred at the time of his or her death. On the other hand, the transfer should be taxed under section 2037: D's power to revoke the trust is a reversionary interest in the property worth more than five percent of the value of the transferred property immediately before D's death, and X's possession or enjoyment of the remainder in the property is dependent upon outliving D. However, since A's life estate is vested and not dependent upon D's life or death, it should be excluded from the taxable amount.

ANSWER TO SAMPLE EXAM QUESTION IV

The issue raised here is that of the "reciprocal trust doctrine" and its application under these facts to produce a tax under section 2036. Prior to the Supreme Court's decision in *United States v. Grace* in 1969, it is unlikely that either trust would have been taxed in D's or W's estate. At that time, courts insisted that technical, common law consideration was the touchstone for determining the "actual" transferor. Quite typically, the courts were unable to find such consideration in connection with husband-wife reciprocal trusts; even where the trusts were created at the same time and pursuant to an apparently integrated plan, the authorities were inclined to view the transaction as merely a division of marital property and not a bargained-for agreement supported by consideration.

In *Grace*, the Supreme Court swept aside the requirement of "consideration," holding that application of the reciprocal trust doctrine requires only that the trusts be ***interrelated*** and that the arrangement, to the extent of mutual value, leave the settlors in approximately the ***same economic position*** as they would have been in had they created the trusts naming themselves as life beneficiaries. However, the Court failed to delineate the scope of its holding, and thus *Grace* presents some problems of interpretation.

If *Grace* adopted a strict "net effect" approach, the trusts here will be subject to the reciprocal trust doctrine; W will be deemed the actual transferor of the D trust, and D will be deemed the actual transferor of the W trust. However, if the trusts must be "interrelated" in the sense that they are established pursuant to a mutual plan or understanding between the parties, then reciprocal trusts might not be found. As presented, the facts actually fall somewhere in between mere parallelism and a mutual, prearranged plan. While there was no prearranged plan, there was a parallel disposition of property undertaken for purposes of avoiding the estate tax but at the same time achieving an economic position identical to the position each transferor would have been in had he or she made a taxable transfer. With this in mind, it would certainly be reasonable to conclude that the reciprocal trust doctrine could and should be applied in this case.

ANSWER TO SAMPLE EXAM QUESTION V

The proceeds of the policy are not taxable to D's estate under section 2042. Nor will premiums paid by D within three years of his death be taxed under section 2035.

Section 2042 does not tax insurance payable to beneficiaries other than the estate of the insured unless the insured possessed incidents of ownership in the insurance at his death. Consequently, the insurance is not exposed to the section 2042 tax in D's estate. Nor could the insurance be taxed under section 2035 because the transfer from D to A took place more than three years prior to D's death. (Note that section 2035 would continue to interact with section 2042 if incidents of ownership are transferred within three years of death.)

In 1967, the Service undertook to use section 2035 to reach a portion of the proceeds of a life insurance policy, even though the insurance had been irrevocably assigned more than three years before death, where the decedent continued to pay premiums up to (and including the three years before) death. The Service's theory was that since the continued payment of premiums kept the insurance in force, and since payments within three years of the decedent's death were "in contemplation of death," section 2035 would reach not only the three years' premiums but a portion of the policy proceeds proportionate to the ratio of premiums paid during the last three years to total premiums paid. This position, however, was rejected by the courts as an improper attempt to reintroduce into the 1954 Code the "premium payment test" which Congress had specifically eliminated in 1954. The Service, in a 1971 ruling, conceded this point and announced that it would not tax a portion of the policy proceeds under this theory, but it would undertake to tax the last three years' premiums under section 2035. Prior to 1982, the taxation of the actual amount of the last three years' premiums was appropriate since these payments ***were*** gifts (albeit indirect) to the owner of the insurance policy. However, the 1981 Act amendments, which limit the scope of section 2035, prevent inclusion of such "outright" (albeit indirect) gifts.

ANSWER TO SAMPLE EXAM QUESTION VI

(a) No. All of the elements of a nondeductible terminable interest of the first class are present here—*i.e.*, an interest in the same property in which the terminable interest passes to Wilbur (surviving spouse) also passes for less than adequate consideration to Samuel (third person) who can possess and enjoy the property only after Wilbur's interest terminates. The fact that Samuel acquired his interest under a different instrument and at a different time than Wilbur acquired his is immaterial.

(b) Under these facts, the term for years which passed to Wilbur would no longer be a nondeductible terminable interest and would qualify for the marital deduction.

The fact that Samuel acquired his interest in the property from Dolores for adequate and full consideration in money or money's worth prevents Wilbur's interest from being a nondeductible terminable interest. Therefore, the marital deduction is available even though Wilbur took an interest in the property that would terminate or fail and an interest in the same property passed to another (by virtue of which he may enjoy the property after the termination of Wilbur's interest).

ANSWER TO SAMPLE EXAM QUESTION VII

Yes. W's interest is not a nondeductible terminable interest since no one other than the surviving spouse or her estate acquires any interest in the property. This is a so-called marital deduction estate trust. Unlike the power of appointment trust, it does not have to meet the requirements for the life estate power of appointment exception to the terminable interest rule: It qualifies for the marital deduction, not as an exception to the terminable interest rule, but as an interest that is not a nondeductible terminable interest. This type of trust may be used as an alternative to the marital deduction power of appointment trust (or a Q-tip) and may be preferred where it is not desirable to pay all the income out annually to the surviving spouse, as is required in the case of a marital deduction power of appointment or Q-tip trust.

ANSWER TO SAMPLE EXAM QUESTION VIII

(a) A made a taxable gift of the entire trust property less the value of his reversionary interest.

(b) At A's death, the trust property—to the extent of C's remainder—is taxable to his estate under section 2037 as a transfer taking effect at death.

When A created the trust, he clearly made a complete transfer and a taxable gift of B's estate pur autre vie. He also made a taxable gift of C's remainder, since he retained no power to revoke the transfer.

Although the remainder is subject to divestment because the property will revert to A if he outlives C, this does not make the transfer of the remainder incomplete for gift tax purposes. Nor does A's reversionary interest coupled with the fact that C must survive A in order to possess or enjoy the property make C's remainder nontaxable under the gift tax.

Since A retained his reversionary interest in the trust property, instead of giving it away, the value of this interest will be subtracted from the amount of A's taxable gift, if it can be valued. Here, it can be valued by comparing the life expectancies of A and C and A's chance of surviving C.

The estate tax exposure under section 2037 is clear: C's possession and enjoyment is contingent upon surviving A and A retained a reversionary interest, the value of which meets the "de minimis rule."

ANSWER TO SAMPLE EXAM QUESTION IX

When A created the trust, she made a completed, and hence taxable, gift of the remainder. The gift was complete because A could only revoke the remainder with the consent of a person possessing a substantial adverse interest in that part of the trust (D). Moreover, the annual exclusion is not available because this was a gift of a future interest.

A did not make a taxable gift of the life estate when she created the trust; at that time the gift was incomplete for gift tax purposes because A retained the power to revoke the life estate without the consent of a person possessing a substantial adverse interest in that part of the trust. On the other hand, a taxable gift was made from A to C when the trustee paid C the $25,000 income from the trust. However, A can claim the exclusion against the tax since it was a gift of a present interest.

TABLE OF CITATIONS TO INTERNAL REVENUE CODE

TABLE OF CASES

Allen v. United States - §§115, 117, 221
Allen, Commissioner v. - §76
Alperstein v. Commissioner - §481
Anderson v. Commissioner - §807
Arents v. Commissioner - §156
Awtry v. Commissioner - §665

Bahen, Estate of v. United States - §§369, 378, 381
Becklenberg v. Commissioner - §151
Bel v. United States - §§539, 540
Billings v. Commissioner - §512
Bischoff v. Commissioner - §139
Blodgett v. Holden - §750
Boeing, Commissioner v. - §756
Borner, Estate of v. Commissioner - §§417, 418
Bosch, Estate of, Commissioner v. - §§91, 92, 603
Bowling, Estate of v. Commissioner - §704
Brandon, Estate of v. Commissioner - §652
Bray, Estate of, Commissioner v. - §608
Bremer v. Luff - §405
Bressani, Estate of v. Commissioner - §440
Bridgeport City Trust Co., Commissioner v. - §332
Brodrick v. Gore - §977
Bromley v. McCaughn - §11
Bronson, Commissioner v. - §583
Bronston, Estate of v. Commissioner - §735
Bull v. United States - §§58, 59
Burnet v. Guggenheim - §§782, 783
Bushman v. United States - §423
Byrum, United States v. - §§199, 200, 203

Camp v. Commissioner - §795
Canfield v. Commissioner - §143
Carson v. Commissioner - §810
Cartwright, United States v. - §978
Central Trust Co. v. United States - §315
Chandler, United States v. - §93
Chase Manhattan Bank, Commissioner v. - §545
Chase National Bank, Commissioner v. - §329
Chown v. Commissioner - §50
Chrysler v. Commissioner - §§172, 215
Church's Estate, Commissioner v. - §127
City National Bank v. United States - §75
Commissioner v. - *see* name of party
Commonwealth Trust Co. v. Driscoll - §323
Connecticut Bank & Trust Co. v. United States - §46
Cook v. Commissioner - §329
Crown v. Commissioner - §761
Cunha, Estate of v. Commissioner - §§664, 668
Curry v. United States - §93

Detroit Bank & Trust Co. v. United States - §539
Dickman v. Commissioner - §762
Diehl v. United States - §160
Dimock v. Corwin - §399
Drazen, Estate of v. Commissioner - §408
DuPont v. Commissioner - §785
DuPont, Estate of - §162
DuPont's Estate v. Commissioner - §49
DuVal's Estate v. Commissioner - §590
Dwight's Estate, Commissioner v. - §168

Ellis, Commissioner v. - §691
Empire Trust Co. v. Commissioner - §97
Endicott Trust Co. v. United States - §404
Erie Railroad Co. v. Tompkins - §91
Estate of - *see* name of party

Farnum v. Commissioner - §142
Fidelity-Philadelphia Trust Co. v. Smith - §§153, 373
Field, United States v. - §§82, 444
Finley v. United States - §481
First National Bank v. United States - §603
First National Bank of Midland v. United States - §537
First Trust & Deposit Co. v. Shaughnessy - §534
Fleishmann v. Commissioner - §794
Fondren v. Commissioner - §§851, 854
Forster v. Sauber - §351
Frazier v. United States - §71
Freedman v. United States - §544
Freeman v. Commissioner - §481
Friedman, Estate of v. Commissioner - §808
Fruehauf, Estate of v. Commissioner - §§528, 529, 531
Fry v. Commissioner - §213
Fusz, Estate of v. Commissioner - §375

Garstin v. United States - §971
Gelb v. Commissioner - §682
Geller v. Commissioner - §861
Giannini v. Commissioner - §809
Gilbert v. Commissioner - §259
Glaser v. United States - §418
Goodman v. Commissioner - §917
Goodman v. Granger - §§63, 918
Goodyear, United States v. - §§431, 433
Gorkey, Estate of v. Commissioner - §168
Grace, United States v. - §§138, 139
Green, Estate of v. United States - §668
Greene, Commissioner v. - §735
Gregory, Estate of v. Commissioner - §§134, 438
Griswold v. Commissioner - §791
Gutchess v. Commissioner - §§159, 164

INDEX

L

M

gilbert

LAW SUMMARIES

ESTATE & GIFT TAX

John H. McCord

Taxpayer Relief Act of 1997
and
IRS Restructuring and Reform Act of 1998
Supplement

HARCOURT BRACE LEGAL AND PROFESSIONAL PUBLICATIONS, INC.
EDITORIAL OFFICES: 111 W. Jackson Blvd., 7th Floor, Chicago, IL 60604

gilbert
LAW SUMMARIES

REGIONAL OFFICES: Chicago, Dallas, Los Angeles, New York, Washington, D.C.
Distributed by: **Harcourt Brace & Company** 6277 Sea Harbor Drive, Orlando, FL 32887 (800)787-8717

SUPPLEMENT TO GILBERT "ESTATE & GIFT TAX" SUMMARY
(15th Edition)

August 1998

TAXPAYER RELIEF ACT OF 1997 AND IRS RESTRUCTURING AND REFORM ACT OF 1998

Introduction

1. **Purpose and Scope of This Supplement:** Federal tax courses must address the significant changes introduced by the Taxpayer Relief Act of 1997 ("1997 Act") and the amendments thereto in the IRS Restructuring and Reform Act of 1998 ("1998 Act"). These changes will be reflected in new editions of casebooks and in the revised edition of the Gilbert *Estate & Gift Tax Summary* ("Summary") now in progress. However, the new editions are unlikely to be available for the 1998-1999 academic year. This supplement undertakes to fill the gap with a summary of the recent amendments affecting the gift, estate, and generation-skipping taxes.

2. **Organization:** The relevant provisions of the 1997 Act and the amendments made in 1998 are reviewed in the order in which they appear in the 1997 Act. The 1998 Act amendments are incorporated with the applicable provisions of the 1997 Act. First addressed is Title V of the 1997 Act, and then, Title XIII. The discussion of each amendment begins with a summary statement of prior law, followed by an outline of the changes made by the 1997 Act and amendments to that Act made by the 1998 Act. Except in the case of amendments which introduce entirely new provisions, the statement of "prior law" contains a cross-reference to relevant sections of the Gilbert Summary.

3. **Income Tax Provisions:** Some of the amendments address income tax issues involving estates and trusts. Since income tax issues are not addressed in the Gilbert *Estate & Gift Tax Summary,* the income tax amendments are not discussed in this supplement.

4. **Appendices:** Many of the casebooks and statutory supplements available to students were published before the effective date of the 1997 Act; all were published prior to the 1998 Act. Consequently, they are not likely to contain the language of the Acts. Therefore, the relevant amendments are reproduced in two appendices to this supplement: the 1997 Act in Appendix 1, and the 1998 Act in Appendix 2. These appendices are cross-referenced by page number.

5. **Effective Dates:** Except as otherwise noted, the amendments contained in Title V of the 1997 Act (and the 1998 Act's amendments thereto) apply to gifts made or estates of decedents dying after December 31, 1997. The effective date of most of the amendments made by Title XIII of the 1997 Act is the day after the date of enactment—August 6, 1997. However, the effective dates for Title XIII amendments are sometimes confusing. In some cases, an amendment applies not to transactions occurring after the relevant effective date but to transactions occurring in "taxable years ***beginning*** after the date of enactment"—which translates as "beginning in calendar or fiscal year 1998." And to compound the confusion, some amendments apply to "taxable years ***ending*** after the date of enactment"—which would include, *e.g.*, calendar year 1997. Effective dates are not particularly interesting subjects for study, but since one cannot assume a single "effective date" for Title XIII, the effective date for each amendment in this Title is noted.

6. **Cross-References:** As noted above, the Gilbert Summary to which this supplement relates and the statutory appendices are cross-referenced in this supplement. In addition, the following page contains a cross-reference table from Internal Revenue Code section to the 1997 and 1998 Act sections and the page(s) at which amendments are outlined in this supplement.

Cross-Reference Table—From Internal Revenue Code Section

I.R.C. Section	1997 Act Section	1998 Act Section	Supplement page(s)
2001	501(a)(1)(D)		4
	506(a)	6007(e)	15, 17
2010	501(a)(1)(A), (B)		3, 6
2031	508	6007(g)	17-18
2032A	501(b)		4
	504		15
	508		19
	1313		22
2033A (new)	502		6-14
2035	1310		20-21
2053	503(b)		14
2056	1311		21
2056A	1303		20
	1312		22
	1314		22
2057 (new)		6007(b)	6-14
2102	501(a)(1)(E)		4
2105	1304		20
2207A (and 2207B)	1302		20
2503	501(c)		4
2504	506(d)	6007(e)	15-17
2505	501(a)(2)		3
2631	501(d)		5
2651 (and 2612)	511		19
6018	501(a)(1)(C)		3
6019	1301		19
6166 (and 6601(j))	501(e)		5
	503(d)	6007(c)	14
6501	506(a), (b)		15-16
7477 (new)	506(c)		16
7479 (new)	505	6007(d)	14-15

TITLE V—ESTATE, GIFT, AND GENERATION-SKIPPING TAX PROVISIONS

A. UNIFIED CREDIT [1997 Act §501(a)(1)(A), (B) and (a)(2), amending I.R.C. §§2010, 2505; *see* Appendix 1, p. 1]

1. **Prior Law:** Since 1986, the unified credit has been $192,800 ($600,000 exemption equivalent). [*See* I.R.C. §§2505 (gift tax), 2010 (estate tax); *and see* Summary §§994-1001, 1014-1016]

2. **1997 Act:** Beginning in 1998, an increasing unified credit, called the "applicable credit," is phased in over a nine-year period. The applicable credit will be the tentative tax computed at I.R.C. section 2001(d) rates (former I.R.C. section 2001(c)) on the "applicable exclusion amount." The increasing applicable exclusion amount is set out in a table in new I.R.C. section 2001(c). This table, followed by the applicable credit computed at current rates, is as follows:

In the case of estates of decedents dying, and gifts made, during:	The applicable exclusion amount is:	Applicable credit (at current rates) will be:
1998	$ 625,000	$202,050
1999	$ 650,000	$211,300
2000 & 2001	$ 675,000	$220,550
2002 & 2003	$ 700,000	$229,800
2004	$ 850,000	$287,300
2005	$ 950,000	$326,300
2006 & thereafter	$1,000,000	$345,800

3. **Comments**

   a. **Slow phase-in:** Note the back-loaded phase-in of the increased credit. Significant increases are deferred until 2004.

   b. **Credit defined by exclusion amount:** The use of the new "applicable exclusion amount" to define the unified credit is more obscure than a stated dollar amount of credit. The rationale appears to be twofold:

      (1) The credit is directly tied to tax rates. An increase or decrease in rates will produce a corresponding increase or decrease in the credit, but the amount of the taxable estate effectively excluded from tax will remain constant.

      (2) The annual exclusion amount is used to define the estate tax filing requirement and the new "family-owned business exclusion" (*see infra*).

4. **Related Amendments in Section 501(a) of the 1997 Act** [*See* Appendix 1, p. 1]

   a. **Filing requirement:** The estate tax filing requirement tracks the "applicable exclusion amount." [1997 Act §501(a)(1)(C), amending I.R.C. §6018(a)] In 1998, therefore, no estate tax return need be filed for a decedent whose gross estate is $625,000 or less. [*See* Summary §1045]

   b. **Phase-out of graduated rates:** The "phase-out of graduated rates and unified credit" is not limited to the present top end of $21,040,000. Rather, the additional 5% added to the top bracket rate for taxable estates in excess of $10,000,000 remains in effect through "the amount at which the average tax rate . . . is 55 percent." [1997 Act §501(a)(1)(D), amending I.R.C. §2001(c)(2), now redesignated as I.R.C. §2001(d)(2); *and see* Summary §990]

c. **Unified credit for nonresident aliens' estates:** The unified credit for estates of nonresident aliens is allowed in the "applicable credit amount." [1997 Act §501(a)(1)(E), amending I.R.C. §2102(c)(3)(A)]

B. OTHER "INFLATION ADJUSTMENTS"

1. **In General:** A number of existing gift, estate, and generation-skipping exclusions and exemptions will be allowed annual cost-of-living ("CPI") adjustments determined in a manner similar to the adjustments allowed for the income tax rate brackets by I.R.C. section 1(f), with the following modification: The adjustment for these items is the percentage by which the CPI for the year of the transfer exceeds the CPI for calendar year 1997.

   a. **Note:** I.R.C. section 1(f)(3) specifies that the CPI adjustment for any year is the ". . . percentage (if any) by which . . . the CPI for the preceding calendar year exceeds the CPI for calendar year 1992." Substituting "1997" for "1992" in the case of the 1997 Act's inflation adjustment, it appears that ***no adjustment will be available until 1999***: For gifts made or estates of decedents dying in 1998, the relevant adjustment under section 1(f)(3) is the difference between the 1997 CPI (preceding year) and the (same) 1997 CPI.

2. **Code Sections Now Subject to Inflation Adjustment**

   a. **Special use valuation of I.R.C. section 2032A** [1997 Act §501(b), amending I.R.C. §2032A(a); *see* Appendix 1, p. 2]

      (1) **Prior law:** The reduction in the value of real property cannot exceed $750,000. [*See* Summary §934]

      (2) **1997 Act:** This $750,000 cap will be increased by the CPI adjustment allowed for the year of death by I.R.C. section 1(f)—using, however, calendar year 1997 as the base year.

         (a) **Limitation:** The adjustment is allowed only in multiples of $10,000 and is rounded down to lowest multiple of $10,000.

         (b) **Example:** If the allowable CPI adjustment for 1998 is 3.2% greater than the 1997 CPI, the value-reduction cap for decedents dying in 1999 is $770,000: 3.2% of $750,000 equals $24,000, but the increase in the cap is limited to the lower multiple of $10,000, *i.e.*, $20,000.

   b. **Annual gift tax exclusion** [1997 Act §501(c), amending I.R.C. §2503(b); *see* Appendix 1, p. 2]

      (1) **Prior law:** The annual gift tax exclusion of I.R.C. section 2503(b) is limited to $10,000 per donee. [*See* Summary §842]

      (2) **1997 Act:** The annual exclusion is also subject to the CPI adjustment.

         (a) **Limitation:** This adjustment is allowed only in multiples of $1,000 and is rounded down to the lowest multiple of $1,000.

(b) **Example:** Assuming, again, that the allowable CPI adjustment for 1998 is 3.2%, the annual exclusion for gifts made in that year ***and*** in 1999 would remain at $10,000: As noted above, the comparison years under I.R.C. section 1(f)(3) are the preceding calendar year (1997 for 1998) and the base year (1997 under the Act). Nor would there be any increase in the exclusion in 1999 because the inflation adjustment (3.2% x $10,000) does not equal or exceed $1,000. Further assuming that the CPI increases at 3.2% annually, the annual exclusion will not increase to $11,000 until 2002 when the aggregate CPI for the four computation years (1998-2001) finally exceeds the 10% necessary to produce an adjustment in excess of $1,000.

c. **Generation-skipping tax exemption** [1997 Act §501(d), amending I.R.C. §2631; *see* Appendix 1, p. 2]

(1) **Prior law:** In determining the rate of the generation-skipping transfer tax ("GST") applicable to a "direct skip" or generation-skipping transfer from a trust, an aggregate $1,000,000 "exemption" is allocated among the direct skips and the trusts. [*See* Summary §1105]

(2) **1997 Act:** The $1,000,000 GST exemption will be increased by the CPI adjustment.

(a) **Limitation:** The adjustment is allowed only in multiples of $10,000 and is rounded down to the lowest $10,000.

(b) **Example:** If the allowable CPI adjustment for 1998 is 3.2%, the maximum GST exemption for direct skips or transfers to trust in 1999 is $1,030,000: 3.2% of $1,000,000 equals $32,000, but the increase in the allowable exclusion is limited to the lowest multiple of $10,000, *i.e.*, $30,000. Furthermore, assuming that the transferor had previously allocated the full $1,000,000 GST exemption, the transferor could allocate the additional $30,000 to direct skips or transfers to trust made in 1999.

(c) **Comment:** Congress had been urged to coordinate the exemption equivalent of the unified credit with the GST exemption, *i.e.*, allow the same $1,000,000 "exemption" for all three transfer taxes. It failed to do so. As previously noted, the "exclusion amount" for estate and gift tax purposes is phased in to $1,000,000 over nine years and is not subject to any inflation adjustment. The GST exemption remains at $1,000,000 and is allowed an inflation adjustment (based on CPI) beginning in 1998. Thus, the GST exemption is disconnected even further from the exemption equivalent of the unified credit!

(3) **1998 Act:** The 1998 Act limits any increase of the GST exemption to generation-skipping transfers made during or after the calendar year to which the increase is applicable. It also denies any inflation adjustment for calendar years after the year of the transferor's death. [1998 Act §6007(a), amending I.R.C. §2631(c); *see* Appendix 2, p. 1]

d. **Amount subject to reduced interest rate for installment payments of estate tax under I.R.C. section 6166** [1997 Act §501(e), amending I.R.C. §6601(j); *see* Appendix 1, pp. 2-3]

(1) **Prior law:** Installment payments of the estate tax liability attributable to the first $1,000,000 in value of a closely held business interest (up to $345,800 of estate taxes) are subject to an especially low interest rate. [*See* Summary §1057]

(2) **1997 Act:** The $1,000,000 cap is adjusted for CPI.

(a) **Limitation:** The adjustment is allowed in multiples of $10,000 and is rounded down to the lowest $10,000.

3. **Comments**

a. Insofar as non-merit-based increases in wage and salary income may be based on increases in the CPI, there is a rough logic in the I.R.C. section 1(f) adjustment of the income tax rate brackets based on the CPI. However, the logical and economic relation of CPI to investment experience and to the fair market value of property is considerably more problematic.

b. It is not clear whether Congress intended to defer inflation adjustments until 1999. However, application of an immediate inflation adjustment for gifts made, etc., in 1998 would present practical problems: The CPI for a calendar year is not determinable until after the close of the year. Consequently, if the inflation adjustment were allowed in the difference between the CPI for the year of the transfer and the base year, the amount of the exclusion, exemption, etc., for any year could not be known until the year after the transfer is made!

C. FAMILY-OWNED BUSINESS INTERESTS [1997 Act §502, adding new I.R.C. §2033A; *and see* Appendix 1, pp. 3-8]

1. **Prior Law:** A closely held business is accorded various forms of relief under the estate tax:

a. ***Attributable estate taxes may be paid in installments***, and a low rate of interest is allowed for the taxes on the first $1,000,000 of its estate tax value. [I.R.C. §6166; *and see* Summary §1057]

b. ***Real property held by the business*** may qualify for some relief under the special use valuation provisions of I.R.C. section 2032A. [*See* Summary §934]

2. **1997 Act:** Section 502 of this Act added new I.R.C. section 2033A entitled "Family-Owned Business Exclusion." Under this new section, all or a portion of the value of "qualified family-owned business interests" is excluded from the gross estate of the deceased owner.

3. **1998 Act:** The exclusion is converted to a deduction, and I.R.C. section 2033A is redesignated as I.R.C. section 2057. The principal thrust of the 1998 amendment is the substitution of new subsection (a). The remaining subsections of former section 2033A are retained with, however, some technical, conforming, and clarifying amendments. [1998 Act §6007(b), adding new I.R.C. §2057 and redesignating I.R.C. §2033A as §2057; *see* Appendix 2, pp. 1-3] New subsection (a) and the clarifying amendments are discussed below in connection with the substantive provisions to which they relate.

4. **Amount of 1997 Exclusion**

a. **Statute:** The exclusion was in the amount of lesser of the "adjusted value of the family-owned business interests of the decedent otherwise includible in the estate," or $1,300,000 less the "applicable exclusion amount" in effect for the year of the owner's death. [*See* former I.R.C. §2033A(a)(1), (2)]

b. **Elaboration:** The "applicable exclusion amount" was phased in over a nine-year period from 1998 until 2006. [*See* 1997 Act §501(a)(1)(B), amending I.R.C. §2010, above] The effect was that the cap on the family-owned business exclusion would decrease over the same period, as follows:

In the case of estates of decedents dying during:	The applicable exclusion amount is:	The I.R.C. §2033A exclusion cap would be:
1998	$ 625,000	$675,000
1999	$ 650,000	$650,000
2000 & 2001	$ 675,000	$625,000
2002 & 2003	$ 700,000	$600,000
2004	$ 850,000	$450,000
2005	$ 950,000	$350,000
2006 & thereafter	$1,000,000	$300,000

5. **Deduction under 1998 Act:** I.R.C. section 2057(a) now allows a deduction in the amount of the "adjusted value of the qualified family-owned business interest(s)" of the decedent, or $675,000, ***whichever is less***.

    a. **Rationale:** An exclusion operates like a deduction. It reduces the taxable estate at the top end and therefore reduces tax liability at the highest marginal rate of tax applicable to the estate. On the other hand, unified credit reduces tax liability at the lowest marginal rates of tax. As illustrated in the schedule above, the exclusion allowed by former I.R.C. section 2033A was continually reduced as the "applicable exclusion amount" of the unified credit was increased between 1998 and 2006. Thus the tax benefit of the family-owned business exclusion was correspondingly reduced. New I.R.C. section 2057(a) effectively fixes the maximum family-owned business deduction at the 1998 level of the former family-owned business exclusion.

    b. **Coordination with unified credit:** However, taxpayers are not allowed both a fixed family-owned business deduction and an increasing unified credit. New I.R.C. section 2057(a)(3) requires that if the allowable family-owned business deduction is in the full amount of the maximum of $675,000, the "applicable exclusion amount" which defines the unified credit will also remain at the 1998 level, *i.e.*, an "applicable exclusion" of $625,000 which produces a unified credit of $202,050. If, however, the allowable family-owned business deduction is less than $675,000, the applicable exclusion amount will be the lesser of (i) $625,000 plus the difference between $675,000 and the family-owned business deduction allowed, or (ii) the applicable exclusion amount for the year of the decedent's death.

    c. **Examples:** Suppose D dies in 2002 when the applicable exclusion amount of the unified credit is $700,000, and that D's estate includes a qualified family-owned business interest.

        (1) If the value the qualified family-owned business interest is $1,000,000, D's estate could claim the maximum deduction of $675,000 under new I.R.C. section 2057(a). However, the unified credit allowed to D's estate would be $202,050, based on the 1998 applicable exclusion amount of $625,000.

        (2) If the value of the qualified family-owned business interest is $500,000, D's estate could deduct only this $500,000 value. D's estate would be allowed a unified credit in the full amount of the year 2002 credit of $229,800, determined as follows:

            (a) The difference between the maximum deduction under I.R.C. section 2057(a) and the amount allowed as a deduction is $175,000 ($675,000 - $500,000).

(b) This amount added to the 1998 applicable exclusion amount is $800,000 ($175,000 + $625,000).

(c) Since $800,000 exceeds the applicable exclusion amount for year 2002 ($700,000), the unified credit allowed to D's estate is limited to the year 2002 amount—producing an allowable unified credit of $229,800.

6. **Requirements for Deduction:** The four basic requirements for this deduction are reminiscent of those applicable to the special use valuation of I.R.C. section 2032A. [*See* former I.R.C. §2033A(b)(1), redesignated as I.R.C. §2057(b)(1)] The requirements are:

   a. The decedent must be a ***United States citizen or resident***.

   b. The executor must ***elect the exclusion and file an "agreement"*** made by the qualified heirs to be subject to a recapture tax (*see* 9. and 10., *infra*).

   c. ***The "adjusted value"*** of the "includible qualified family-owned business interests" included in the gross estate ***plus*** the "includible gifts of such interests" must exceed 50% of the "adjusted gross estate."

   d. During the eight-year period preceding death, there must have been periods ***aggregating five years*** during which the decedent (or a member of the decedent's family) ***owned the interest(s) and materially participated*** in the operation of the business.

7. **Elaboration**

   a. The third requirement is elaborated in a congeries of definitions next summarized in 8., below.

   b. The material participation required prior to the decedent's death is the same as the similar requirement under I.R.C. section 2032A special use valuation, including the special rules for decedents who were retired or disabled and for surviving spouses. [*See* former I.R.C. §2033A(b)(1)(D)(ii), (i)(3)(A), (B), redesignated as some subsections of I.R.C. §2057]

8. **Definitions**

   a. **"Includible qualified family-owned business interests":** [*See* former I.R.C. §2033A(b)(2), redesignated as I.R.C. §2057(b)(2)] In determining the 50% of adjusted gross estate requirement (above), the relevant interest(s) must be "qualified family-owned business interests" which:

      (1) Are included in determining the value of the gross estate—without the application of this exclusion.

      (2) Pass from the decedent to a qualified heir—by bequest, inheritance, survivorship, interest in a trust, or other arrangement in which an interest in property is deemed to pass from the decedent for estate tax purposes and, in particular, under I.R.C. sections 2032A(e)(9) and 1014(b).

   b. **"Includible gifts of interests":** [*See* former I.R.C. §2033A(b)(3), redesignated as I.R.C. §2057(b)(3)] For purposes of the 50% of adjusted gross estate requirement, there is also included:

      (i) ***The value of all lifetime gifts of qualified family-owned business interests*** which were made by the decedent to family members and which are included as adjusted taxable gifts under I.R.C. section 2001(b)(1)(B).

(ii) ***Plus*** the amount of any annual exclusions allowed under I.R.C. section 2503(b) for these gifts—but only if the transferred interests were continuously held by the donee family members (other than the decedent's spouse) from the time of the gift until the decedent's death.

(1) **1998 Act:** Former I.R.C. section 2033A(b)(3)(B) required the subtraction from this sum of ". . . the value of such gifts that are included in the decedent's gross estate." The 1998 Act eliminates this subtraction. This is actually a clarifying amendment since the definition of adjusted taxable gifts in I.R.C. section 2001(b)(1)(B) already excludes such gifts.

c. **"Family member":** The term "family member" has the same meaning for purposes of this exclusion as for purposes of the I.R.C. section 2032A special use valuation. [*See* former I.R.C. §2033A(i)(2), redesignated as I.R.C. §2057(i)(2), cross-referencing I.R.C. §2032A(e)(2)]

d. **"Qualified heir":** This term includes a family member. [*See* former I.R.C. §2033A(i)(2), redesignated as I.R.C. 2057(i)(2), cross-referencing the special use valuation definition of "qualified heir" in I.R.C. §2032A(e)(1)] Also, for purposes of this new exclusion, "qualified heir" includes "an active employee" of the qualified family-owned business if ". . . such employee has been employed by such trade or business for a period of at least 10 years before the date of the decedent's death." [*See* former I.R.C. §2033A(i)(1), redesignated as I.R.C. §2057(i)(1)]

e. **"Qualified family-owned business interest":** Former I.R.C. section 2033A(e) [redesignated as I.R.C. §2057(e)] defines this term as follows:

(1) **Family ownership rules**

(a) The business qualifies if it is a trade or business carried on as a ***proprietorship*** (wholly owned by decedent).

(b) If the trade or business is carried on as an ***entity*** (partnership, corporation, etc.), the entity must be a "***family business***." Specifically, it must be at least:

(i) 50% owned by the decedent or a member of the decedent's family; or

(ii) If two families are involved, at least 70% owned by the two families; or

(iii) If three families are involved, at least 90% owned by the three families.

If two or three families are involved, at least 30% of the entity must be owned by the decedent and the decedent's family. [*See also* former I.R.C. §2033A(e)(3), redesignated as I.R.C. §2057(e)(3), for special rules determining ownership of entities]

(2) **United States business:** The principal place of business must be in the United States.

(3) **Closely held business:** The interest does not qualify if its stock or debt was readily tradeable on an established securities (or secondary) market within three years of the decedent's death.

(4) **Trade or business:** That portion of the business attributable to assets generating specific types of "passive income" does not qualify.

(a) Cash or marketable securities in excess of reasonable day-to-day working capital needs are disregarded. (The Committee Reports emphasize that liquid assets accumulated for capital improvements are not to be treated as working capital needs.)

(b) Also disregarded are assets producing certain types of passive income described in section 543(a) (Personal Holding Company income) or section 954(c)(1) (Controlled Foreign Corporation income).

(c) ***The 1998 Act adds*** that a decedent will be treated as engaged in a trade or business if a member of the decedent's family is so engaged. [1998 Act §6007(b)(5)(A), amending redesignated I.R.C. §2057(e)(1); *see* Appendix 2, p. 3] Also, a net cash lease from a decedent to a member of the decedent's family is not treated as "passive" or Personal Holding Company income if the activity of the lessee family member meets the active trade or business requirement. [1998 Act 6007(b)(3)(C), amending redesignated I.R.C. §2057(e)(2); *see* Appendix 2, p. 2]

f. **"Adjusted gross estate":** [*See* former I.R.C. §2033A(c), redesignated as I.R.C. §2057(c)] This is the total value of the decedent's gross estate, less claims against the estate and unpaid mortgages which are deductible by the estate under I.R.C. section 2053(a)(3) or (4), but increased by:

(1) ***The total of "includible gifts of interests"*** (above), ***and also*** gifts made by the decedent to the decedent's spouse within 10 years of the decedent's death, and any other gifts by the decedent within three years of death (other than annual exclusion gifts to family members).

(2) ***Less*** the amount of these gifts that are included in the decedent's gross estate.

g. **"Adjusted value of the qualified business interest":** [*See* former I.R.C. §2033A(d), redesignated as §2057(d)] This is the value of any such interest for purposes of the estate tax (determined without regard to the present family-owned business deduction), reduced by the excess of:

(1) Any claims against the estate and unpaid mortgages deductible under I.R.C. section 2053(a)(3) or (4).

(2) ***Less*** the following types of deductible amounts:

(a) Indebtedness relating to a qualified residence on which interest is deductible under I.R.C. section 163(h)(3).

(b) Indebtedness relating to the payment of medical or educational expenses of the decedent or the decedent's spouse or dependents.

(c) Other debts not exceeding $10,000.

9. **Recapture of Estate Tax Saved** [*See* former I.R.C. §2033A(f), redesignated as I.R.C. §2057(f)]

a. **10-year recapture rule:** A 10-year recapture rule similar to the recapture under I.R.C. section 2032A applies if:

(1) **Failure of material participation:** The qualified heir (or family member) must continue to materially participate in the business. [*See* redesignated I.R.C. §2057(f)(1)(A), and note the cross-reference to material participation requirements for special use valuation in I.R.C. §2032A(c)(6)(B)]

(2) **Disposition of interest:** The qualified heir must continue to own thc qualificd business interest. A disposition of the interest, other than to a family member or ". . . through a qualified conservation contribution under section 170(h)," triggers recapture. [*See* redesignated I.R.C. §2057(f)(1)(B)]

(3) **Loss of citizenship:** The qualified heir must continue to be a citizen of the United States. [*See* new I.R.C. §2057(f)(1)(B)] However, the recapture will not occur if the heir's interest is held in a "qualified trust" similar to a qualified domestic trust ("QDT") allowed for marital deduction purposes. [*See* redesignated I.R.C. §2057(g)]

(4) **Business moves out of United States:** The principal place of the business must continue to be located in the United States. [*See* new I.R.C. §2057(f)(1)(D)]

(5) **1998 Act:** The 1998 Act clarified that the qualified heir will not be treated as ceasing to be engaged in a trade or business so long as the property is used in a trade or business by a member of the qualified heir's family. [1998 Act 6007(b)(5)(B), adding new paragraph (3) to redesignated I.R.C. §2057(f); *see* Appendix 2, p. 3]

b. **Recapture amount:** [*See* new I.R.C. §2033A(f)(2), redesignated as I.R.C. 2057(f)(2)] The "applicable percentage" of the "adjusted tax difference attributable to the qualified . . . interest" is subject to recapture.

(1) **Adjusted tax difference attributable to interest:** This is, essentially, the proportionate estate tax that was saved as a result of the application of the deduction to the interest which is the subject of recapture.

(a) Under the 1997 Act, this was " . . . determined under rules similar to the rules of section 2032A(c)(2)(B)." [*See* former I.R.C. §2033A(f)(2)(A)(i)]

(b) ***The 1998 Act*** uncoupled the determination from I.R.C. section 2032A by deleting the phrase quoted above, and by adding a new subparagraph (C) to redesignated I.R.C. section 2057(f)(2) which defines the "adjusted tax difference with respect to the interest" as " . . . the excess of what would have been the estate tax liability but for the election . . . " over the estate tax liability actually paid. [1998 Act §6007(b)(4); *see* Appendix 2, pp. 3-4]

(2) **Applicable percentage:** [*See* redesignated I.R.C. §2057(f)(2)(B)] This is 100% for years 1 through 6. It declines thereafter as follows:

Year	**Applicable percentage**
7	80%
8	60%
9	40%
10	20%

(3) **Interest:** Interest is charged on the recapture amount from the date the decedent's estate tax was due. [*See* redesignated I.R.C. §2057(f)(2)(A)(ii)]

10. **Election and Agreement:** [*See* new I.R.C. §2033A(h), redesignated as I.R.C. §2057(h)] To qualify for the exclusion, the executor must elect its application and the qualified heirs who acquire an interest in the qualified business must consent to assume the obligation to pay the recapture tax in the event it is imposed.

11. **Other Applicable Rules**

a. **Cross-reference to I.R.C. section 2032A (and some other sections):** Redesignated I.R.C. section 2057(i)(3) provides that "rules similar to the following rules" shall apply:

(1) Section 2032A(b)(4)—relating to decedents who are retired or disabled.
(2) Section 2032A(b)(5)—relating to special rules for surviving spouses.
(3) Section 2032A(c)(2)(D)—relating to partial dispositions.
(4) Section 2032A(c)(3)—relating to only one additional tax imposed with respect to any single portion.
(5) Section 2032A(c)(4)—relating to due date.
(6) Section 2032A(c)(5)—relating to liability for tax, and the furnishing of a bond.
(7) Section 2032A(c)(7)—relating to no tax if use begins within two years, and active management by eligible qualified heir being treated as material participation.
(8) Paragraphs (1) and (3) of section 2032A(d)—relating to election and agreement.
(9) Section 2032A(e)(10)—relating to community property.
(10) Section 2032A(e)(14)—relating to treatment of replacement property acquired in section 1031 or 1033 transactions.
(11) Section 2032A(f)—relating to statutes of limitations.
(12) Section 6166(b)(3)—relating to farmhouses and other structures taken into account.
(13) Subparagraphs (B), (C), and (D) of section 6166(g)(1)—relating to acceleration of payment.
(14) Section 6324B—relating to the special lien for additional estate tax.

b. **1998 Act:** The Act added two additional cross-references for applicable rules [1998 Act §6007(b)(7); *see* Appendix 2, p. 3]:

(1) To section 2032A(g)—relating to application to interests in partnerships, corporations, and trusts.

(2) To sections 2032A(h) and (i)—relating to transfers incident to involuntary conversions and like-kind exchanges.

c. **Comments on "applicable rules"**

(1) One cannot but be concerned about a statutory announcement that complex operating rules are to be ***similar*** to those of another complex provision. Are they to be the same, or might they embody subtly nuanced differences?

(2) If not otherwise obvious from a reading of the prior subsections of redesignated I.R.C. section 2057, this concluding paragraph of the statute demonstrates how the new exclusion was "pasted together" from another non-revenue provision which has engendered over 20 years of confusion and controversy.

12. **Relation to Other Relief Provisions:** The Committee Reports accompanying the 1997 Act indicated that the exclusion allowed by former I.R.C. section 2033A would operate ***in addition***

to the special use valuation rules of I.R.C. section 2032A and the favorable installment payment of estate taxes allowed by I.R.C. section 6166. The deduction allowed by redesignated I.R.C. section 2057 will operate similarly.

a. **I.R.C. section 6166:** This section operates in regard to the "taxable amount" of the closely held business interest. Hence, favorable installment payments will apply to the estate tax attributable to the value of the business after taking into account:

   (1) Any reduced value of business real property under I.R.C. section 2032A.

   (2) The new I.R.C. section 2057 exclusion.

   (3) The "applicable exclusion amount" of the unified credit.

b. **I.R.C. section 2032A:** The interrelationship of former I.R.C. section 2033A with the special use valuation allowed by I.R.C. section 2032A was less clear, and the Committee Reports accompanying the 1997 Act were less than helpful. However, the generally accepted interpretation was that qualification for the former exclusion and the amount of the exclusion would be determined after the application of I.R.C. section 2032A. The validity of this approach is even clearer now that former family-owned business exclusion has been recast as a deduction.

   (1) **Application:** Three steps are involved:

      (a) I.R.C. section 2032A is first applied (if applicable) to determine the value of the business real property qualifying for special use valuation.

      (b) Under new I.R.C. section 2057, the value of the gross estate (and "adjusted gross estate") and the value of the qualified family-owned business (and its "adjusted value") is determined with regard to the special use valuation assigned to the business's real property under I.R.C. section 2032A.

      (c) If the family-owned business qualifies for the new I.R.C. section 2057 deduction, this deduction will be based on the value of the business interests as finally determined after the application of special use value to its real property.

   (2) **Example:** D dies in 1998. A farming business owned by D has farmland with a fair market value of $2,000,000, and machinery and equipment with a fair market value of $500,000. D's other gross estate assets are valued at $1,000,000. For simplicity, assume that D made no lifetime gifts, and that the estate has no liabilities deductible under I.R.C. section 2053(a)(3) or (4). Also assume that D met the pre-death ownership, use, and material participation requirements of both I.R.C. sections 2032A and 2057, and that D's entire estate passes to a "qualified heir."

      (a) D's estate would qualify for special use valuation under I.R.C. section 2032A. Assume special use valuation is elected and produces an includible value of $1,250,000 for the farmland (maximum $750,000 reduction).

      (b) Even with the $750,000 reduction of the value of the land, the value of D's business interest exceeds 50% of the "adjusted gross estate" ($1,750,000: $2,750,000).

      (c) Assuming D's business interest otherwise qualifies for the family-owned business deduction of new I.R.C. section 2057, D's estate may deduct $675,000, the lesser of the value of the interest in the gross estate ($1,750,000) or the deduction cap of $675,000.

13. **Income Tax Basis to Qualified Heirs:** Under I.R.C. section 1014, the basis of the business interest in the hands of the qualified heir will be the fair market value at the decedent's death (or the special use value if I.R.C. section 2032A was also applicable). In the above example, the qualified heir would take the farmland with a basis of $1,250,000, but the basis of the business assets, *i.e.*, the date of death value of the machinery and equipment ($500,000) and special use value of the land ($1,250,000), is not affected by the $675,000 deduction.

D. OTHER CLOSELY HELD BUSINESS PROVISIONS

1. **Interest Rate Under I.R.C. Section 6166** [1997 Act §503, amending I.R.C. §§6601(j), 2053(c), 163; *see* Appendix 1, pp. 8-9]

   a. **Prior law:** Where installment payments for the estate tax on a closely held business interest are allowed, the interest on the deferred payments is established by statute at a relatively low rate. [*See* Summary §1057]

   b. **1997 Act:** The Act offers further relief—at a new cost:

      (i) The interest rate on the "four percent portion" (up to $1,000,000 value) is reduced to 2%, and the interest on the excess is set at 45% of the "regular" annual rate. [1997 Act §503(a), amending I.R.C. §6601(j)] Recall that the "2-percent portion" is now subject to an "inflation adjustment." [1997 Act §501(e)—*see* above]

      (ii) ***But*** no deduction is allowed for "section 6166 interest" for either estate or income tax purposes. [1997 Act §503(b), amending I.R.C. §§2053(c), 163]

   c. **Election for decedents dying before 1998:** If the decedent's executor made an election under I.R.C. section 6166 and if some installments remain to be paid, the executor may elect to have the new rates apply to installments that become due after the effective date of the election. [*See* 1997 Act §503(d)(2)—and note limitations]

   d. **1998 Act:** The 1998 Act clarifies that the 2-percent interest rate does not apply to non-readily-tradable business interests or to holding companies described, respectively, in I.R.C. section 6166(b)(7)(A) and (8)(A). [1988 Act §6007(c), amending I.R.C. §6166(b)(7), (8); *see* Appendix 2, p. 3]

2. **Judicial Review of Eligibility for Installment Payments Under I.R.C. Section 6166** [1997 Act §505, adding new I.R.C. §7479; *see* Appendix 1, pp. 9-10]

   a. **Prior law:** An IRS denial of eligibility is generally not subject to judicial review unless the estate pays the entire tax liability and then sues. [*See* Summary §1057]

   b. **1997 Act:** An estate may petition the Tax Court for a declaratory judgment on this issue where it contests an adverse determination by the IRS ("or a failure . . . to make a determination . . ."), and a decision by the Tax Court is ". . . reviewable as such."

      (1) **Limitations:** Special limitations are set out in new I.R.C. section 7479(b), including the requirements that the taxpayer exhaust all administrative remedies, and that the taxpayer file the petition before the 91st day after the IRS determination of ineligibility is mailed.

(2) **Effective date:** This new provision applies to estates of decedents dying after August 5, 1997. [*See* 1997 Act §505(c)]

(3) **Comment:** It has been suggested that the declaratory judgment jurisdiction here created (and in 1997 Act section 506(c), below) will add an estimated 1,500 cases annually to the Tax Court's docket.

c. **1998 Act:** The 1998 Act clarifies that the declaratory judgment jurisdiction of the Tax Court extends to determining not only whether an estate qualifies for installment payments of the estate tax but also to what business interests are eligible for the deferred payments. [1998 Act §6007(d), amending I.R.C. §7479(a); *see* Appendix 2, p. 3]

3. **Cash Rental of Real Property Subject to I.R.C. Section 2032A Special Use Valuation:** [1997 Act §504, amending I.R.C. §2032A(c)(7) by adding new paragraph (E); *see* Appendix 1, p. 9]

a. **Prior law:** In order to avoid the recapture tax, a qualified heir is required to materially participate in the operation of the specially valued real property. In general, the leasing of the property on a net cash rent basis does not constitute material participation. [*See* Summary §935]

b. **1997 Act:** A qualified heir who is the surviving spouse or lineal descendent of the decedent may rent the property to a member of the spouse's or descendent's family on a net cash basis without triggering the recapture tax.

(1) **Effective date:** This allowance is retroactive; it applies to leases entered into after December 31, 1976.

E. REVALUATION OF GIFTS AFTER EXPIRATION OF STATUTE OF LIMITATIONS [1997 Act §506, amending I.R.C. §§2001, 2504(c), 6501(c)(9), and adding new I.R.C. §7477; *see* Appendix 1, pp. 10-11]

1. **Prior Law:** The IRS has taken the position that adjusted taxable gifts may be revalued for purposes of the estate tax computation after the expiration of the statute of limitations for assessment of any gift tax liability or deficiency on the lifetime transfer. Furthermore, I.R.C. section 2504(c) prevented revaluation of prior taxable gifts for purposes of the cumulative gift tax computation only if the statute of limitations had run with respect to the prior gift(s) ***and*** a gift tax liability was due and was paid with respect to the gifts. [*See, e.g.*, Rev. Rul. 84-11, 1984-1 C.B. 201 and Tech. Adv. Mem. 9718004; *see* Summary §1010]

2. **1997 Act:** Revaluation of gifts for both estate and gift taxes is addressed.

a. **Estate tax:** An "adjusted taxable gift" may not be revalued if the statute of limitations has run ***and*** if the value of the prior gift is shown on the gift tax return ". . . or is disclosed in such return or in a statement attached to the return, in a manner adequate to apprise the . . . [IRS] of the nature of the gift." [1997 Act §506(a), adding new subsection (f) to I.R.C. §2001]

b. **Gift tax:** The Act allows assessment and collection of the gift tax on any gift not reported or disclosed on a gift tax return, even though a return was filed and even though the statute of limitations has run. However, if the gift has been disclosed the Act appears to prevent revaluation after the expiration of the period of limitation.

(1) ***1997 Act section 506(b),*** captioned "Modification of Application of Statute of Limitations" amends I.R.C. section 6501(c)(9) (captioned "Gift Tax on Certain Gifts not shown on Return").

(a) The first sentence of amended I.R.C. section 6501(c)(9) provides that the statute of limitations will not bar assessment of the gift tax on any gift not "shown" on a gift tax return.

(b) The second sentence, however, provides that the bar of the statute will apply to ". . . any item which is disclosed on such return, or in a statement attached to the return, in a manner adequate to apprise the . . . [IRS] of the nature of such item."

(c) The amended paragraph concludes that "[t]he value of any item which is so disclosed may not be redetermined by the . . . [IRS] after the expiration of the . . . [statute of limitations]."

(2) ***1997 Act Section 506(d),*** captioned "Conforming Amendment," amends I.R.C. section 2504(c) by deleting the troublesome phrase ". . . and if a tax under this chapter [gift tax] . . . has been assessed or paid for such preceding calendar year."

(3) ***The Committee Report states:*** "It is intended that, in order to revalue a gift that has been adequately disclosed . . . , the IRS must issue a final notice of redetermination of value (a 'final notice') within the statute of limitations applicable to the gift for gift tax purposes (generally, three years). This rule is applicable even where the value of the gift as shown on the return does not result in any gift tax (*e.g.*, through use of the unified credit). It is also anticipated that the IRS will develop an administrative appeals process whereby a taxpayer can challenge a redetermination of value by the IRS prior to the issuance of a final notice."

c. **Declaratory judgment authorized:** The Act adds new I.R.C. section 7477. [*See* 1997 Act §506(c)] Under this new section, the donor may seek a declaratory judgment from the Tax Court as to the value of a gift if:

(1) ***An actual controversy exists*** involving the IRS's determination of the value of a gift.

(2) ***The petitioner has exhausted all available administrative remedies*** within the IRS.

(3) ***The petition is filed before the 91st day after any determination of value is mailed*** to the petitioner by the IRS.

d. **Effective dates:** The rule as to revaluation of gifts for estate tax purposes, and the authorization of declaratory judgment jurisdiction, applies to gifts made after August 5, 1997. The amendment related to the statute of limitations on gifts (and revaluation thereof) applies to gifts made in 1997 (and thereafter).

e. **Comment:** The statute was not clearly drafted. Its import with respect to revaluation of gifts for gift tax purposes became clear only when read together with the accompanying House Ways and Means Committee Report. This defect was addressed in the Tax Technical Corrections Bill of 1997, which was incorporated as part of section 6007 of the 1998 Act.

3. **1998 Act:** I.R.C. sections 2001(f) and 2504(c) are completely rewritten so as to make clear that revaluation of prior taxable gifts is prohibited for both the cumulative gift and estate tax

computations after there has been a final determination of the value of such prior gifts under Chapter 12 (gift tax). [1998 Act §6007(e), amending I.R.C. §§2001(f) and 2504(c): *see* Appendix 2, pp. 3-4]

a. **Final determination:** For these purposes, a "final determination" is defined as either (i) the expiration of the statute of limitations with respect to a gift tax return on which the value of the prior gift is reported and not contested by the IRS; (ii) the failure of taxpayer to timely contest a value for the prior gift specified by the IRS; or (iii) the determination of the value of the prior gift by a court or under a settlement agreement between the taxpayer and the IRS. [*See* new I.R.C. §§2001(f)(2) and 2504(c) (last clause)]

b. **Payment of gift tax unnecessary:** Both the House and Senate Reports emphasize that the "final determination" of the value of the prior gifts operates to preclude revaluation ". . . even if no gift tax was assessed or paid on that gift."

F. ESTATE TAX VALUE OF LAND SUBJECT TO A CONSERVATION EASEMENT [1997 Act §508, amending I.R.C. §2031 by adding new subsection (c); *see* Appendix 1, pp. 12-14]

1. **Prior Law:** Qualified contributions of conservation easements are allowed income, gift, and estate tax charitable deductions. [*See* I.R.C. §§170(h), 2522(d), 2055(f)] No special valuation rule or exclusion applies to land subject to such an easement.

2. **1997 Act:** The Act amends I.R.C. section 2031 to provide that a decedent's executor may elect to exclude a portion of the value of land included in the gross estate if the land is subject to a "qualified conservation easement." This is a very complex valuation-based exclusion. In summary:

a. **"Qualified conservation easement":** New I.R.C. section 2031(c)(8) adopts, as a basic definition, that of I.R.C. section 170(h): a perpetual restriction limiting the use of property exclusively for certain designated conservation purposes (except certain historic preservation purposes) which is granted to a "qualified organization." For purposes of the new exclusion, however, special rules are applicable:

(1) ***The land subject to the easement must have been owned by the decedent*** or a family member at all times ***during the three-year period*** ending on the date of the decedent's death.

(2) ***The easement can be an existing easement or one granted after the death*** of the decedent (but before the date of the executor's election), but it must be granted ***by the decedent***, a family member, the decedent's executor, or a trustee holding the land.

(3) ***The land subject to the easement must be located*** within 25 miles of a metropolitan area (defined by the Office of Management and Budget) or a national park or wilderness area which is part of the National Wilderness Preservation System, or within 10 miles of an Urban National Forest.

b. **Limitations**

(1) **Debt-financed property:** The exclusion is not allowed for property which, at decedent's death, is subject to an "acquisition indebtedness." [*See* new I.R.C. §2031(c)(4)]

(2) **Retained development right:** The exclusion does not apply to the extent of the value of any retained "development right." A development right, for this purpose, is any right to use the land for any commercial purpose, except commercial purposes that are subordinate to and directly supportive of use of the land for farming. [*See* new I.R.C. §2031(c)(5)(A), (D)] However, the exclusion will be allowed if every person who has an interest in the land files an agreement to permanently extinguish the retained development right. This agreement must be filed by the date the estate tax return is due, and must be implemented within two years of the decedent's death. [*See* new I.R.C. §2031(c)(5)(B), (C)]

c. **Amount of exclusion:** [*See* new §2031(c)(1)] The exclusion is the ***lesser*** of:

(i) The "applicable percentage" of the value of the land subject to the qualified conservation easement, less any charitable deduction allowed to the decedent's estate under section 2055(f) with respect to this land; or

(ii) The "exclusion limitation."

(1) **Applicable percentage:** [*See* new I.R.C. §2031(c)(2)] This is 40% of the value of the land, reduced by 2% for each percentage point by which the value of the easement is less than 30% of the value of the land.

(2) **Exclusion limitation:** [*See* new §2031(c)(3)] This is a fixed dollar amount which increases from $100,000 to $500,000 over a five-year period, as follows:

Year of death:	**Exclusion limitation:**
1998	$100,000
1999	$200,000
2000	$300,000
2001	$400,000
2002 and thereafter	$500,000

(3) **Example:** Assume that D dies in 1999, that land included in D's estate is subject to a qualified conservation easement, that none of the limitations apply, and that the land is valued at $400,000 and the easement is valued at $100,000. D's executor could elect to exclude $120,000: The value of the easement is 25% of the value of the land, reducing the "applicable percentage" by 10 points (2 x (30-25)). The computed exclusion is, then $120,000 (30% x $400,000), and this is less than the 1999 exclusion limitation. Note that if D's estate was entitled to a charitable deduction for a grant of the easement, the exclusion would be $20,000 (the above applicable percentage less the $100,000 charitable deduction.)

d. **Carryover basis in excluded land:** To the extent of the exclusion allowed by new section 2031(c), the basis of the land will be the same as its basis in the hands of the decedent. [*See* 1997 Act §508(b), amending I.R.C. §1014(a)]

3. **1998 Act:** The 1998 Act clarifies that the grant of a qualified conservation easement made by a decedent's executor or trustee will qualify for the estate tax deduction allowed by new I.R.C. section 2055(f), but that no income tax deduction is allowed with respect to such post-mortem conservation easements. [1998 Act §6007(g), amending I.R.C. §2031(c); *see* Appendix 2, p. 5]

4. **Related Amendments:** Apart from the new exclusion, the 1997 Act section 508 contains two amendments relating to conservation contributions.

   a. **Amendment to section 2032A:** A qualified conservation contribution will not be considered a "disposition" by the qualified heir of land subject to special use valuation. [1997 Act §508(c)] Thus, qualified heirs may transfer a conservation easement or make a qualified contribution of the entire interest without triggering the recapture tax.

   b. **Amendment to section 170(h):** Under prior law, the retention of under-surface mineral rights would not defeat the charitable deduction for a qualified conservation contribution if the surface estate and mineral rights were "separated" prior to June 13, 1976. The 1997 Act section 508(d) allows this rule to apply without regard to the time of such separation.

5. **Effective Date:** The amendments apply to estates of decedents dying after December 31, 1997, and to qualified contributions made after that same date.

6. **Comment:** This is frankly not a revenue measure. It is designed to use the estate tax to encourage transfers of conservation easements. One wonders, however, whether the complexity of the allowance, valuation problems, etc., will frustrate its purpose.

G. GENERATION-SKIPPING TAX EXCEPTION FOR TRANSFERS TO PERSONS WHOSE PARENTS ARE DEAD [1997 Act §511, amending §2612(c) by deleting paragraph (2) and amending §2651 by adding a new subsection (e); *see* Appendix 1, p. 15]

1. **Prior Law:** Direct skips to lineal descendants of the transferor are not generation-skipping transfers if the parent of the transferee is dead. [*See* present §2612(c)(2); *see* Summary §1093]

2. **1997 Act:** The Act extends this exception to:

   (i) Transfers to lineal descendants of the parents of the transferor (*e.g.,* grandnephews or grandnieces), but only if the transferor has no living lineal descendants.

   (ii) All forms of generation-skipping transfers—taxable distributions and taxable terminations as well as direct skips.

   a. **Effective date:** The Act applies to taxable terminations, distributions, and transfers after December 31, 1997.

   b. **Comments:** The amendment extends a logical exception somewhat beyond the initial logic. But note that the extended exception is very limited in scope: It applies only to childless granduncles/grandaunts whose nephew/niece predeceased them.

TITLE XIII—SIMPLIFICATION PROVISIONS RELATING TO ESTATE AND GIFT TAXES

H. GIFTS TO CHARITIES—FILING REQUIREMENTS [1997 Act §1301, amending §6019; *see* Appendix 1, pp. 15-16]

1. **Prior Law:** A gift tax return is required for any gift made in the year, except gifts excluded under section 2503(b) or (e) (annual and medical/educational exclusions) and gifts deductible under section 2523 (marital deduction). [*See* Summary §1029]

2. **1997 Act:** The Act adds an exception for gifts deductible under section 2522 (charitable deduction), but only if the entire interest of the donor is transferred to the charity and no interest in the property is or was transferred to a noncharitable person or use.

   a. **Effective date:** The Act applies to gifts made after August 5, 1997.

I. WAIVER OF RIGHTS OF RECOVERY UNDER SECTIONS 2207A AND 2207B [1997 Act §1302, amending §§2207A and 2207B; *see* Appendix 1, p. 16]

1. **Prior Law:** A decedent's will (or trust) might inadvertently waive the estate's right to recover applicable estate taxes from a Q-tip trust [§2207A] or retained interest trust [§2207B]. [*See* Summary §§706, 1036, 1052]

2. **1997 Act:** The Act requires a specific waiver in the decedent's will (or trust).

   a. **Effective date:** The Act applies to estates of decedents dying after August 5, 1997.

J. PRE-1990 QUALIFIED DOMESTIC [MARITAL] TRUSTS FOR NONCITIZEN SPOUSE [1997 Act §1303, transitional rule under §2056A; *see* Appendix 1, p. 16]

1. **Prior Law:** The original iteration of the QDT marital trust required that all trustees be United States persons, but did not require estate tax withholding for corpus distributions (since the United States trustee could be personally liable). The 1990 Act (Revenue Reconciliation Act of 1990) allows that a QDT need only have one United States trustee, but imposed a withholding requirement if any corpus distributions were made by the trust. [*See* Summary §720]

2. **1997 Act:** The Act provides a retroactive transitional rule which, in effect, waives the withholding requirement for pre-1990 QDTs where all the trustees are United States persons.

   a. **Effective date:** This provision is retroactive to the effective date of the 1990 Act.

   b. **Comment:** This "transitional rule" is independently operative; it does not amend the I.R.C.

K. ESTATE TAX TREATMENT OF SHORT-TERM OBLIGATIONS OF NONRESIDENT ALIENS [1997 Act §1304, amending §2105(b); *see* Appendix 1, p. 16]

1. **Prior Law:** Section 2105(b) excluded certain bank deposits and debt obligations from inclusion in the estate of a nonresident alien. [*See* Summary §24]

2. **1997 Act:** The Act extends this exclusion to certain original issue discount debt obligations.

   a. **Effective date:** The Act applies to estates of nonresidents dying after August 5, 1997.

L. GIFTS WITHIN THREE YEARS OF DEATH [1997 Act §1310, rewriting and amending §2035; *see* Appendix 1, p. 17]

1. **Prior Law:** Section 2035 (transfers within three years of death) was the subject of a number of "paste-on" amendments since 1976. Also, controversies developed in regard to the proper treatment of transfers from revocable trusts within three years of death. [*See* Summary §§103-109]

2. **1997 Act:** The Act rewrites section 2035 in a more logical form. It also resolves the controversies involving distributions from revocable trusts by treating them as if made directly by the decedent.

a. **Rewrite of section**

(1) Subsection (d)(2) of the prior section 2035 was, in fact, the principal operative provision. It is now stated as the principal rule in new subsection (a).

(2) The "gross up" rule for gift taxes paid or payable on account of gifts made within three years of death—formerly subsection (c)—is restated in new subsection (b).

(3) The special rules for grossing up gifts made within three years of death for purposes of determining the application of sections 303, 2032A, 6166, etc.—formerly in subsections (d)(3) and (4)—are contained in new subsection (c). New subsection (c) also excepts annual exclusion gifts (other than life insurance) from these special rules.

(4) The exception for transfers for consideration—formerly in subsection (b)(1)—is restated in new subsection (d).

b. **Distributions from revocable trusts**

(1) **Prior law:** There was a split of authority as to whether distributions from a revocable trust within three years of the decedent's death (or the direct or indirect exercise of a power to appoint property from the trust) should be treated as the release or exercise of the power subject to the estate tax under former subsection (d)(2) or as a direct gift by the decedent, which was not subject to the estate tax. [*Compare, e.g.*, Estate of Jalkut v. Commissioner, 96 T.C. 675, *acq.*, 1991-2 C.B. 1, *and* Tech. Adv. Mem. 9226007 and 9309003, *with* Kisling v. Commissioner, 32 F.2d 1222 (8th Cir. 1994); McNeely v. United States, 16 F.3d 303 (8th Cir. 1994)]

(2) **1997 Amendment:** New subsection (e) of section 2035 provides that ". . . any transfer of any portion of a trust during any period that such portion was treated under section 676 as owned by the decedent by reason of a power in the grantor . . . shall be treated as a transfer made directly by the decedent."

(a) The effect is that distributions from a revocable trust will be treated as gifts made directly by the decedent. If otherwise qualifying for the annual exclusion, the annual exclusion may be applied, and the distributions will not be included in the decedent's gross estate whether or not made within three years of death.

(b) The House Committee Report states that this amendment ". . . codifies the rule set forth in the *McNeely* and *Kisling* cases. . . ." The Conference Committee Report states that it ". . . is not intended to modify the result in the *Kisling* case."

c. **Effective date:** The amendment applies to estates of decedents dying after August 5, 1997.

M. TREATMENT OF SURVIVOR ANNUITIES UNDER Q-TIP RULES [1997 Act §1311, amending §2056(b)(7)(C); *see* Appendix 1, p. 18]

1. **Prior Law:** There was some confusion about gross estate inclusion and the application of the Q-tip marital deduction where a nonparticipant spouse who has a community property interest in a qualified retirement annuity predeceases the participating spouse. [*See* Summary §§697-704]

2. **1997 Act:** The Act clarifies that the community property interest ***is includible*** in the predeceasing spouse's gross estate and ***may be allowed the Q-tip marital deduction***.

a. **Effective date:** The Act applies to estates of decedents dying after August 5, 1997.

N. **TREATMENT OF NON-TRUST ARRANGEMENTS UNDER QDT RULES** [1997 Act §1312, amending §2056A(c); *see* Appendix 1, p. 18]

1. **Prior Law:** The "qualified domestic trust" rules were literally applicable only to formal trust arrangements. [*See* Summary §720]

2. **1997 Act:** The Act authorizes the Treasury to prescribe Regulations extending the QDT rules to arrangements "which have substantially the same effect as a trust."

   a. **Effective date:** The Act applies to estates of decedents dying after August 5, 1997.

O. **REASONABLE TIME TO CORRECT ELECTION AND AGREEMENT UNDER SECTION 2032A** [1997 Act §1313, amending §2032A(d)(3); *see* Appendix 1, p. 18]

1. **Prior Law:** Modification of the election and agreement required for special use valuation was allowed only if the original election substantially complies with the statute and applicable Regulations. [*See* Summary §935(f)]

2. **1997 Act:** The "substantial compliance" provision is deleted from the statute. If there is a timely notice of election, but the notice (or the agreement) does not contain all required information or signatures, the executor "will have a reasonable period of time (not exceeding 90 days) after notification of such failures to provide such information or signatures."

   a. **Effective date:** The Act applies to estates of decedents dying after August 5, 1997.

P. **WAIVER OF UNITED STATES TRUSTEE REQUIREMENT FOR QDT** [1997 Act §1314, amending §2056A(a)(1)(A); *see* Appendix 1, p. 18]

1. **Prior Law:** A qualified domestic trust must have at least one trustee who is a citizen of the United States. Apparently there are some countries that prohibit a trust from having a foreign (U.S.) trustee. [*See* Summary §720]

2. **1997 Act:** The Act authorizes Regulations that will specify exceptions to this requirement.

   a. **Effective date:** The Act applies to estates of decedents dying after August 5, 1997.

Appendix 1: Taxpayer Relief Act of 1997[1]

Public Law No. 105-34
August 5, 1997

TITLE V — ESTATE, GIFT, AND GENERATION-SKIPPING TAX PROVISIONS

SUBTITLE A—ESTATE AND GIFT TAX PROVISIONS

SEC. 501. COST-OF-LIVING ADJUSTMENTS RELATING TO ESTATE AND GIFT TAX PROVISIONS.

(a) INCREASE IN UNIFIED ESTATE AND GIFT TAX CREDIT —

(1) ESTATE TAX CREDIT —

(A) IN GENERAL — Subsection (a) of section 2010 (relating to unified credit against estate tax) is amended by striking "$192,800" and inserting "*the applicable credit amount*".

(B) APPLICABLE CREDIT AMOUNT — Section 2010 is amended by redesignating subsection (c) as subsection (d) and by inserting after subsection (b) the following new subsection:

c) APPLICABLE CREDIT AMOUNT — For purposes of this section, the applicable credit amount is the amount of the tentative tax which would be determined under the rate schedule set forth in section 2001(c) if the amount with respect to which such tentative tax is to be computed were the applicable exclusion amount determined in accordance with the following table:

In the case of estates of decedents dying, and gifts made, during:	*The applicable exclusion amount is:*
1998	*$ 625,000*
1999	*$ 650,000*
2000 and 2001	*$ 675,000*
2002 and 2003	*$ 700,000*
2004	*$ 850,000*
2005	*$ 950,000*
2006 and thereafter	*$1,000,000*

(C) ESTATE TAX RETURNS — Paragraph (1) of section 6018(a) is amended by striking "$600,000" and inserting "*the applicable exclusion amount in effect under section 2010(c) for the calendar year which includes the date of death*".

(D) PHASEOUT OF GRADUATED RATES AND UNIFIED CREDIT — Paragraph (2) of section 2001(c) is amended by striking "$21,040,000" and inserting "*the amount at which the average tax rate under this section is 55 percent*".

(E) ESTATES OF NONRESIDENTS NOT CITIZENS — Subparagraph (A) of section 2102(c)(3) is amended by striking "$192,800" and inserting "*the applicable credit amount in effect under section 2010(c) for the calendar year which includes the date of death*".

(2) UNIFIED GIFT TAX CREDIT — Paragraph (1) of section 2505(a) is amended by striking "$192,800" and inserting "*the applicable credit amount in effect under section 2010(c) for such calendar year*".

---

[1] New matter is in italics. [JHM]

(b) ALTERNATE VALUATION OF CERTAIN FARM, ETC., REAL PROPERTY— Subsection (a) of section 2032A is amended by adding at the end the following new paragraph:

(3) INFLATION ADJUSTMENT — In the case of estates of decedents dying in a calendar year after 1998, the $750,000 amount contained in paragraph (2) shall be increased by an amount equal to —

(A) $750,000, multiplied by

(B) the cost-of-living adjustment determined under section 1(f)(3) for such calendar year by substituting "calendar year 1997" for "calendar year 1992" in subparagraph (B) thereof.

If any amount as adjusted under the preceding sentence is not a multiple of $10,000, such amount shall be rounded to the next lowest multiple of $10,000.

(c) ANNUAL GIFT TAX EXCLUSION — Subsection (b) of section 2503 is amended —

(1) by striking the subsection heading and inserting the following:

(b) EXCLUSIONS FROM GIFTS —

(1) IN GENERAL —,

(2) by moving the text 2 ems to the right, and

(3) by adding at the end the following new paragraph:

(2) INFLATION ADJUSTMENT — In the case of gifts made in a calendar year after 1998, the $10,000 amount contained in paragraph (1) shall be increased by an amount equal to:

(A) $10,000, multiplied by

(B) the cost-of-living adjustment determined under section 1(f)(3) for such calendar year by substituting "calendar year 1997" for "calendar year 1992" in subparagraph (B) thereof.

If any amount as adjusted under the preceding sentence is not a multiple of $1,000, such amount shall be rounded to the next lowest multiple of $1,000.

(d) EXEMPTION FROM GENERATION-SKIPPING TAX — Section 2631 (relating to GST exemption) is amended by adding at the end the following new subsection:

(c) INFLATION ADJUSTMENT — In the case of an individual who dies in any calendar year after 1998, the $1,000,000 amount contained in subsection (a) shall be increased by an amount equal to —

(1) $1,000,000, multiplied by

(2) the cost-of-living adjustment determined under section 1(f)(3) for such calendar year by substituting "calendar year 1997" for "calendar year 1992" in subparagraph (B) thereof.

If any amount as adjusted under the preceding sentence is not a multiple of $10,000, such amount shall be rounded to the next lowest multiple of $10,000.

(e) AMOUNT SUBJECT TO REDUCED RATE WHERE EXTENSION OF TIME FOR PAYMENT OF ESTATE TAX ON CLOSELY HELD BUSINESS — Subsection (j) of section 6601 is amended by redesignating paragraph (3) as paragraph (4) and by inserting after paragraph (2) the following new paragraph:

(3) INFLATION ADJUSTMENT — In the case of estates of decedents dying in a calendar year after 1998, the $1,000,000 amount contained in paragraph (2)(A) shall be increased by an amount equal to —

(A) $1,000,000, multiplied by

(B) the cost-of-living adjustment determined under section 1(f)(3) for such calendar year by substituting "calendar year 1997" for "calendar year 1992" in subparagraph (B) thereof.

If any amount as adjusted under the preceding sentence is not a multiple of $10,000, such amount shall be rounded to the next lowest multiple of $10,000.

(f) EFFECTIVE DATE — The amendments made by this section shall apply to the estates of decedents dying, and gifts made, after December 31, 1997.

SEC. 502. FAMILY-OWNED BUSINESS EXCLUSION.

(a) IN GENERAL — Part III of subchapter A of chapter 11 (relating to gross estate) is amended by inserting after section 2033 the following new section:

SEC. 2033A. FAMILY-OWNED BUSINESS EXCLUSION.

(a) IN GENERAL — In the case of an estate of a decedent to which this section applies, the value of the gross estate shall not include the lesser of —

(1) the adjusted value of the qualified family-owned business interests of the decedent otherwise includible in the estate, or

(2) the excess of $1,300,000 over the applicable exclusion amount under section 2010(c) with respect to such estate.

(b) ESTATES TO WHICH SECTION APPLIES —

(1) IN GENERAL — This section shall apply to an estate if —

(A) the decedent was (at the date of the decedent's death) a citizen or resident of the United States,

(B) the executor elects the application of this section and files the agreement referred to in subsection (h),

(C) the sum of —

(i) the adjusted value of the qualified family-owned business interests described in paragraph (2), plus

(ii) the amount of the gifts of such interests determined under paragraph (3),

exceeds 50 percent of the adjusted gross estate, and

(D) during the 8-year period ending on the date of the decedent's death there have been periods aggregating 5 years or more during which —

(i) such interests were owned by the decedent or a member of the decedent's family, and

(ii) there was material participation (within the meaning of section 2032A(e)(6)) by the decedent or a member of the decedent's family in the operation of the business to which such interests relate.

(2) INCLUDIBLE QUALIFIED FAMILY-OWNED BUSINESS INTERESTS — The qualified family-owned business interests described in this paragraph are the interests which —

(A) are included in determining the value of the gross estate (without regard to this section), and

(B) are acquired by any qualified heir from, or passed to any qualified heir from, the decedent (within the meaning of section 2032A(e)(9)).

(3) INCLUDIBLE GIFTS OF INTERESTS — The amount of the gifts of qualified family-owned business interests determined under this paragraph is the excess of —

(A) the sum of —

(i) the amount of such gifts from the decedent to members of the decedent's family taken into account under subsection 2001(b)(1)(B), plus

(ii) the amount of such gifts otherwise excluded under section 2503(b), to the extent such interests are continuously held by members of such family (other than the decedent's spouse) between the date of the gift and the date of the decedent's death, over

(B) the amount of such gifts from the decedent to members of the decedent's family otherwise included in the gross estate.

(c) ADJUSTED GROSS ESTATE — For purposes of this section, the term "adjusted gross estate" means the value of the gross estate (determined without regard to this section) —

(1) reduced by any amount deductible under paragraph (3) or (4) of section 2053(a), and

(2) increased by the excess of —

(A) the sum of —

(i) the amount of gifts determined under subsection (b)(3), plus

(ii) the amount (if more than de minimis) of other transfers from the decedent to the decedent's spouse (at the time of the transfer) within 10 years of the date of the decedent's death, plus

(iii) the amount of other gifts (not included under clause (i) or (ii)) from the decedent within 3 years of such date, other than gifts to members of the decedent's family otherwise excluded under section 2503(b), over

(B) the sum of the amounts described in clauses (i), (ii), and (iii) of subparagraph (A) which are otherwise includible in the gross estate.

For purposes of the preceding sentence, the Secretary may provide that de minimis gifts to persons other than members of the decedent's family shall not be taken into account.

(d) ADJUSTED VALUE OF THE QUALIFIED FAMILY-OWNED BUSINESS INTERESTS — For purposes of this section, the adjusted value of any qualified family-owned business interest is the value of such interest for purposes of this chapter (determined without regard to this section), reduced by the excess of —

(1) any amount deductible under paragraph (3) or (4) of section 2053(a), over

(2) the sum of —

(A) any indebtedness on any qualified residence of the decedent the interest on which is deductible under section 163(h)(3), plus

(B) any indebtedness to the extent the taxpayer establishes that the proceeds of such indebtedness were used for the payment of educational and medical expenses of the decedent, the decedent's spouse, or the decedent's dependents (within the meaning of section 152), plus

(C) any indebtedness not described in subparagraph (A) or (B), to the extent such indebtedness does not exceed $10,000.

(e) QUALIFIED FAMILY-OWNED BUSINESS INTEREST —

(1) IN GENERAL — For purposes of this section, the term "qualified family-owned business interest" means —

(A) an interest as a proprietor in a trade or business carried on as a proprietorship, or

(B) an interest in an entity carrying on a trade or business, if —

(i) at least —

(I) 50 percent of such entity is owned (directly or indirectly) by the decedent and members of the decedent's family,

(II) 70 percent of such entity is so owned by members of 2 families, or

(III) 90 percent of such entity is so owned by members of 3 families, and

(ii) for purposes of subclause (II) or (III) of clause (i), at least 30 percent of such entity is so owned by the decedent and members of the decedent's family.

(2) LIMITATION — Such term shall not include —

(A) any interest in a trade or business the principal place of business of which is not located in the United States,

(B) any interest in an entity, if the stock or debt of such entity or a controlled group (as defined in section 267(f)(1)) of which such entity was a member was readily tradable on an established securities market or secondary market (as defined by the Secretary) at any time within 3 years of the date of the decedent's death,

(C) any interest in a trade or business not described in section 542(c)(2), if more than 35 percent of the adjusted ordinary gross income of such trade or business for the taxable year which includes the date of the decedent's death would qualify as personal holding company income (as defined in section 543(a)),

(D) that portion of an interest in a trade or business that is attributable to —

(i) cash or marketable securities, or both, in excess of the reasonably expected day-to-day working capital needs of such trade or business, and

(ii) any other assets of the trade or business (other than assets used in the active conduct of a trade or business described in section 542(c)(2)), which produce, or are held for the production of, income of which is described in section 543(a) or in section 954(c)(1) (determined without regard to subparagraph (A) thereof and by substituting "trade or business" for "controlled foreign corporation").

(3) RULES REGARDING OWNERSHIP —

(A) OWNERSHIP OF ENTITIES — For purposes of paragraph (1)(B) —

(i) CORPORATIONS — Ownership of a corporation shall be determined by the holding of stock possessing the appropriate percentage of the total combined voting power of all classes of stock entitled to vote and the appropriate percentage of the total value of shares of all classes of stock.

(ii) PARTNERSHIPS — Ownership of a partnership shall be determined by the owning of the appropriate percentage of the capital interest in such partnership.

(B) OWNERSHIP OF TIERED ENTITIES — For purposes of this section, if by reason of holding an interest in a trade or business, a decedent, any member of the decedent's family, any qualified heir, or any member of any qualified heir's family is treated as holding an interest in any other trade or business —

(i) such ownership interest in the other trade or business shall be disregarded in determining if the ownership interest in the first trade or business is a qualified family-owned business interest, and

(ii) this section shall be applied separately in determining if such interest in any other trade or business is a qualified family-owned business interest.

(C) INDIVIDUAL OWNERSHIP RULES — For purposes of this section, an interest owned, directly or indirectly, by or for an entity described in paragraph (1)(B) shall be considered as being owned proportionately by or for the entity's shareholders, partners, or beneficiaries. A person shall be treated as a beneficiary of any trust only if such person has a present interest in such trust.

(f) TAX TREATMENT OF FAILURE TO MATERIALLY PARTICIPATE IN BUSINESS OR DISPOSITIONS OF INTERESTS —

(1) IN GENERAL — There is imposed an additional estate tax if, within 10 years after the date of the decedent's death and before the date of the qualified heir's death —

(A) the material participation requirements described in section 2032A(c)(6)(B) are not met with respect to the qualified family-owned business interest which was acquired (or passed) from the decedent,

(B) the qualified heir disposes of any portion of a qualified family-owned business interest (other than by a disposition to a member of the qualified heir's family or through a qualified conservation contribution under section 170(h)),

(C) the qualified heir loses United States citizenship (within the meaning of section 877) or with respect to whom an event described in subparagraph (A) or (B) of section 877(e)(1) occurs, and such heir does not comply with the requirements of subsection (g), or

(D) the principal place of business of a trade or business of the qualified family-owned business interest ceases to be located in the United States.

(2) ADDITIONAL ESTATE TAX —

(A) IN GENERAL — The amount of the additional estate tax imposed by paragraph (1) shall be equal to —

(i) the applicable percentage of the adjusted tax difference attributable to the qualified family-owned business interest (as determined under rules similar to the rules of section 2032A(c)(2)(B)), plus

(ii) interest on the amount determined under clause (i) at the underpayment rate established under section 6621 for the period beginning on the date the estate tax liability was due under this chapter and ending on the date such additional estate tax is due.

(B) APPLICABLE PERCENTAGE — For purposes of this paragraph, the applicable percentage shall be determined under the following table:

If the event described in paragraph (1) occurs in the following year of material participation:	*The applicable percentage is:*
1 through 6	*100*
7	*80*
8	*60*
9	*40*
10	*20*

(g) SECURITY REQUIREMENTS FOR NONCITIZEN QUALIFIED HEIRS —

(1) IN GENERAL — Except upon the application of subparagraph (F) or (M) of subsection (i)(3), if a qualified heir is not a citizen of the United States, any interest under this section passing to or acquired by such heir (including any interest held by such heir at a time described in subsection (f)(1)(C)) shall be treated as a qualified family-owned business interest only if the interest passes or is acquired (or is held) in a qualified trust.

(2) QUALIFIED TRUST — The term 'qualified trust' means a trust —

(A) which is organized under, and governed by, the laws of the United States or a State, and

(B) except as otherwise provided in regulations, with respect to which the trust instrument requires that at least 1 trustee of the trust be an individual citizen of the United States or a domestic corporation.

(h) AGREEMENT — The agreement referred to in this subsection is a written agreement signed by each person in being who has an interest (whether or not in possession) in any property designated in such agreement consenting to the application of subsection (f) with respect to such property.

(i) OTHER DEFINITIONS AND APPLICABLE RULES — For purposes of this section —

(1) QUALIFIED HEIR — The term "qualified heir" —

(A) has the meaning given to such term by section 2032A(e)(1), and

(B) includes any active employee of the trade or business to which the qualified family-owned business interest relates if such employee has been employed by such trade or business for a period of at least 10 years before the date of the decedent's death.

(2) MEMBER OF THE FAMILY — The term "member of the family" has the meaning given to such term by section 2032A(e)(2).

(3) APPLICABLE RULES — Rules similar to the following rules shall apply:

(A) Section 2032A(b)(4) (relating to decedents who are retired or disabled).

(B) Section 2032A(b)(5) (relating to special rules for surviving spouses).

(C) Section 2032A(c)(2)(D) (relating to partial dispositions).

(D) Section 2032A(c)(3) (relating to only 1 additional tax imposed with respect to any 1 portion).

(E) Section 2032A(c)(4) (relating to due date).

(F) Section 2032A(c)(5) (relating to liability for tax; furnishing of bond).

(G) Section 2032A(c)(7) (relating to no tax if use begins within 2 years; active management by eligible qualified heir treated as material participation).

(H) Paragraphs (1) and (3) of section 2032A(d) (relating to election; agreement).

(I) Section 2032A(e)(10) (relating to community property).

(J) Section 2032A(e)(14) (relating to treatment of replacement property acquired in section 1031 or 1033 transactions).

(K) Section 2032A(f) (relating to statute of limitations).

(L) Section 6166(b)(3) (relating to farmhouses and certain other structures taken into account).

(M) Subparagraphs (B), (C), and (D) of section 6166(g)(1) (relating to acceleration of payment).

(N) Section 6324B (relating to special lien for additional estate tax).

(b) CLERICAL AMENDMENT— The table of sections for part III of subchapter A of chapter 11 is amended by inserting after the item relating to section 2033 the following new item:

Sec. 2033A. Family-owned business exclusion.

(c) EFFECTIVE DATE— The amendments made by this section shall apply to estates of decedents dying after December 31, 1997.

SEC. 503. MODIFICATIONS TO RATE OF INTEREST ON PORTION OF ESTATE TAX EXTENDED UNDER SECTION 6166.

(a) IN GENERAL— Paragraphs (1) and (2) of section 6601(j) (relating to 4-percent rate on certain portion of estate tax extended under section 6166) are amended to read as follows:

(1) IN GENERAL— If the time for payment of an amount of tax imposed by chapter 11 is extended as provided in section 6166, then in lieu of the annual rate provided by subsection (a)—

(A) interest on the 2-percent portion of such amount shall be paid at the rate of 2 percent, and

(B) interest on so much of such amount as exceeds the 2-percent portion shall be paid at a rate equal to 45 percent of the annual rate provided by subsection (a).

For purposes of this subsection, the amount of any deficiency which is prorated to installments payable under section 6166 shall be treated as an amount of tax payable in installments under such section.

(2) 2-PERCENT PORTION— For purposes of this subsection, the term "2-percent portion" means the lesser of—

(A)(i) the amount of the tentative tax which would be determined under the rate schedule set forth in section 2001(c) if the amount with respect to which such tentative tax is to be computed were the sum of $1,000,000 and the applicable exclusion amount in effect under section 2010(c), reduced by

(ii) the applicable credit amount in effect under section 2010(c), or

(B) the amount of the tax imposed by chapter 11 which is extended as provided in section 6166.

(b) DISALLOWANCE OF INTEREST DEDUCTION—

(1) ESTATE TAX— Paragraph (1) of section 2053(c) is amended by adding at the end the following new subparagraph:

(D) SECTION 6166 INTEREST— No deduction shall be allowed under this section for any interest payable under section 6601 on any unpaid portion of the tax imposed by section 2001 for the period during which an extension of time for payment of such tax is in effect under section 6166.

(2) INCOME TAX—

(A) Section 163 is amended by redesignating subsection (k) as subsection (l) and by inserting after subsection (j) the following new subsection:

(k) SECTION 6166 INTEREST— No deduction shall be allowed under this section for any interest payable under section 6601 on any unpaid portion of the tax imposed by section 2001 for the period during which an extension of time for payment of such tax is in effect under section 6166.

(B) Subparagraph (E) of section 163(h)(2) is amended by striking "or 6166" and all that follows and inserting a period.

(c) CONFORMING AMENDMENTS —

(1) Paragraphs (7)(A)(iii) and (8)(A)(iii) of section 6166(b) are amended by striking "4-percent" each place it appears (including the heading) and inserting "*2-percent*".

(2) Paragraph (4) of section 6601(j), as redesignated by section 501(e), is amended by striking "4-percent" each place it appears and inserting "*2-percent*".

(3) The subsection heading for section 6601(j) is amended by striking "4 PERCENT" and inserting "*2-PERCENT*".

(d) EFFECTIVE DATE —

(1) IN GENERAL — The amendments made by this section shall apply to estates of decedents dying after December 31, 1997.

(2) ELECTION — In the case of the estate of any decedent dying before January 1, 1998, with respect to which there is an election under section 6166 of the Internal Revenue Code of 1986, the executor of the estate may elect to have the amendments made by this section apply with respect to installments due after the effective date of the election; except that the 2-percent portion of such installments shall be equal to the amount which would be the 4-percent portion of such installments without regard to such election. Such an election shall be made before January 1, 1999 in the manner prescribed by the Secretary of the Treasury and, once made, is irrevocable.

SEC. 504. EXTENSION OF TREATMENT OF CERTAIN RENTS UNDER SECTION 2032A TO LINEAL DESCENDANTS.

(a) GENERAL RULE — Paragraph (7) of section 2032A(c) (relating to special rules for tax treatment of dispositions and failures to use for qualified use) is amended by adding at the end the following new subparagraph:

(E) CERTAIN RENTS TREATED AS QUALIFIED USE — For purposes of this subsection, a surviving spouse or lineal descendant of the decedent shall not be treated as failing to use qualified real property in a qualified use solely because such spouse or descendant rents such property to a member of the family of such spouse or descendant on a net cash basis. For purposes of the preceding sentence, a legally adopted child of an individual shall be treated as the child of such individual by blood.

(b) CONFORMING AMENDMENT — Section 2032A(b)(5)(A) is amended by striking the last sentence.

(c) EFFECTIVE DATE — The amendments made by this section shall apply with respect to leases entered into after December 31, 1976.

SEC. 505. CLARIFICATION OF JUDICIAL REVIEW OF ELIGIBILITY FOR EXTENSION OF TIME FOR PAYMENT OF ESTATE TAX.

(a) IN GENERAL — Part IV of subchapter C of chapter 76 of the Internal Revenue Code of 1986 (relating to declaratory judgments) is amended by adding at the end the following new section:

SEC. 7479 DECLARATORY JUDGMENTS RELATING TO ELIGIBILITY OF ESTATE WITH RESPECT TO INSTALLMENT PAYMENTS UNDER SECTION 6166.

(a) CREATION OF REMEDY — In a case of actual controversy involving a determination by the Secretary of (or a failure by the Secretary to make a determination with respect to) —

(1) whether an election may be made under section 6166 (relating to extension of time for payment of estate tax where estate consists largely of interest in closely held business) with respect to an estate, or

(2) whether the extension of time for payment of tax provided in section 6166(a) has ceased to apply with respect to an estate,

upon the filing of an appropriate pleading, the Tax Court may make a declaration with respect to whether such election may be made or whether such extension has ceased to apply. Any such declaration shall have the force and effect of a decision of the Tax Court and shall be reviewable as such.

(b) LIMITATIONS —

(1) PETITIONER — A pleading may be filed under this section, with respect to any estate, only —

(A) by the executor of such estate, or

(B) by any person who has assumed an obligation to make payments under section 6166 with respect to such estate (but only if each other such person is joined as a party).

(2) EXHAUSTION OF ADMINISTRATIVE REMEDIES — The court shall not issue a declaratory judgment or decree under this section in any proceeding unless it determines that the petitioner has exhausted all available administrative remedies within the Internal Revenue Service. A petitioner shall be deemed to have exhausted its administrative remedies with respect to a failure of the Secretary to make a determination at the expiration of 180 days after the date on which the request for such determination was made if the petitioner has taken, in a timely manner, all reasonable steps to secure such determination.

(3) TIME FOR BRINGING ACTION — If the Secretary sends by certified or registered mail notice of his determination as described in subsection (a) to the petitioner, no proceeding may be initiated under this section unless the pleading is filed before the 91st day after the date of such mailing.

(b) CLERICAL AMENDMENT — The table of sections for part IV of subchapter C of chapter 76 of such Code is amended by adding at the end the following new item:

Sec. 7479. Declaratory judgments relating to eligibility of estate with respect to installment payments under section 6166.

(c) EFFECTIVE DATE — The amendments made by this section shall apply to the estates of decedents dying after the date of the enactment of this Act.

SEC. 506. GIFTS MAY NOT BE REVALUED FOR ESTATE TAX PURPOSES AFTER EXPIRATION OF STATUTE OF LIMITATIONS.

(a) IN GENERAL — Section 2001 (relating to imposition and rate of estate tax) is amended by adding at the end the following new subsection:

(f) VALUATION OF GIFTS — If —

(1) the time has expired within which a tax may be assessed under chapter 12 (or under corresponding provisions of prior laws) on the transfer of property by gift made during a preceding calendar period (as defined in section 2502(b)), and

(2) the value of such gift is shown on the return for such preceding calendar period or is disclosed in such return, or in a statement attached to the return, in a manner adequate to apprise the Secretary of the nature of such gift,

the value of such gift shall, for purposes of computing the tax under this chapter, be the value of such gift as finally determined for purposes of chapter 12.

(b) MODIFICATION OF APPLICATION OF STATUTE OF LIMITATIONS — Paragraph (9) of section 6501(c) is amended to read as follows:

(9) GIFT TAX ON CERTAIN GIFTS NOT SHOWN ON RETURN— If any gift of property the value of which (or any increase in taxable gifts required under section 2701(d) which) is required to be shown on a return of tax imposed by chapter 12 (without regard to section 2503(b)), and is not shown on such return, any tax imposed by chapter 12 on such gift may be assessed, or a proceeding in court for the collection of such tax may be begun without assessment, at any time. The preceding sentence shall not apply to any item which is disclosed in such return, or in a statement attached to the return, in a manner adequate to apprise the Secretary of the nature of such item. The value of any item which is so disclosed may not be redetermined by the Secretary after the expiration of the period under subsection (a).

(c) DECLARATORY JUDGMENT PROCEDURE FOR DETERMINING VALUE OF GIFT —

(1) IN GENERAL — Part IV of subchapter C of chapter 76 is amended by inserting after section 7476 the following new section:

SEC. 7477. DECLARATORY JUDGMENTS RELATING TO VALUE OF CERTAIN GIFTS.

(a) CREATION OF REMEDY— In a case of an actual controversy involving a determination by the Secretary of the value of any gift shown on the return of tax imposed by chapter 12 or disclosed on such return or in any statement attached to such return, upon the filing of an appropriate pleading, the Tax Court may make a declaration of the value of such gift. Any such declaration shall have the force and effect of a decision of the Tax Court and shall be reviewable as such.

(b) LIMITATIONS —

(1) PETITIONER — A pleading may be filed under this section only by the donor.

(2) EXHAUSTION OF ADMINISTRATIVE REMEDIES — The court shall not issue a declaratory judgment or decree under this section in any proceeding unless it determines that the petitioner has exhausted all available administrative remedies within the Internal Revenue Service.

(3) TIME FOR BRINGING ACTION — If the Secretary sends by certified or registered mail notice of his determination as described in subsection (a) to the petitioner, no proceeding may be initiated under this section unless the pleading is filed before the 91st day after the date of such mailing.

(2) CLERICAL AMENDMENT — The table of sections for such part IV is amended by inserting after the item relating to section 7476 the following new item:

Sec. 7477. Declaratory judgments relating to value of certain gifts.

(d) CONFORMING AMENDMENT — Subsection (c) of section 2504 is amended by striking ", and if a tax under this chapter or under corresponding provisions of prior laws has been assessed or paid for such preceding calendar period".

(e) EFFECTIVE DATES —

(1) IN GENERAL — The amendments made by subsections (a) and (c) shall apply to gifts made after the date of the enactment of this Act.

(2) SUBSECTION (b) — The amendment made by subsection (b) shall apply to gifts made in calendar years ending after the date of the enactment of this Act.

SEC. 507. REPEAL OF THROWBACK RULES APPLICABLE TO CERTAIN DOMESTIC TRUSTS.

This amendment of the ***income tax*** is omitted from this appendix.

SEC. 508. TREATMENT OF LAND SUBJECT TO A QUALIFIED CONSERVATION EASEMENT.

(a) ESTATE TAX WITH RESPECT TO LAND SUBJECT TO A QUALIFIED CONSERVATION EASEMENT — Section 2031 (relating to the definition of gross estate) is amended by redesignating subsection (c) as subsection (d) and by inserting after subsection (b) the following new subsection:

(c) ESTATE TAX WITH RESPECT TO LAND SUBJECT TO A QUALIFIED CONSERVATION EASEMENT—

(1) IN GENERAL— If the executor makes the election described in paragraph (6), then, except as otherwise provided in this subsection, there shall be excluded from the gross estate the lesser of—

(A) the applicable percentage of the value of land subject to a qualified conservation easement, reduced by the amount of any deduction under section 2055(f) with respect to such land, or

(B) the exclusion limitation.

(2) APPLICABLE PERCENTAGE — For purposes of paragraph (1), the term "applicable percentage" means 40 percent reduced (but not below zero) by 2 percentage points for each percentage point (or fraction thereof) by which the value of the qualified conservation easement is less than 30 percent of the value of the land (determined without regard to the value of such easement and reduced by the value of any retained development right (as defined in paragraph (5)).

(3) EXCLUSION LIMITATION— For purposes of paragraph (1), the exclusion limitation is the limitation determined in accordance with the following table:

In the case of estates of decedents dying during:	*The exclusion limitation is:*
1998	*$ 100,000*
1999	*$ 200,000*
2000	*$ 300,000*
2001	*$ 400,000*
2002 or thereafter	*$ 500,000*

(4) TREATMENT OF CERTAIN INDEBTEDNESS —

(A) IN GENERAL— The exclusion provided in paragraph (1) shall not apply to the extent that the land is debt-financed property.

(B) DEFINITIONS — For purposes of this paragraph —

(i) DEBT-FINANCED PROPERTY — The term "debt-financed property" means any property with respect to which there is an acquisition indebtedness (as defined in clause (ii)) on the date of the decedent's death.

(ii) ACQUISITION INDEBTEDNESS — The term "acquisition indebtedness" means, with respect to debt-financed property, the unpaid amount of—

(I) the indebtedness incurred by the donor in acquiring such property,

(II) the indebtedness incurred before the acquisition of such property if such indebtedness would not have been incurred but for such acquisition,

(III) the indebtedness incurred after the acquisition of such property if such indebtedness would not have been incurred but for such acquisition and the incurrence of such indebtedness was reasonably foreseeable at the time of such acquisition, and

(IV) the extension, renewal, or refinancing of an acquisition indebtedness.

(5) TREATMENT OF RETAINED DEVELOPMENT RIGHT —

(A) IN GENERAL — Paragraph (1) shall not apply to the value of any development right retained by the donor in the conveyance of a qualified conservation easement.

(B) TERMINATION OF RETAINED DEVELOPMENT RIGHT — If every person in being who has an interest (whether or not in possession) in the land executes an agreement to extinguish permanently some or all of any development rights (as defined in subparagraph (D)) retained by the donor on or before the date for filing the return of the tax imposed by section 2001, then any tax imposed by section 2001 shall be reduced accordingly. Such agreement shall be filed with the return of the tax imposed by section 2001. The agreement shall be in such form as the Secretary shall prescribe.

(C) ADDITIONAL TAX — Any failure to implement the agreement described in subparagraph (B) not later than the earlier of —

(i) the date which is 2 years after the date of the decedent's death, or

(ii) the date of the sale of such land subject to the qualified conservation easement,

shall result in the imposition of an additional tax in the amount of the tax which would have been due on the retained development rights subject to such agreement. Such additional tax shall be due and payable on the last day of the 6th month following such date.

(D) DEVELOPMENT RIGHT DEFINED — For purposes of this paragraph, the term "development right" means any right to use the land subject to the qualified conservation easement in which such right is retained for any commercial purpose which is not subordinate to and directly supportive of the use of such land as a farm for farming purposes (within the meaning of section 2032A(e)(5)).

(6) ELECTION — The election under this subsection shall be made on the return of the tax imposed by section 2001. Such an election, once made, shall be irrevocable.

(7) CALCULATION OF ESTATE TAX DUE — An executor making the election described in paragraph (6) shall, for purposes of calculating the amount of tax imposed by section 2001, include the value of any development right (as defined in paragraph (5)) retained by the donor in the conveyance of such qualified conservation easement. The computation of tax on any retained development right prescribed in this paragraph shall be done in such manner and on such forms as the Secretary shall prescribe.

(8) DEFINITIONS — For purposes of this subsection —

(A) LAND SUBJECT TO A QUALIFIED CONSERVATION EASEMENT — The term "land subject to a qualified conservation easement" means land —

(i) which is located —

(I) in or within 25 miles of an area which, on the date of the decedent's death, is a metropolitan area (as defined by the Office of Management and Budget),

(II) in or within 25 miles of an area which, on the date of the decedent's death, is a national park or wilderness area designated as part of the National Wilderness Preservation System (unless it is determined by the Secretary that land in or within 25 miles of such a park or wilderness area is not under significant development pressure), or

(III) in or within 10 miles of an area which, on the date of the decedent's death, is an Urban National Forest (as designated by the Forest Service),

(ii) which was owned by the decedent or a member of the decedent's family at all times during the 3-year period ending on the date of the decedent's death, and

(iii) with respect to which a qualified conservation easement has been made by an individual described in subparagraph (C), as of the date of the election described in paragraph (6).

(B) QUALIFIED CONSERVATION EASEMENT — The term "qualified conservation easement" means a qualified conservation contribution (as defined in section 170(h)(1)) of a qualified real property interest (as defined in section 170(h)(2)(C)), except that clause (iv) of section 170(h)(4)(A) shall not apply, and the restriction on the use of such interest described in section 170(h)(2)(C) shall include a prohibition on more than a de minimis use for a commercial recreational activity.

(C) INDIVIDUAL DESCRIBED — An individual is described in this subparagraph if such individual is —

(i) the decedent,

(ii) a member of the decedent's family,

(iii) the executor of the decedent's estate, or

(iv) the trustee of a trust the corpus of which includes the land to be subject to the qualified conservation easement.

(D) MEMBER OF FAMILY — The term "member of the decedent's family" means any member of the family (as defined in section 2032A(e)(2)) of the decedent.

(9) APPLICATION OF THIS SECTION TO INTERESTS IN PARTNERSHIPS, CORPORATIONS, AND TRUSTS — This section shall apply to an interest in a partnership, corporation, or trust if at least 30 percent of the entity is owned (directly or indirectly) by the decedent, as determined under the rules described in section 2033A(e)(3).

(b) CARRYOVER BASIS — Section 1014(a) (relating to basis of property acquired from a decedent) is amended by striking "or" at the end of paragraphs (1) and (2), by striking the period at the end of paragraph (3) and inserting "*, or*" and by adding at the end the following new paragraph:

(4) to the extent of the applicability of the exclusion described in section 2031(c), the basis in the hands of the decedent.

(c) QUALIFIED CONSERVATION CONTRIBUTION IS NOT A DISPOSITION — Subsection (c) of section 2032A (relating to alternative valuation method) is amended by adding at the end the following new paragraph:

(8) QUALIFIED CONSERVATION CONTRIBUTION IS NOT A DISPOSITION — A qualified conservation contribution (as defined in section 170(h)) by gift or otherwise shall not be deemed a disposition under subsection (c)(1)(A).

(d) QUALIFIED CONSERVATION CONTRIBUTION WHERE SURFACE AND MINERAL RIGHTS ARE SEPARATED — Section 170(h)(5)(B)(ii) (relating to special rule) is amended to read as follows:

(ii) SPECIAL RULE — With respect to any contribution of property in which the ownership of the surface estate and mineral interests has been and remains separated, subparagraph (A) shall be treated as met if the probability of surface mining occurring on such property is so remote as to be negligible.

(e) EFFECTIVE DATES —

(1) EXCLUSION — The amendments made by subsections (a) and (b) shall apply to estates of decedents dying after December 31, 1997.

(2) EASEMENTS — The amendments made by subsections (c) and (d) shall apply to easements granted after December 31, 1997.

SUBTITLE B—GENERATION-SKIPPING TAX PROVISION

SEC. 511. EXPANSION OF EXCEPTION FROM GENERATION-SKIPPING TRANSFER TAX FOR TRANSFERS TO INDIVIDUALS WITH DECEASED PARENTS.

(a) IN GENERAL — Section 2651 (relating to generation assignment) is amended by redesignating subsection (e) as subsection (f) and by inserting after subsection (d) the following new subsection:

(e) SPECIAL RULE FOR PERSONS WITH A DECEASED PARENT —

(1) IN GENERAL — For purposes of determining whether any transfer is a generation-skipping transfer, if —

(A) an individual is a descendant of a parent of the transferor (or the transferor's spouse or former spouse), and

(B) such individual's parent who is a lineal descendant of the parent of the transferor (or the transferor's spouse or former spouse) is dead at the time the transfer (from which an interest of such individual is established or derived) is subject to a tax imposed by chapter 11 or 12 upon the transferor (and if there shall be more than 1 such time, then at the earliest such time),

such individual shall be treated as if such individual were a member of the generation which is 1 generation below the lower of the transferor's generation or the generation assignment of the youngest living ancestor of such individual who is also a descendant of the parent of the transferor (or the transferor's spouse or former spouse), and the generation assignment of any descendant of such individual shall be adjusted accordingly.

(2) LIMITED APPLICATION OF SUBSECTION TO COLLATERAL HEIRS — This subsection shall not apply with respect to a transfer to any individual who is not a lineal descendant of the transferor (or the transferor's spouse or former spouse) if, at the time of the transfer, such transferor has any living lineal descendant.

(b) CONFORMING AMENDMENTS —

(1) Section 2612(c) (defining direct skip) is amended by striking paragraph (2) and by redesignating paragraph (3) as paragraph (2).

(2)Section 2612(c)(2) (as so redesignated) is amended by striking "section 2651(e)(2)" and inserting "section 2651(f)(2)".

(c) EFFECTIVE DATE — The amendments made by this section shall apply to terminations, distributions, and transfers occurring after December 31, 1997.

TITLE XIII — SIMPLIFICATION PROVISIONS RELATING TO ESTATE AND GIFT TAXES

SEC. 1301. GIFTS TO CHARITIES EXEMPT FROM GIFT TAX FILING REQUIREMENTS.

(a) IN GENERAL — Section 6019 is amended by striking 'or' at the end of paragraph (1), by adding 'or' at the end of paragraph (2), and by inserting after paragraph (2) the following new paragraph:

(3) a transfer with respect to which a deduction is allowed under section 2522 but only if —

(A) (i) such transfer is of the donor's entire interest in the property transferred, and

(ii) no other interest in such property is or has been transferred (for less than adequate and full consideration in money or money's worth) from the donor to a person, or for a use, not described in subsection (a) or (b) of section 2522, or

(B) such transfer is described in section 2522(d),

(b) EFFECTIVE DATE — The amendment made by this section shall apply to gifts made after the date of the enactment of this Act.

SEC. 1302. CLARIFICATION OF WAIVER OF CERTAIN RIGHTS OF RECOVERY.

(a) AMENDMENT TO SECTION 2207A — Paragraph (2) of section 2207A(a) (relating to right of recovery in the case of certain marital deduction property) is amended to read as follows:

(2) DECEDENT MAY OTHERWISE DIRECT — Paragraph (1) shall not apply with respect to any property to the extent that the decedent in his will (or a revocable trust) specifically indicates an intent to waive any right of recovery under this subchapter with respect to such property.

(b) AMENDMENT TO SECTION 2207B — Paragraph (2) of section 2207B(a) (relating to right of recovery where decedent retained interest) is amended to read as follows:

(2) DECEDENT MAY OTHERWISE DIRECT — Paragraph (1) shall not apply with respect to any property to the extent that the decedent in his will (or a revocable trust) specifically indicates an intent to waive any right of recovery under this subchapter with respect to such property.

(c) EFFECTIVE DATE — The amendments made by this section shall apply with respect to the estates of decedents dying after the date of the enactment of this Act.

SEC. 1303. TRANSITIONAL RULE UNDER SECTION 2056A.

(a) GENERAL RULE — In the case of any trust created under an instrument executed before the date of the enactment of the Revenue Reconciliation Act of 1990, such trust shall be treated as meeting the requirements of paragraph (1) of section 2056A(a) of the Internal Revenue Code of 1986 if the trust instrument requires that all trustees of the trust be individual citizens of the United States or domestic corporations.

(b) EFFECTIVE DATE — The provisions of subsection (a) shall take effect as if included in the provisions of section 11702(g) of the Revenue Reconciliation Act of 1990.

SEC. 1304. TREATMENT FOR ESTATE TAX PURPOSES OF SHORT-TERM OBLIGATIONS HELD BY NONRESIDENT ALIENS.

(a) IN GENERAL — Subsection (b) of section 2105 is amended by striking "and" at the end of paragraph (2), by striking the period at the end of paragraph (3) and inserting ", and", and by inserting after paragraph (3) the following new paragraph:

(4) obligations which would be original issue discount obligations as defined in section 871(g)(1) but for subparagraph (B)(i) thereof, if any interest thereon (were such interest received by the decedent at the time of his death) would not be effectively connected with the conduct of a trade or business within the United States.

(b) EFFECTIVE DATE — The amendment made by this section shall apply to estates of decedents dying after the date of the enactment of this Act.

SEC. 1305. CERTAIN REVOCABLE TRUSTS TREATED AS PART OF ESTATE.

This section, and the 4 following sections [Act §§1306-1309], amend ***income tax*** provisions, and thus they are omitted from this appendix. (The titles of Act §§1306-1309 are — §1306: "Distributions During First 65 Days of Taxable Year of Estate"; §1307: "Separate Share Rules Available to Estates"; §1308: "Executor of Estate and Beneficiaries Treated as Related Persons for Disallowance of Losses, Etc."; §§1308, 1309: "Treatment of Funeral Trusts".)

SEC. 1310. ADJUSTMENTS FOR GIFTS WITHIN 3 YEARS OF DECEDENT'S DEATII.

(a) GENERAL RULE — Section 2035 is amended to read as follows:

SEC. 2035. ADJUSTMENTS FOR CERTAIN GIFTS MADE WITHIN 3 YEARS OF DECEDENT'S DEATH.

(a) INCLUSION OF CERTAIN PROPERTY IN GROSS ESTATE – If—

(1) the decedent made a transfer (by trust or otherwise) of an interest in any property, or relinquished a power with respect to any property, during the 3-year period ending on the date of the decedent's death, and

(2) the value of such property (or an interest therein) would have been included in the decedent's gross estate under section 2036, 2037, 2038, or 2042 if such transferred interest or relinquished power had been retained by the decedent on the date of his death,

the value of the gross estate shall include the value of any property (or interest therein) which would have been so included.

(b) INCLUSION OF GIFT TAX ON GIFTS MADE DURING 3 YEARS BEFORE DECEDENT'S DEATH — The amount of the gross estate (determined without regard to this subsection) shall be increased by the amount of any tax paid under chapter 12 by the decedent or his estate on any gift made by the decedent or his spouse during the 3-year period ending on the date of the decedent's death.

(c) OTHER RULES RELATING TO TRANSFERS WITHIN 3 YEARS OF DEATH —

(1) IN GENERAL – For purposes of—

(A) section 303(b) (relating to distributions in redemption of stock to pay death taxes),

(B) section 2032A (relating to special valuation of certain farms, etc., real property), and

(C) subchapter C of chapter 64 (relating to lien for taxes),

the value of the gross estate shall include the value of all property to the extent of any interest therein of which the decedent has at any time made a transfer, by trust or otherwise, during the 3-year period ending on the date of the decedent's death.

(2) COORDINATION WITH SECTION 6166 — An estate shall be treated as meeting the 35 percent of adjusted gross estate requirement of section 6166(a)(1) only if the estate meets such requirement both with and without the application of paragraph (1).

(3) MARITAL AND SMALL TRANSFERS — Paragraph (1) shall not apply to any transfer (other than a transfer with respect to a life insurance policy) made during a calendar year to any donee if the decedent was not required by section 6019 (other than by reason of section 6019(2)) to file any gift tax return for such year with respect to transfers to such donee.

(d) EXCEPTION — Subsection (a) shall not apply to any bona fide sale for an adequate and full consideration in money or money's worth.

(e) TREATMENT OF CERTAIN TRANSFERS FROM REVOCABLE TRUSTS — For purposes of this section and section 2038, any transfer from any portion of a trust during any period that such portion was treated under section 676 as owned by the decedent by reason of a power in the grantor (determined without regard to section 672(e)) shall be treated as a transfer made directly by the decedent.

(b) CLERICAL AMENDMENT — The table of sections for part III of subchapter A of chapter 11 is amended by striking "gifts" in the item relating to section 2035 and inserting "certain gifts".

(c) EFFECTIVE DATE — The amendments made by this section shall apply to the estates of decedents dying after the date of the enactment of this Act.

SEC. 1311. CLARIFICATION OF TREATMENT OF SURVIVOR ANNUITIES UNDER QUALIFIED TERMINABLE INTEREST RULES.

(a) IN GENERAL — Subparagraph (C) of section 2056(b)(7) is amended by inserting "*(or, in the case of an interest in an annuity arising under the community property laws of a State, included in the gross estate of the decedent under section 2033)*" after "section 2039".

(b) EFFECTIVE DATE — The amendment made by this section shall apply to estates of decedents dying after the date of the enactment of this Act.

SEC. 1312. TREATMENT UNDER QUALIFIED DOMESTIC TRUST RULES OF FORMS OF OWNERSHIP WHICH ARE NOT TRUSTS.

(a) IN GENERAL — Subsection (c) of section 2056A (defining qualified domestic trust) is amended by adding at the end the following new paragraph:

> *(3) TRUST — To the extent provided in regulations prescribed by the Secretary, the term 'trust' includes other arrangements which have substantially the same effect as a trust.*

(b) EFFECTIVE DATE — The amendment made by this section shall apply to estates of decedents dying after the date of the enactment of this Act.

SEC. 1313. OPPORTUNITY TO CORRECT CERTAIN FAILURES UNDER SECTION 2032A.

(a) GENERAL RULE — Paragraph (3) of section 2032A(d) (relating to modification of election and agreement to be permitted) is amended to read as follows:

> *(3) MODIFICATION OF ELECTION AND AGREEMENT TO BE PERMITTED — The Secretary shall prescribe procedures which provide that in any case in which the executor makes an election under paragraph (1) (and submits the agreement referred to in paragraph (2)) within the time prescribed therefor, but —*
>
> > *(A) the notice of election, as filed, does not contain all required information, or*
> >
> > *(B) signatures of 1 or more persons required to enter into the agreement described in paragraph (2) are not included on the agreement as filed, or the agreement does not contain all required information,*
>
> *the executor will have a reasonable period of time (not exceeding 90 days) after notification of such failures to provide such information or signatures.*

(b) EFFECTIVE DATE — The amendment made by subsection (a) shall apply to the estates of decedents dying after the date of the enactment of this Act.

SEC. 1314. AUTHORITY TO WAIVE REQUIREMENT OF UNITED STATES TRUSTEE FOR QUALIFIED DOMESTIC TRUSTS.

(a) IN GENERAL — Subparagraph (A) of section 2056A(a)(1) is amended by inserting "*except as provided in regulations prescribed by the Secretary,*" before "requires".

(b) EFFECTIVE DATE — The amendment made by this section shall apply to estates of decedents dying after the date of the enactment of this Act.

Appendix 2: Internal Revenue Service Restructuring and Reform Act of 1998[1]

Public Law No. 105-206
July 22, 1998

TITLE VI — TECHNICAL CORRECTIONS

SEC. 6007. AMENDMENTS RELATED TO TITLE V OF 1997 ACT.

(a) AMENDMENTS RELATED TO SECTION 501 OF 1997 ACT —

(1) Subsection (c) of section 2631 of the 1986 Code is amended to read as follows:

(c) INFLATION ADJUSTMENT —

(1) IN GENERAL — In the case of any calendar year after 1998, the $1,000,000 amount contained in subsection (a) shall be increased by an amount equal to —

(A) $1,000,000, multiplied by

(B) the cost-of-living adjustment determined under section 1(f)(3) for such calendar year by substituting "calendar year 1997" for "calendar year 1992" in subparagraph (B) thereof.

If any amount as adjusted under the preceding sentence is not a multiple of $10,000, such amount shall be rounded to the next lowest multiple of $10,000.

(2) ALLOCATION OF INCREASE — Any increase under paragraph (1) for any calendar year shall apply only to generation-skipping transfers made during or after such calendar year; except that no such increase for calendar years after the calendar year in which the transferor dies shall apply to transfers by such transferor.

(2) Subsection (f) of section 501 of the 1997 Act is amended by inserting *"(other than the amendment made by subsection (d))" after "this section".*

(b) AMENDMENTS RELATED TO SECTION 502 OF 1997 ACT —

(1) (A) Section 2033A of the 1986 Code is hereby moved to the end of part IV of subchapter A of chapter 11 of the 1986 Code and redesignated as section 2057.

(B) So much of such section 2057 (as so redesignated) as precedes subsection (b) thereof is amended to read as follows:

SEC. 2057. FAMILY-OWNED BUSINESS INTERESTS.

(a) GENERAL RULE —

(1) ALLOWANCE OF DEDUCTION — For purposes of the tax imposed by section 2001, in the case of an estate of a decedent to which this section applies, the value of the taxable estate shall be determined by deducting from the value of the gross estate the adjusted value of the qualified family-owned business interests of the decedent which are described in subsection (b)(2).

---

[1] New matter is in italics. [JHM]

(2) MAXIMUM DEDUCTION — The deduction allowed by this section shall not exceed $675,000.

(3) COORDINATION WITH UNIFIED CREDIT —

(A) IN GENERAL — Except as provided in subparagraph (B), if this section applies to an estate, the applicable exclusion amount under section 2010 shall be $625,000.

(B) INCREASE IN UNIFIED CREDIT IF DEDUCTION IS LESS THAN $675,000— If the deduction allowed by this section is less than $675,000, the amount of the applicable exclusion amount under section 2010 shall be increased (but not above the amount which would apply to the estate without regard to this section) by the excess of $675,000 over the amount of the deduction allowed.

(C) Subparagraph (A) of section 2057(b)(2) of the 1986 Code (as so redesignated) is amended by striking "(without regard to this section)".

(D) Subsection (c) of section 2057 of the 1986 Code (as so redesignated) is amended by striking "(determined without regard to this section)".

(E) The table of sections for part III of subchapter A of chapter 11 of the 1986 Code is amended by striking the item relating to section 2033A.

(F) The table of sections for part IV of such subchapter is amended by adding at the end the following new item:

Sec. 2057. Family-owned business interests.

(2) Section 2057(b)(3) of the 1986 Code (as so redesignated) is amended to read as follows:

(3) INCLUDIBLE GIFTS OF INTERESTS — The amount of the gifts of qualified family-owned business interests determined under this paragraph is the sum of —

(A) the amount of such gifts from the decedent to members of the decedent's family taken into account under section 2001(b)(1)(B), plus

(B) the amount of such gifts otherwise excluded under section 2503(b), to the extent such interests are continuously held by members of such family (other than the decedent's spouse) between the date of the gift and the date of the decedent's death.

(3) (A) Section 2057(e)(2)(C) of the 1986 Code (as so redesignated) is amended by striking "(as defined in section 543(a))" and inserting "*(as defined in section 543(a) without regard to paragraph (2)(B) thereof) if such trade or business were a corporation*".

(B) Clause (ii) of section 2057(e)(2)(D) of the 1986 Code (as so redesignated) is amended by striking "income of which is described in section 543(a) or" and inserting "*personal holding company income (as defined in subparagraph (C)) or income described*".

(C) Paragraph (2) of section 2057(e) of the 1986 Code (as so redesignated) is amended by adding at the end the following new flush sentence:

In the case of a lease of property on a net cash basis by the decedent to a member of the decedent's family, income from such lease shall not be treated as personal holding company income for purposes of subparagraph (C), and such property shall not be treated as an asset described in subparagraph (D)(ii), if such income and property would not be so treated if the lessor had engaged directly in the activities engaged in by the lessee with respect to such property.

(4) Paragraph (2) of section 2057(f) of the 1986 Code (as so redesignated) is amended —

(A) by striking "(as determined under rules similar to the rules of section 2032A(c)(2)(B))"; and

(B) by adding at the end the following new subparagraph:

(C) ADJUSTED TAX DIFFERENCE — For purposes of subparagraph (A) —

(i) IN GENERAL — The adjusted tax difference attributable to a qualified family-owned business interest is the amount which bears the same ratio to the adjusted tax difference with respect to the estate (determined under clause (ii)) as the value of such interest bears to the value of all qualified family-owned business interests described in subsection (b)(2).

(ii) ADJUSTED TAX DIFFERENCE WITH RESPECT TO THE ESTATE — For purposes of clause (i), the term "adjusted tax difference with respect to the estate" means the excess of what would have been the estate tax liability but for the election under this section over the estate tax liability. For purposes of this clause, the term "estate tax liability" means the tax imposed by section 2001 reduced by the credits allowable against such tax.

(5) (A) Paragraph (1) of section 2057(e) of the 1986 Code (as so redesignated) is amended by adding at the end the following new flush sentence:

For purposes of the preceding sentence, a decedent shall be treated as engaged in a trade or business if any member of the decedent's family is engaged in such trade or business.

(B) Subsection (f) of section 2057 of the 1986 Code (as so redesignated) is amended by adding at the end the following new paragraph:

(3) USE IN TRADE OR BUSINESS BY FAMILY MEMBERS — A qualified heir shall not be treated as disposing of an interest described in subsection (e)(1)(A) by reason of ceasing to be engaged in a trade or business so long as the property to which such interest relates is used in a trade or business by any member of such individual's family.

(6) Paragraph (1) of section 2057(g) of the 1986 Code (as so redesignated) is amended by striking "or (M)".

(7) Paragraph (3) of section 2057(i) of the 1986 Code (as so redesignated) is amended by redesignating subparagraphs (L), (M), and (N) as subparagraphs (N), (O), and (P), respectively, and by inserting after subparagraph (K) the following new subparagraphs:

(L) Section 2032A(g) (relating to application to interests in partnerships, corporations, and trusts).

(M) Subsections (h) and (i) of section 2032A.

(c) AMENDMENTS RELATED TO SECTION 503 OF THE 1997 ACT—

(1) Clause (iii) of section 6166(b)(7)(A) of the 1986 Code is amended to read as follows:

(iii) for purposes of applying section 6601 (j), the 2-percent portion (as defined in such section) shall be treated as being zero.

(2) Clause (iii) of section 6166(b)(8)(A) of the 1986 Code is amended to read as follows:

(iii) 2-PERCENT INTEREST RATE NOT TO APPLY — For purposes of applying section 6601 j), the 2-percent portion (as defined in such section) shall be treated as being zero.

(d) AMENDMENT RELATED TO SECTION 505 OF THE 1997 ACT — Paragraphs (1) and (2) of section 7479(a) of the 1986 Code are each amended by striking "an estate," and inserting *"an estate (or with respect to any property included therein),"*.

(e) AMENDMENTS RELATED TO SECTION 506 OF THE 1997 ACT —

(1) Paragraph (1) of section 506(e) of the 1997 Act is amended by striking "and (c)" and inserting *", (c), and (d)"*.

(2) (A) Paragraph (9) of section 6501 (c) of the 1986 Code is amended by striking the last sentence.

(B) Subsection (f) of section 2001 of the 1986 Code is amended to read as follows:

(f) VALUATION OF GIFTS —

(1) IN GENERAL — If the time has expired under section 6501 within which a tax may be assessed under chapter 12 (or under corresponding provisions of prior laws) on —

(A) the transfer of property by gift made during a preceding calendar period (as defined in section 2502(b)); or

(B) an increase in taxable gifts required under section 2701(d),

the value thereof shall, for purposes of computing the tax under this chapter, be the value as finally determined for purposes of chapter 12.

(2) FINAL DETERMINATION—For purposes of paragraph (1), a value shall be treated as finally determined for purposes of chapter 12 if —

(A) the value is shown on a return under such chapter and such value is not contested by the Secretary before the expiration of the time referred to in paragraph (1) with respect to such return;

(B) in a case not described in subparagraph (A), the value is specified by the Secretary and such value is not timely contested by the taxpayer; or

(C) the value is determined by a court or pursuant to a settlement agreement with the Secretary.

(B) Subsection (c) of section 2504 of the 1986 Code is amended to read as follows:

(c) VALUATION OF GIFTS — If the time has expired under section 6501 within which a tax may be assessed under this chapter 12 (or under corresponding provisions of prior laws) on —

(1) the transfer of property by gift made during a preceding calendar period (as defined in section 2502(b)); or

(2) an increase in taxable gifts required under section 2701(d),

the value thereof shall, for purposes of computing the tax under this chapter, be the value as finally determined (within the meaning of section 2001(f)(2)) for purposes of this chapter.

(f) AMENDMENTS RELATED TO SECTION 507 OF 1997 ACT—

(1) Paragraph (3) of section 1(g) of the 1986 Code is amended by striking subparagraph (C) and by redesignating subparagraph (D) as subparagraph (C).

(2) Section 641 of the 1986 Code is amended by striking subsection (c) and by redesignating subsection (d) as subsection (c).

(3) Paragraph (4) of section 1361(e) of the 1986 Code is amended by striking "section 641(d)" and inserting *"section 641(c)"*.

(4) Subparagraph (A) of section 6103(e)(1) of the 1986 Code is amended by striking clause (ii) and by redesignating clauses (iii) and (iv) as clauses (ii) and (iii), respectively.

(g) AMENDMENTS RELATED TO SECTION 508 OF 1997 ACT—

(1) Subsection (c) of section 2031 of the 1986 Code is amended by redesignating paragraph (9) as paragraph (10) and by inserting after paragraph (8) the following new paragraph:

(9) TREATMENT OF EASEMENTS GRANTED AFTER DEATH—In any case in which the qualified conservation easement is granted after the date of the decedent's death and on or before the due date (including extensions) for filing the return of tax imposed by section 2001, the deduction under section 2055(f) with respect to such easement shall be allowed to the estate but only if no charitable deduction is allowed under chapter 1 to any person with respect to the grant of such easement.

(2) The first sentence of paragraph (6) of section 2031 (c) of the 1986 Code is amended by striking all that follows "shall be made" and inserting *"on or before the due date (including extensions) for filing the return of tax imposed by section 2001 and shall be made on such return."*

Notes

Notes

Notes

Notes

Notes

Notes

Notes

gilbert LAW SUMMARIES

Conflict of Laws

By Dean Herma Hill Kay, U.C. Berkeley

Domicile; Jurisdiction (including Notice and Opportunity to be Heard, Minimum Contacts, Types of Jurisdiction); Choice of Law (including Vested Rights Approach, Most Significant Relationship Approach, Governmental Interest Analysis); Choice of Law in Specific Substantive Areas; Traditional Defenses Against Application of Foreign Law; Constitutional Limitations and Overriding Federal Law (including Due Process Clause, Full Faith and Credit Clause, Conflict Between State and Federal Law); Recognition and Enforcement of Foreign Judgments.

ISBN: 0-15-900424-1 Pages: 250 $20.95

Constitutional Law

By Professor Jesse H. Choper, U.C. Berkeley

Powers of Federal Government (including Judicial Power, Powers of Congress, Presidential Power, Foreign Affairs Power); Intergovernmental Immunities, Separation of Powers; Regulation of Foreign Commerce; Regulation of Interstate Commerce; Taxation of Interstate and Foreign Commerce; Due Process, Equal Protection; "State Action" Requirements; Freedoms of Speech, Press, and Association; Freedom of Religion.

ISBN: 0-15-900375-X Pages: 312 $21.95

Contracts

By Professor Melvin A. Eisenberg, U.C. Berkeley

Consideration (including Promissory Estoppel, Moral or Past Consideration); Mutual Assent; Defenses (including Mistake, Fraud, Duress, Unconscionability, Statute of Frauds, Illegality); Third-Party Beneficiaries; Assignment of Rights and Delegation of Duties; Conditions; Substantial Performance; Material vs. Minor Breach; Anticipatory Breach; Impossibility; Discharge; Remedies (including Damages, Specific Performance, Liquidated Damages).

ISBN: 0-15-900014-9 Pages: 278 $21.95

Corporations

By Professor Jesse H. Choper, U.C. Berkeley, and Professor Melvin A. Eisenberg, U.C. Berkeley

Formalities; "De Jure" vs. "De Facto"; Promoters; Corporate Powers; Ultra Vires Transactions; Powers, Duties, and Liabilities of Officers and Directors; Allocation of Power Between Directors and Shareholders; Conflicts of Interest in Corporate Transactions; Close Corporations; Insider Trading; Rule 10b-5 and Section 16(b); Shareholders' Voting Rights; Shareholders' Right to Inspect Records; Shareholders' Suits; Capitalization (including Classes of Shares, Preemptive Rights, Consideration for Shares); Dividends; Redemption of Shares; Fundamental Changes in Corporate Structure; Applicable Conflict of Laws Principles.

ISBN: 0-15-900342-3 Pages: 282 $21.95

Criminal Law

By Professor George E. Dix, University of Texas

Elements of Crimes (including Actus Reus, Mens Rea, Causation); Vicarious Liability; Complicity in Crime; Criminal Liability of Corporations; Defenses (including Insanity, Diminished Capacity, Intoxication, Ignorance, Self-Defense); Inchoate Crimes; Homicide; Other Crimes Against the Person; Crimes Against Habitation (including Burglary, Arson); Crimes Against Property; Offenses Against Government; Offenses Against Administration of Justice.

ISBN: 0-15-900217-6 Pages: 271 $20.95

Criminal Procedure

By Professor Paul Marcus, College of William and Mary, and Professor Charles H. Whitebread, U.S.C.

Exclusionary Rule; Arrests and Other Detentions; Search and Seizure; Privilege Against Self-Incrimination; Confessions; Preliminary Hearing; Bail; Indictment; Speedy Trial; Competency to Stand Trial; Government's Obligation to Disclose Information; Right to Jury Trial; Right to Counsel; Right to Confront Witnesses; Burden of Proof; Insanity; Entrapment; Guilty Pleas; Sentencing; Death Penalty; Ex Post Facto Issues; Appeal; Habeas Corpus; Juvenile Offenders; Prisoners' Rights; Double Jeopardy.

ISBN: 0-15-900376-8 Pages: 244 $20.95

Estate and Gift Tax

By Professor John H. McCord, University of Illinois

Gross Estate; Allowable Deductions Under Estate Tax (including Expenses, Indebtedness, and Taxes, Deductions for Losses, Charitable Deduction, Marital Deduction); Taxable Gifts; Deductions; Valuation; Computation of Tax; Returns and Payment of Tax; Tax on Generation-Skipping Transfers.

ISBN: 0-15-900425-X Pages: 298 $20.95

Evidence

By Professor Jon R. Waltz, Northwestern University, and Roger C. Park, University of Minnesota

Direct Evidence; Circumstantial Evidence; Rulings on Admissibility; Relevancy; Materiality; Character Evidence; Hearsay and the Hearsay Exceptions; Privileges; Competency to Testify; Opinion Evidence and Expert Witnesses; Direct Examination; Cross-Examination; Impeachment; Real, Demonstrative, and Scientific Evidence; Judicial Notice; Burdens of Proof; Parol Evidence Rule.

ISBN: 0-15-900385-7 Pages: 342 $22.95

Federal Courts

By Professor William A. Fletcher, U.C. Berkeley

Article III Courts; "Case or Controversy" Requirement; Justiciability; Advisory Opinions; Political Questions; Ripeness; Mootness; Standing; Congressional Power Over Federal Court Jurisdiction; Supreme Court Jurisdiction; District Court Subject Matter Jurisdiction (including Federal Question Jurisdiction, Diversity Jurisdiction); Pendent and Ancillary Jurisdiction; Removal Jurisdiction; Venue; Forum Non Conveniens; Law Applied in the Federal Courts (including Erie Doctrine); Federal Law in the State Courts; Abstention; Habeas Corpus for State Prisoners; Federal Injunctions Against State Court Proceedings; Eleventh Amendment.

ISBN: 0-15-900232-X Pages: 270 $21.95

Future Interests & Perpetuities

By Professor Jesse Dukeminier, U.C.L.A.

Reversions; Possibilities of Reverter; Rights of Entry; Remainders; Executory Interest; Rules Restricting Remainders and Executory Interest; Rights of Owners of Future Interests; Construction of Instruments; Powers of Appointment; Rule Against Perpetuities (including Reforms of the Rule).

ISBN: 0-15-900218-4 Pages: 162 $19.95

Income Tax I - Individual

By Professor Michael R. Asimow, U.C.L.A.

Gross Income; Exclusions; Income Splitting by Gifts, Personal Service Income, Income Earned by Children, Income of Husbands and Wives, Below-Market Interest on Loans, Taxation of Trusts; Business and Investment Deductions; Personal Deductions; Tax Rates; Credits; Computation of Basis, Gain, or Loss; Realization; Nonrecognition of Gain or Loss; Capital Gains and Losses; Alternative Minimum Tax; Tax Accounting Problems.

ISBN: 0-15-900421-7 Pages: 279 $21.95

Income Tax II - Partnerships, Corporations, Trusts

By Professor Michael R. Asimow, U.C.L.A.

Taxation of Partnerships (including Current Partnership Income, Contributions of Property to Partnership, Sale of Partnership Interest, Distributions, Liquidations); Corporate Taxation (including Corporate Distributions, Sales of Stock and Assets, Reorganizations); S Corporations; Federal Income Taxation of Trusts.

ISBN: 0-15-900384-9 Pages: 210 $19.95

Labor Law

By Professor James C. Oldham, Georgetown University, and Robert J. Gelhaus

Statutory Foundations of Present Labor Law (including National Labor Relations Act, Taft-Hartley, Norris-LaGuardia Act, Landrum-Griffin Act); Organizing Campaigns, Selection of the Bargaining Representative; Collective Bargaining (including Negotiating the Agreement, Lockouts, Administering the Agreement, Arbitration); Strikes, Boycotts, and Picketing; Concerted Activity Protected Under the NLRA; Civil Rights Legislation; Grievance; Federal Regulation of Compulsory Union Membership Arrangements; State Regulation of Compulsory Membership Agreements; "Right to Work" Laws; Discipline of Union Members; Election of Union Officers; Corruption.

ISBN: 0-15-900340-7 Pages: 221 $19.95

Legal Ethics

By Professor Thomas D. Morgan, George Washington University

Regulating Admission to Practice Law; Preventing Unauthorized Practice of Law; Contract Between Client and Lawyer (including Lawyer's Duties Regarding Accepting Employment, Spheres of Authority of Lawyer and Client, Obligation of Client to Lawyer, Terminating the Lawyer-Client Relationship); Attorney-Client Privilege; Professional Duty of Confidentiality; Conflicts of Interest; Obligations to Third Persons and the Legal System (including Counseling Illegal or Fraudulent Conduct, Threats of Criminal Prosecution); Special Obligations in Litigation (including Limitations on Advancing Money to Client, Duty to Reject Certain Actions, Lawyer as Witness); Solicitation and Advertising; Specialization; Disciplinary Process; Malpractice; Special Responsibilities of Judges.

ISBN: 0-15-900026-2 Pages: 221 $20.95

Legal Research, Writing and Analysis

By Professor Peter J. Honigsberg, University of San Francisco

Court Systems; Precedent; Case Reporting System (including Regional and State Reporters, Headnotes and the West Key Number System, Citations and Case Finding); Statutes, Constitutions, and Legislative History; Secondary Sources (including Treatises, Law Reviews, Digests, Restatements); Administrative Agencies (including Regulations, Looseleaf Services); Shepard's Citations; Computers in Legal Research; Reading and Understanding a Case (including Briefing a Case); Using Legal Sourcebooks; Basic Guidelines for Legal Writing; Organizing Your Research; Writing a Memorandum of Law; Writing a Brief; Writing an Opinion or Client Letter.

ISBN: 0-15-900436-5 Pages: 162 $17.95

Multistate Bar Examination

By Professor Richard J. Conviser, Chicago Kent

Structure of the Exam; Governing Law; Effective Use of Time; Scoring of the Exam; Jurisdictions Using the Exam; Subject Matter Outlines; Practice Tests, Answers, and Subject Matter Keys; Glossary of Legal Terms and Definitions; State Bar Examination Directory; Listing of Reference Materials for Multistate Subjects.

ISBN: 0-15-900246-X Pages: 776 $24.95

Personal Property

Gilbert Staff

Acquisitions; Ownership Through Possession (including Wild Animals, Abandoned Chattels); Finders of Lost Property; Bailments; Possessory Liens; Pledges, Trover; Gift; Accession; Confusion (Commingling); Fixtures; Crops (Emblements); Adverse Possession; Prescriptive Rights (Acquiring Ownership of Easements or Profits by Adverse Use).

ISBN: 0-15-900360-1 Pages: 118 $14.95

Professional Responsibility

(see Legal Ethics)

Call To Order: 1-800-787-8717 or Order On-Line at http://www.gilbertlaw.com

gilbert LAW SUMMARIES

AMERICA'S BEST SELLING OUTLINES

Property
By Professor Jesse Dukeminier, U.C.L.A.

Possession (including Wild Animals, Bailments, Adverse Possession); Gifts and Sales of Personal Property; Freehold Possessory Estates; Future Interests (including Reversion, Possibility of Reverter, Right of Entry, Executory Interests, Rule Against Perpetuities); Tenancy in Common; Joint Tenancy; Tenancy by the Entirety; Condominiums; Cooperatives; Marital Property; Landlord and Tenant; Easements and Covenants; Nuisance; Rights in Airspace and Water; Right to Support; Zoning; Eminent Domain; Sale of Land (including Mortgage, Deed, Warranties of Title); Methods of Title Assurance (including Recording System, Title Registration, Title Insurance).

ISBN: 0-15-900426-8 Pages: 445 $22.95

Remedies
By Professor John A. Bauman, U.C.L.A., and Professor Kenneth H. York, Pepperdine University

Damages; Equitable Remedies (including Injunctions and Specific Performance); Restitution; Injuries to Tangible Property Interests; Injuries to Business and Commercial Interests (including Business Torts, Inducing Breach of Contract, Patent Infringement, Unfair Competition, Trade Defamation); Injuries to Personal Dignity and Related Interests (including Defamation, Privacy, Religious Status, Civil and Political Rights); Personal Injury and Death; Fraud; Duress, Undue Influence, and Unconscionable Conduct; Mistake; Breach of Contract; Unenforceable Contracts (including Statute of Frauds, Impossibility, Lack of Contractual Capacity, Illegality).

ISBN: 0-15-900325-3 Pages: 349 $22.95

Sale and Lease of Goods
By Professor Douglas J. Whaley, Ohio State University

UCC Article 2; Sales Contract (including Offer and Acceptance, Parol Evidence Rule, Statute of Frauds, Assignment and Delegation, Revision of Contract Terms); Types of Sales (including Cash Sale Transactions, Auctions, "Sale or Return" and "Sale on Approval" Transactions); Warranties (including Express and Implied Warranties, Privity, Disclaimer, Consumer Protection Statutes); Passage of Title; Performance of the Contract; Anticipatory Breach; Demand for Assurance of Performance; Unforeseen Circumstances; Risk of Loss; Remedies; Documents of Title; Lease of Goods; International Sale of Goods.

ISBN: 0-15-900367-9 Pages: 196 $19.95

Secured Transactions
By Professor Douglas J. Whaley, Ohio State University

Coverage of Article 9; Creation of a Security Interest (including Attachment, Security Agreement, Value, Debtor's Rights in the Collateral); Perfection; Filing; Priorities; Bankruptcy Proceedings and Article 9; Default Proceedings; Bulk Transfers.

ISBN: 0-15-900231-1 Pages: 191 $18.95

Securities Regulation
By Professor David H. Barber, and Professor Niels B. Schaumann, William Mitchell College of Law

Jurisdiction and Interstate Commerce; Securities Act of 1933 (including Registration Requirements and Exemptions); Securities Exchange Act of 1934 (including Rule 10b-5, Tender Offers, Proxy Solicitations Regulation, Insider Transactions); Regulation of the Securities Markets; Multinational Transactions; State Regulation of Securities Transactions.

ISBN: 0-15-9000437-3 Pages: 421 $22.95

Torts
By Professor Marc A. Franklin, Stanford University

Intentional Torts; Negligence; Strict Liability; Products Liability; Nuisance; Survival of Tort Actions; Wrongful Death; Immunity; Release and Contribution; Indemnity; Workers' Compensation; No-Fault Auto Insurance; Defamation; Invasion of Privacy; Misrepresentation; Injurious Falsehood; Interference With Economic Relations; Unjustifiable Litigation.

ISBN: 0-15-900220-6 Pages: 400 $22.95

Trusts
By Professor Edward C. Halbach, Jr., U.C. Berkeley

Elements of a Trust; Trust Creation; Transfer of Beneficiary's Interest (including Spendthrift Trusts); Charitable Trusts (including Cy Pres Doctrine); Trustee's Responsibilities, Power, Duties, and Liabilities; Duties and Liabilities of Beneficiaries; Accounting for Income and Principal; Power of Settlor to Modify or Revoke; Powers of Trustee Beneficiaries or Courts to Modify or Terminate; Termination of Trusts by Operation of Law; Resulting Trusts; Purchase Money Resulting Trusts; Constructive Trusts.

ISBN: 0-15-900039-4 Pages: 238 $20.95

Wills
By Professor Stanley M. Johanson, University of Texas

Intestate Succession; Simultaneous Death; Advancements; Disclaimer; Killer of Decedent; Elective Share Statutes; Pretermitted Child Statutes; Homestead; Formal Requisites of a Will; Revocation of Wills; Incorporation by Reference; Pour-Over Gift in Inter Vivos Trust; Joint Wills; Contracts Relating to Wills; Lapsed Gifts; Ademption; Exoneration of Liens; Will Contests; Probate and Estate Administration.

ISBN: 0-15-900040-8 Pages: 262 $21.95

Gilbert Law Summaries FIRST YEAR PROGRAM

Includes Five Gilbert Outlines:

- **Civil Procedure**
  By Professor Thomas D. Rowe, Jr. Duke University Law School, and Professor Richard L. Marcus U.C. Hastings School Of Law
- **Contracts**
  By Professor Melvin A. Eisenberg U.C. Berkeley School Of Law
- **Criminal Law**
  By Professor George E. Dix University Of Texas School Of Law
- **Property**
  By Professor Jesse Dukeminier U.C.L.A. Law School
- **Torts**
  By Professor Marc A. Franklin Stanford University Law School

Plus—

- **Gilbert's Dictionary Of Legal Terms**
- **The 8 Secrets Of Top Exam Performance In Law School**
  By Professor Charles H. Whitebread USC Law School

All titles are packaged in a convenient carrying case with handle. $130 if purchased separately. $95 if purchased as a set. Save $35.

ISBN: 0-15-900254-0 Set $95

Gilbert's Pocket Size Law Dictionary
Gilbert

A dictionary is useless if you don't have it when you need it. If the only law dictionary you own is a thick, bulky one, you'll probably leave it at home most of the time — and if you need to know a definition while you're at school, you're out of luck!

With Gilbert's Pocket Size Law Dictionary, you'll have any definition you need, when you need it. Just pop Gilbert's dictionary into your pocket or purse, and you'll have over 4,000 legal terms and phrases at your fingertips. Gilbert's dictionary also includes a section on law school shorthand, common abbreviations, Latin and French legal terms, periodical abbreviations, and governmental abbreviations.

With Gilbert's Pocket Size Law Dictionary, you'll never be caught at a loss for words!

Available in your choice of 5 colors

- **Brown** ISBN: 0-15-900252-4 $7.95
- **Blue** ISBN: 0-15-900362-8 $7.95
- **Burgundy** ISBN: 0-15-900366-0 $7.95
- **Green** ISBN: 0-15-900365-2 $7.95

Limited Edition: Simulated Alligator Skin Cover

- **Black** ISBN: 0-15-900364-4 $7.95

The Eight Secrets Of Top Exam Performance In Law School
Charles Whitebread

Wouldn't it be great to know exactly what your professor's looking for on your exam? To find out everything that's expected of you, so that you don't waste your time doing anything other than maximizing your grades?

In his easy-to-read, refreshing style, nationally recognized exam expert Professor Charles Whitebread will teach you the eight secrets that will add precious points to every exam answer you write. You'll learn the three keys to handling any essay exam question, and how to add points to your score by making time work for you, not against you. You'll learn flawless issue spotting, and discover how to organize your answer for maximum possible points. You'll find out how the hidden traps in "IRAC" trip up most students… but not you! You'll learn the techniques for digging up the exam questions your professor will ask, before your exam. You'll put your newly-learned skills to the test with sample exam questions, and you can measure your performance against model answers. And there's even a special section that helps you master the skills necessary to crush any exam, not just a typical essay exam — unusual exams like open book, take home, multiple choice, short answer, and policy questions.

"The Eight Secrets of Top Exam Performance in Law School" gives you all the tools you need to maximize your grades — quickly and easily!

ISBN: 0-15-900323-7 $9.95

Call To Order: 1-800-787-8717 or Order On-Line at http://www.gilbertlaw.com

LAW SCHOOL LEGENDS
SERIES
America's Greatest Law Professors on Audio Cassette
Wouldn't it be great if all of your law professors were law school legends — the kind of professors whose classes everyone fights to get into? The professors whose classes you'd take, no matter what subject they're teaching. The kind of professors who make a subject sing. You may never get an opportunity to take a class with a truly brilliant professor, but with the Law School Legends Series, you can now get all the benefits of the country's greatest law professors...on audio cassette!
Call To Order: 1-800-787-8717 or Order On-Line at http://www.gilbertlaw.com

Criminal Procedure
By Professor Charles H. Whitebread
USC School of Law

TOPICS COVERED: Incorporation Of The Bill Of Rights; Exclusionary Rule; Fruit Of The Poisonous Tree; Arrest; Search & Seizure; Exceptions To Warrant Requirement; Wire Tapping & Eavesdropping; Confessions (Miranda); Pretrial Identification; Bail; Preliminary Hearings; Grand Juries; Speedy Trial; Fair Trial; Jury Trials; Right To Counsel; Guilty Pleas; Sentencing; Death Penalty; Habeas Corpus; Double Jeopardy; Privilege Against Compelled Testimony.
3 Audio Cassettes
ISBN: 0-15-900281-8 $39.95

Evidence
By Professor Faust F. Rossi
Cornell Law School

TOPICS COVERED: Relevance; Insurance; Remedial Measures; Settlement Offers; Causation; State Of Mind; Rebuttal; Habit; Character Evidence; "MIMIC" Rule; Documentary Evidence; Authentication; Best Evidence Rule; Parol Evidence; Competency; Dead Man Statutes; Examination Of Witnesses; Present Recollection Revived; Past Recollection Recorded; Opinion Testimony; Lay And Expert Witness; Learned Treatises; Impeachment; Collateral Matters; Bias, Interest Or Motive; Rehabilitation; Privileges; Hearsay And Exceptions.
5 Audio Cassettes
ISBN: 0-15-900282-6 $45.95

Family Law
Professor Roger E. Schechter
George Washington University Law School

TOPICS COVERED: Marital Relationship; Formalities And Solemnization; Common Law Marriage; Impediments; Conflict Of Laws; Non-Marital Relationship; Void And Voidable Marriages; Annulment; Divorce; Separation; Full Faith And Credit; Temporary Orders; Property Division; Community Property Principles; Equitable Distribution And Reimbursement; Marital And Separate Property; Alimony; Child Support; Enforcement Of Orders; Antenuptial And Postnuptial Agreements; Separation And Settlement Agreements; Custody; Visitation Rights; Termination Of Parental Rights; Adoption; Illegitimacy; Paternity Actions.
3 Audio Cassettes
ISBN: 0-15-900283-4 $39.95

Federal Courts
Professor John C. Jeffries
University of Virginia School of Law

TOPICS COVERED: History Of The Federal Court System; "Court Or Controversy" And Justiciability; Congressional Power Over Federal Court Jurisdiction; Supreme Court Jurisdiction; District Court Subject Matter Jurisdiction—Federal Question Jurisdiction, Diversity Jurisdiction And Admiralty Jurisdiction; Pendent And Ancillary Jurisdiction; Removal Jurisdiction; Venue; Forum Non Conveniens; Law Applied In The Federal Courts; Federal Law In The State Courts; Collateral Relations Between Federal And State Courts; The Eleventh Amendment And State Sovereign Immunity.
3 Audio Cassettes
ISBN: 0-15-900372-5 $39.95

Federal Income Tax
By Professor Cheryl D. Block
George Washington University Law School

TOPICS COVERED: Administrative Reviews; Tax Formula; Gross Income; Exclusions For Gifts; Inheritances; Personal Injuries; Tax Basis Rules; Divorce Tax Rules; Assignment Of Income; Business Deductions; Investment Deductions; Passive Loss And Interest Limitation Rules; Capital Gains & Losses; Section 1031, 1034, and 121 Deferred/Non Taxable Transactions.
4 Audio Cassettes
ISBN: 0-15-900284-2 $45.95

Future Interests
By Dean Catherine L. Carpenter
Southwestern University Law School

TOPICS COVERED: Rule Against Perpetuities; Class Gifts; Estates In Land; Rule In Shelley's Case; Future Interests In Transferor and Transferee; Life Estates; Defeasible Fees; Doctrine Of Worthier Title; Doctrine Of Merger; Fee Simple Estates; Restraints On Alienation; Power Of Appointment; Rules Of Construction.
2 Audio Cassettes
ISBN: 0-15-900285-0 $24.95

Law School Exam Writing
By Professor Charles H. Whitebread
USC School of Law

TOPICS COVERED: With "Law School Exam Writing," you'll learn the secrets of law school test taking. Professor Whitebread leads you step-by-step through his innovative system, so that you know exactly how to tackle your essay exams without making point draining mistakes. You'll learn how to read questions so you don't miss important issues; how to organize your answer; how to use limited exam time to your maximum advantage; and even how to study for exams.
1 Audio Cassette
ISBN: 0-15-900287-7 $19.95

Professional Responsibility
By Professor Erwin Chemerinsky
USC School of Law

TOPICS COVERED: Regulation of Attorneys; Bar Admission; Unauthorized Practice; Competency; Discipline; Judgment; Lawyer-Client Relationship; Representation; Withdrawal; Conflicts; Disqualification; Clients; Client Interests; Successive And Effective Representation; Integrity; Candor; Confidences; Secrets; Past And Future Crimes; Perjury; Communications; Witnesses; Jurors; The Court; The Press; Trial Tactics; Prosecutors; Market; Solicitation; Advertising; Law Firms; Fees; Client Property; Conduct; Political Activity.
3 Audio Cassettes
ISBN: 0-15-900371-7 $39.95

Real Property
By Professor Paula A. Franzese
Seton Hall Law School

TOPICS COVERED: Estates—Fee Simple, Fee Tail, Life Estate; Co-Tenancy—Joint Tenancy, Tenancy In Common, Tenancy By The Entirety; Landlord-Tenant Relationship; Liability For Condition Of Premises; Assignment & Sublease; Easements; Restrictive Covenants; Adverse Possession; Recording Acts; Conveyancing; Personal Property.
4 Audio Cassettes
ISBN: 0-15-900289-3 $45.95

Remedies
By Professor William A. Fletcher
University of California at Berkeley, Boalt Hall School of Law

TOPICS COVERED: Damages; Restitution; Equitable Remedies; Tracing; Rescission and Reformation; Injury and Destruction of Personal Property; Conversion; Injury to Real Property; Trespass; Ouster; Nuisance; Defamation; Trade Libel; Inducing Breach of Contract; Contracts to Purchase Personal Property; Contracts to Purchase Real Property (including Equitable Conversion); Construction Contracts; and Personal Service Contracts.
4 Audio Cassettes
ISBN: 0-15-900353-9 $45.95

Sales & Lease of Goods
By Professor Michael I. Spak
Chicago Kent College of Law

TOPICS COVERED: Goods; Contract Formation; Firm Offers; Statute Of Frauds; Modification; Parol Evidence; Code Methodology; Tender; Payment; Identification; Risk Of Loss; Warranties; Merchantability; Fitness; Disclaimers; Consumer Protection; Remedies; Anticipatory Repudiation; Third Party Rights.
3 Audio Cassettes
ISBN: 0-15-900291-5 $39.95

Secured Transactions
By Professor Michael I. Spak
Chicago Kent College of Law

TOPICS COVERED: Collateral; Inventory; Intangibles; Proceeds; Security Agreements; Attachment; After-Acquired Property; Perfection; Filing; Priorities; Purchase Money Security Interests; Fixtures; Rights Upon Default; Self-Help; Sale; Constitutional Issues.
3 Audio Cassettes
ISBN: 0-15-900292-3 $39.95

Securities Regulation
By Professor Therese H. Maynard
Loyola University Law School **NEW**
4 Audio Cassettes
ISBN: 0-15-900359-8 $39.95

Torts
By Professor Richard J. Conviser
Chicago Kent College of Law

TOPICS COVERED: Essay Exam Techniques; Intentional Torts—Assault, Battery, False Imprisonment, Intentional Infliction Of Emotional Distress, Trespass To Land, Trespass To Chattels, Conversion; Defenses. Defamation—Libel, Slander; Defenses; First Amendment Concerns; Invasion Of Right Of Privacy; Misrepresentation; Negligence—Duty, Breach, Actual And Proximate Causation, Damages; Defenses; Strict Liability, Products Liability; Nuisance; General Tort Considerations.
4 Audio Cassettes
ISBN: 0-15-900185-4 $45.95

Wills & Trusts
By Professor Stanley M. Johanson
University of Texas School of Law

TOPICS COVERED: Attested Wills; Holographic Wills; Negligence; Revocation; Changes On Face Of Will; Lapsed Gifts; Negative Bequest Rule; Nonprobate Assets; Intestate Succession; Advancements; Elective Share; Will Contests; Capacity; Undue Influence; Creditors' Rights; Creation Of Trust; Revocable Trusts; Pourover Gifts; Charitable Trusts; Resulting Trusts; Constructive Trusts; Spendthrift Trusts; Self-Dealing; Prudent Investments; Trust Accounting; Termination; Powers Of Appointment.
4 Audio Cassettes
ISBN: 0-15-900294-X $45.95

Law School Legends Series
FIRST YEAR PROGRAM

Includes Five Law School Legends Titles:

- **Civil Procedure**
  By Professor Richard D. Freer
  Emory University Law School
- **Contracts**
  By Professor Michael I. Spak
  Chicago Kent College Of Law
- **Criminal Law**
  By Professor Charles H. Whitebread
  USC School of Law
- **Real Property**
  By Professor Paula A. Franzese
  Seton Hall Law School
- **Torts**
  By Professor Richard J. Conviser
  Chicago Kent College of Law

Plus—

- **Law School Exam Writing**
  By Professor Charles H. Whitebread
  USC Law School

All titles are packaged in a convenient carry case. $250 if purchased separately. $195 if purchased as a set. Save $55.

ISBN: 0-15-900306-7 Set $195

If you accidentally damage a tape within five years from the date of purchase we'll replace it for FREE— No questions asked!

GILBERT LAW AUDIO TAPES · TAPE REPLACEMENT GUARANTEE · FIVE YEAR

Call To Order: 1-800-787-8717 or Order On-Line at http://www.gilbertlaw.com

SAVE
Hundreds
Of HOURS
On Your
READING
Assignments!
Legalines
Torts
Legalines
Civil Procedu
galines
Evidence

100% Comprehensive, 100% Authoritative, 100% of What You Need

CASEBRIEFS FOR WINDOWS

Detailed Briefs Of Every Major Case— At Your Fingertips!

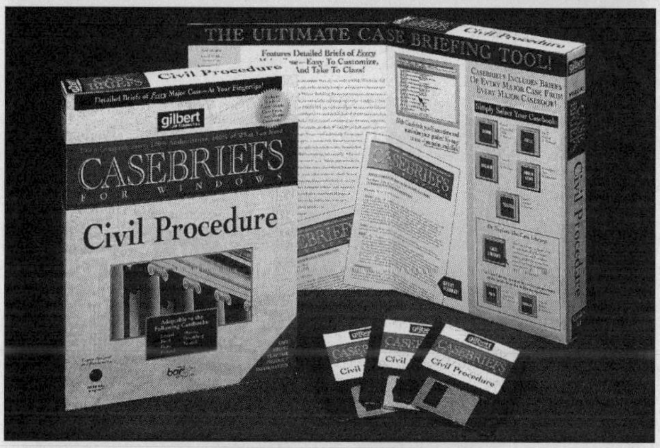

Casebriefs Interactive Software For Windows

As a law student you can't afford to waste a minute. That's why you need Casebriefs Software. With Casebriefs you simply click on the name of the case you're looking for, and you instantly have an expert brief of it at your fingertips! The facts. The issue. The holding. The rationale. Expert commentary. You'll get everything you need, whether you're preparing for class or studying for your final exam!

When you use Casebriefs, you can focus solely on the cases covered in your casebook, or you can use the Case Library, which includes briefs of all of the major cases from every major casebook. The Case Library is ideal for researching cases for writing assignments, moot court briefs, law review and other periodicals.

With Casebriefs, searching for cases is a breeze. You can search by topic. You can search alphabetically. You can search the cases in the order in which they appear in your casebook. You can even enter the date you'll cover different cases in class, and sort them by those dates. No matter how you want to look for a case, Casebriefs will help you find it instantly!

For each brief, you can add your own notes, or leave it "as is." Whether you customize the briefs or not, you can print them out and take them to class with you. You can even configure Casebriefs to access Lexis/Nexis and Westlaw directly from the Casebriefs screen (with Lexis/Nexis or Westlaw software and account). Whether you want to compare your own briefs to expert briefs, fill in gaps in your class notes, or research cases for your legal writing class, moot court, law review or other periodicals— Casebriefs is the source you'll turn to, over and over again!

Administrative Law
Includes briefs of all of the major cases from the Breyer, Gellhorn and Schwartz casebooks, many of the major cases from the Bonfield and Mashaw casebooks, plus a Case Library.
ISBN# 0-15-900190-0 $27.95

Antitrust
Includes briefs of all of the major cases from the Areeda and Handler casebooks, many of the major cases from the Sullivan casebook, plus a Case Library.
ISBN# 0-15-900400-4 $27.95

Civil Procedure
Includes briefs of all of the major cases from the Cound, Field, Hazard, Rosenberg and Yeazell casebooks, many of the major cases from the Marcus and Levin casebooks, plus a Case Library.
ISBN# 0-15-900191-9 $27.95

Commercial Law
Includes briefs of all of the major cases from the Farnsworth casebook, plus a Case Library.
ISBN# 0-15-900407-1 $27.95

Conflict Of Laws
Includes briefs of all of the major cases from the Cramton and Reese casebooks, many of the major cases from the Brilmayer casebook, plus a Case Library.
ISBN# 0-15-900192-7 $27.95

Constitutional Law
Includes briefs of all of the major cases from the Brest, Cohen, Gunther, Lockhart, Rotunda and Stone casebooks, plus a Case Library.
ISBN# 0-15-900193-5 $27.95

Contracts
Includes briefs of all of the major cases from the Calamari, Dawson, Farnsworth, Fuller, Kessler and Murphy casebooks, many of the major cases from the Burton, Crandall, Hamilton, Knapp, and Rosett casebooks, plus a Case Library.
ISBN# 0-15-900194-3 $27.95

Corporations
Includes briefs of all of the major cases from the Cary, Choper, Hamilton and Vagts casebooks, many of the major cases from the O'Kelley and Solomon casebooks, plus a Case Library.
ISBN# 0-15-900195-1 $27.95

Criminal Law
Includes briefs of all of the major cases from the Boyce, Dix, Johnson, Kadish and La Fave casebooks, many of the major cases from the Dressler, Johnson, Kaplan, Moenssens and Weinreb casebooks, plus a Case Library.
ISBN# 0-15-900196-X $27.95

Criminal Procedure
Includes briefs of all of the major cases from the Kamisar casebook, many of the major cases from the Allen, Haddad and Saltzburg casebooks, plus a Case Library.
ISBN# 0-15-900197-8 $27.95

Domestic Relations
Includes briefs of all of the major cases from the Clark and Wadlington casebooks, plus a Case Library.
ISBN# 0-15-900408-X $27.95

Estate & Gift Taxes
Includes briefs of all of the major cases from the Surrey casebook, plus a Case Library.
ISBN# 0-15-900396-2 $27.95

Evidence
Includes briefs of all of the major cases from the Sutton, Waltz, and Weinstein casebooks, many of the major cases from the Strong and Mueller casebooks, plus a Case Library.
ISBN# 0-15-900198-6 $27.95

Family Law
Includes briefs of all of the major cases from the Areen casebook, many of the major cases from the Clark, Ellman, Krause and Wadlington casebooks, plus a Case Library.
ISBN# 0-15-900199-4 $27.95

Federal Courts
Includes briefs of all of the major cases from the McCormick casebook, many of the major cases from the Bator, Currie, Low and Redish casebooks, plus a Case Library.
ISBN# 0-15-900409-8 $27.95

Income Tax
Includes briefs of all of the major cases from the Freeland and Klein casebooks, many of the major cases from the Burke and Graetz casebooks, plus a Case Library.
ISBN# 0-15-900200-1 $27.95

Labor Law
Includes briefs of all of the major cases from the Cox and Merrifield casebooks, many of the major cases from the Harper, Leslie and Meltzer casebooks, plus a Case Library.
ISBN# 0-15-900410-1 $27.95

Property
Includes briefs of all of the major cases from the Casner, Cribbet, Dukeminier and Rabin casebooks, many of the major cases from the Donahue, Johnson, Kurtz, and Singer casebooks, plus a Case Library.
ISBN# 0-15-900201-X $27.95

Remedies
Includes briefs of all of the major cases from the Re and York casebooks, many of the major cases from the Leavell and Shoben casebooks, plus a Case Library.
ISBN# 0-15-900202-8 $27.95

Securities Regulation
Includes briefs of all of the major cases from the Jennings casebook, many of the major cases from the Cox casebook, plus a Case Library.
ISBN# 0-15-900411-X $27.95

Torts
Includes briefs of all of the major cases from the Epstein, Franklin, Henderson, Keeton and Prosser casebooks, many of the major cases from the Christie, Dobbs and Shulman casebooks, plus a Case Library.
ISBN# 0-15-900203-6 $27.95

Wills, Trusts & Estates
Includes briefs of all of the major cases from the Dukeminier casebook, many of the major cases from the Wagoner casebook, plus a Case Library.
ISBN# 0-15-900204-4 $27.95

Call To Order: 1-800-787-8717 or Order On-Line at http://www.gilbertlaw.com

Employment Guides

A collection of best selling titles that help you identify and reach your career goals.

Guerrilla Tactics for Getting the Legal Job of Your Dreams
Kimm Alayne Walton, J.D.

Whether you're looking for a summer clerkship or your first permanent job after school, this revolutionary book is the key to getting the job of your dreams!

Guerrilla Tactics for Getting the Legal Job of Your Dreams leads you step-by-step through everything you need to do to nail down that perfect job! You'll learn hundreds of simple-to-use strategies that will get you exactly where you want to go. You'll Learn:

- The seven magic opening words in cover letters that ensure you'll get a response.
- The secret to successful interviews every time.
- Killer answers to the toughest interview questions they'll ever ask you.
- Plus Much More!

Guerrilla Tactics features the best strategies from the country's most innovative law school career advisors. The strategies in *Guerrilla Tactics* are so powerful that it even comes with a guarantee: Follow the advice in the book, and within one year of graduation you'll have the job of your dreams ... or your money back!

Pick up a copy of *Guerrilla Tactics* today ... you'll be on your way to the job of your dreams!

ISBN: 0-15-900317-2 $24.95

Proceed With Caution: A Diary Of The First Year At One Of America's Largest, Most Prestigious Law Firms
William R. Keates

Prestige. Famous clients. High-profile cases. Not to mention a starting salary approaching six figures.

In *Proceed With Caution*, the author takes you behind the scenes, to show you what it's really like to be a junior associate at a huge law firm. After graduating from an Ivy League law school, he took a job as an associate with one of New York's blue-chip law firms.

He also did something not many people do. He kept a diary, where he spelled out his day-to-day life at the firm in graphic detail.

Proceed With Caution excerpts the diary, from his first day at the firm to the day he quit. From the splashy benefits, to the nitty-gritty on the work junior associates do, to the grind of long and unpredictable hours, to the stress that eventually made him leave the firm — he tells story after story that will make you feel as though you're living the life of a new associate.

Whether you're considering a career with a large firm, or you're just curious about what life at the top firms is all about — *Proceed With Caution* is a must read!

ISBN: 0-15-900181-1 $17.95

The Official Guide To Legal Specialties
Lisa Shanholtzer

With *The Official Guide To Legal Specialties* you'll get a behind the scenes glimpse at dozens of legal specialties. Not just lists of what to expect, real life stories from top practitioners in each field. You'll learn exactly what it's like to be in some of America's most desirable professions. You'll get expert advice on what it takes to get a job in each field. How much you'll earn and what the day-to-day life is really like, the challenges you'll face, and the benefits you'll enjoy. With *The Official Guide To Legal Specialties* you'll have a wealth of information at your fingertips!

Includes the following specialties:

Banking	Intellectual Property
Communications	International
Corporate	Labor/Employment
Criminal	Litigation
Entertainment	Public Interest
Environmental	Securities
Government Practice	Sports
Health Care	Tax
Immigration	Trusts & Estates

ISBN: 0-15-900391-1 $17.95

Beyond L.A. Law: Inspiring Stories of People Who've Done Fascinating Things With A Law Degree
National Association for Law Placement

Anyone who watches television knows that being a lawyer means working your way up through a law firm — right?

Wrong!

Beyond L.A. Law gives you a fascinating glimpse into the lives of people who've broken the "lawyer" mold. They come from a variety of backgrounds — some had prior careers, others went straight through college and law school, and yet others have overcome poverty and physical handicaps. They got their degrees from all different kinds of law schools, all over the country. But they have one thing in common: they've all pursued their own, unique vision.

As you read their stories, you'll see how they beat the odds to succeed. You'll learn career tips and strategies that work, from people who've put them to the test. And you'll find fascinating insights that you can apply to your own dream, whether it's a career in law or anything else!

From Representing Baseball In Australia. To International Finance. To Children's Advocacy. To Directing a Nonprofit Organization. To Entrepreneur.

If You Think Getting A Law Degree Means Joining A Traditional Law Firm — Think Again!

ISBN: 0-15-900182-X $17.95

America's Greatest Places To Work With A Law Degree
Kimm Alayne Walton, J.D.

"Where do your happiest graduates work?" That's the question that author Kimm Alayne Walton asked of law school administrators around the country. Their responses revealed the hundreds of wonderful employers profiled in *America's Greatest Places To Work With A Law Degree.*

In this remarkable book, you'll get to know an incredible variety of great places to work, including:

- Glamorous sports and entertainment employers — the jobs that sound as though they would be great, and they are!
- The 250 best law firms to work for between 20 and 600 attorneys.
- Companies where law school graduates love to work and not just as in-house counsel.
- Wonderful public interest employers – the "white knight" jobs that are so incredibly satisfying.
- Court-related positions, where lawyers entertain fascinating issues, tremendous variety, and an enjoyable lifestyle.
- Outstanding government jobs, at the federal, state, and local level.

Beyond learning about incredible employers, you'll discover:

- The ten traits that define a wonderful place to work ... the sometimes surprising qualities that outstanding employers share.
- How to handle law school debt, when your dream job pays less than you think you need to make.
- How to find — and get! — great jobs at firms with fewer than 20 attorneys.

And no matter where you work, you'll learn expert tips for making the most of your job. You'll learn the specific strategies that distinguish people headed for the top ... how to position yourself for the most interesting, high-profile work ... how to handle difficult personalities ... how to negotiate for more money ... and what to do now to help you get your next great job!

ISBN: 0-15-900180-3 $24.95

About The Author

Kimm Alayne Walton is the author of numerous books and articles including two national best seller's — *America's Greatest Places To Work With A Law Degree* and *Guerrilla Tactics For Getting The Legal Job Of Your Dreams.* She is a renowned motivational speaker, lecturing at law schools and bar associations nationwide, and in her spare time, she has taken up travel writing, which has taken her swimming with crocodiles in Kakadu, and scuba diving with sharks on the Great Barrier Reef.

E-mail the Job Goddess with your own legal job search questions!

Visit www.gilbertlaw.com for details.

Call To Order: 1-800-787-8717 or Order On-Line at http://www.gilbertlaw.com

Employment Guides

A collection of best selling titles that help you identify and reach your career goals.

The National Directory Of Legal Employers
National Association for Law Placement

The National Directory of Legal Employers brings you a universe of vital information about 1,000 of the nation's top legal employers— *in one convenient volume!*

It includes:

- Over 22,000 job openings.
- The names, addresses and phone numbers of hiring partners.
- Listings of firms by state, size, kind and practice area.
- What starting salaries are for full time, part time, and summer associates, plus a detailed description of firm benefits.
- The number of employees by gender and race, as well as the number of employees with disabilities.
- A detailed narrative of each firm, plus much more!

The National Directory Of Legal Employers has been the best kept secret of top legal career search professionals for over a decade. Now, for the first time, it is available in a format specifically designed for law students and new graduates. *Pick up your copy of the Directory today!*

ISBN: 0-15-900434-9 $39.95

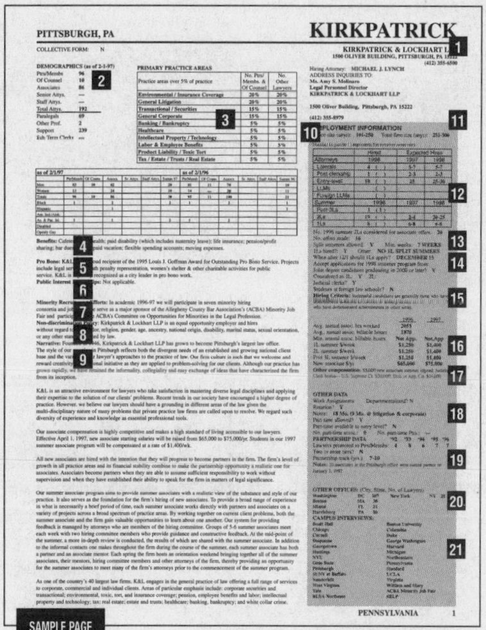

SAMPLE PAGE

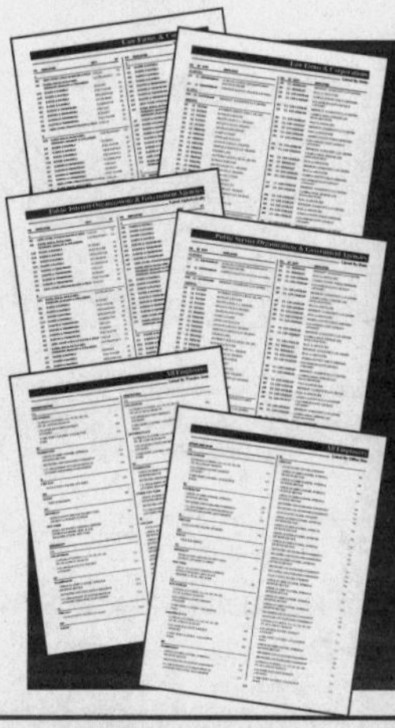

Everything You Need To Know About 1,000 Of the Nation's Top Legal Employers— Fully Indexed For Quick Reference!

Including:

Law Firms and Corporations
Listed Alphabetically

Law Firms and Corporations
Listed by State

Public Interest Organizations and Government Agencies
Listed Alphabetically

Public Interest Organizations and Government Agencies
Listed by State

All Employers
Listed By Practice Area

All Employers
Listed By Office Size

Company Information

1. *Name, Address, and Phone Number Of Hiring Partner*
2. *Demographics*
3. *Primary Practice Areas*
4. *Benefits*
5. *Pro Bono*
6. *Public Interest Fellowships*
7. *Minority Recruitment Efforts*
8. *Non-Discrimination Policy*
9. *Narrative*

Employment Information

10. *Office Size*
11. *Total Firm Size*
12. *Job Opportunities*
13. *Summer Associate Information*
14. *Application Timeline For Summer Associates*
15. *Hiring Criteria For All Job Openings*
16. *Salary Information*
17. *Other Compensation*
18. *Other Data*
19. *Partnership Data*
20. *Other Offices*
21. *Campus Interviews*

The Best Of The Job Goddess
Kimm Alayne Walton, J.D.

In her popular **Dear Job Goddess** column, legal job-search expert Kimm Alayne Walton provides the answers to even the most difficult job search dilemmas facing law students and law school graduates. Relying on career experts from around the country, the Job Goddess provides wise and witty advice for every obstacle that stands between you and your dream job!

ISBN: 0-15-900393-8 $14.95

SAMPLE COLUMN

Business Card Resumes: Good Idea, Or Not?

Dear Job Goddess,

One of my friends showed me something called a "business card resume." What he did was to have these business cards printed up, with his name and phone number on one side, and highlights from his resume on the other side. He said a bunch of people are doing this, so that when they meet potential employers they hand over these cards. Should I bother getting some for myself?

Curious in Chicago

Dear Curious,

Sigh, You know, Curious, that the Job Goddess takes a fairly dim view of resumes as a job-finding tool, even in their full-blown bond-papered, engraved 8-1/2x11" incarnation. And here you ask about a business card resume, two steps further down the resume food chain. So, no, you *shouldn't* bother with business card resumes. Here's why.

Think for a moment, Curious, about the kind of circumstance in which you'd be tempted to whip out one of these incredible shrinking resumes. You're at a social gathering. You happen to meet Will Winken, of the law firm Winken, Blinken, and Nod, and it becomes clear fairly quickly that Will is a) friendly, and b) a potential employer. The surest way to turn this chance encounter into a job is to use it as the basis for future contact. As Carolyn Bregman, Career Services Director at Emory Law School, points out, "Follow up with a phone call or note, mentioning something Winken said to you." You can say that you'd like to follow up on whatever it is he said, or that you've since read more about him and found that he's an expert on phlegm reclamation law and how that's a topic that's always fascinated you, and invite him for coffee at his convenience so you can learn more about it. What have you done? *You've taken a social encounter and turned it into a potential job opportunity.* And that makes the Job Goddess very proud.

But what happens if you, instead, whip out your business card resume, and say, "Gee, Mr. Winken, nice meeting you. Here's my business card resume, in case you ever need anybody like me." *Now* what have you done? You have, with one simple gesture, wiped out any excuse to follow up! Instead of having a phone call or a note from you that is personalized to Winken, you've got a piddling little standardized card with your vital statistics on it. Ugh. I know you're much more memorable, Curious, than anything you could possibly fit on the back of a business card.

So there you have it, Curious. Save the money you'll spend on a business card resume, and spend it later, when you have a *real* business card to print, reading, "Curious, Esq. Winken, Blinken, and Nod, Attorneys at Law."

Yours Eternally,

The Job Goddess

Call To Order: 1-800-787-8717 or Order On-Line at http://www.gilbertlaw.com

AMERICA'S GREATEST PLACES TO WORK WITH A LAW DEGREE
AND HOW TO MAKE THE MOST OF ANY JOB, NO MATTER WHERE IT IS!
By Kimm Alayne Walton, J.D.
Features Hundreds Of Traditional and Non-Traditional Employers
Discover The Places Where Law School Graduates Love To Work!
Available At Your Law School Bookstore
Order Toll-Free: 1-800-787-8717
Order Online: www.gilbertlaw.com
THE BEST OF THE JOB GODDESS
GUERRILLA TACTICS
OF YOUR DREA
Proceed with Caution
BEYOND L.A. LAW
BREAK THE TRADITIONAL "LAWYER" MOLD
National Directory Of Legal Employers
1999-2000 Edition
22,000 GREAT JOB OPENINGS
NALP